D1191476

A HANDBOOK FOR THE AMATEUR THEATRE

THE SHAPE OF THINGS TO COME

...del of the proposed new Questors Theatre at Ealing

A HANDBOOK FOR THE AMATEUR THEATRE

by
PETER COTES

OLDBOURNE PRESS

OLDBOURNE PRESS
121–128 Fleet Street
London, E.C.4

First published 1957

PRINTED IN GREAT BRITAIN
BY WESTERN PRINTING SERVICES LTD BRISTOL

Dedicated to my friend
Lois McLean
— Amateur turned Professional —
Without whose unfailing enthusiasm
this book, once started, might never
have been completed.

CONTENTS

LIST OF ILLUSTRATIONS

INTRODUCTION

"THE AMATEUR"

SOME six years ago, a book of mine entitled *No Star Nonsense*, dealing largely with the theatre, contained a chapter on the Amateur which stimulated at the time a considerable amount of comment and controversy. It also brought me a large correspondence from amateur actors and producers, most of whom agreed wholeheartedly with what I had said. Moreover, my views were in the main endorsed by a number of theatrical publications, amateur as well as professional. When the publishers of the present volume requested me to undertake a practical handbook for the Amateur Theatre which might be of service to theatrical societies throughout the British Isles, I remembered the interest already evinced in my previous writings in this field and gladly accepted the invitation to aid, if possible, the countless workers whom I knew to exist in the amateur theatre movement, a large number of whom are now personal friends.

To preface the book I would like to reintroduce my former chapter on the amateur, because it seems to me upon re-reading it, and in the light of further study, that these same comments are as valid today as they were when *No Star Nonsense* was first written.

THE AMATEUR

I recently escaped from the roar of London theatre-life to the welcome peace of an East Anglian market-town to enjoy a week-end "away from it all". Outside the public library my attention was arrested by a hand-painted poster, announcing a performance by the local amateur dramatic society of *Night Must Fall*. I wondered if such a production was really justified. A long time ago, one May night in 1935, to be exact, the leading parts had been brilliantly played at the Duchess Theatre in London by Emlyn Williams, Angela Baddeley and Dame May Whitty. How could a group of amateurs in a country town, with only a smattering of the actor's art, hope to emulate those fine performances? Why bother to do indifferently a job which has previously been done so well by professional artists? At first glance it seems to be little more than a waste of time. On the other hand, such a production gives considerable pleasure to the people in the cast and possibly to a number of inhabitants in the town, and what is even more important, it may give some actor-in-embryo his first taste of the boards. Emlyn Williams himself had a scholastic career in mind until he went to Oxford and became a member of the O.U.D.S., which gave him some idea of the satisfaction he would derive from becoming a professional actor, and possibly a dramatist as well. Hundreds of others must have entered the professional theatre as a result of early amateur experience —so the amateur theatre has some justification for its existence.

It was the amateur theatre that gave us Mrs. Patrick Campbell. She was a very young married woman with two babies and a sick husband. Her friends said it would cheer her and amuse her to play the leading part in a production being staged by the Anomalies Dramatic Club. One of the members had fallen ill, and so she decided to appear in Mark Quinton's play, *In His Power*, which was produced in 1886. *The Stage* sent a representative to the show and he remarked:

> The Anomalies are fortunate in counting Mrs. Campbell as one of their members. It was this lady's first appearance on any stage on Thursday, and her performance was therefore the more extraordinary. Mrs. Campbell possesses a natural depth of pathos and yet a power and earnestness, which, joined to a graceful, easy manner and charming presence, render her a most valuable acquisition.

Mr. Patrick Campbell went abroad for his health. He only sent money at irregular intervals, so his wife, with two babies on her hands, considered taking up the stage professionally, on the strength of her success with the Anomalies Dramatic Club, for whom she also played in *Blow for Blow* and *The Money Spinner*. Through an agent she discovered that Hermann Vezin was looking for a leading lady, but he could only pay 50s. a week and the actress had to supply her own dresses. Thus, in 1888 at the Alexandra Theatre in Liverpool, Mrs. Pat made her first professional appearance, billed as Miss Stella Campbell in *Bachelors*. Five years later she was to create Paula Tanqueray at the St. James's and to make theatre history. But for her experience as an amateur, she would probably never have turned to the stage as a means of making both ends meet.

Casting to type is not the same curse in the amateur world as in the professional. Perhaps conceit is in some degree responsible for that state of affairs. The amateur "big shot" has no small opinion of himself. He thinks that most parts are within his grasp and he tries his hand at every part that comes his way. He has nothing to lose if he happens to misfire, as his livelihood in no way depends on his performance at the parish hall. His work on the bank ledger or as secretary of the local golf club is still as secure as ever, even if he makes an appalling mess of playing Churdles Ash or Charles the Second. His public will congratulate him and will be rather proud to think that there is someone in their little circle capable of playing the part at all. With the professional actor it is different. He may desire to experiment, but dare not risk complete failure in a world where he has begun to earn some sort of a reputation. He is often compelled to play for safety and accept only those parts which the managers offer him, parts similar to those in which he has made good. The unadventurous managers have living proof that he can play that type of part without letting them down, so they can offer similar parts with complete confidence. The actor soon becomes a specialist rather than a versatile artist. The amateur has a much freer hand to experiment and put his own powers to the test. He rarely suffers the agony of frustration.

Amateurs worth their salt can benefit the professional theatre by making people in their district theatre-conscious. Their plays are less perfectly presented than in the theatre at its best, but most amateurs worthy of the name can work to ensure that their performance is as good as, if not better than, the average production one sees at a weekly repertory theatre. The top-flight repertory companies are capable of putting most West End productions to shame, as the Liverpool Repertory Company proved when they played *The Cherry Orchard* at the St. James's, but a vast chasm yawns between their work and that of the third-rate companies of the smaller towns, where, for the most part, there is little or no direction, and only a collection of actors who do little more than learn their lines and repeat them each night for a week, with the aid of a few conventional gestures. They have neither the time nor the heart to do anything better. The amateurs, on the other hand, have weeks in which to prepare their play and to give serious thought to their individual parts in the peace of their homes. They should be capable—but rarely are—of putting up a much finer performance than the repertory players, as their working conditions are so much more favourable, and they need only prepare one play at a time. The wretched repertory actor is rehearsing one part by day and playing another by night, with half an eye on a third part that will be coming along the week after next.

If the standard of amateur productions could be raised they would undoubtedly be patronized by the public at large, not only by friends and relations of the cast, but by the man-in-the-street, who would as willingly spend his money on a thoughtfully produced amateur show as on a hastily flung together professional one. Amateurs, incidentally, can provide an excellent audience for professionals. At their best they can give the public a taste for the theatre and provoke discussion on plays and acting in general. The theatre will come to mean something in the life of the town where amateurs operate. It will get a hold on the population, who might quite feasibly start making plans to provide some means of inviting professional players to entertain them.

In many of the theatreless districts the only live drama has been provided by amateurs for years. In such theatreless wastes as the South Wales and Durham coalfields groups of amateurs have given splendid entertainment to thousands of people over many years, long before the Arts Council ever dreamed of their experiments. As the *Durham Chronicle* remarked on 5 March 1948, the people of the North are very proud of their amateurs:

> They have extracted sheer joy from the rehearsals, and the productions, generally over six nights, have been immensely enjoyed by audiences representing every house in the respective localities for miles around. Little jealousies there may have been, but they have nothing to do with the professional stage and if one of the actors throws his chest out and regards himself as the natural inheritor of the mantle of Sir Henry Irving, then that is scarcely a crime. It is pardonable pride in a job done to the best of his ability.

> Had it not been for these amateurs on the stage, the people of this county would have had a lean time. After all, the professional companies appear at theatres far removed from the villages and are inaccessible to thousands of people, but, even so, hundreds of amateurs have gone to much expense in order to see how the professional actors and actresses interpret and present their parts. Gilbert and Sullivan operas have always been popular in this county, and whenever any of them have been staged by professionals in the county or at Newcastle, the audiences have consisted largely of amateurs who have appeared in these operas on the local amateur stage.

As certain amateurs are frequently held in such high esteem by their fellowmen, who seem interested in their work as something to be maintained in the life of the community, it seems obvious that the amateur movement can play a vital part in the battle for civic theatres which will go on raging in this country until such institutions become as commonplace as public libraries. Local authorities now have the power to bring civic theatres into being, but they are hardly likely to do so unless there is a strong public demand for them. Through their audiences, amateurs can build up public appreciation and a keen desire for a theatre which will be a driving force to bring civic theatres into being. Many people stupidly resent a charge on the rates for pleasures which do not appeal to them. These same people say nothing about that fraction of the rates which goes towards the upkeep of a park

PROFESSIONAL

Joan Miller as Clara Dennison in *The Wooden Dish*; starring twenty years later at the Phoenix Theatre, London, in 1954.

————— INTO —————

AMATEUR

Joan Miller as "Elizabeth the Queen", for which performance she was adjudged Best Actress at the Dominion Drama Festival held in Ottawa, Canada, in 1934.

in which they never walk and a public library from which they never borrow a book. They must be taught that the charge upon the rates will only be a temporary measure while the theatre is being established. Once it has opened and is being properly run, it will be self-supporting. Many people have more leisure now than in the past, and more money with which to enjoy it. It is only right that the theatre should play a major part in our enjoyment of that leisure, as it is a temple where so many of the arts can be practised—music, art, drama and dancing can all find expression on that stage which should give added pleasure to any town in which it is established.

Amateurs should keep a watchful eye on the premises, as in so many cases they will be responsible for the agitation which will eventually bring these civic theatres into being. Any old hall with a platform and curtains is not enough. The theatre must be something that will last for years, and not a makeshift four walls and a platform defying the creation of that atmosphere so vital to the production of plays. Theatre technicians must be called in at the beginning, so that they can help to plan the premises. These experts have back-stage knowledge. They have helped to create magic in the professional theatre. Their co-operation at the beginning is invaluable, so that if an existing hall has to be converted, they can make the best of what may look like a bad job on the surface. The British Drama League is pressing for the provision of civic theatres and urges each individual amateur dramatic society to make a positive move by passing resolutions at their annual meetings, calling upon their local authorities to provide them. Such a widely organized campaign should establish the theatre in this country on a more solid foundation than ever before.

Too frequently the amateur and the professional theatre view each other with distaste and contempt. As each of the two worlds are peopled by a few intelligent beings who respect the drama sufficiently, steps should be taken to bring them together, thereby strengthening the position of both. The best amateur societies should be a stimulant to dramatic art, and should be looked upon as a subsidiary branch of the professional theatre. A good deal of plain speaking concerning the amateur and the professional stage was heard at the conference in Newcastle in March 1948. The proceedings were convened by the Arts Council in order to hear the views of the general public of north-eastern England with regard to the policy of the coalfields tours. The views expressed by Llewellyn Rees, at that time Drama Director of the Arts Council, and André van Gyseghem, whose production of *Caste* toured the coalfields, are worth recalling.

Llewellyn Rees said that by sending out professional companies to theatreless districts, the Arts Council aimed at stimulating an interest in drama; they wanted to set a standard for the work of the amateur societies and to so create an interest in drama in the region, that facilities, now in many cases lacking, would be provided by the people to whom they presented the plays. It was hoped that halls would be improved and that conditions would be made bearable for visiting artists. Turning to the relationship between the amateur and the professional theatre, Mr. Rees said:

"Unless the amateurs support the professional theatre I don't think the amateur societies are very much good, except as a means of amusing themselves and their relations. They can be of great use to the theatre if they will regard themselves as part of the theatre. We want to see a closer link between amateur and professional companies. In the past there have been mutual suspicions, and sometimes little antagonisms which have arisen, partly on the professional side because of economic reasons, and partly on the amateur side because of a peculiar sort of conceit that they can do better than the professionals. That, of course, is most unlikely, as all intelligent amateurs will agree. Technical training in any profession must count, and that is being realized more and more by the intelligent amateur who can be of great help to the professional theatre."

On this same occasion André Van Gyseghem, who has a wide knowledge of the professional theatre, both in this country and in Russia, deplored the bitter opposition between the amateur and the professional and wondered why the two could not unite.

"A great number of amateur theatres exist solely as a means of exhibitionism for their members. They like to get up and be seen on platforms by their friends and enjoy these mutual admiration societies. Such amateur societies are of no use either to man or beast; they could be closed down.

In my adjudications I have told them that quite half of the groups who belong to the Drama League ought not to be in existence because they are not serious. If they are not serious theatre productions I don't care two hoots for them. If the art of the theatre becomes a secondary consideration to some other object, then I am not interested. That is not the ground in which the seeds of a healthy theatre should be sown. It is art all the time and should be approached with humility demanding full concentration. If you cannot approach it in that way, then finish. Some amateur societies have this attitude to their work and are doing an admirable service.

We see in the amateur theatre bumptiousness and jealousy. We have heard those people who say that their society have done the particular play presented by a professional company and that they have 'done it rather better'. We have all met the man who has played for a long time in his local society and who never goes to see a professional production. That is not a very unusual attitude. Isolation from the general life of the theatre is a very bad thing. You cannot thrive on isolation, but only when in contact with the general pattern of the theatre. If you cut yourself off from contacts you become sterile and your work is of little value."

Mr. Van Gyseghem urged amateur societies to keep alive plays that were not being staged in the commercial theatre. The worst thing they could do was to copy the commercial theatre. No truly creative work came from copying. The work of adjudication at amateur drama festivals was a good thing because it brought in the outside mind to view h eir work.

"It is impossible for you to judge your own work and that of your friends. I decry the organisation which refuses to enter a festival. You must keep contacts if your work is to remain fresh, vital and alive. When you have gifted amateurs with a right attitude to their work there is no reason why they should not be drafted into the professional companies and make it a full-time job. That is where we find some of our most talented players.

What is not understandable is that because an amateur society has performed a certain play, the members do not wish to see anyone else do it because they cannot think that anyone else can do it better. The professionals resent the criticism of those who have had less experience than them at the theatre and all it implies. It is only the ignorant and the inexperienced who will try to be didactic in their criticism of the professional stage. Professional players like to get to know the people before whom they are performing in a warm, friendly and human way. Amateur players can educate the public to a more constructive approach to the theatre, and professional people should do all they can in the training of the amateur. The more we can do to break down the spirit of antagonism between the audience, the amateur theatre and the stage, the more we know about each other, the more we can perfect our art."

As E. Martin Browne has pointed out, the professional theatre is apt to be rather cold in its reception of the people who go to it; it might do well to make an attempt to establish for itself a more definite place in the life of the community. What could be better, as a first move, than some sort of an understanding with amateurs, who should not be regarded as serious rivals? They are generally bodies of local people who have no sort of ulterior motive and simply enjoy playing the parts

b

for which the producer considers them best fitted. In their leisure-time stage work they are not considering whether they are competing with the commercial theatre or presenting problem and propaganda plays. They are acting for the joy of it, and no one would wish to discourage them. They are consistent supporters of the commercial theatre and openly confess that much of the success of their work is due to their study of the professional stage.

Amateurs could best win the respect of professionals and so help to bridge the gap, by following the footsteps of such conscientious amateur producers as Thelma Niklaus, and the Unity Theatre in North London, where much good work has been done under the supervision of Joe MacColum. On that small stage I saw some of the finest amateur productions of my experience, including *Winkles and Champagne*, *Match Girls* and *The Whole World Over*. These plays were worth doing. They were not plays that had previously been staged by professionals, but they were acted by people who were inspired by their parts. They had modelled themselves on the best professionals, under the guidance of Frank Godwin and Bill Rowbotham, bringing an air of professionalism to their productions and putting up outstandingly good performances.* I have heard that the Unnamed Society in Manchester, as well as the Maddermarket at Norwich, has been responsible for some exceedingly accomplished work, but while, generally speaking, the work of amateurs is good, it is rarely outstanding. It will never improve until they are prepared to judge their work by the highest possible standards. They must always strive to touch professional heights. Never must they excuse themselves by saying that they are only amateurs. It is fatal to become slipshod in the knowledge that friends and relations in the audience will make allowances. It should be the constant ambition of the amateur to impress those people who are not friends and relations. If he can move them he is half-way to calling himself an artist.

As a handful of amateurs have proved that their work can be impressive, it is up to the others to take stock of the general failings of the non-professional theatre in an attempt to correct them. As I told the Drama School of the Pontypool Educational Settlement some years ago, I think plays chosen by amateurs are often unsuitable and uninspired. Before they select a play they should face the fact that they have not perfected the art of acting and they should rely on the dramatist for compensation. With the best plays of the world to choose from, they should decide upon something for which they are ideally

---

* Since the above was first written, Ted Willis, a dramatist of strength and sincerity, who was discovered at Unity through the production of his play *Buster*, has been hailed in the professional theatre as "one of the white hopes of British Drama".

suited. The play should satisfy the audience, even if the acting leaves something to be desired. The two together should make a worthwhile evening. A good play is the first essential, and I am in favour of one which makes some sort of comment. Shaw, Ibsen and Shakespeare are good material for amateurs. I think Chekhov and Strindberg are rather too difficult to act, but the other three wrote plays that give audiences something to think about and can be relied upon to compensate for the shortcomings of the actors. The total effect gives the audience something to talk about . . . in short, something to take home. It is one of the hall-marks of satisfying entertainment.

I am not suggesting that amateurs should confine themselves to propaganda plays, or their productions will become little more than political meetings carried out in costume. But they should choose plays with a certain thought content. The plays of Sheridan and Pinero are unsuitable because they call for stylish acting to put them across. *George and Margaret* and *French Without Tears* are always being played by amateurs in some part of the country, probably because the committees of the various societies think that they call forth a good laugh and will cheer the people who come to see them. Despite their long West End runs—*George and Margaret* ran for 799 performances and *French Without Tears* for 1,039—I count these empty pieces. They need to be very well-dressed and speedily played if they are to be really satisfactory from a production point of view. The discussion play of the Shavian school has such potent and pregnant dialogue that no particularly imaginative stage action is required to keep them alive. In a good discussion-play actors can for long passages afford to do little more than sit round and talk, and still the interest of the house is held. They in no way tax the limitations of the producer or the artists, and still the play itself is good enough to get across.

Amateurs are sometimes prone to imitate professional actors slavishly in everything they do, so that an amateur production is little more than a blurred carbon copy of the original professional one. There is more than one way of looking at most serious plays, and consequently more than one way of producing them. No laws of right and wrong can be laid down. Each producer interprets a play according to his own viewpoint as he understands the writer, and if the amateur feels that he has a new angle on a play, he should have the courage to say so and carry it out, provided it is not a stupid stunt staged purely for the sake of sensationalism. I am against the wholesale hiring of sets and properties which fail to strike any note of originality or atmosphere. Let the company try and design their own set and build it out of materials available on the spot. They will have many problems to solve, but the result will be far more effective than the hired set, which we have all

seen on so many previous occasions. Specialist sections should be
formed in each amateur group to look after such vital contributions as
decor, costumes, lighting and properties. Such sections would give
added interest to the non-playing members of the society and break
down any tendency to stereotyped production. What amusement they
could have staging *R.U.R.* or *The Insect Play*, to say nothing of the first
part of *Back to Methuselah* or *Macbeth*, with their robots, beetles, serpents
and witches. Such plays offer endless scope for imaginative and
original production.

Enterprise, originality and individuality should be encouraged in
amateur societies if they are to create a deeper love for the theatre
generally. In this manner they might attract young people to a greater
extent than they do at present. Some of those youngsters who love
going to camp, lighting fires, in the pouring rain and erecting tents in
the teeth of a gale, would be delighted to build a set out of a few feet
of timber and a roll of processed paper. Apart from being valuable
recruits, they would become life-long patrons of the theatre of tomorrow.
There is much to be said about Youth drama, and Douglas Powell,
drama adviser to the Bristol Youth Committee, covered some excellent
ground in an article in *The Amateur Stage*:

"Give youth something to occupy its time seems to be generally
accepted in theory and practice. One argument is that if this is done
there will be less time for juvenile delinquency. As an object this is
laudable, as an excuse for fooling with drama it is damnable. . . .
Knowledge of any art or craft should lead to a greater appreciation
of it. Does it in Youth Drama? Is anything achieved by 'putting
on a play' and receiving the plaudits of friends and relations? Yes,
given a good producer, a sense of discipline may result, team spirit
may be created, some care in speech may be taken—if a high standard is set, even though it may not be attained.

Unless drama means more than producing a play, it can be
dangerous. It encourages self-exploitation, it inflates the Ego and
makes people unbearable. Young folk are psychologically unstable
and easily influenced by injudicious flattery. Acting in a play is
always dangerous because of this—for youth or adult.

How can it be countered? The answer is in the approach to
drama. Drama is instinctive in all of us, it is inseparable from life,
it has influenced fashions, social conditions, the development of
civilization, politics, religion, and all that we call culture. It is not
confined to acting on a stage and cannot be appreciated solely from
this angle.

I believe that drama should never be superficial, that it is futile considered merely as a pleasant pastime. The technique involved in the production of a play, both from the production and the acting side, should be explained to the players, reasons given for moves, grouping, pace, etc., and the producer should show his players how he has interpreted and created a picture from the author's words.

If the players can see how the play has been built up for performance, if they are encouraged to criticize (not during a rehearsal, but in a break), if they discuss points with the producer, their critical faculties will be sharpened and used when they visit the amateur or professional theatre.

There is a danger of conceited criticism, but a producer who knows his job will make his players realize how little any amateur can really know about the theatre. However much time an amateur gives to it, how can he compete with a professional, whose life it is? A humble approach will reveal the unending discoveries which can be made about drama.

Sometimes it is said that young people are not interested in an analysis of drama or its technique. If so, then they act for personal satisfaction only. They may not display a great interest at first, but it can be built up and, I am convinced, is only dormant in many of them.

Improvised drama, especially of items taken from the daily papers, can arouse great interest, besides demonstrating how an author builds up a play and how the actors produce the effects he wants. Improvisation, besides being good fun, can be used as subtle way of teaching technique, but its greatest value is in the discussion among the players."

Quite obviously the amateur movement can be a boon to the professional theatre as long as their relationship is clearly defined and appreciated. One of the crying needs is for a general raising of the amateur standard of production. The increasing number of amateur drama festivals held up and down the country should help to bring this about, but care should be exercised in the choice of adjudicators. They must be practical men of the theatre, who can offer good solid advice on the work they see, and not the mere theoreticians who quote Stanislavsky without being able to translate his theories into practice on the stage.

We all love a story. Drama is the most exciting way of telling a story, hence it is fundamental to human nature to go in for drama. It offers that escape and emotional expression which have made dramatic performances enjoyable since the darkest ages. It is a pastime that should be encouraged on all sides, whether amateur or professional. If

Hitler had played Shylock for the Pontypool Educational Settlement there might have been no persecution of the Jews in Germany, and certainly no Second World War. It would probably have offered a cure for his emotional repression.

Something must be done to define amateur and professional spheres of activity, so that one is not confused with the other. After reading annual reports of the Arts Council and the official organ of the British Drama League, as well as taking an interest in numerous amateur productions up and down the country, I have come to the conclusion that a hopeless muddle exists over the question of amateur and professional. Educational authorities give financial support to such organizations as the Scottish National Players and the Community Drama Association, despite the fact that they are amateur. What is more regrettable is the fact that the Arts Council contributes financially to certain amateur organizations. There are far too many unemployed actors and actresses to let these meagre public funds go to the local Squire's lady and the farmer's boy both of whom may have a genuine desire to "depict", but only limited talent to offer their small circle of acquaintances. It is doubtful whether amateurs could possibly reach artistic perfection, yet the Arts Council supports them, though the chief professed aim of that august body is to improve the general standard of public taste. From the fundamental Trade Union point of view the amateur should not get "official" help unless Parliament makes a special grant and sets up an individual organization to look after the amateur. For some time past, both in the big cities and in the smaller towns there has been a general tendency to mix amateurs and professionals, which may be one reason why art is not viewed as seriously as it should be, either by the Government or by the people. After all, in both films and sport, the amateur modestly erects a self-imposed segregation between himself and the professional, and this principle has proved beneficial to all concerned.

ACKNOWLEDGMENTS

I WOULD like to express my gratitude for invaluable assistance in compiling this book, to the following: for the help and advice of Miss Joan Miller, John Stannard, Eric J. Batson, Eric Blore, Miss Pauline Brown, Miss E. Smith, Edmund Cooper, Mrs. Olive Dodds, Kit Dodds, Alfred E. J. Emmet, E. N. Hogben, John L. Hughes, Lyndesay G. Langwell, Richard MacDonald, Miss Ngaio Marsh, Mrs. Thelma Niklaus, Doctor Robert Niklaus, Brendan O'Brien, S. Pollitzer, Miss Marjorie Spink, Charles Rodda and Norman S. Jefferies.

For the kind co-operation of all the contributors of articles and drawings amongst, whom Miss Felicity Gray, Eric Maschwitz, Miss Thea Neu, Peter Mullings, and Frank Drury have all worked in the past as successful technicians in various productions I have had the opportunity of directing in the professional theatre.

For information from: the Amateur Drama Council of Ireland, the British Drama League, the Little Theatre Guild of Great Britain, the National Operatic and Dramatic Association, the Religious Drama Society of Great Britain, the Scottish Community Drama Association, the Standing Conference of Drama Associations, and the many Little Theatres and Societies throughout the country who have co-operated wholeheartedly in the search for material.

For permission to print excerpts from: the *N.O.D.A. Yearbook*; *No Star Nonsense* (publishers: Rockliff Publishing Corporation); extracts from Shaw's writings by courtesy of the Public Trustee and the Society of Authors; photographs of Lighting Equipment from the Strand Electric and Engineering Company Limited; colour chart from Messrs. Leichner Limited.

And last but by no means least my renewed thanks to Miss Lois McLean for assistance in research and compiling material.

I. THE PLAYWRIGHT

THE word "Drama" means an action which is executed (or performed) where one or more persons collect to watch. That is the main point for the playwright, and indeed all workers in the theatre, to bear in mind. The action of the play is of first importance and no great dramatist, however profound his thoughts or lofty his language, has neglected this basic requirement. It has been levelled against Shaw, not without some truth, that he disregarded action altogether when he felt like it and made of the theatre a place for discussion and argument, depending instead on his brilliant wit and originality. But having admitted this truth in connection with some of his plays, let it never be forgotten that few playwrights have understood better the value of action in the theatre, or have known better, upon occasion, how to employ it. Contrast the long drawn out static arguments in the middle acts of *Back to Methuselah* with the brilliantly theatrical opening act, "In the Beginning". The construction and action throughout *Candida* have scarcely been equalled by another playwright. That discerning judge of plays and players, Mr. George W. Bishop once told me that he considered *Candida*'s third act the best constructed ever written.

In its early forms drama was little else than a spectacle-dance and movement. Later the emotions were broadly appealed to and finally the mind. Masses of people who gathered in huge amphitheatres to witness a spectacle changed to gatherings in much smaller spaces in market places and inn yards, and eventually, audiences congregated in theatres of variously changing types and sizes to listen as much as to watch.

Drama covers such a wide field in the present day that one is debarred from making broad or arbitrary rules about it because what may be essential to one form is inappropriate to another. Drama, in its broadest sense, covers all forms of human expression before an audience: ballet, ice shows, musical comedy, opera, pageants, circuses, puppets and, finally, the performance of plays. This last form of drama is our particular concern.

Fundamental needs in the human being have been satisfied throughout the centuries by the performance and the witnessing of these various types of physical expression: the simple childhood pleasures of "Let's pretend!" which is never absent from any sort of acting, the opportunity for expression of primitive sexual and religious instincts and the elevation and release of emotions. Eventually, as thought provoking

C   I

plays began to be written, a stimulation of mind was provided as well
as emotional outlet and entertainment.

The Elizabethan theatre was the first of any importance in England.
There must have been considerable numbers of bands of players
wandering around the country performing in such vehicles as *The
Misfortunes of Arthur*, which was acted before Queen Elizabeth, or
The Famous Victories of Henry the Fifth, or *The Troublesome Raigne of King
John*, because in 1572 an act came into force which decreed that all
common players were to be designated as rogues and vagabonds unless
they were under the patronage of a lord of the realm. Shortly afterwards the Lord Chamberlain's Men, which included Shakespeare and
Burbage, and the Lord Admiral's Men, which sponsored Edward
Allyn, the rival of Burbage, became established and as respectable as
theatre folk could be in those days. Similar to the problem in our own
time, these companies needed homes and eventually both of them had
their own playhouses: "The Theater" and "The Curtain" were the
first permanent theatres in England.

There was great talent in all walks of life in the Elizabethan period
and the theatre, even without the world's greatest poet, was generously
populated with gifted men, notably Christopher Marlowe and Ben
Jonson. But Shakespeare grasped all the essentials of the theatre in a
way which no one has ever equalled. Of his many rare gifts his most
valuable was for characterization. He was the first dramatist to understand the importance of action as well as greatness of thought and beauty
of language, and it was through action that he developed his characters
as much as by dialogue.

Almost from the beginning of the theatre in England a censorship
was imposed which has prevailed, to the detriment of playwriting, to
the present day. The duties of censor were given to an official called
The Master of the Revels, and it was not until 1737 that this authority
was vested in the then Lord Chamberlain. All political reference had
to be strictly guarded and it is noticeable that Shakespeare, who must
have had the strongest desire to speak of the social injustices of his time
in the same way that he did of human frailties, refrained from doing so
altogether or so wrapped up his comment that no objection could be
lodged. With his great humanity and capacity for pity he must undoubtedly have been horrified by the use of the rack for instance, as
a means of obtaining confessions. When he expressed his disapproval,
however, he did it lightly in a love scene between Portia and Bassanio:

> Ay, but I fear you speak upon the rack,
> Where men, enforced, do speak anything.

The Theatre continued to flourish up to the outbreak of the Civil

War when all theatres were closed and public performances forbidden. The Restoration brought with it a rebirth and prosperity for the drama which led to new companies being formed and theatres being built. The accent of Restoration playwriting was on comedy—comedy of manners—and the plays of Congreve and Vanbrugh are constantly revived today—often with great success. Few serious works of merit were written and those attempted were stiff and formal copies of the accepted French model. The great plays of the Elizabethan period were ruthlessly mutilated to suit the fancy of actors playing the leading roles. Farce was firmly established in the eighteenth century and has remained a favourite English form of playwriting to the present time. The plays of Goldsmith, particularly *She Stoops to Conquer*, remain as producible in our present time as in the period for which they were written. Finally Sheridan, the master of stylish comedy, still the foremost British writer of satire, gave the greatest lustre to eighteenth-century drama output with *The School for Scandal* and *The Rivals*.

Although the nineteenth century produced some of England's greatest poets and novelists the adverse conditions in the rapidly changing world of the theatre discouraged playwriting of merit. With the single exception of Shelley's *The Cenci* no work of value was produced until T. W. Robertson, under the Bancroft management, wrote *Caste*. The famous actor Hare, who was a member of the company, wrote of Robertson, "As nature was the basis of his work, so he sought to make actors understand that it should be theirs. He thus founded a school of natural acting which completely revolutionized the then existing method and, by so doing, did incalculable good to the stage."

The reason for this halt in dramatic progress is not difficult to define. The industrial age was upon us and with its growth the commercial theatre, as we know it today, began to be established. The art of the theatre was changing into an industry. The "long run" became a financial necessity and took the place of the classical repertory. Cheap, sentimental and melodramatic plays were produced for the growing leisured classes, plays that were tailor-made for the first "commercial" star actors. There were reactions against this new trend, of course, just as there are today against a state of affairs in the theatre which is all too similar. Samuel Phelps, lessee of Sadler's Wells, did great service to Shakespeare by returning, in his productions, to the original texts and throwing out the abominable "versions" and "adaptations" of the plays which had grown in number throughout the eighteenth century. New writers, however, were not encouraged to do more than turn out endless replicas of farce and melodrama in the French tradition or adapt already existing ones. Any potential original talent was stifled and playwrights were mere hacks in the pay of the new commercial regime. Robertson was a lone voice in this changed world of the theatre. It was the heyday of the actor manager and the head of each company, having the finances as well as the artistic merits of his productions to consider, was careful to provide pieces which would be unfailingly popular with an audience which, though wealthy, had limited taste and were averse to any theatrical fare which might make mental demands upon them.

So Beerbohm Tree at the Haymarket, apart from revivals of the classics, carried on with adaptations and translations of unworthy foreign plays and refused to take the risk of presenting untried English writing talent. Another famous management, however, Mr. and Mrs. Bancroft, with whom Robertson worked, made a valuable contribution to the theatre of their period, gaining for it a respectability which it had never enjoyed before. With the growing ease of transportation they were able to send out tours complete with scenery which were almost replicas of their London productions and provincial audiences, for the first time, had the opportunity of witnessing stage presentations which were well mounted and well acted. As these companies gained in popularity so the old stock companies which had previously toured a repertory of plays, fell upon hard times and their method of using their players for many and varied parts, which demanded great versatility and resilience, fell into disuse. Actors, touring only one play and playing the same part month after month became specialists in certain types of parts. As a result the practice of type casting was adopted and is in use to the present time.

If, during the early and mid-Victorian period, no new playwrights of outstanding worth were produced in the British theatre at least there were fine actors—men and women of unique personality. Their acknowledged leader was Henry Irving. By his example he further respectablized his calling and, although the new plays he presented were almost all worthless pieces of writing he gave them a transitory appearance of value through the greatness of his performances.

It is seldom, in the theatre, that the ideal state of affairs is achieved where all the separate arts which go to make a unified whole attain an approximate degree of excellence. If the playwright is in the ascendant the actors are inferior, or if great individual actors abound they must rely on classical roles for expression because no contemporary dramatist is capable of writing plays worthy of them—or the producer and playwright have somehow fused their talents together to produce a memorable result, but the actors are unable to live up to the standard demanded of them. Occasionally the miracle does happen and then we have players of the calibre of Arthur Sinclair, Sara Allgood, Maire O'Neill and Sydney Morgan acting in one masterpiece after another by

Synge, O'Casey, Yeats, Padriac Colum, St. John Ervine among other fine writers. Still, if the ideal situation occurs but seldom, it is an invariable fact that whatever is wrong will change. Towards the end of the nineteenth century after the triumphs of Irving, Ellen Terry, Tree, Mrs. Patrick Campbell, Bernhardt and Duse—only a few of the great names when one considers the world theatre—the pendulum started to swing and the playwright slowly began to regain his rightful position. But there had been a lapse of one hundred years. The last *great* British play to have been written was *The School for Scandal*. The art of the theatre is necessarily ephemeral depending as it does on the spoken word, the direction of the play, and the personality and talent of actors. What is permanent, besides those accounts of performance and production recorded by bygone critics, is the work of the dramatist.

Henry Arthur Jones and Pinero were the first writers of skill to emerge after the long silence. They were quickly followed by men of widely differing types of talent: Oscar Wilde, Bernard Shaw and J. M. Barrie. Contemporary with these outstanding writers was a genius, still unknown in England but widely followed on the Continent, who was to have the profoundest influence on the theatre since Shakespeare. Ibsen was a great realist. He introduced the Play of Ideas. The parts, he wrote for actors were as demanding and as rewarding as the great characters created by Shakespeare. In a period which was shackled by false, unhealthy moral values especially on the subject of sex, where the ordinary rights of man and woman were disregarded, Ibsen spoke freely and forthrightly to a shocked public on subjects which they scarcely admitted to themselves existed. He insisted on the intelligent participation of his audience. Although his following in England has never been large, his influence on the theatre as a whole and on methods of acting and production, which had to alter to meet the demands he made upon them, is incalculable. The flowering of his genius seemed a signal to the theatre workers of the entire world to make a new, simpler, and truer approach to their art. In Russia, Stanislavsky developed his famous method of realistic acting and Chekhov, responding gladly to an opportunity for sympathetic treatment and understanding, wrote his great plays.

J. T. Grein, founder of the Independent Theatre introduced Ibsen to England with a production of *Ghosts*. Shortly afterwards he presented *Widower's Houses*, Shaw's first play to be produced. With the establishment of the great Irishman the attitude of the theatre going public altered. The theatre began to be regarded as an art form as well as a means by which commercialists made money by presenting frivolous entertainment to an escapist audience. The theatre proper was more firmly established than at any time since Shakespeare.

Dramatists again became what they should always be: the chroniclers of their times. There are few important modern British playwrights who have not owed their initial opportunity to such experimental theatres as the Independent Theatre, the Stage Society (in its early days), the Royal Court under Vedrenne and Barker, Miss Horniman in Manchester, Barry Jackson in Birmingham, William Armstrong in Liverpool, Peter Godrey at The Gate, Norman McDermott at The Everyman and Ashley Dukes at The Mercury. Although these theatres often showed a considerable loss on the debit side, on the credit side they could point to memorable first productions of plays by such writers as: Granville Barker, Bernard Shaw, Allan Monkhouse, John Masefield, Stanley Houghton, St. John Ervine, Arnold Bennett, Edward Knoblock, Somerset Maugham, T. S. Eliot, Christopher Fry and John Galsworthy.

With the end of the First World War, and in the period afterwards, when many of these momentous events were taking place in the small theatres, the reign of the actor-manager had given way before the growing power of the businessmen. The control they gained at that time has grown until, at the present time, the entire professional theatre is in the hands of an all-powerful monopoly. Just as in the early and mid-Victorian period, when the financial side of the theatre was given first priority, the promising new dramatists, writing to order, are dissipating their talent and producing little of integrity or permanent value. One way of demonstrating this is to examine the theatre column of a daily paper.* The theatres in the West End of London were being used in the following way.

> Five English Musicals;
> Five American Musicals;
> Three English Revues;
> Seven American Plays (including one revival. All these plays were established successes in the U.S.A. before they were presented in England);
> Two Plays translated from the French;
> Two Shakespearean productions;
> One Opera company;
> Emlyn Williams as Dylan Thomas;
> Two Ice Shows;
> Three Variety Shows;
> *Dry Rot* (which is much more a variety entertainment than a play);
> Seven British Plays.

* National Press, 18 July 1955.

Of these seven plays two were thrillers by Agatha Christie and one was a light-hearted romp called *Home and Away*. There were two plays by solidly established writers—Terence Rattigan and William Douglas Home. Of the remaining two, *Sailor Beware* was transferred to the West End complete with the repertory company who first presented it and therefore took the initial risk. The final offering, *Shadow of a Doubt*, was the only play by a new author being shown in London at the time. With the future of British playwriting in mind it is an uninspiring list. One looks in vain for the young Priestleys and Galsworthys, the Arnold Bennetts and St. John Ervines. Where are the up-and-coming dramatists who can write a *Jane Clegg*, *An Inspector Calls*, *Candida*, *To What Red Hell*, *The Silver Box*, *The Grain of Mustard Seed*, *The Voysey Inheritance*? Asking for plays of this calibre, and for the people who can write them, is not asking for an Ibsen, a Chekhov or an O'Casey. It is asking for the same kind of fine craftsmen with their unerring dramatic instinct who gave the British theatre its backbone and its guts until the recent past. H. M. Harwood for example.*

A dramatist must have a platform. In order to develop and perfect the difficult technique required he must see his plays in production. Playwrights have always flourished when they have been encouraged through presentations of their work by established companies.

As it appears useless for the vital new writers to look to the commercial managements for encouragement, and as the professional experimental theatre and the repertory movement are both in the doldrums, the responsibility of fostering their talent falls directly on the shoulders of serious groups in the amateur theatre movement. It is to these groups that the dramatist of tomorrow must be able to look for support.

* This writer produced and wrote many successes of note, mostly in association with his wife, F. Tennyson Jesse, and Robert Gore Browne, when he owned the Ambassadors Theatre in the thirties.

II. THE PRODUCER

THERE is an unfortunate confusion connected with the title given to the person who is in charge of producing or directing a play. In the era of the actor-manager the play was "staged" by the great man himself. That usually meant that he gave himself an impressive build-up prior to his first entrance, arranged the entrance so that the eye of every player, as well as every member of the audience, was glued on him. The majority of his lines were delivered stage centre, while the members of his company were placed, at his discretion, downstage with their backs to the audience. Thanks to this method he could scarcely fail to "stand out", and his admiring public applauded his genius enthusiastically although frequently they remembered little of the play and nothing of the supporting players.

When the theatre fell into the hands of the businessmen they called themselves "managers", which was the correct title, and they hired producers to do the artistic work for them—that is, to produce the play. About this time, following the practice in Hollywood, American managers on Broadway began to call themselves producers, and the men who produced the play they called directors. Although for the most part the terms manager and producer are still in use in England there have been recent productions where the American titles have appeared. To add to the confusion there is still another term used to describe the same office. When a man is given the artistic control of a theatre, usually with a board advising him, he is called the artistic director.

It is only in the last century that the producer has emerged as a figure of central importance in the theatre. His unique position in today's world theatre derives principally from the influence of Reinhardt and Jessner in Germany, and Stanislavsky and Meyerhold in Russia. These artists and reformers led the way for the outstanding directorial talents that were shortly to blossom: David Belasco in America, who fought for realism, and Gordon Craig, the son of Ellen Terry was an imaginative lover of beauty who demanded that all the individual facets of the theatre be merged into a creative unity. Along with these came Granville Barker, Basil Dean, and in our own time, Elia Kazan. These men were the foremost to demonstrate that a single dominating mind was necessary to shape a production, giving it character and clarity, and, by combining the separate sections of a stage presentation, produce for an audience not the remembrance of a scene, a performance or a setting, but of a work of art.

8

The producer is to a cast what a conductor is to an orchestra, and in his relation to an author's play his function is precisely the same as that of a musical director to the score he conducts.

Plays are written not so much to be read as to be acted and no new play really comes to life until it is seen in production. In the hands of a skilful director a play can sometimes take on a life that not even the author had imagined for it. The producer owes his first duty and allegiance to the play. The dramatist is the most important figure in the theatre and it falls to the producer to try to understand and interpret his intention and, from a written page, create through the medium of the theatre a work of vitality and life. The producer's loyalty to, and affection for, the play should preclude him from being willing to produce a "copy" of some other person's production. His approach to the work should be original and the interpretation should be his own. This is one of the main reasons why I have suggested else-where the importance of engaging, whenever possible, a professional producer for the early part of an amateur society's existence. To pro-duce well requires so much experience and, until very recently, in the professional theatre, an artist was not considered competent to attempt this most important of all jobs unless he had gone through other branches of theatre work, notably stage management and stage direc-torship, with, if possible a background of acting. He must have mastered the intricacies of lighting and must understand the functioning and difficulties of all departments backstage.

When a producer has performed a really accomplished job the audience should be conscious only of the play and the acting. He should never, in his interpretation, draw attention to himself at the expense of the play. The audience must not realize how greatly the good impression they received was influenced by lighting, tempo, mood, the skilful obtaining of dramatic effects, the interplay between actors. In a good production these many important facets are finally merged together by the producer, and the audience should not be permitted to see how the final effect was achieved.

As the interpreter of the play, the producer should first of all try to understand what was in the author's mind when he wrote it. If the author is alive his task is simplified (although it is considered by some a mixed blessing to have the author hovering anxiously because Miss Snooks, our *ingénue*, has said at a rehearsal, "There is no other course left to me", instead of "There is no other way"). At any rate, having studied the play and discussed it with the author (if possible) the pro-ducer then sets out to interpret in theatrical terms, the basic message, meaning, or theme of the work. The materials for achieving his object are several. First the set, including furnishings and props: having

digested and come to an understanding with the play, the set is almost
the first priority after casting. Actually both matters are attended to
simultaneously but it must never be forgotten that casting is the first
concern. In an emergency a play can be done without a set, but
never without actors, and this thought is something which should be
taken to heart in these days when, chiefly influenced by America, the
setting and lighting often take precedence over everything, including
the play. Nevertheless the set is probably next in importance and long
discussions between producer and scenic artist take place very early on
in production planning. Having studied the play carefully the scenic
artist, at a meeting with the producer, irons out numerous technical
difficulties. The producer explains what he wants and the scenic
artist goes away to make a sketch and a model for the producer's
approval. It is only after the producer is completely satisfied that the
work of constructing the set can begin. If there is a costume designer
the producer will meet him and pass sketches for the clothes of the
various characters. Should the making of them be attempted by the
society it is a laudable but lengthy and complicated business. Enlist
the aid of a member with a flair for clothes and a knowledge of period:
if she is industrious and capable in addition, she will prove a treasure
and should be made wardrobe mistress. If clothes are hired it is still
of great importance that sketches should be made and sent to the
costumiers so that mistakes of period will not arise, colours will blend,
and garments appropriate to each character will be dispatched.

Make-up discussions come later unless dyeing of hair or weight
reduction are involved. Make-up should have due consideration, for
it plays a large part in the overall effect.

Lighting can mar, and sometimes almost make a play. In Great
Britain it is still expected of every professional producer that he will
understand how to light a play. In America a separate department of
scenic artists and lighting experts, with their attendant unions, are in
control, and sometimes they achieve quite remarkable effects. I think,
however, that our system is preferable for no one knows better than the
producer all the nuances and intricacies of the mood of the play he is
producing, and if the same effect can be achieved by doing the job
personally it cuts out endless conferences with the lighting expert and,
in the precious period of the final rehearsals, saves hours of time. As we
are discussing amateur productions I need not add that it also saves a
great deal of money. My own experience in New York may have been
particularly unfortunate but, in a play which I was directing, the
rehearsals were arranged in such a way, and my protests fell upon deaf
ears, that the initial lighting was done while the dress rehearsals were
n progress. This meant that actors, playing delicate scenes, had to

compete with a raucous voice out front bellowing instructions through a microphone to the electricians on the stage. Even had the result been wonderful it would not have been adequate compensation, because the strain on the actors' already overwrought and exhausted nerves was too great. In this country the producer and stage staff carry out the first, long, difficult lighting rehearsal by themselves, going through the entire lighting plot, which the producer has worked out beforehand, and each lighting cue is rehearsed until, at that rehearsal, it is accurate. No actor is present while this preliminary lighting rehearsal is in progress. As the dress rehearsals commence the lighting is further experimented with and perfected.

Now we come to the most important facet of the production—the acting. It is hoped that the producer, having been given a free hand, will not have indulged in type casting. To find the actor who can best play the part is the achievement. Amateurs can be independent on this point. Professional managers frequently choose actors with names, mannerisms and other qualities which they suppose will attract the public without fully considering their value to the play. In numberless cases a leading part has been cast with a star recognized as "box office" and the whole venture, or adventure, has failed because he or she was unsuitable. So, please, eschew type casting.

It is necessary that everyone connected with a production should have faith and belief in the producer. When this belief fails it is sometimes the producer's fault, sometimes the fault of those surrounding him. There is always the danger of too many sets of loyalties, too much self-centredness. Where there is a complete allegiance to *the play* there is the greatest possibility of success for the project. If it is felt that the people working with the producer have not got faith in what he is doing he should go; there is no alternative. Without co-operation he cannot contribute work of any value at all.

Having completed the casting of the play, almost the first thing the producer must make the chosen players aware of is that most of what is done in acting is interdependent. If an actor will give everything in his nature to another actor and that actor will reciprocate, the result is teamwork or, that highly suspect word these days because it has been so bandied about and misunderstood, "group acting". Sean O'Casey, perhaps the only living playwright who qualifies for the mantle of the much-abused term "genius", has said so rightly, "Actors should be trained together like a football team and stay together for at least five years." This means that with the producer's guidance actors can find out their own strength and weakness, and the strength and weakness of their fellow players—the people they are working *with*. "With" is the operative word. If actors will not work together to help and heighten each others' performances the entire production can go for "naught". There is no other form of expression, with the exception of an orchestra, where it is so necessary for all those participating to give and take; give of their best to each other and take gratefully.

The producer's first job in rehearsal is to see that all actors are *au fait* not only with their own parts but with the play as a whole. It is essential that the cast should care about the other characters as well as their own if only for the selfish reason that each character reacts to and depends on the other and, in the general effect, all characters are deeply involved with each other.

The rehearsals start with readings of the play; how many there are depends on the producer. The theatre is a place for practical work. Naturally theory has its place but it should never take precedence over the active side of the performance. The very word "act" demonstrates that it means "to do". There are certain "arty crafty" elements in the theatre who would talk for weeks before getting down to the physical business of acting. It is noticeable in these cases that the discussions are more impressive, as a rule, than the performance. It should be realized that these theoreticians have gained a support from people who feel a need to protest, or react, against the outdated method, often still in use in repertory, where the company never reads or discusses the play at all, but starts rehearsing immediately under a director who blocks out a series of often meaningless moves which he has obtained from the "acting edition" of some previous production. This sort of direction is almost always bad. A compromise between these two methods should be striven for; the play should be read in concert, perhaps several times. The producer should discuss his opinion of the author's intention. The actors should be given the opportunity to express their opinions. Throughout the entire rehearsal period, providing it is remembered that the producer is completely in control, and has the final word—an atmosphere of experiment and discovery should be encouraged. The producer who sees the overall performance of the play more clearly than any single player, must inspire the cast with confidence and, in every way possible stimulate and encourage their imagination. He and the actors are creative artists and should work side by side to achieve a common end. It must always be remembered, however, that the actor, finally, has only his own part to worry about while the producer must constantly bear in mind every facet of the play and the production. He must think of the characters not only individually but collectively, and in their relation one to another, and the especial bearing each one of them has on the principal theme of the play. A performance can be achieved in many different ways which becomes increasingly effective as the artists gather more experience and gain developed imagination. The producer must realize this always, and although he makes the final decision on how a speech or a scene is to be interpreted, must have an open mind, and be willing to change and adapt his first conception when he sees an actor performing creatively and imaginatively, providing that the play is being served by the actor. The actor should make every effort to keep his mind receptive at all times and be adaptable to different points of view. The player who is rigid about a method of interpretation is almost always limited and therefore not useful in the sort of company we are discussing. The producer should constantly bear in mind the varying degrees of talent and experience among the actors in his cast, and be careful not to ask inexperienced performers to do things beyond their ability. He must be quick to see and exploit the virtues they do possess. A producer should make the following rule: never to ask an actor to do something which he could not do himself. By that I don't mean that a middle-aged producer should be able to vault over a settee with the same agility as the eighteen-year-old juvenile, but he must be sure that such a movement is possible for that particular young player and if it is not, he must think of an alternative movement. The actor should be helped by the producer to feel mentally and physically comfortable in all that he is asked to do. However much assistance and inspiration the producer is able to give his cast during rehearsal he must never forget that, finally, he must withdraw as the curtain is going up on the first night and leave everything in the hands of the players.

Many mediocre plays have been strengthened and made worth while by the performance of the actors playing in them. Even the greatest plays depend for their continued life on the interpretation given to the various parts by the succeeding generations of actors. But for the best result the actor must be outstanding only because of his talent and the original and exciting conception that he is able to bring to a part. He should never be propped up by tricks, either his own or the producer's, to stand out at the expense of the play.

For the sake of the whole (and his *own* performance) an actor playing a part should never be in charge of the production. Some of our finest actors, Olivier and Gielgud frequently, take on this dual role but however gifted they may be, both the play and their playing may suffer as a result. The work of production is so wide in scope, covering every facet of putting a play onto the stage that it is not wise to combine it with another highly responsible job which, by itself, requires such intense concentration.

The rehearsal period should be a time of experiment between the producer and the actors when characterization is slowly built up and when the individual talents of each artist are assisted by the producer to develop and mature. He will obtain his best results by guidance and stimulation. The actors, given the opportunity to be creative, will respond to such suggestion and inspiration until they are all working together to bring out the best in themselves and each other.

There are no hard and fast rules in methods of production but certain points can be mentioned with advantage: the producer who is capable of *demonstrating* what he means to an actor is invaluable but he should use such a talent only when necessary. If he can get the same result by suggestion it is better for the actor, who should try always not to be an imitator. The producer would be wise to refrain, whenever possible, from asking actors to copy his interpretation of lines and his inflections. Again he should ask for a result and help the actor to find the method. However, where actors are beginners and the producer is experienced, to learn by imitation may be the only way in which any results can be obtained at all. If this is the case the cast should be grateful for a producer who is also an actor and can help them over the first difficult period, when there seems everything to learn, by showing them physically how things are done.

The producer should insist that if there are difficult or foreign skills required by an artist in a particular part he must master them from the early stages of rehearsal. If the part calls for a special dialect, dance steps, singing, fights, falls, special curtseys, tumbles over furniture, etc., these must be done at all rehearsals, and not passed over until some later period. If a kiss and passionate embrace are indicated they must be practised at every rehearsal, so that the performance will be easy and natural; if sobbing is required in a breakdown of emotions, let the actress, or the actor, weep in reality. In the professional theatre this advice would be unnecessary but, among amateurs, things which might cause embarrassment to an actor before he has discovered how to "lose" himself in a part even while rehearsing, may be left until it is too late to learn to do them well. It is a golden rule that the most difficult parts of a play, should be rehearsed most and mastered first. Beware of an actor who says, "I shall be able to do it when I have the costume on." If he can't learn to do a thing naturally and effectively in his ordinary clothes, imagining what he will finally wear, no costume is going to help him very much.

When the rehearsal period has advanced sufficiently to allow the actors to get a flow in mood, movement, and lines, the producer should interrupt as little as possible and should content himself with letting a scene carry through and *then* make alterations and corrections. There is nothing more difficult for players to contend with than the producer who will not stop talking and let the actors act.

It is important that a producer should be incisive and have decision.

Even quite inexperienced actors know almost immediately when a producer is "padding" either through insufficient knowledge of the script, inexperience, a paucity of ideas, or nervousness with his cast. Making quite radical alterations late in the rehearsal period is not what I mean by lack of decision. Often, as the production takes shape and characterizations develop, and the separate scenes begin to build towards their climaxes and knit together, the producer may see many more effective methods of getting the result for which he is aiming. The actors must be adaptable to such changes up to the very last moment.

It is desirable that the producer should appreciate the talents and potentialities of his cast and not be slow to express his satisfaction when their efforts begin to bear fruit, and the production, through development of mood and atmosphere, character and teamwork, pace and tempo, commences to express the author's intention which was the goal from the beginning. It is equally important that when an actor is not developing and is holding up the progress of the production, not always through lack of talent, or even experience, but through an error of casting, the producer must not hesitate, after giving the actor all the help in his power, to make a change in the cast before the damage is irreparable. This has sometimes to be done in the professional theatre and naturally is one of the unhappiest experiences possible for all concerned, especially as there is the risk that the artist being replaced may suffer damage to his reputation. Among amateurs, the hurt feelings would be just as great, but to accept such an unhappy decision gracefully is the greatest service the person who is asked to withdraw can do for the play and the success of the society. In another part and play the same actor might give an excellent performance.

The amount of rehearsal is at the discretion of the producer. If he has used the ninety hours scheduled with skill and there has been no time wasted, and if the cast has worked hard and done adequate home study there may be no need for extra rehearsals as the time for the dress rehearsals draws near. If there is need—if the actors are not word-perfect, or have not completely mastered all physical business, if the scenes are not knitting together, or the production is ragged in any way, the producer should issue extra "calls" ruthlessly. He may be unpopular at the time, but how grateful everyone will be that they did that additional work, as they wait for those last agonizing moments to pass before the curtain goes up on the first performance!

At the final rehearsal, prior to the dress rehearsals, it is wise, after giving long and copious notes to players and stage management, to advise the actors to get as much rest as possible before the first dress rehearsal as they may very well be up most of the night. They should come provided with food and hot drinks as there is seldom an opportunity to break long enough to get out of the theatre for refreshment. The actors are given their first dress rehearsal call and dismissed. The real ordeal for the producer, stage management, stage crew, and all those vitally important workers backstage whose great efforts are so often unremarked when all is over, begins. The producer, who will now be taxed to his utmost until the rise of the curtain on the first night, turns his attention away from the actors with whom he has worked so hard in the preceding months and concentrates entirely, for the time being, on the various jobs being handled by the people backstage. Because he is now so completely immersed in this other side of the production I will continue to discuss the director's function, in this final phase, in a later chapter entitled Stage Management.

COSTUMES THROUGH THE AGES
Drawings by Thea Neu

2. Roman.

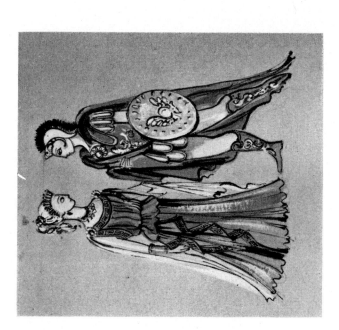

1. Greek.

4. Italian Renaissance.

3. Medieval.

III. THE ACTOR

THE actor may not be as important in the general scheme of things as certain professional players like to think he is, but it must never be forgotten that it is usually the actor or actress that audiences pay to see. Folks like to *see* plays; few of them have the urge to read them. It is by the actor's art that the printed page becomes transformed into the magic of make-believe. For the best type of theatre this art is propped up, padded, endorsed, and bettered by the worthwhile script, skilful director, imaginative settings and good team-work, which help to make the play and production a symphonic unity. In the past when poor pieces like *The Lyons Mail*, *The Bells* and *Sweet Nell of Old Drury* were performed regularly, actors proved their worth and consolidated their authority by using such vehicles to show off their personalities. Many of these pieces would be jeered off the stage if performed today. It was largely this sort of performance which established the convention that the actor, from the audience stand-point, is without peer in the matter of importance. Without him the playwright is like the proverbial fuel without fire, but without a good playwright it has been shown, in the past, that the actor can frequently shine. On the surface the leading actor, because convention has decreed thus, is independent of script, director, even fellow actors. They, on the other hand, are dependent upon him; his art, personality, genius, call it what you like. These qualities of greatness were quite capable in the old days of attracting, silencing, enthralling audiences who cared little about the play, but said, "The player's the thing." *In the old days*. Yes, I dare say, but not in the practical theatre of today. Convention has been handed down, the great tradition surrounded by cliches ("The show must go on", and "Loyalty to the public", are but two of them; I won't bore you with the Pagliacci theme!), and so when choosing your company it is well to bear in mind that to the layman, whether he be a member of the audience who has paid for admission, the reporter from the local newspaper, or even the chap who sells tickets at the door, it is the amateur's performance as an actor, and not the producer, scenic artist, dancer or musician, which will be observed most closely, and discussed afterwards at perhaps such great length.

Of course, any of us who has had much connection with stage productions knows how many contributory factors must be taken into account when presenting plays today. The actor, to all who work backstage, is an important cog in the wheel, but no more important from the technical standpoint, than the electrician, the stage manager or carpenter, the producer or the conductor of the orchestra—if there is an orchestra. This is what the merest novice backstage knows, but it is frequently overlooked by audiences who come for the most part so superficially minded, and so conditioned by a past theatre lauding the importance of the player over the play, that they cannot see that a series of independent factors, all of which knitted together under the guidance of a producer, all depending one upon the other, go to make up the result—a Production. However, because of this conditioned thought where everything is seen through the actor's physique, utterance, attitude and action, it is as well to remember to provide the best conditions to surround his efforts when he is depicting a part.

Most people with a creative talent are aware at a very early age, in a vague way, that there is a particular thing they want to do: paint, make music, dance, write, etc. Certainly, however shy they may be in normal circumstances, "natural" actors have the desire by the time they are four or five to "perform in front of people". If this urge is encouraged—or if it is just left alone—the possessors of it will find their own way, almost inevitably, into some branch of "show business". Of course, they may have other, greater talents, or compensating traits of character which warn them against being "pro's", and when this is the case they usually become the mainstays of the amateur theatre. The important point is that people who have this *instinct* for dramatic expression make up the rank and file of the theatre—professional or amateur.

Millions of words have been written on the art of acting. There are many first-rate books to recommend on the subject (some of which are mentioned in the bibliography at the back of this book) and perhaps, in addition there is room for certain advice to the serious amateur from one, like myself, who has spent all his life, from childhood, working in various phases of the professional theatre.

Dancers like Ulanova and Fonteyn, musicians of the calibre of Heifitz and Menuhin, actors of the stamp of Thorndyke, Olivier, Ashcroft and Guinness, are professional to their fingertips. Apart from their expert talents, they have conquered, long ago, the fundamental requirements of their respective arts. If the amateur actor is unable to master his craft with the many obstacles placed in the way of all those who follow a profession half-time, there are certain basic factors he can absorb, thus following in the footsteps of the most professional of the best professionals.

There is one point on the art of acting about which all thoughtful players can agree—however divergent their views may be on method—and that is: you never stop learning to the end of your life.

Regardless of how one starts on an acting career, whether as an amateur, a student at a dramatic academy, in a repertory company or as an assistant stage manager, one frequently starts with a fear of performing in public. This is what is termed in the theatre as "stage-fright". The urge to act is so strong that it outweighs this emotion but it is there, nevertheless, and is something quite apart from the nervous tension from which no actor ever frees himself, however experienced he may become. It is necessary that this initial fear should be con-quered. If it can't be got rid of the possessor of it should give up the stage—and indeed many gifted people have left the theatre because they found it impossible to defeat this fundamental drawback. Its effect on an actor is to cause inhibitions which prevent him ever gaining complete mastery over his voice, body and mind and make impossible the development of the concentration which is essential to a good performance. This fear is usually due to a destructive type of self-consciousness. Young people particularly go through agonies of suffering because they are wrapped up in assessing the impression they make on other human beings, instead of being interested to find out about those other human beings, or the subject or activity under dis-cussion. At the moment when a person transfers his interest and atten-tion from himself to another person, or subject, apart from himself, he becomes interesting to other people and he becomes free, unself-con-scious. This type of unself-consciousness must be achieved by every actor. At the same time that an actor rids himself of an obsession with self he must learn to develop another kind of self-consciousness—or critical observation of self. A good actor is aware, and in control, of every slight movement of his body and inflection of voice. While one part of him is lost in playing or "living" the part he is enacting, another part of him is standing by, completely master of each detail of his playing, gauging the effect of his performance and the perfor-mance as a whole on the audience, noting the reaction of fellow players, rising immediately to any sudden emergency on the stage, and all without disturbing or upsetting the part of him which is immersed in playing, the part which is the artist engaged on the moment to moment progress of the action and atmosphere of the play. An actor is like two people, both intensely concentrated on the job in hand. If the actor is not freed at the very beginning of his acting life from a self-centred interest in his own, often very unimportant personality, how can he possibly learn to develop the concentration which is necessary in order to play even a simple, straightforward part success-fully?

It has been said that all actors are exhibitionists, and I suppose to a lesser or greater extent this is true. Therefore, it is clear that the inhibited and repressed types are useless in the theatre, as actors, until they lose their represssions and inhibitions. To steep oneself in a character, to be interested in how such a character looks, talks, sees and walks, to the total exclusion of self, soon rids oneself of that embarrassment which all too many men and women feel when they are called upon to play characters who, as people, are unfamiliar to them. Complete concentration *can* be acquired if constant and uncompromising work is spent on developing it, and it is the most important basic keynote for the good actor. The sense of stillness in an actor on the stage is of paramount importance. How many times have we been distracted when, during a vital scene between two characters, a third has failed to concentrate, and we have been divorced from the proceedings? Concentration is required to an even greater degree from an actor who must be on-stage but is not part of the immediate action.

There is a tendency among beginners in certain sections of the theatre, especially in America, to approach the study of acting from the wrong end. A sort of theatrical "mish mush" language has been born (an apt term coined by Lillian Hellman as we discussed this new "trend" over lunch in her New York apartment in 1953). Young professionals, with little knowledge and often even less experience, discourse learnedly on "motivation", "the inner creative state", "the understanding of the subconscious", etc. These are pretentious expressions for the sort of advanced knowledge and understanding towards which all experienced actors should constantly aim. In students they stem largely from an inexpert study of the Stanislavsky method of acting. To start one's work entirely from this point of view is comparable with a student musician commencing a study of the piano by attempting a concerto instead of five-finger exercises.

An amusing story is told of an American producing a play in England, and saying to the late Arthur Sinclair, one of the great Irish Players, "Mr. Sinclair, I want you to physicalize your comedic dynamics." And Sinclair replying, "You mean you want me to fall flat on my arse?" I doubt if the Irish Players ever called their remarkable style of acting by any particular name but no group of artists, not the American Group Theatre, splendid though they were, nor, I am convinced, Stanislavsky's own company, The Moscow Arts Theatre, understood better or displayed more memorably the virtues of the naturalistic school of acting.

Having mastered, or while mastering, the elementary requirements of acting, which I shall outline in a moment, the actor can turn his attention to the involved difficult means by which highly skilled actors get their effects. The influence of Stanislavsky's Theory of Naturalism on the modern theatre is incalculable. He has caused a revolution in the approach to acting throughout the world. His theory demands complete sincerity and naturalness from the actor. The player should be able to identify himself, through his own experiences, with the character he is playing, so completely, that he gives the impression of living the author's character in actuality each time he plays it. This is precisely the correct approach to the art of acting but, although it was absent from the stage for many years, it is not new. Great actors have always used it. When one reads the reports of noted critics of the past, on the performances of the really great, we are forced to the conclusion, that whatever those actors called their method of acting the result was as thrilling as any which grew out of a study and expert understanding of the "Stanislavsky method". I will quote from two great critics discussing two of the memorable artists of their period. First, a description by Julian Charles Young of Mrs. Sarah Siddons playing Volumnia in *Coriolanus*: "In the second scene of the second act of *Coriolanus*, after the victory of the battle of Corioli, an ovation in honour of the victor was introduced with great and imposing effect by John Kemble. Now in this procession, and as one of the central figures in it, Mrs. Siddons had to walk. Had she been content to follow in the beaten track of her predecessors in the part, she would have marched across the stage, from right to left, with the solemn, stately, almost funeral, step conventional. But at the time, as she often did, she forgot her own identity. She was no longer Sarah Siddons, tied down to the direction of the prompter's book, or trammelled by old tradition. She was Volumnia, the proud mother of a proud son and conquering hero. So that, when it was time for her to come on, instead of dropping each foot at equidistance in its place, with mechanical exactitude and cadence subservient to the orchestra; deaf to the guidance of her woman's ear, but sensitive to the throbbings of her haughty mother's heart, with flashing eye, and proudest smile, and head erect, and hands pressed firmly on her bosom as if to repress by manual force its triumphant swellings, she towered above all around and rolled and almost reeled across the stage; her very soul as it were, dilating and rioting in its exultation; until her action lost all grace and yet became so true to nature, so picturesque and so descriptive that pit and gallery sprang to their feet, electrified by the transcendent execution of an original conception."

In George Henry Lewes's great book of criticism called *Actors, and The Art of Acting*, he says of the third act of Edmund Kean's Othello, "From the third act onwards all was wrought out with a mastery over the resources of expression such as has been seldom approached. In the successive unfolding of these great scenes he represented with incomparable effect the lion-like fury, the deep and haggard pathos, the forlorn sense of desolation alternating with gusts of stormy cries for vengeance, the misgivings and sudden reassurances, the calm and deadly resolution of one not easily moved, but who, being moved, was stirred to the very depths. Kean was a consummate master of passionate expression. People generally spoke of him as a type of the 'impulsive actor'. But if by this they meant one who abandoned himself to the impulse of the moment without forethought or pre-arranged effect, nothing could be wider from the mark. He was an artist, and in Art all effects are regulated. The original suggestion may be, and generally is, sudden and unprepared—'inspired', as we say; but the alert intellect recognizes its truth, seizes on it, regulates it. Without nice calculation no proportion could be preserved; we should have a work of fitful impulse, not a work of enduring Art. Kean vigilantly and patiently rehearsed every detail, trying the tones until his ear was satisfied, practising looks and gestures until his artistic sense was satisfied; and having once regulated these he never changed them. The consequence was that, when he was sufficiently sober to stand and speak, he could act his part with the precision of a singer who has thoroughly learned his air. . . . Hence it was that he was always the same; not always in the same health, not always in the same vigour, but always master of the part, and expressing it through the same symbols. The voice on some nights would be more irresistibly touching in 'But, oh! the pity of it, Iago!'—or more musically forlorn in 'Othello's occupation's gone'—or more terrible in 'Blood; Iago; blood, blood!' but always the accent and rhythm were unchanged."

A report in the *Observer* of 1 May 1955, by Kenneth Tynan, describes most graphically the results achieved when "The Method" is used successfully in the present-day theatre on Broadway. "In New York one is always conscious of the theatrical revolution wrought by 'the method'—the holy work of Stanislavsky, handed down by the Group Theatre in the thirties and now enshrined in Elia Kazan's Actors' Studio. Beside the 'method actors', most American players over forty-five (and most English players of any age are breaths of stale air; the young inhabit a tradition of realism as radical and lively as any on earth. Some accuse them of acting too exclusively with their nerves, like the restless actress at whom a director hissed: 'Don't just *do* something, *stand* there!' Others, such as the brilliant television writer Paddy Chayefsky, assert that 'method actors' frequently lack 'talent refined enough to play what their intelligence has uncovered'.

"A perfect answer to these criticisms lies in the performance I have mentioned. The actress, Eileen Heckart, plays a bereaved mother, tipsy and listless, with such total identification that one of the rarest things in all theatre takes place: the audience is allowed to form its own opinion of the character. Most players would have implied a moral judgment on the part; would have made it either pathetic or hateful, would have invited either love or loathing; for actors love to 'editorialize'. Miss Heckart leaves that to us. Simply the thing she is shall make her live; and live she does, abundantly, tactfully and in depth."

Side by side with Tynan's appreciation of that beautifully sensitive actress, Eileen Heckart, whose performance, on Broadway, in William Inge's *Picnic* I shall long remember, is a sad little story of an earnest young actress I directed in a New York production and had finally and most reluctantly to replace. She played only a small part in the opening scene and unfortunately for her almost all her lines were exposition. After struggling with her inadequacy for some days she told me that she thought her difficulty lay in the fact that she really didn't fully understand the "inner compulsion" of the character. My answer was, "I daresay you don't, my dear, but if you could just speak the lines clearly and loudly enough so that I could hear them beyond the first two rows of the stalls it would be a basis on which to work." I tell this story in order to illustrate my point that every actor —or would-be actor—*must* master certain elementary requisites as well as, or preferably before, trying to conquer the subtle and delicate intricacies which make acting an art. He must:

1. Be able to memorize without difficulty.
2. Be willing to work harder than he ever thought possible. There is great truth in the saying, "Genius is 10 per cent talent and 90 per cent hard work."
3. Have a professional attitude to the theatre at all times whether he earns money from it or not. This advice can apply in these times equally to the professional and the amateur. An actor must, at all times, abide by the discipline of the theatre and obey all rules set down for the good of the production.
4. Be audible.
5. Be able to project.

It is regrettable that such an elementary point as audibility should ever have to be mentioned to an actor. The two physical tools of his trade are his voice and his body and the possibilities of expression of each one of them are infinite. To control body and voice should be an actor's primary interest in life. The voice can be considered from many aspects but, basically, it is the instrument used to convey the story or message of the play to the audience. Apart from the movement of the actors and the action of the play, the voice is the only means by which the audience can comprehend what is being presented to them. So it follows that they must be able to hear and understand what the actors are saying. Wrapped up with audibility is projection, not only of voice but of personality. The actor must know that distance from an audience calls for broader and more elaborate gestures, and additional volume of voice. This is what is termed "projection" and "size". Its absence from the professional stage is sorely missed. It should not be confused with "ham" acting, which is bad acting; bad, because it is unreal. True, *Big* acting is often bad acting, but the Big acting of those who project realistically, possess an actor's sense and sensibility to mark the occasion and commemorate the Big part by an actor's genius, is the major achievement in the theatre from the actor's viewpoint. An audience can experience a feeling of greatness.

The result of projection is referred to in slang usage as "getting over". It is brought about by every movement being clear-cut and decisive. Although gestures and movement, including facial expression are heightened in stage performance, it is of vital importance that the actor should know exactly how much exaggeration or heightening is necessary because, from the audience's point of view, the result should look absolutely natural and unexaggerated. The same rule applies to vocal performance. The voice must be pitched to stage level and placed so that it can be easily heard in all parts of the theatre. All words must be articulated more clearly and decidedly than would be necessary in ordinary speech and the actor must know how to point his lines to get the maximum dramatic effect. As with the body the result must appear to be entirely natural and spontaneous. An experienced actor knows how to whisper and yet be heard to the furthermost part of the theatre. The most delicate, restrained performance can still be projected so that it is as powerful in dramatic effect as Shakespeare's "Friends, Romans, and Countrymen".

Some great actors—Henry Irving for one—have had limited rasping voices and stilted, affected mannerisms, but for all that, so great a talent and expertness accompanied these drawbacks that they were made to appear virtues. Great actors, when exceptions to the general rule, are however, no good example for the amateur, who, to hold his audience, must be able to enunciate clearly. The study of diction, which has been getting steadily worse down the years should always be regarded as of the utmost importance.

One famous actor is said to have remarked, "In order to perfect his art an actor must devote all his attention to three things: voice, voice and voice!" That is an exaggeration, especially today. But, while appreciating development and reforms in styles of acting, it is dangerous to follow the modern tendency to overlook the fact that the voice is the main tool of the actor's craft. An actor deprived of the use of his legs and arms can still act effectively and powerfully provided his voice, brain and emotions remain intact.

It is important that an actor should be able to speak his own language without any accent or dialect at all. He should discover and correct faults of affectation and slovenliness often found in certain, so-called, "educated" accents, and mispronunciations and carelessness when the accent is regional. There is an accepted standard English which all actors should strive to learn and master. Some actors may have a natural flair for speaking dialects. The possessor of such a gift is fortunate for it is given to few people. Much time should be devoted to the study of dialects and accents, for when mastered, they broaden an actor's range immeasurably and, more than that, such knowledge helps his powers of auditory observation. A man's speech is one of the most telling clues to his character, and an actor should be constantly occupied in the study of character and characteristics. It is impossible not to be immensely assisted in playing a part if an actor realizes the fundamental character differences between, for example, a person who speaks with a lilting, musical, romantic Irish or Welsh accent and the firm, practical, down-to-earth voice of the inhabitant of Yorkshire or Lancashire. An actor must be observant of life around him. He must watch people at home, at work, on buses, trains, in the streets. He must watch the walk of a tired workman, the skipping of a schoolboy, the reaction of an irate passenger taken past his bus stop, the way a bent old woman stirs the sugar in her tea and nibbles her biscuit in a teashop. An actor gets into the habit of storing these impressions unconsciously. More than watching life around one, which is, after all, only the noting of outside behaviour, is the understanding and storing of one's own and other people's emotional experiences. The more facets an actor can develop to his own character the greater his range will be in performance. When an actor can identify himself *completely* with a character, he achieves almost perfect success. It is not necessary to *be* a Don Juan, a monk, a murderer, a Rothschild, a Hitler, a martyr, a saint, or a devil, but it is necessary that an actor should understand the basic emotional impetus of such outstanding characters and that he should have experienced emotions approximating to each type. Then, with his hard-won technical equipment—mastery of his voice and body, ability to use these instruments to convey thoughts and emotions, understanding of the behaviour and speech of many types and classes of people, he can imagine and amplify his experience until he can faithfully portray the jealousy of an Iago prompting the noble Othello to jealousy, the passionate love of a Romeo, the blind ambition of a Lady Macbeth, the ruined power of a Borkman, the repression and frustration of a Hedda Gabler, the rugged simplicity and saintliness of a St. Joan, the artificiality covering the basic sincerity of a Lady Teazle.

But we have gone ahead of ourselves. We are still, in the beginning, mainly concerned with gaining mastery over our body and our voice. There is great satisfaction to be derived from their growing response to the demands made upon them. The hard work entailed offers rich rewards. It is essential to gain complete control over breathing, to learn to place the voice properly so that its quality will constantly improve, and its possessor will be enabled to speak with full strength at stage pitch, hour after hour, for days on end, without straining or injuring the vocal chords. Resonance must be developed over the entire range of the voice so that, as an instrument, it will be capable of obeying the performer's dictates. The actor must learn to pronounce and enunciate clearly and absolutely distinctly. He must learn the value and use of vowels and consonants. He must learn to phrase short speeches and sentences within long speeches, with infinite variety and dramatic effectiveness so that he can hold the interest of an audience indefinitely. Finally, and most important, his voice must become the flexible, controlled instrument which conveys with subtlety and accuracy every shade of thought and emotion which the actor's interpretation of a part demands.

The student of acting usually finds that he can rid his voice of nervous self-conscious mannerisms more easily and early than he can his body. The reason there is such difficulty in achieving even elementary physical relaxation and repose can be traced to our old enemy, self-centredness. There are various methods of freeing oneself from this crippling state.

1. Genuinely transfer your interest from yourself to an object, another person, or a subject.
2. Learn to concentrate easily and completely and sincerely.
3. Teach your voice and your body to react to thought and feeling. Force every feeling from your heart, from your brain, to your hands—to your fingertips—to your feet.

Long before you have taught your body to express *all* shades of feeling and thought, it will respond with truth, up to a point, if you are honestly concentrating on *what* you are doing and not on *how* you are doing it. It is wrong to show an actor how to "put out his arms in entreaty", for instance, or "throw up his hands in despair". The actor must first genuinely experience the emotion of wanting to "entreat" and let the emotion flow through his body; then in some way or other, in the way most natural for the particular person—the body will express the feeling. In one person a large flamboyant movement will be the result, in another person perhaps a very slight one. But if the movement is the result of the *actual emotion* the gesture will be true and the onlookers will recognize the feeling whether there is speech to accompany the physical action or not. Often the face can record most graphically a series of emotions while the hands and feet feel like lead and express nothing but the most miserable embarrassment. This is understandable, in a way, inasmuch as the feet and hands are the outposts of the body. To masses of people hands are merely the instruments with which they pick up objects or perform daily tasks, and feet are provided for walking. To an accomplished actor the feet have infinite possibilities of expression and the hands are comparable with the most expressive and useful feature of all—the eyes.

People spend large sums—more than they can afford usually—on decorating the body. Great efforts are made to enhance physical assets and disguise defects, but few people use their inner powers of mind and heart to make their bodies and their faces more attractive and expressive. Youth, or its semblance, is the everlasting Eldorado. An actor, if he has mastered his art, can go from age to age serenely, each phase of life bringing new and exciting experiences. No period of human life is undramatic. The most telling example of such a person in the professional theatre, at the present time, is Sybil Thorndyke. This splendid actress has had an outstandingly distinguished career. At no point has she clung to a particular age group. She has lived her own full life from year to year, as beloved privately as she is publicly. She has managed to extract the richest and best from each phase of her life from the time when she created Shaw's St. Joan to the present day, when she has achieved a beauty which surely comes from her inner resources and seems to surpass the loveliness of any actress on the stage today. It is rare that a person grows more beautiful with age. It is a sentimental fallacy when such an idea is paraded. But in the case of this fine actress it is exactly what has happened. Year by year she achieves greater beauty. It would be infinitely boring if all people remained young. The mental, emotional, and physical states of man during his various stages of life present the actor with an endless field of study.

At the commencement of an acting life the most useful qualities are natural gifts—either dramatic or comic. The possessor of such talents will be able to do by instinct, many of the things which less gifted people take years to learn. But the natural actor must "learn" also. He must become aware of how he gets effects so that he may reproduce them at will whether he feels like it or not. Some of the things a "natural" *sometimes* understands automatically are "timing", "making use of dramatic pauses", getting and keeping "pace", getting legitimate "laughs", "holding" an audience at a dramatic moment so that the proverbial "pin-dropping" may be heard.

Instinctive actors can usually do these things almost from the beginning, up to a point, and of course they master the things they cannot do very quickly. But let us reject, for the moment, the notion that it is at all common for the professional or amateur actor to be, like so many of the Irish Players of the 'twenties, that rare and blessed thing, a "natural"; instead let us approach the art of acting as something where faults have to be overcome, where experience must be accompanied by homework. This homework should include, whenever possible, seeing the best professional actors and productions. Some alleged professionals have little to teach the amateur, but we can eradicate our worst faults by noting them in others, and perfecting those good points we are fortunate enough to possess. Sincerity on the stage, like sincerity in life, is worth so very much indeed and it must come from the heart as well as the mind. No theorist can say, "You must be sincere", because this must be a matter of temperament. What the theorist can say with authority however, is that *unless* you are sincere, have studied the play as a whole, so that your characterization becomes an integral part of that whole, then you will never be an actor. The foregoing points are only a few of many which must be learnt whether the actor be a "natural" or not. Every actor, however talented, has to learn the all-important art of teamwork, how to gauge an audience and control it, how to keep a part so completely fresh that it is as real and apparently spontaneous after three hundred performances, as it was on the first night when excitement and apprehension carried one along.

Thankfully, in this country, we still have at least the remnants of the system of theatrical apprenticeship. No other method, whatever people are told, will ever replace it. No school, university or study, can possibly be a substitute for practical experience. Certainly, in the theatre, so filled with the most subtle intricacies, the constant day-to-day familiarity with problems, crises, fulfilment, do more to teach than any academy. That is why the amateur theatre is healthy and, more than at any previous time, essential. People who can act must get onto a stage. They must be given a chance to perform. The golden opportunities, as in the United States, are getting less and less. Repertory companies are closing down all over the country. The repertory movement has always been the training ground for the future: many fine actors, actresses, producers and, in some cases, playwrights have been given their first chances by them. This field of expression is rapidly narrowing. The amateur theatre, free of overwhelming financial responsibilities, can continue calmly in its usual way providing, as it does, an alternative to the professional repertory theatre and, in that way keep the legitimate theatre alive. There is no reason why the amateur should not make a clarion call throughout Great Britain to save the "live theatre". His may well be the only voice which will be heeded—or even heard.

IV. THE AUDIENCE

WE have discussed the playwright, the producer, the actor; the fourth indispensable part of the cornerstone is the audience. However much atmosphere the set lends, however beautiful the costumes and luxurious and convenient the theatre, the production will make little impact if the four elementary necessities have no quality. How many times are cast and audience alike distracted and their concentration ruined by late comers, constant smoking and clicking of cigarette lighters, audible discussion of the play while it is in progress, the banging of tip-up seats, belated and noisy requests for programmes, and rattling of crockery in the auditorium. On the other hand what pleasure and satisfaction a cast feels when, after the first disappointment of finding that there are very few people in front, they realize that though small in quantity their audience is great in quality. Being good troupers the artists are, as usual, giving of their very best, and the warmth, attentiveness and appreciation which come over the footlights to them make them feel happy and fulfilled. It seems to them the most rewarding performance of the week.

Audiences would be astonished if they knew how greatly their performance in front of the curtain influences the performance they see on the stage. Artistic success in the theatre depends on a give-and-take attitude. The more the player is capable of giving to fellow artists, the audience, and, primarily, to the play, the more will be given back to *him*. This applies also to an audience.

One of the greatest differences between the amateur and the professional is that because of the much wider and more constant opportunities, the professional learns to recognize and handle various types of audiences. It is an accepted fact that, when touring, certain towns are "difficult" or "sticky". The audiences of Scotland and Wales are quite different in their response to the same play, but they are both considered wonderful audiences. But then, the audiences of Edinburgh and Glasgow are different too. A first night West End audience is unlike any other audience on earth—fortunately! A matinee house requires all the persuasiveness an actor can muster, while a Saturday-night public must often be disciplined early and firmly if the performance is to be kept up to standard.

The theatregoer's point of view must be discussed too. Many a lover of the legitimate theatre turns out in any kind of weather to see a new or familiar play with the most pleasurable feelings of anticipation; willing and anxious to be perfectly quiet, diffident, attentive—or loudly appreciative—depending on the piece. Consider his sense of frustration when he sees a shoddily or pretentiously presented play, inadequately rehearsed, with artists bored to distraction, and quite often walking through their parts or, even worse, having private jokes with each other during the performance. The latter situation does not arise in an amateur production because no actor repeats a performance often enough to become tired of it, and indeed, no first-rate professional allows a performance to get stale. But the former can and does happen all too frequently in amateur and in repertory companies. In such cases the audience must not be blamed for lack of response or for indignant protests. People giving their time and money to witness the playing of a piece in which they are interested, have the right to expect to see a well-presented play which has been adequately rehearsed.

It is often impossible for amateur companies, especially before they get their own theatre, to offer their patrons the most elementary comforts of the professional theatre. But even when the theatre has no rake and therefore the sight line is bad, where the hall has no tip-up seats attached to the floor, and consequently chairs have to be hired, with the distracting attendant noise whenever a member of the audience moves—even with such seriously important drawbacks, certain things can and must be done for the comfort of the customers:

1. The hall must be kept warm in winter and as cool as possible in summer.
2. Patrons should be greeted with courtesy and friendliness. Their complaints should be investigated and attended to.
3. All front-of-house attendants should remain absolutely quiet during the performance. They must be particularly vigilant regarding this after the first few performances when they themselves are no longer interested in watching the play.
4. Tea-cups and glasses must be washed up and money counted, out of the hearing of the audience. If these duties are carried out near the back of the auditorium they should be done with the utmost quietness so that the concentration of the audience is not disturbed.
5. Curtains at the back or sides of the hall should not be opened during the performance in case distracting beams of light from outside are suddenly cast on the audience or players.
6. All refreshments should be served outside the auditorium. It is a mistake to emulate that worst of all customs in the professional theatre of serving trays of tea or coffee in the house, thereby causing untold irritation to players and other members of the audience.

7. If at all possible late-comers should not be shown to their seats until the end of a scene or act. To arrive late for a theatre is one of the most unpleasant and discourteous examples of bad theatre-going behaviour. A sensitive member of the audience will not wish to inconvenience the artists and fellow-members of the audience by being shown to his seat after the curtain has risen.

Before the war a theatre programme was sometimes a little booklet containing interesting information as well as advertisements, the cast list and synopsis of scenes and acts. During the war and since, however, it has become an uninspired and limited document, but the price has never been reduced. Until recently I have frequently complained that audiences are asked to pay so much for so little. However, now that conditions in the theatre are seriously straightened I am reluctantly forced to agree that no form of income, be it ever so small, should be overlooked or disregarded. I would suggest, though, that the programmes be made as original, attractive and informative as possible. Especially in an amateur society where the audience, for the most part, are members and feel a stronger sense of participation than an ordinary theatre going audience, the programme can be made into a charming memento of a memorable occasion.

I have spoken and written on many occasions regarding my feelings about atmosphere music in the theatre. The music selected for use before the curtain goes up on the first act and the music between the acts should be chosen with extreme care. It is as much part of the production as the lighting, and deciding on the works to be played is part of the producer's job. A live orchestra adds greatly to the cost of a professional production, hence the almost universal use of "canned" music in the intervals of a straight play. An amateur society would not be faced by extra expense in this matter and there might be, among the members, talented instrumentalists who could form themselves into a trio or quartet and render invaluable aid to all the productions. They must, of course, rehearse as assiduously as the folk backstage, and not agree to appear until their performance together (for this is the most telling example of teamwork) has reached a high standard. The chief advantage the legitimate theatre has over the films, or any kind of relayed or filmed entertainment, is the pleasure derived from the artists and the audience taking part together in the occasion. They are all "in the flesh". The spell that is cast on an audience and cast alike can be immeasurably heightened if the musicians are also "in the flesh".

Bad manners in an audience are notorious but when a performance receives an unfavourable reaction throughout and finally a poor

6. Restoration—Court Dress.

5. Elizabethan.

8. Empire.

7. Restoration—Puritan Dress.

10. Late Victorian.

9. Early Victorian.

12. World War I.

11. Edwardian.

reception the producer and actors, stage staff and playwright should look to themselves for the cause. If a laugh is received when there should be a deathly hush or if an actor has a comedy line or situation which can't miss getting a laugh—but he doesn't get it—the fault is seldom with the audience.

It is important that the curtain should go up at the advertised time unless the crowds pouring into the theatre are so great that they cannot be seated quickly enough. The atmosphere on such happy—all too rare—occasions is so cheerful that a wait is permissible. The folk backstage, however, should never keep a curtain waiting. If the programme states that the interval is twelve minutes it should be exactly that length of time.

It is unnecessary to state that a performance "goes" better when there is a full, or nearly full, house. The artists are stimulated by the audience and the audience by each other. This is particularly true when the play is a comedy. Knowing this, actors should be particularly on their guard, when the house is poor, to give their very best performance. It is the test of a good actor to be able to play to bad houses and still play as well as he would to a packed and appreciative house. If twenty-five people have turned out to see a play they have the same right to witness a first-rate performance as they would if the "House Full" notice was proudly displayed outside.

In many cases the only difference between an amateur and a professional is that one gets paid for the work and the other does it from interest and a desire for self-expression. It is claimed in the professional theatre, however, that there is a further difference. The amateur, it is said, gives a good performance when he feels like it and the professional gives a good performance whether he feels like it or not. This is not necessarily true, of course, because there are occasions when professionals, getting fabulous salaries, give performances which are most unimpressive, to say the least.

In any case it is worth bearing in mind, whether the player be amateur or professional, because the secret of keeping a performance fresh and inspired is a difficult one to learn and calls for much experience. But it is almost the best secret of all for a player to know.

E

V. FORMING AN AMATEUR SOCIETY

THE determination in a person, or a group of people, to form a theatrical society may derive from a recognized need in the community. More often than not, however, it comes from a personal compulsion for some sort of expression in dramatic form: writing, producing, acting or designing. Once in a century a group is formed by a lover of the theatre—a patron—who has the financial means to satisfy an urge to create a living playhouse in the community. It is this patron's project—and it is enhanced considerably if there is courage, taste and integrity behind it—which has the greatest chance of success. Any theatre, professional or amateur, requires financial stability plus the patience and imagination necessary to nurse a new project through years of struggle and loss to artistic triumph and sometimes, but only, alas, very occasionally, material success.

Financial figures for the serious professional theatre are more readily accessible than are those for amateur endeavours, and the balance sheets of a few of the most notable ventures in the former sphere make sorry reading. Some, of course, have been sponsored personally by philanthropists of the calibre of Sir Barry Jackson who for over twenty years shouldered the losses at the Birmingham Repertory Theatre. There was also that golden era at Manchester, nearly half a century ago, when the great Miss Horniman founded her famous theatre, made a proud reputation and lost a vast fortune in so doing. There was the Royal Court Theatre in London, which was headed by Vedrenne and Granville Barker. The story of that noble venture, and experiment in high theatrical art, has been most faithfully recorded by Desmond McCarthy in his well-known book, *The Court Theatre 1904–1907*. It was a tale made vivid by the courage of its two creators and, as McCarthy has said: "Audiences sat enthralled through a play, delighted by acting unlit by the light of a star, which was obviously and incomparably the better for that. Here they found a play, the roots of which struck among the interests of the time, which presented types of character delightfully recognizable yet new to the stage, in which a most natural sequence of events carried them along by the series of ingeniously contrived surprises, and left them with plenty to think over, laugh over, and dispute over when the curtain fell; in short, here was a new play, full of qualities which the critics had been arraigning the London stage for not possessing. No wonder, when the question of going to the theatre next came up, people would ask themselves what was being done at the Court."

Certainly, against the astronomical financial losses sustained by such pioneers as Barry Jackson, Vedrenne and Barker, Miss Horniman and those folk who chose to present the play of ideas, must be placed on the credit side the discovery and establishment of some of the finest playwrights in the world. Bernard Shaw and Galsworthy were two whom the Royal Court found and favoured; the Manchester Group included Stanley Houghton, Allan Monkhouse, Harold Brighouse, to name but a few of the most outstanding. Then there were those wonderful Irish Players who introduced us to Sean O'Casey, Yeats, Synge and Lady Gregory, who were in turn followed by Lennox Robinson, Denis Johnstone and countless more who had, to enact the wonderful characters of these lords of the language, such players as Sidney Morgan, Sarah Allgood, Maire O'Neill, Arthur Sinclair and W. G. Fay; most of whom, alas, have passed on.

The Birmingham Repertory gave Edith Evans, Cedric Hardwicke and Margaret Leighton their first golden opportunities, whilst Sybil Thorndyke, Estelle Winwood and Lewis Casson were among the great of the Manchester Horniman group. Incidentally Bernard Shaw, who after his early successes suffered, if not a total eclipse certainly a partial one, was "re-discovered" by Sir Barry Jackson and had some of his most difficult plays (by the word "difficult" I mean the most complex and difficult to stage) performed at the Birmingham Repertory Theatre. George W. Bishop's famous book on Barry Jackson and the Birmingham Repertory is priority reading for all serious students of the amateur theatre. In it they will find much information dealing with the struggles of a theatre which, through the enthusiasm of an idealist, jumped from a high amateur category into that of Britain's leading professional repertory theatre; the training ground of many producers and actors, as well as the experimental home of a number of those who have since become acknowledged as our leading playwrights.

These are the types of theatres which have made the most valuable contribution to the drama of this country during our present lifetime. They approximate most closely to the serious amateur groups of today; companies like the Norwich Maddermarket, the Ealing Questors, the Unnamed Society in Manchester, the Tyneside People's Theatre, the Tavistock and Unity in London; each having an impressive record of achievement for many years past.

The motivating reasons for starting a group or forming a society are various, but the method—if you wish to survive—is simple, direct and of the greatest possible importance. You must start, and continue, on a business-like basis. The "guiding spirit", that is, the most ardent enthusiast, must arrange a gathering together of all the people interested in the idea. At this meeting practical points of view should be exchanged and discussed. The type of play to be produced should be agreed upon, and the method of presentation. The serious problem of the theatre, or building, to be used for early productions should be tackled at the outset. The nucleus of an active group should be organized—people who are interested in and have some qualifications for directing, acting, scene-designing, stage management, lighting, costume-making, business management and publicity.

Unless the project is headed by a patron with considerable financial means, the subject of cold, hard cash will monopolize a large part of the first, and many of the subsequent meetings. At this initial gathering it is imperative that the matters of organization and finance should be discussed fully. Without a sound, practical, business organization, no scheme will succeed. Without high artistic principles, and an adventurous outlook, no scheme is worth bothering about.

In the theatre, professional or amateur, the individual is of paramount importance. There is no such thing as a cypher; each job is vitally important to the success of the enterprise as a whole; each person must be constantly encouraged to give of his best.

In forming a society, the organization should take more or less the following form and should not start a production until such preliminaries are complete and in sound working order.

The president of the society is an honorary post—or should I say the presidency of the society is an honorary post—and should be filled by someone of local consequence. If it is a group gathered together from those working in a store, factory, or one of the large utility public services, certain key members of the organization should be approached if possible (perhaps a benevolent managing director might be inclined to fill this position). Selecting a chairman to the society is more difficult because it must be some one of importance who is also prepared to be active. The welfare and success of the movement should be close to his heart. Thus we look for a good businessman who, at the same time, possesses some knowledge of, and regard for, the theatre. An understanding should be reached regarding these two nominations at the very beginning of the plans and, if the consent of the people who have been approached has been obtained, they should be elected at the first, or preliminary meeting. The secretary and treasurer, as well as the business and publicity managers, should also be decided upon. These are appointments of the greatest possible importance. The secretary is the person who will have, perhaps, the closest contact with the public as well as with members and with friends of members; the latter are potential members. The secretary must possess tact, friendliness and patience, plus organizing ability, a capacity for detail, and the ability to deal ably with a vast correspondence. He should also have a clear and logical mind; if possible one with some sense of finance and, although this is not an absolute essential, a knowledge of shorthand and typewriting. If you should be fortunate enough to find such a paragon, value him (or her) deeply. Apart from the producer, the secretary will most probably put in more intensive work than anyone in the unit. The perfect secretary is willing to make a contribution of long hours and complete selflessness in his behaviour and approach to the problems of the society. If the secretarial duties are not carried out efficiently, chaos will result. These duties are, more or less, as follows:

1. Be responsible for all the correspondence of the society.
2. Be responsible for keeping up to date and in perfect order a well-organized, simple, filing system.
3. Keep a record of all members.
4. Be responsible for circularizing the membership at regular intervals.
5. Collect dues from all members regularly on the dates on which they fall due.
6. Call and attend all meetings: meetings of the board, meetings of main and sub committees, meetings of members, general annual meeting.
7. At all meetings have particulars ready of business to be discussed. Take down minutes of meetings—enter them in a Minute Book—and send copies to all affected by the decisions arrived at.
8. At the annual general meeting prepare and read a report of the season's work.

The treasurer is responsible for the financial records of the society. He keeps the books, prepares production and other estimates and accounts, collects subscriptions, and administers transactions for plays and all the many other agreements into which the society may enter. Too frequently, the financial aspect of affairs in amateur dramatic societies is left to take care of itself, but this department of the theatre is never "all right on the night" unless it is organized most carefully, and on a professional basis, at the very beginning. Like the production itself the financial aspect cannot be left to chance.

Business management and publicity each have a chapter to themselves in this book. They are two of the lifelines of the society so we shall give them much space later and only a word or two now. Of the publicity manager, suffice it to say that if a person with the necessary qualifications for this post can be found the results of his work will show most gratifyingly at the box-office.

The business manager obtains all necessary licences and permissions regarding productions. He completes arrangements for the hiring of the hall or theatre which will house each production. He controls the front of house and box-office; he organizes programmes, programme-sellers and box-office attendants and clerks. He looks after the comfort of the press. He is responsible for cash takings from all sources: he banks the takings after each performance.

The remainder of the board—four members will suffice—should represent various important parts of the community; an educational body, a representative of local government, someone socially prominent, and a one-hundred-per-cent voluble enthusiast who will help to spread the gospel of the society's work far and wide (this is a friend indeed!).

Now we come to, perhaps, the most important person in the set-up, the artistic director, or producer. He is the most important only because he has the most work to do and carries the greatest load of responsibility. He *must* be experienced.

In forming an amateur society, it might be advisable to follow the method used by non-profit-making professional companies which are organized very similarly to the above plan. In these organizations the artistic director usually produces all the plays, but this is not a cast-iron rule; however, he is responsible for implementing the policy laid down by the society's committees and co-ordinating the various de-partments. He is also ultimately responsible for the smooth working and presentation of all productions. The artistic success of a venture will depend on the person who fills this role and, if it is at all possible, the society will be well advised to engage a professional with wide experience for at least the first year after the society's formation. This engagement, it is true, will eat into the resources, but the standard of the first productions would be so immeasurably improved by the appointment of the right type of person, that the box-office returns could not fail to justify the decision. Remember the late Sir James Barrie's "First impressions are awfully important"? Another old saying, about a woman's work never being finished, applies equally to the artistic director: certainly in the professional theatre, he can work sixteen hours out of twenty-four, for seven days each week, and never fully meet the demands made upon him. In an amateur society his duties would be less arduous, because there would be only intermittent productions, but he would, nevertheless, be well able to fill a full work-ing day if he did the job well. Apart from his work as a producer, which has been dealt with in another chapter, his responsibilities include the following:

1. Attendance at all meetings of the Board of Directors to report progress, discuss policy, give, and take, advice.
2. Be the controlling figure at all executive meetings.

3. Read all plays submitted to him by the play-reading committee.
4. Hold himself in readiness to accept invitations from various organizations to speak to them. This should enable him to make friends for the society and swell the membership and the audience.
5. Preside when visiting speakers address the society.
6. Arrange and organize play-readings and discussion groups within the society.

When it is decided that such-and-such a play will be produced, it is necessary for the artistic director to study and work out his conception of the production. He will confer with the scenic artist and costume designer, both of whom will adapt their designs to meet the needs of his production. It is important that an early date be fixed for this conference, shortly after the decision to launch the specific play has been decided upon. He will, doubtless, hold auditions among the members who wish to take part in the play, so that he may cast his production from the best of the available talent. From the first reading of the script until the curtain goes up on the first night, the producer must be completely responsible for everything that takes place. He will, of course, light the play, and at a costume parade will pass or reject each costume. His approval, or the reverse, also applies to the settings, furniture, props and make-up. When he finally leaves the stage, as the curtain is going up on the first performance, to watch the result from some dark corner in the auditorium where he can groan unseen and unheard, his responsibility, for the moment, is at an end— and the stage director is in charge. The latter is, like the captain of the proverbial ship, in complete command until the fall of the curtain, and even the producer must obey his directives when going back-stage during the performance. The artistic director is the only member of the production or back-stage staff who will be discussed in this chapter.

Although I devoted a short chapter, in the early part of this book, to the artistic side of the producer's work, I have found it necessary, when enlarging in detail on the key people connected with a production, to deal again and again with the producer's relation to them, or theirs to him.

From the above officers will be chosen the executive committee. These members will really be the governing body of the society. Apart from the executive committee there are two sub-committees which are absolutely essential: the membership and the play-reading sections. Both of these bodies will work in close collaboration with the executive committee. If there is limited finance, then the society's lifeblood will be supplied by the fees from those members who have their group's welfare passionately at heart, are good mixers and popular in the com-

munity. If they don't want to perform, so much the better. Members
of the play-reading committee should scan dozens of plays and finally
submit those which are, in their opinion, the likeliest ones for possible
production by the society. The artistic director, to whom these are
shown, will put up to the Board for approval those scripts he is able to
endorse. The members of the play-reading committee should, of course,
have some knowledge of plays and of the theatre. They should have
taste and discrimination. It is important they take into consideration
the limitations of the stage on which the play will be performed and
they should know pretty well the potentialities of all active members—
particularly actors. There is no point in deciding to do *Romeo and Juliet*
if the available talent is only capable of attempting a performance of—
say—*Worm's Eye View*. There is no reason to suppose, however, that
two seasons hence the society will not be able to handle a difficult play
without turning a hair.

So far we have chosen the president, chairman, a board of directors,
an executive committee, the business and publicity managers, the
secretary, treasurer, artistic director, the membership and play-reading
committees. Now we must give our attention to the form or "Constitution" and "The Rules" of the society. It is the creative people who
usually set the ball in motion to start a society of this kind and they will
be apt to feel, in the beginning, that so much preliminary organization
is unnecessary, but I can assure them that this planning is a foundation
on which their edifice will shortly commence to rise. The constitution
of the society should cover the following points:

1. Name of the society.
2. Objects of society.
3. Membership (types).
4. President.
5. Officers.
6. Executive committee (duties and powers).
7. Accounts.
8. Subscriptions.
9. Annual General Meeting.
10. Extraordinary General meetings.
11. Alterations in Constitution.

The rules of the society may be altered quite frequently and must be
drawn up for the needs of each particular society. The following is a
specimen of what might be found satisfactory:

No member of the society has the right to enter into any financial
transaction of behalf of the society without the authority of the
executive committee.

No member in arrears with his or her subscription shall be entitled to take an active part in any production or attend any meetings of the society.

If any members participating in a production, in any capacity, fail to attend a rehearsal when they have been called, without satisfactory explanation, or if they are not amenable to stage discipline, the committee shall have the right to replace those artists without further notification.

All members taking part in a production as actors shall be considered to be on trial for a period of five rehearsals and can be replaced if not satisfactory.

Any member, in rehearsal for a production, who is aware that, for any reason, he or she may not be able to perform on the night or nights of the performance, must give warning to the producer at the earliest possible date. Any member, failing to appear at a performance without giving due warning, shall forfeit his membership to the society.

These above rules can be considered as a guide to various societies who may desire quite a different set.

When all the foregoing points have been dealt with, in a businesslike fashion, and the wheels can actually be said to have been "set in motion", it will be found that a group has been formed for the productions of plays by a new amateur society. The organization of such a society may seem laborious and far removed from the initial desire for exciting artistic activity, which motivated the instigators of the scheme in the first place. Nevertheless, such an organization must be aspired to; once it is accomplished the creative ones—they whose brain-child it is—can forge ahead, secure in the knowledge that the costumes *will* arrive, the play is theirs for the playing, the hall is actually hired, tickets printed, the public aware of the society's existence. They might even —who knows?—attend the performance. All that our members now have to do, those of them on the other side of the curtain, is produce— in more ways than one—the Play!

VI. THE NEW SOCIETY'S FIRST PRODUCTION

ONCE the organization of the new society is established, the different committees will start functioning. The play-reading committee will have short-listed a number of plays—having discarded, at least for the time being, those unsuitable for performance by the society at present. The remainder will have been passed to the artistic director. He will consider all of them carefully and, after further weeding out, will put the few he considers suitable up to the board for a final decision. The choice of the first play is very important.

At least some part of the potential acting strength will already be known. These people are almost certain to have been among the original group wishing to start the society. It is most desirable to use every means possible to discover further available talent in the society —talent in every phase of theatrical production. The ways by which it can be discovered are often tedious and difficult. A little-known fact, but one which should never be overlooked, is that it is invariably the most talented people who have little ability to "push" themselves. The search for actors should include patient and exhaustive auditions as well as unofficial (that is without an audience) "play-readings". It should be ascertained whether members can sing or dance. They will have filled in a form when they joined, if they wish to be active members, stating their qualifications and past experience, but I urge a constant search for ability within the society. Talent is sometimes found where it is least expected.

Having considered the company available for the first play, the next concern is the building which will house the production. If the group happens to be one formed from members of a large organization such as a store, factory, university, or some other such body, there may be a hall or even something approaching a theatre in some part of the building where the daily occupation is located. Those who have the advantage of starting their activities "at home", so to speak, are among the lucky ones. In this case they will, most likely, also have the favourable eye, "the patronage", of the "powers that be"—those who are in control of the particular building where they will function. In this case, providing they carefully carry out all the instructions in the chapter "Forming a Society", their path should be fairly smooth. They may be able to choose, as their first production, the play they would really *like* to do—the one which suits their aims and the talent

42

available. But, supposing it is only a small group of people in a village or town which has no theatre free for amateur productions. This is the society with a problem! Before it can choose its first play, even if there are a dozen good actors to perform it, the society must find a home in which to perform.

Most villages have a workmen's hall or an institute, and many of the smaller towns, a Town Hall, which is available at given times for theatrical presentations—providing the authorities are not expected to contribute financially towards the production expenses. Some of these stages were built initially *for* stage productions. In the old days—"the good old days"—before the competition of the cinema, radio and television, theatre companies frequently toured these small towns. Certain veteran actors of today will tell with loving memory of playing "Abergavenny in Monmouthshire in 1920", or thereabouts. Those were the days when the country was being toured from end to end by professional companies. All the public had by way of entertainment outside their homes was "the theatre". I confess to looking back upon such an era with a certain nostalgia—although it was partly before my time. How rich and rewarding is a performance on the stage in "flesh and blood"—whether it be good or bad—compared with some of the "canned" varieties of mediocre entertainment, neither good nor bad, ladled out to us today. Let us admit just how unsatisfying much of the "canned" entertainment is; more often than not it is just as untalented as our old fourth-rate touring company sometimes, but not always, may have been.

If the society in the village or small town is fortunate, the stage available will have adequate depth and width. If it has been built for theatrical performances it will, of course, have these elementary requisites, plus space for storing scenery. But some groups may be faced with a platform (never intended for the presentation of a play), thirty feet wide and twelve feet deep—with no space in the wings at all and no switchboard or lighting equipment. If this is the case, they must not lose heart, but accept it. They must choose their first play very carefully; a play with one set, obviously, and look to the time when they will have their *own* building.

The next necessary point to be taken into consideration is the amount of money available for the first production. If there is a "patron", a costume play is not a risk; if there is very little financial backing it is wise to choose a play with one set and not more than about nine characters. For a modern play the actors will supply their own clothes —and there will, in all probability, be no wig hires. If possible, the set should not require expensive furniture unless it can be borrowed from tradespeople sympathetic to the group effort.

It is also of the greatest importance, particularly in the beginning, to choose a play which will be popular with the public. A society knows its audience. If it is composed of students at a university, or some comparable body, Ibsen is a wonderful choice, because of the economy in production of most of this great author's plays. It must be known, of course, that there are the producer and the actors available who can do something like justice to such a piece. When I advocate "horses for courses", I never mean a group should stoop too low in order to produce some dreary farce which may have been running in London for five years; such a run really doesn't mean anything. It is no unusual occurrence for a low calibre play once it has been established in the West End (often at great initial loss), to keep going automatically. It is doubtful whether anybody ever asks members of the audience who go and see such a play after it has been running for years, whether they enjoyed it. No one cares. The unthinking patrons, and their members are legion, only go *becuase* it has been running for such a long time.

Let us accept the fact that the first play is chosen, bearing in mind the available talent, the building in which it will be played, and the finances at the society's disposal.

Now the production must be cast.

From the moment the play is decided upon, the fate of the first production is in the hands of the artistic director. As soon as the decision is made he will study the script most carefully in order to form his opinions about ideal casting, and he will ask that auditions of available talent be organized immediately. He will exercise the greatest patience, kindness, sympathy and helpfulness at all these auditions, which may try him exceedingly. If he is exasperated, he must never show it; his task is to find actors and he must search for them in the most unlikely people who often turn out to be the finest actors. He must be completely ruthless in casting (that is, he must never cast anyone, however sympathetic he may personally be towards them, if he knows they are unsuitable) and, at the same time, he must be endlessly kind and encouraging to all aspirants for parts.

Auditions may continue for many days for so much depends on the final choice. It is particularly difficult to cast the first production when members have never worked together before, because it is only during the testing time of the final period of rehearsal that people really get to know one another's potentialities.

Although a person comes into a society to work in the theatre in his spare time, there is really no place in *any form* of theatre, amateur or professional, for the dilettante. The amateur actor must be prepared to give all his talent, experience, loyalty, energy and spare time, to such a project. Although a hobby, it must be realized that it is a most demanding one; one in which much more will be asked than could ever have been imagined, and a serious amateur must be ready to give selflessly with a willing spirit. Great satisfaction will be found by following this credo.

There may be great disappointment in many hearts when the final decisions on casting are known. This is the case in the professional theatre as well. There are always scores of eager applicants for every good part; only one person can be cast for it in the end. Disappointment must be accepted philosophically. There is nothing so degrading or unpleasant in the theatre, professional or amateur, as jealousy. Everybody's turn may come. If it doesn't it is best to forget it, and not worry over another's triumphs. It must be realized that the producer's word on casting is law and his decisions should be accepted graciously.

During the time the producer has been holding auditions he has also been conferring with the scenic artist and the stage director in working out his production. The scenic artist will submit a sketch of the set to the producer after having read the play and studied it with great care. The producer will, in all likelihood, also ask for a model of the set to scale. This will give him a much better idea of what the set will really be like on completion. The scenic artist will also provide a ground plan to exact scale, which will be given to the stage director so that he may mark out the rehearsal space exactly to the measurements of the final set. This ground plan will be explained to the actors, by the stage director, at the first rehearsal. Usually the actors are shown the design and model of the set so they may get some idea of the "atmosphere" of the space in which they will finally be working.

The leading actors will have been supplied with full scripts and, if possible, though this is not always convenient or economical to the management, all actors should be supplied with a complete copy of the play. It is one of the worst traditions of the professional theatre which has drifted into the amateur theatre that actors are supplied with "sides", that is, just their own lines with cues. At the very least actors should know and care about the play as a whole. They cannot do this if they have never studied or even read it. However, if, for reasons of economy, the society has seen fit to type a few full copies for the stage management and the producer, and the wretched players are fobbed off with part copies, then the opportunity should be given to every actor taking part in the play to read the entire script at leisure before the first rehearsal. The particular value of the first reading of the play by the cast finally chosen, is that they may grow acquainted with one another and, more important, that the producer listening to the texture of the voices, one against the other, may assess the balance, at this very early stage, of the type of material he has to work with.

At the end of the first reading the producer will, no doubt, address the company in general terms, giving them his views about the play and the approach he hopes to get from them. He may tell some particular artist that the reading was not in keeping with the overall conception. At any rate, it will be a session given up to a general approach to the play. Actors should be very much on the alert to gauge other interpretations so that their own particular reading fits into the general tone. It is necessary to realize first and foremost that "the play's the thing". The producer and the artists concerned with the production are there with one idea; to interpret the author's work. At the end of the first reading the time for the first rehearsal will be announced.

No two producers conduct rehearsals in the same way. Once the early general approach to the play by the entire company is dealt with and the slow, but interesting work of blocking out movement and generally working on mechanics begins, most producers, aided by their stage director, see that only the actors directly concerned with the scenes to be rehearsed are called. This means the careful working out of a rehearsal schedule by the stage director in consultation with the producer. It is an awkward moment for a stage director—provided the producer is adhering to the schedule agreed to—if an actor's entrance cue comes half an hour before he has been told to arrive.

In the professional theatre an "ordinary" play—that is a play which presents no special difficulties from a presentation or technical point of view—is normally rehearsed for a minimum of six hours a day for three weeks. Work during the week-end is done at the producer's discretion. The production week-end, which is frequently in the provinces, often presents great difficulty from a time point of view. The set-up starts by 8 a.m. on Sunday—sometimes earlier. Occasionally the stage staff build all night or as soon as the scenery for the previous production is out of the theatre. The set should be up by 1 p.m. or 2 p.m. on Sunday and the producer then proceeds to light the play. If it is a straightforward lighting job, he may be ready to start a first dress rehearsal by 7 p.m. This will be a slow-motion rehearsal and there should be at least two subsequent dress rehearsals before the curtain goes up on the first night. These two or three days are great periods of strain in the theatre, to which everyone rises gallantly. Indeed, it is from these occasions that workers in the theatre derive their greatest satisfaction. Everyone works as a team. Experience, resourcefulness and patience are utilized to their utmost. This is the part of the professional attitude which the amateur would do well to emulate.

Too often commercial managements are not unduly worried if a production is inexpert on its opening night in the provinces. They expect it to be a little rough. They think of the preliminary tour as a period of pruning and polishing while the company proceeds week after week towards the all-important first night in the West End of London when every detail must glisten. Why? Because it is this performance which will be judged by the London critics. It is on this performance that great reputations and large sums of money are staked. It is very often *this* performance which decides whether the play shall run for a week or for twelve months. I feel, personally, that the production seen by the out-of-town, first-night audiences should have the same care lavished on it as the first night in London. I feel, and many people in the theatre would agree with me, that an audience paying its money to see the opening of a play in Edinburgh, Cardiff, Birmingham, Manchester or Timbuctoo, should have the same right to witness an expert performance as the first-night audiences in London. I also believe such an end can be, and of course often is, achieved; and what I feel about the professional theatre applies with even greater force to the amateur theatre because all too often the amateur has only one opportunity to make an impression. All the weeks of preparation may be for a single performance. If this is the case, it is most praiseworthy; and if such a great effort is taken seriously by all members it will not be long before there will be three performances of each play, and then five. The growth from small beginnings of some of our leading amateur companies makes stirring reading.

In dealing with the subject of rehearsal I felt it was necessary to state briefly the method used in the professional theatre because I think the amateur should follow it as closely as possible—that is:

1. Approximately ninety hours' preliminary rehearsal.
2. A strict rehearsal schedule to which everyone adheres and which summons only those artists whose scenes will be rehearsed.
3. Production rehearsals:
   Set-up.
   Lighting rehearsal.
   Slow-motion dress rehearsal.
   Second dress rehearsal.
   One, and if possible, two dress rehearsals exactly as the play will be performed before an audience.

Producers map out their rehearsal period in different ways. The method I have found most satisfactory is to block out the first scene, or the first part of the first act, and develop that portion fairly fully before continuing. I shall deal with this at length in the chapter on "The Producer". Some producers prefer to block out the entire play early on. In other words, having blocked out the play in the first few days, the rehearsals run as follows: morning, act one; afternoon, act two; following morning, act two again; afternoon, act three; and so on. Producers discover from experience how they get their best results.

In the conducting of a rehearsal there must be one controlling voice —the producer's. The stage director, among his other duties, enforces discipline and meets small outside emergencies as they arise, such as the noise upstairs or downstairs which prevents concentration in the rehearsal rooms; the sudden entrance of the stranger, unannounced, who is looking for the Water Board; endless phone messages about timber, costumes, props, etc. When one says the producer "conducts" a rehearsal, that is exactly the right word. He is like a musical conductor, and the members of the orchestra, i.e. the actors and stage management (each one of whom is of great importance to the whole) must be constantly on the alert to follow their conductor's direction.

Alertness and concentration are the two most valuable states of mind a company should have while rehearsing. One hopes for talent, and once in a long while for inspiration, but even when these two elusive qualities are not overwhelmingly noticeable, alertness and concentration go a long way towards making up for their absence. An actor must take direction not only obediently but with a will. He has every right to ask the Producer to give him alternative business or movement if he feels that he has been asked to do something too intricate for his present stage of development. A producer is usually sympathetic to an actor's difficulties and one of his chief qualities should be an ability to adapt his conception of a role to the personality and capability of the person playing it.

Sometimes it is necessary to drive actors and staff very hard in order to achieve the necessary high standard by the opening performance, and on these occasions the tired company, convinced that it is already doing its utmost, may feel rather hard done by. But members must realize that their producer sees the play as a whole, and is in the best position to gauge how much more ground must be covered before the desired result is achieved. Actors must co-operate with a will although they may believe they may never survive the ordeal. This extra effort, if well directed, almost makes the difference between mediocrity and something quite outstanding.

Some producers work out the mechanics of movement rigidly before rehearsals commence and ask the actors to adapt themselves to these moves. This is a bad method. If puppets were being used the result would be satisfactory, but living, and sometimes creative human beings are the performers. When an actor does an imaginative and exciting thing a good producer will immediately note it, and, if necessary, alter

THE
AMATEUR MAKES
UP

The Rag Picker in *The Madwoman of Chaillot*—The Highbury Little Theatre, Sutton Coldfield.

Falstaff in *The Merry Wives of Windsor* — The Great Hucklow Village Players.

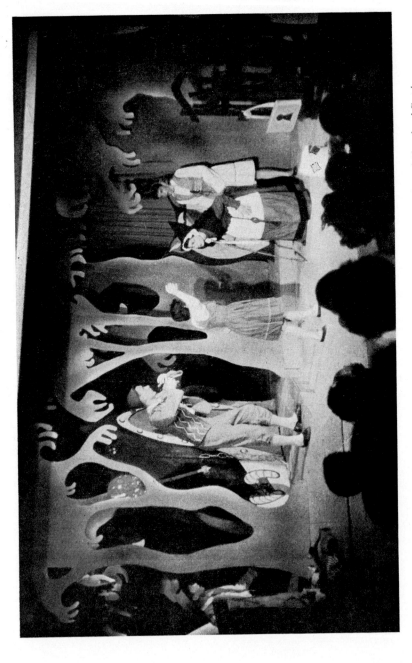

The Holiday Theatre, Vancouver, Canada in a children's theatre presentation of *Hansel and Gretel*.

or adapt his own conception in order to make use of it. For this reason, among others, the early moves in rehearsal may be tentative and often altered as the production shapes and develops. This is a good thing so long as the producer is experienced and knows what he is doing. Thus, in the early stages of rehearsals, all moves should be marked, as they are given, into the prompt book in pencil (so they can be changed if necessary). It is absolutely essential that a member of the stage management should understand and mark in *every move* given by the producer; and that whenever an actor forgets a move or makes a false one, he should be corrected by the prompter *at the time of the mistake*. There is often considerable confusion and embarrassment over points of this kind. In the chapter on Stage Management I have dealt with them thoroughly.

In spite of the reputation theatre people get for being easygoing and often unreliable, actually, especially when working at their job, they are the opposite; they have to be. We have said that there is one voice only in control in a rehearsal room—the producer's or, if he is absent, the stage director's. He gives the orders and does any criticizing there is to be done. A strict rule to enforce is that one actor may not offer advice to another actor on how to play his part. If an actor feels that his own performance is being hampered by another actor, he should speak to the producer about it, preferably in the hearing of the actor being discussed. All remarks by actors regarding the action of the play should be addressed to the producer; and if the actor is in doubt about a line or already set down move, he should consult the prompter.

There is no set rule about the time it should take to memorize a part. Some producers prefer actors to have the book out of their hands at an early date and perhaps in the case of amateurs, for whom freedom of movement is not automatic, this is a good rule. For my part, as long as I know the actor is not a poor study, I prefer to go slowly and let the lines come mainly through thought, feeling and movement. I don't mean by this that there should be no home study. There should be a very great deal. But sometimes the over-quick study has a tendency to be mechanical. Which ever method serves the actor's performance best should be encouraged. Of course, no actor should leave the learning of his part so late that he inconveniences the movement or pace of the play or the performances of the other actors. If the company is rehearsing for six weeks it is safe to require actors to be "word-perfect" by the end of the fourth week.

The six weeks of the preliminary rehearsals draw to an end, and the production rehearsals begin. First comes the set-up. If the group is one of the lucky ones, with its own hall or theatre, the set-up presents no urgent difficulties. It should be started far enough ahead so that

F

the set will be completely ready for the lighting and dress rehearsals. If, however, it has been necessary to hire a hall or theatre where the stage staff are not allowed to work until the day before the first dress rehearsal, every minute will count, and success will depend on a tireless and willing carpenter, stage crew and stage management, headed by a clear-headed, methodical stage director who has everything planned in advance and knows how to get it. The scenic artist will, of course, be in attendance from the start of the set-up until the final dress rehearsal, making last-minute adjustments. Details of the set-up are dealt with in the chapter on stage management.

It is very important that, if possible, however limited or even non-existent the lighting equipment is, sufficient lighting should be hired to do justice to the play and the production. If an experienced producer is in charge he will understand what equipment is necessary and how to get the effects he desires. If the producer is inexperienced in these technical matters his best course is to find an electrician (there may be a member longing to express himself in this particular department of the theatre), and with his help, work out a lighting plot. There is a great deal of information on lighting equipment in the chapter on "Lighting", by Peter Mullings, an ex-member of one of my groups. When lighting such intricate productions as revivals of *John Gabriel Borkman* and *Miss Julie*, as well as such complicated modern pieces as *Home of the Brave*, I always found Mr. Mullings' assistance on the electrics staff to be quite invaluable. However the matter is resolved, the producer will have agreed with the electrician about the type and amount of lighting required and at the lighting rehearsal, where the stage director is really the 'voice' issuing commands received from the producer, every lighting cue in the play will be worked out one by one and, when the producer is satisfied with the result, marked on a lighting plot by the electrician, he will then follow this plot faithfully at subsequent dress rehearsals and all performances.

The first dress rehearsal is sometimes referred to as the "slow motion" rehearsal. Actors are dressed in costume and made up for this rehearsal. It is a rehearsal with frequent stops, a slow, patient, rehearsal at which actors get used to the set, their costumes, the furniture, unfamiliar props, etc.; at which the electrician becomes acquainted with his lighting cues and corrects errors he makes; where the stage management practise the giving of cues for lighting, music, sound effects, front of house music lights and curtain cues, etc. They also rehearse the speed of curtains desired by the producer at the ends of scenes or acts, as: slow, medium or fast. At this rehearsal it is discovered that "the drawer won't open", "the flex on the telephone won't reach", "the chair is too low", "they forgot to put that letter on the mantelpiece", "the door sticks, it squeaks, it won't open, it's closed, it won't stay open". The list goes on and on. The golden rule is: *never leave any point that needs adjusting until it has been put right and until there is no reason at all for it to go wrong again.* That is primarily what this first, slow dress rehearsal is for. Everyone connected with the production must *say* when anything is wrong, and not hope that it will be better next time. It won't, unless something is done about it. If basic difficulties are not straightened out at this rehearsal the second dress rehearsal will be held up, whereas it should be, by comparison, an easy straightforward run-through.

The second dress rehearsal is an attempt to go through the play smoothly but there are bound to be many mistakes. These *must* be put right at the time, and again in such a manner that they will not occur again. But this rehearsal will be less arduous than the first. Of course, everyone will be much more exhausted, so it may *seem* equally terrible to all concerned. After consultation with the producer, the stage director should post a list of the curtain calls on the notice board, and all actors should look at the list and memorize their positions at each call. At the end of the second rehearsal the curtain calls should be rehearsed so that they are taken with a maximum of speed, efficiently and quietly.

It is *essential* that there should be at least one and, if possible, two, dress rehearsals with every detail of the performance conducted as it will be "on the night". There should be no interruptions, and any difficulties that may arise must be got over exactly as though before an audience. These rehearsals should start with the half hour being called, with exact intervals allowed between scenes and acts. The curtain calls, having been rehearsed earlier, should be taken at the finish of the performance again before an invisible audience.

At the end of each dress rehearsal the producer gives the cast and stage staff notes. It is of vital importance that the mistakes he points out at the end of one rehearsal should not occur at the next, or indeed, ever again. At the final dress rehearsal the producer talks to the company generally, giving them last-minute advice and encouragement. In amateur companies it is difficult, of course, to have a rehearsal on "the day of the show". In all likelihood the last run-through will have been the night before, and the artists and stage staff will have the nervous ordeal of working at their regular jobs all the following day knowing the great testing time is ahead of them. The professional actor has an advantage here. It is a much more single-minded business. Usually, on the day of an opening performance one works until four or five p.m. on the final run-through. There is just time for a cup of tea before making up for "the night". How much more difficult for the amateur actor to recapture the all-important concentration that one must have on a first night. It is "do or die". In fact one always feels that "The Charge of the Light Brigade" was a pretty small affair compared with the ordeal one is about to embark on.

At any rate, the night has arrived. The actors are all at the place of performance at *least a half-hour* before the curtain is due to go up. The call-boy goes round the dressing-rooms calling, "half an hour please—half an hour please". One actress thinks nervously, "I must just wish the boys good luck", and she knocks at the room next door. All the male members of the company are very eager to hide their nerves. No sooner is she back in her own room than Bill knocks at the door. "Good luck, dear", he says. She looks into her leading man's eyes. "Good luck, Bill", she whispers weakly, grabbing him with one hand while the other waves a mascara brush in the air. "Good luck". "Quarter of an hour", chants the call-boy, and she starts to pray. There is a small knock at the door. "Come in", she says in a trembling voice. The Producer enters. He seems full of confidence, not at all the man who said those awful things last night. He looks at her, tells her that she will be wonderful, what faith he has in her; her spirits soar. Of course she will be wonderful. The producer goes on to the other dressing-rooms leaving comfort and reassurance in his wake, which he does not in the least feel himself. Then he visits the stage again. Everybody, list in hand, is checking and rechecking to make sure nothing is forgotten; everything is in place. The stage director is quietly in command of everything and everyone on the stage. The stage manager or A.S.M. is in 'the corner' in complete control of that vitally important small area. His prompt script is expertly and accurately marked, and he knows it so well, that there is no possibility of failing to give a cue to the various departments depending on him, or of giving a wrong one. The A.S.M., working the panatrope knows exactly what she has to do; every record is marked and in its proper order, every prop for which she is responsible is in its place, and ready. The electrician has made a lighting plot which is absolutely "foolproof", he could do it now in his sleep. The carpenter has worked up to the last half-hour, perhaps putting right the various details connected with the set which were wrong during the dress rehearsals. The scenic artist may still have his paint-brush in his hand. Nervously each worker checks, and checks again.

"Five minutes", is called. The audience is coming in. It sounds like a good house. The Overture begins. The stage director says, "Call beginners", and off goes the call-boy. "Beginners please", he knocks on the first door; "Beginners please", his voice dies away as he goes on to the other dressing-rooms. The actors take a last look in the mirrors and go towards the stage, terrified and exhilarated, wondering why they ever took on this ridiculous job in the first place. When they arr ve on the stage it is strangely calm; they feel the air of discipline. The producer is there, smiling, and quietly confident. They hear the lovely sound of the rustle, babble and laughter of the audience. 'Places please", says the stage director. "Good luck," whispers the producer to the actors. "Good luck", he says to the stage staff. He leaves the stage. The actors are in their places. "Fade the music", says the stage director; the front-of-house music fades down. "House lights", is the next command. The lights out front go down, the audience becomes still—waiting; the electrician brings up the lighting on stage for the opening of the play.

"All right," says the stage director, "Curtain going up". You hear the almost silent swish of the curtain rising; you sense the expectancy of the audience; there is a tiny pause—The First Performance has begun!

VII. BUSINESS MANAGEMENT

THE organization and operation of the business side of an amateur society must be efficiently planned and carried out in order to make the artistic side fully successful. Too frequently, haphazard budgeting, careless handling of money, ignorance of official rules regarding licensing of plays, theatres, and arrangement of royalties, entertainments duty and insurance can bring disaster to a group. Failure to observe official regulations can result in serious court cases and faulty business management may mean audiences too small to enable the society to continue.

Business management is a "cut and dried" phase of the theatre. There are certain procedures which must always be followed, whether the society be large or small, and although systems of book-keeping, ticket selling and banking may differ slightly, their overall patterns and the general results are much the same.

In what follows, I have attempted to outline certain basic rules and regulations and suggestions for business routine. It is rare to find one person who can capably combine the business and artistic aspects of the theatre. There have, of course, been many notable examples of successful actor-managers in the professional theatre, people like Henry Irving, for example, and Beerbohm Tree, Frank Benson, Fred Terry, George Alexander, Charles Wyndham and Mary Moore. Both Donald Wolfit and Laurence Olivier in our own time have run their companies with varying degrees of success. But although these artists may have controlled, and some are still controlling, general business policy, it is an indubitable fact that their highly skilled business managers were, and are, responsible for the smooth running of their organizations and companies. Irving upon more than one occasion paid tribute to Harry Loveday, his business manager, and to Bram Stoker,* his general factotum. Thus in the amateur theatre it will be rare to find a producer who can combine artistic direction and the handling of business affairs. He must have someone on whose judgement he relies absolutely; someone with practical business experience and with the initiative to go ahead with financial plans once they have been approved by the society's executive.

The general duties of the business manager have been outlined in a previous chapter under the heading "Forming an Amateur Society". Now we shall deal with these duties in far greater detail. Following this will be a section on the Treasurer and his practical duties with

* The author of the famous old melodrama, *Dracula*.

reference to the budgeting and book-keeping involved. Then we shall have a section on the selling of tickets and box-office bookings. The sale of tickets should take place not only at the box-office but at various sites in the area where the production is to be performed. Music shops, libraries, even the local post office may display posters and sell tickets upon behalf of the society.

THE PLAY AND ITS COPYRIGHT

One of the first things the business manager must ascertain after the play has been chosen is the holder of the copyright. Unless it is an original work by a society member it will almost surely be registered under the Copyright Act of 1911 which covers all original literary, dramatic, musical and artistic works. The owner of the copyright may be the author, composer, or an agent. Just inside the first few pages of a printed play will be found notices similar to either of the following:

"No performance or reading of this play may be given unless a licence has been obtained in advance from the author's agent, Messrs..........of..........Street, London, and no copy of the play or any part thereof may be reproduced for any purpose whatsoever by any printing or duplicating or photographic or other method without written permission obtained in advance from the publishers."

An alternative to the above notice or, shall we say, injunction, is to be found in the following:

"Applications for a licence to perform this play by companies of amateurs in the British Empire (except Canada) must be addressed to Messrs. Samuel French & Co. Ltd., 26 Southampton Street, Strand, London, W.C.2, or to their authorized representatives. No performance may take place unless a licence has been obtained."

The copyrights continue from the date of publication or of first performance during the author's life-time and for fifty years after his death. Then the copyright expires. The play is then "in public domain". Shakespeare, Ibsen, Sheridan, Strindberg, Chekhov, Marlowe, Jonson are all writers who are "in public domain".

Permission for a performance or reading of a play should be applied for well in advance, so that there is no danger of having to change plans at the last minute, should there be a refusal of permission for any reason. The agent, author, or publisher, as the case may be, will quote the fees payable for performances of the play. Many struggling societies feel resentment at having to pay these royalties, but they should always remember that only through royalties does an author get paid for his important work. He does not earn a regular salary but depends entirely on the unpredictable earnings from his pen. Payment of royalties should never be regretted, for the playwright is a highly skilled craftsman, a sensitive artist, and the most necessary of all workers in the theatre. His talents should be gratefully and practically acknowledged. Sometimes a play will not be available for amateur performance because it is still being professionally performed. Generally release is given after a West End run, provincial tour, and professional repertory performances are completed. Because a play is being performed by a neighbouring amateur society, it does not mean it is generally available. The rights may have been withdrawn because a West End revival is contemplated. Sometimes this happens after a great many amateur societies have performed a piece. Therefore, a fresh application for permission must be made for each production of a play. It is quite possible to have a clause in the permit covering non-payment of royalties in the case of a cancelled performance. Notice of cancellation must be sent to the copyright owners before a mutually agreed date. When a permit is issued, it must be remembered that this is for the text of the play as published. No dialogue or lyrics may be changed in any way; nor may any portions be copied for reprinting in a programme. Additional dialogue must not be added, nor may the title or names of characters be changed. Permission must be acquired for dramatization of a story or book, and even the singing of a copyright song in a public place must be licensed.

A play reading which is privately arranged by a society for its members and guests can often be given without payment of fees, but again permission should be requested. Various play agents, brokers and authors have different rules about this, but an example of the rules of Messrs. Samuel French Ltd., who control the copyright of many plays performed by amateurs, is that no fees are payable providing a private reading is given to an audience of not more than fifty people; no money may be taken at the door or as a collection of subscriptions; the play must be read from the published copy; no scenery or properties may be used and no action portrayed; there must be no announcement in the Press. If more than fifty people are present, a fee of one guinea for a three-act play and seven and six for a one-act play must be paid for the right to read the work.

According to the Theatre Act of 1843, every stage play must be licensed by the Lord Chamberlain for public performance in Great Britain. "Public performance" means that members of the public have paid admission to see a production in a theatre or building licensed for the performance of stage plays. If the society is a private club where tickets may be purchased by members only and not by the general public, it is not necessary to have a Lord Chamberlain's licence for the play. Productions in aid of charity are not exempted from the

Theatres Act if they are publicly performed and admission charged. In the majority of cases when the play chosen has been performed and published, it will already have been licensed, but the business manager should not take this for granted. Enquiries should be made about every play contemplated for production, because if an unlicensed play is presented a maximum fine of £50 may be imposed on the society and the court dealing with the case has the power under the Criminal Justice Act 1925, to suspend or cancel the theatre's licence. If the play is a new one, the society should not take any steps towards a production before applying for a licence. This law includes every type of entertainment: pantomimes, mimes, opera, sketches, melodramas, as well as full-length straight plays. A copy of the final version of the play must be sent to the Controller, Lord Chamberlain's Office, St. James's Palace, London, S.W.1, at least seven days before the performance date of production, and the name of the theatre must also be supplied. It is the duty of the manager of the theatre in which the play is to be first performed to see that the play has been submitted for licensing by the management presenting the play. Authors, producers or composers may submit their work personally for licensing if they so desire. It is imperative that the business manager should be able to produce the licence at a moment's notice. Full regulations concerning the licensing of plays may be obtained upon application to the Lord Chamberlain's Office. This department will keep the script as a record, but an extra copy will be stamped and returned to the society if desired, upon payment of an additional five shillings.

The following is a list of the licensing fees:

One act, with not more than four scenes: 1 guinea.
One act, with more than four scenes: 2 guineas.
Two acts with not more than four scenes in all: 1 guinea.
Two acts with more than four scenes in all: 2 guineas.
Three or more acts with any number of scenes: 2 guineas.
Additional scenes to plays, reviews or pantomimes already licensed: 1 guinea.

Any alterations made to the script after it is licensed must be sent to the Lord Chamberlain and not performed until he has passed them.

Grounds for banning plays are obscenity, homo-sexual themes, brutality, slander, political reasons; frequently in biographical plays descendants of the character are still alive and object to the play. This latter reason was advanced by the Lord Chamberlain's office in the case of *A Pin to see the Peep Show*, based on the famous Thompson-Bywaters murder case. I produced this play by F. Tennyson Jesse and H. M. Harwood at the New Boltons Theatre Club in 1951 and when it proved very successful I naturally wanted to transfer it to the West End of London for public performance. A number of West End theatrical managers were anxious to make this transfer possible in view of the lyrical press the play, and especially the performance of Joan Miller in the leading role, received. Alas, a licence was refused because a distant relative of Edith Thompson objected. Thus a fine piece of theatre failed to reach the wide public it deserved; later it was publicly presented on Broadway in New York because, of course, plays performed in America do not need a Lord Chamberlain's licence.

Until legislation is introduced to abolish this out-dated unnecessary licensing of plays, let every business manager keep his society out of trouble by complying with the Lord Chamberlain's regulations.

THE LICENSING OF THEATRES

As soon as the place of performance is decided upon, the business manager must make sure that his licence is in order for the performance of stage plays. Again, under the Theatre Act of 1843, it is unlawful to present a public production of a play unless the premises are licensed for that purpose, and heavy fines are imposed for failure to observe this ruling. The majority of theatres, that is those which are regularly used for plays, operas, etc., hold a permanent licence which is renewed annually. In this case a society need not trouble further. However, when a local hall, institute, school auditorium, etc. is used, there is need to obtain a temporary licence as these premises, not usually used for play presentation, will probably not be licensed. Temporary licences cover the exact dates of performances only and cost a few shillings. Full information re application for such licences can be obtained from the local County or Borough Council. In some cases these bodies actually issue the licences, in others they are issued by Justices of the Peace. Theatres holding permanent licences must comply with a high standard of safety regulations including: adequate exits in case of fire; well-maintained fire-fighting equipment; limited authorized standing room or extra seating accommodation; a safety curtain which must be lowered and raised in view of the audience before the beginning of the performance to ensure that it is in working order; open exit doors at the end of a performance; a light marked "Exit" on all doors which lead to safety. There are also a number of regulations controlling a specified closing time each night and the prevention of disorderly conduct. Many professional performances on Sunday, Good Friday and other such days are forbidden in the case of amateur performances. Various rules and regulations may be added by different councils. In the case of temporary licences the regulations are sometimes relaxed slightly on certain points, for example: the provision of the safety curtain. However, local authorities check the premises before issuing such a licence, to make sure that safety regulations are satisfactory, and a member of the Police Force is free to enter the building at any time during the performance for inspection and supervision. In the interests of safety strict fire regulations are made back-stage, and in regular theatres there is a fireman in attendance at all performances, to see that these rules are observed. All scenery, curtains, artificial flowers and other such inflammable properties must be treated with an anti-flame paint spray or dip. When they are hired, this service is customarily performed by the firm hiring out the materials. However, when these are made by the society, the same precautions should be taken, whether in a theatre or a village hall. The fireman has the authority to light a match against such materials to test their flame resistance and may forbid their use if not correctly treated. Smoking back-stage is forbidden, frequently in dressing-rooms as well. Use of electrical appliances such as irons, razors, etc., is also not allowed in most theatre dressing-rooms. A special wardrobe room is provided in those cases, where ironing is permitted before, but not during, the performance.

A building licensed to show a stage play may not have permission to show a film, or music or dancing. Licences may be obtained to cover these additional entertainments. Enquiries should be made if an additional licence is required. In the event of intoxicating liquor being sold in the building, the business manager must make quite certain that an Excise licence is held. Some theatres hold this licence if they are used regularly, but if not it is wise to apply for a temporary licence to the local Justices, and this should be sent, together with an application for an Excise licence, to the local Collector of Customs and Excise.

Licensed hours for the sale of liquor may be extended if a special order of "exemption" is obtained from the District Petty Sessional Courts.

MUSIC AND ITS COPYRIGHT

Apart from full musical plays and operas, which we have already discussed, all music used during the action of a play, on stage or off stage, and all interval music, whether played by live musicians or on gramophone records, must be covered by a licence from the Performing Right Society.

The Copyright Act of 1911 established that copyright owners have the sole right of performance, that no music shall be publicly performed without their permission. In order to aid composers, publishers and authors in protecting their rights, the Performing Right Society Ltd. was formed in 1914. They charge a fee and issue a licence for music used. The fee is later distributed as royalties to the copyright owners.

Some theatres are fully licensed by this Society for the performance of any of the works they control, which are very extensive and include music of all nations. But if such a licence is not held, a special licence must be applied for. Full information re title of production, address of theatre, dates of performances, titles of musical works, composers and the way in which the music is to be used (intermissions, incidental, on-stage, etc.) must be given. From this a fee will be decided upon. This sum must be paid for *all* performances, whether public or private, free or by ticket; club theatres are not exempt. Certain special exemptions may be made in the case of religious worship, music festivals and charity performances when all talent and services are given free. But the business manager must check with the P.R.S. should these cases arise. The address is: The Performing Right Society Ltd., 33 Margaret Street, London, W.1.

When the music is played by gramophone records a further licence is required from Phonographic Performance Ltd., which is an association formed in 1934 for their protection by the major gramophone record companies. A special application form must be filled in by amateur groups which gives them a specially reduced annual fee, for unlimited use of gramophone records. The Society must supply its full name and address, number of productions per year, and date from which the licence is required.

The address is: Phonographic Performance Ltd., 144 Wigmore Street, London, W.1.

ENTERTAINMENT TAX

The actual working out of tax figures will be dealt with by the treasurer, but the business manager should know the general details about it, and will enter into necessary correspondence with the authorities. There is a movement afoot among both amateur and professional theatre groups to have this tax reduced, if not abolished, but at the present time it is still in effect. It was introduced as a war-time measure in 1916 and has lasted ever since, with amendments.

Relief from tax for most amateur societies was ensured in the Financial Bill of 1953 when it was stated that paid producers could be employed for directing plays, provided their work was completed before the first performance. This meant that most societies which present only straight plays are exempt from Entertainment Tax. However, amateur dramatic societies who employ professional conductors and musicians are still liable for the tax. This is rather ironic, since it was the National Operatic and Dramatic Association who fought to have the tax removed. Most of the societies on their books cannot claim exemption.

Exemption from entertainment tax may be claimed by certain amateur societies, and the National Operatic and Dramatic Association has been responsible for widening the sphere of exemptions to a great extent. In collaboration with the Commissioners of Customs and Excise, they have worked out exemption forms for the following:

1. *Completely amateur organizations* where no payment or reward (even expenses) is given for the appearance of any performers of actions constituting entertainment or any part of it, or for any person's services in connection with the entertainment as manager, conductor or member of the orchestra.

2. *Permanent Groups with solely or partly charitable and philanthropic objects.* In this case, proof must be shown that at least one-fifth of the gross receipts are given to charity.

3. *Permanent Educational Establishments* who give performances with present or past registered students.

4. *Partly Educational Societies not conducted for profit,* and whose funds are used for the further encouragement and cultivation of music, drama, etc. These Societies must show that the play they present has definite educative value and contains sufficient merit to justify their choice.

5. *Societies in Rural Areas* where the population does not exceed two thousand, and the seating capacity of the building does not exceed four hundred.

In all of the above cases, forms for exemption should be applied for at least fourteen clear days ahead of the first performance date, to: The Secretary, H.M. Commissioners of Customs and Excise, Kings Beam House, Mark Lane, London, E.C.3. In the case of application for the first time, a copy of the Constitution, Rules and Aims of the Society must be included, together with a copy (if it is not a new society) of the last Financial Statement. Financial Statements must be available for inspection by H.M. Inspectors at any time. Further and fuller details re exemption may be applied for at the above address.

When no exemption is granted, tax must be deducted from each ticket sold, and a careful and accurate account kept of this. At the present time tax is payable at the rate of 1d. for admission exceeding 1s. and not exceeding 1s. 5d.; and 1d. for every 5d. or part of 5d. over 1s. 5d. Thus tax is payable on a 2s. 6d. ticket would be 3d.; on a 5s. ticket—8d.; on a 10s. ticket—1s. 6d.; and on a 15s. ticket—2s. 4d.

Tax is claimed on tickets sold but not used, therefore a voucher system is an excellent idea. The voucher can be bought in advance and exchanged at the box office for a stamped ticket. Complimentary tickets, clearly marked, are free of tax. Private theatre clubs are not exempt unless they fall into one of the aforementioned categories.

The price of all tickets, and a statement as to whether this price is inclusive or exclusive of tax, must be clearly marked on them. When collected, they must be torn in half across the entertainment tax stamp; one portion being retained by the usher, one portion by the patron admitted. Portions kept by the organization must not be destroyed until after midnight on the day following, and each day's portions must be kept separate from those of the previous day.

If the theatre being used, or the society itself, is not bonded to make true returns to the Commissioners of Customs and Excise, then adhesive stamps must be affixed to tickets. These may be obtained in the different values from any post office or from the Customs and Excise Offices in larger towns; government tickets may be purchased in rolls or pads from the Collector of Customs and Excise, Entertainments Duty Branch, Customs House, London, E.C.3; or in Scotland from the Collector of Customs and Excise, 25 Waterloo Place, Edinburgh 1. A remittance must accompany each order. Unused stamps and unsold tickets may be returned and a refund claimed, if they were not purchased more than two years previous to the society's application.

INSURANCE

Insurance is an item which is constantly overlooked by some societies. Nothing has ever happened to their property or personnel in the past, and so they feel it never will. This attitude can be very dangerous. It is worth every shilling spent to feel that the society is completely "covered".

The best kind of safeguard for a business manager to investigate on behalf of his society is the "Combined Policy" which covers almost every eventuality. These policies may be arranged for on behalf of societies through either the British Drama League or the National Operatic and Dramatic Association. The Caledonian Insurance Company and the Mutual Insurance Company issue such special policies; both are fully aware of the needs and circumstances of Amateur Groups.

Combined policies include protection from the following:

1. Loss of expenditure due to abandonment or postponement of the production, which is self-explanatory.
2. Damage to borrowed, hired and other property. This includes protection from fire, loss, theft, water damage, and any kind of accident except normal wear and tear, breakage of china, or injury to property due to negligence. It is wise to have the

insurance policy cover properties, costumes, etc. *in transit*, as well as in the theatre. Any personal valuables such as jewellery, furs, etc., belonging to members of the cast should be included, unless the owner has personal insurance covering them.

3. Liability to public and cast. This third-party risks policy protects the society from damages claims by members of the audience or the company who may be injured in the theatre, or even by falling banners or advertising boards in the street. It also covers the possibility of food poisoning in the case of refreshments being served. If claims are brought against the society legal aid is provided for the policy-holder.

4. Accident insurance for the company and voluntary workers. This covers accidents during rehearsals or performances, for which the society is not legally liable, but feels obliged to pay full compensation. It covers accidents ranging from death to total or partial disablement.

A special 'Pluvius' policy can be taken out for open-air performances as a protection against bad weather. This must be finalized at least a week before the first performance.

Fidelity Guarantees may be arranged to cover officials handling money, and in the case of societies which have a large cash turnover this policy is recommended.

FRONT OF HOUSE

The business manager is responsible for all front of house arrangements, in fact, everything in front of the curtain which divides the audience from the play. Although the business manager is not responsible for supplying the actual production, he is responsible for supplying satisfaction to the audience in every other way, from the time the first ticket is purchased until the last patron has left the last performance. Only if the front of house is organized and run smoothly can the business manager be said to fulfil this responsibility. Some of the arrangements he must make are:

1. *Box Office and Ticket Sales:* this will be discussed in further detail later, as it also involves the Treasurer.

2. *Ushers and Programme Sellers:* this is most often a combined duty. In professional theatres such duties are usually arranged by the permanent management, and would merely be supervised by the business manager. In a small hall, however, the business manager must instruct his ushers, usually members of the society, regarding the exact seating plan and location of various priced seats; provide them with handy purses or boxes in which to collect programme

money, as well as torches for use in the dark. The seating of
latecomers is always an irritating problem in any theatre—professional or amateur; and I, personally, would require all such
offenders to wait either at the back of the theatre, or outside, until
the first interval of any "straight" play of a serious nature where
audience concentration is required. Perhaps, in time, as a result
of such a rule the public would endeavour to come to the playhouse on time. This method is strictly enforced at the Covent
Garden Opera House, and stragglers there are very few! However, this is a matter that must be left to the discretion of each
individual society. If latecomers are seated while the play is in
progress, it is imperative that ushers know the theatre well, for
nothing is more annoying than to have people shown to the wrong
seats and then have to change seats when further latecomers
arrive with the same seat numbers. Such juggling can ruin the
atmosphere of a play. Ushers wearing dark suits or dresses are
less distracting if movement in the dark is necessary.

3. *Programmes:* These should be planned in conjunction with the
producer and publicity manager, but it is the duty of the business
manager to endeavour to make the programmes pay for themselves, plus a small profit for the society. Most programmes are
sold for not less than sixpence although a shilling, and even a
half a crown, may be charged if a special souvenir programme
with pictures included is for sale. Small societies, who duplicate
their own programmes may wish to give them free of charge to
the audience, and it is a pleasurable surprise to be handed a free
programme. Advertisements from local firms pay for the expense
of programme printing, and sometimes guarantee a small profit.
The programme is ideal for advertising future plays and activities
and exchanging news with other societies. To many people who
collect them an attractive well-planned programme will serve as
a reminder of a pleasurable evening, and perhaps encourage
them to attend the society's plays again.

4. *The Refreshments:* In large theatres this too will be looked after by
the management, but in halls, it is part of the business manager's
job to organize the refreshment booth. If liquor is served, care
must be taken to observe the licensing laws as mentioned earlier
in this chapter. The majority of societies playing in halls serve
tea and/or coffee. The business manager would be well advised
to place this duty in the hands of one of the society's lady members. Quite often savouries and cakes donated by members can
provide an extra profit when served with hot drinks. An attractive refreshment booth serving *good* tea and coffee, will earn much

goodwill for the Society. I emphasize "good" beverages, because they are often so unpalatable when made in bulk that bicarbonate of soda should also be provided for the unhappy patrons. Don't let your society be of the "bicarb-after-coffee" variety.

5. *Smoking:* Fire Regulations for the theatre or hall regarding smoking must be investigated, and clear signs displayed if smoking is not permitted. Ushers should be instructed to point this out politely to any members of the audience who smoke when it is not permitted.

6. *Special Guests:* The business manager should liaise with the publicity manager on this matter. It should be arranged that members of the press and specially invited guests be met by a society official, given a free programme, seated without delay, and entertained at the intervals.

7. *Supervision:* The business manager should be "out front" during each performance, in order to supervise personally the various aspects of front-of-house management. He must keep an eye on the box office, and be available to settle smoothly any disputes over tickets, seating, programmes, or anything that might arise to disturb efficiency. By mingling with the audience during the performances and the intervals business managers are in an excellent position to study the audience reaction to the choice of play, production, acting, etc.; this can be most valuable, for after all, it should be the prime wish of each society to please its audience.

BUDGETS

Before a production is started a budget should be worked out by the Treasurer. Accurate forethought in a budget can mean all the difference between a season which is a financial failure or success. Budgets are a part of modern everyday life, and nowhere are they more necessary than in the theatre. Once the budget is completed it should be presented to the executive committee for approval.

On one side should be listed every possible item of expenditure, on the other, possible estimated revenue. The two should balance. Never over-estimate the income and under-estimate the expenditures. It is much better in the long run to practise the opposite. Ticket sales should never be based on a capacity house, but on two-thirds capacity; and income from programmes, refreshments, etc., should not be relied upon to any extent. Mature societies will have past budgets and past productions on which to base their present budgets. Care should be taken to find out whether charges for hire and rentals, etc., have increased since the most recent production. For groups start-

G

ing a new society a simple production budget is shown in the Appendix.

Budgets act as a brake upon expenditure, and indicate to the various heads of departments how much they are authorized to spend. They act as a reminder to the business manager and secretary of items to be dealt with and arranged. In the case of alternative plays being discussed for production a budget will indicate clearly which play would be the best financial risk. Budgets should be carefully kept, so that they may be referred to for future productions. Most important of all, budgets should show how much money is required to finance the show.

TICKET SALES AND THE BOX OFFICE

The business manager helps to organize and supervise this very important phase of business management, but the details of carrying it out are usually left to the treasurer and often to the secretary. In small societies, where the business manager is also the treasurer, it will be the duty of one person, with appointed assistants, to take charge of ticket sales.

Tickets are the main source of income and so must be promoted to the best of the society's ability. There should be one central box office at a local shop or newsagent with members of the society acting as agents for selling tickets. In order to avoid confusion there must be one central authority—either business manager or secretary who issues blocks of tickets to these agents. A receipt should be signed for each lot of tickets taken, and they should be clearly marked off in a ticket record book. There should be a definite date for return of unsold tickets, so that vacant seats may not be discovered at the last moment.

An up-to-date theatre or hall seating plan should be kept for each performance, and as each ticket is paid for, it should be entered on this plan. There may be different markings for different types of sale, e.g. a fully blocked out square for a ticket sold at full price; a half-blocked out square for a child's ticket at half-price; a diagonal line for tickets sold at a special party reduction; a vertical line for tickets sold at a membership reduction rate; a circle in the square for complimentary tickets, etc.; or different coloured pencils may be used instead of markings. Societies will work out systems most convenient to their own particular needs, but the point to remember is to keep the system clear and simple.

The business manager or treasurer must always check to see that there is an actual seat for every ticket sold. Great would be the embarrassment and discomfort of all to discover that, although a front row of seats had been removed to make more room for the orchestra, the tickets had been sold for these non-existent seats!

A constant check must be kept on ticket sellers, to make sure that tickets are "moving". It is not enough to give out blocks of tickets and hope they will be sold. Members must be constantly "jogged" to ensure that they are actually selling tickets. If a member seems to be having no luck at all, his tickets should be recalled without delay and promoted by someone else.

The business manager should at all times have a statement to date showing tickets out, tickets sold, and the amount of money received for these. Enquiries may be made about this at any time by officials of the Customs and Excise officer.

Regular theatres usually provide tickets, marked for their own seating plan, under the terms of the society's contract with them, but if the society has its own tickets printed, care should be taken to have all the essential information given on them, such as name of the society, title and date of the production, price of seat, time of performance, and where it will take place. Different coloured tickets may be used for different nights of the week, or to distinguish between prices of seats.

Some societies use a voucher system for tickets. Members sell vouchers at various prices, and the purchaser himself must exchange them for an actual ticket at the box office for the performance of his choice. However, in most cases, the direct ticket method is more successful. For each performance the treasurer must prepare a detailed statement showing the box-office returns. This can usually be done during the performance. The number of tickets sold must balance with the cash on hand or banked.

The business manager should be absolutely firm about stating a date at least three days before the actual performance, by which money from ticket sales should be returned to him. This will make his work much easier and the records more efficient.

BANKING

It is wise for every society to have a banking account. This is not only a safeguard for the society's finance, but the cheque stubs and paying-in book serve as checking records for income and expenditure. Two signatures should be necessary on each cheque issued, those of the producer and business manager, or secretary and business manager, or as the society decides. The point to remember is that the signatures must be those of responsible people who are regularly available. It would waste much time to have as a signatory, one who travelled a great deal of the time, or who lived in an isolated spot far from the town. Only one signature is necessary for endorsing cheques to be paid into the society's account. If possible the same person should always be responsible for "paying in", perhaps the business manager, treasurer or secretary.

Most accounts, except for very small items, should be paid by crossed cheque. For items like postage, sundry stationery, and other small incidentals, a petty cash "float" should be kept by the secretary or treasurer. Each expenditure should be recorded in a simple petty cash book, and receipts retained regarding those items for which receipts can be issued. A postage book should also be kept, into which all letters or parcels sent are entered, with the appropriate amount of postage used. A petty cash float, recorded in the same manner, should be issued to the stage director to cover each production, for the purchase of small items of additional properties, wardrobe, lights, settings, etc. The stage director is responsible for handing in a detailed account of petty cash spent, together with any cash on hand at the end of each production. These "floats" should be reimbursed by the treasurer or business manager from time to time as required.

All large orders for purchase of materials, hire of wigs, settings, lights, etc., should be confirmed by the business manager before they are placed, and it is often wise to have special order forms (in duplicate) printed for these, which can be signed by the same officer. The accounts should later be paid by cheque.

In order to simplify book-keeping it is necessary for most societies to keep only one cash book (in addition to the petty cash book), and a membership ledger. In general, the procedure is to keep income (from ticket sales, subscriptions, donations, etc.) on the left-hand page and expenditure on the right-hand page. There should be a monthly balance made of these, which should check with Bank Statements. In the case of societies which do only one or two productions a year, this monthly balance, of course, is not necessary; a balance may be struck at the end of each production.

The membership ledger should show all membership fees paid, and the dates they cover. The secretary should be quick to contact members whose subscriptions have lapsed. I have heard of one society who placed the names of long-standing defaulters on the bulletin board for all to see. It wasn't long before the guilty members either paid up or let the secretary know they had left the club.

At the end of each year the society's accounts should be audited by a certified accountant, who will thoroughly examine books, bank statements, cheque-stubs, ticket summaries, in order to satisfy himself that all is in order. The fact that this has been done is stated on the society's balance sheet over the signature of the certified accountant. Many societies may think that auditing is not necessary, but it is very important indeed—as a safeguard and assurance of efficient business management to every member of the society.

VIII. PUBLICITY

ONE of the most important departments in the Drama Society is that section responsible for Publicity. Without imaginative, well-planned publicity there will be poor audiences, and the best written, produced and acted play of the season will not be an unqualified success before a half-empty house. The word *publicity* implies Public, and it is the job of the Publicity Manager to see that the majority of the community are aware of the society's existence and fully informed of its activities. Half-hearted publicity is worse than none. Uninteresting news stories, dull posters and hand-bills, last-minute liaison with the local press, frequently condemn the success of a production from the beginning.

The choice of this Public Relations officer is of prime importance. He or she must be alert, a capable organizer, socially affable, and full of initiative. Such an enterprising person will form a good committee of members who will prove invaluable to the society in suggesting new and original ideas, planning the publicity campaign, and carrying it out efficiently. This committee should consist of representatives of various professions and trades in order to cover the widest possible public. A committee of four might include a school-teacher, a factory-worker, an office-worker or official and a farmer. The choice of persons will vary greatly in different communities, depending largely upon the size and location. In a small group the Publicity Committee may also be the Membership Committee.

It should always be remembered that personal contact is invaluable in publicizing an amateur society. Each member of the society, whether active or an associate member, should at all times know what programme is being planned, which play in rehearsal, and the date or dates of its performance. Then at work, in the home, or at social events, all members may spread the news by word of mouth, and perhaps arrange to sell tickets to business associates, family and friends.

Publicity for the average production (3 acts, 1 setting, a dozen characters) should start about four weeks in advance of the first night, and should follow a well-calculated plan, building each week until the production is over. Publicity should not stop on the opening night; sometimes a concerted effort is required during the run of the play to ensure good houses.

The first step the Publicity Manager and Committee should take is to read the play to be launched in order that they may become thoroughly familiar with it. Too often this precaution is neglected, and consequently, when a member of the public happens to ask what the play is about, the publicist can only say, "Well, *I* haven't read it, but they tell me it's very good." Now, that will not do. The Committee should be able to give a brief outline of the plot if requested to do so, they must be able to tell what type of play it is and in which of the numerous categories—comedy, tragedy, farce, modern, historical, etc. —it should be placed. They must also know members of the cast, and any interesting information about them. The Publicity Manager should make notes as he reads the play of anything unusual that might be used for publicity purposes; for example, period costumes, unusual settings, novel plots, etc.

The next step is a conference with the Producer, during which the latter gives his ideas concerning the aspects he would like stressed in publicity for the sake of the play. The Publicity Manager can then bring forth his ideas, and together they may arrive at a general approach to the press campaign. The Public Relations Officer, or Publicity Manager as he is normally called, then meets with his committee and detailed plans are worked out.

The society's membership should be circularized immediately a play has been decided upon and production dates finalized. This should be done before any public announcement is made, because members usually like to feel that they know what their organization is doing, before the general public does. It gives them a greater sense of "belonging" to the group.

The first public announcement should take the form of a short and accurate news story in the local papers, stressing those aspects of the production to be most publicized; for example, if it is a new play, emphasize the fact that this will be its première; if the playwright is a local person, write a brief paragraph about him (perhaps even more than a brief paragraph, sometimes he's worth a column!). Try and have a photograph inserted with the article in question.

The importance of photo blocks, pictures, sketches, cannot be over-emphasized. The public eye is always caught by these. A newspaper reader will invariably look at the pictures first and read the captions under them. He may not have either the time or inclination to read the article beside the picture, but he will remember the latter. Photographs on posters may be rather costly, but if the society can afford to have a block made and printed, it is usually a worthwhile expenditure. The attention of passers-by will be arrested by a photograph when they might ignore a mere mass of information. Displays of photographs in shop-windows can be of immense value. In these modern times of high-powered publicity campaigns concerning everything from automobiles to soap-flakes, the pictorial lay-out is indispensable.

Early in the publicity campaign, soon after the play is cast, the Press Representative should interview each member of the company in order that biographies can be collected. This applies to the stage management as well as the cast. The most interesting facts in these can form the basis for much good publicity because the personal story can apply to the call-boy every bit as much as it does to the stage manager. This material should then be filed safely away for use in connection with future productions, to ensure that if certain artists are used in several plays, they need only be requested to bring their files up to date. These information sheets should be the sole responsibility of a single member of each Publicity Committee. It will be his duty to keep them in order and see that all forms are up to date. It is frequently a good notion to work out a specimen questionnaire which could quite simply be duplicated. It will record all basic items of relevance. The following is an example of this:

Name ....

(Mr. Mrs. Miss)

Address ....

Tel. No. ....

Length of time in community.......................................

Profession or Trade ....

Acting experience (a) in this society (b) in any other society (c) professionally.

(*Names of plays and parts played to be included—this information can be recorded on the back of the sheet*)

Training ....

Experience in any phase of the Theatre other than acting, e.g.—
Producing, Stage Managing, Lighting, Business Management.

....

....

....

Any other interesting details about yourself or your work which may be used for publicity purposes.

....

....

....

The Publicity Campaign is divided roughly into three categories: Press Publicity, Posters and Handbills and Special Activities.

PRESS PUBLICITY

Newspapers are always looking for unusual pieces of reporting, whether they be merely factual or of the human interest variety. Each drama society should be able to provide good examples of both types. Many local newspapers are most co-operative in printing stories, and for that matter pictures, to advertise the forthcoming attraction or, as it is frequently called, "dramatic event". In return for this profitable gratuitous publicity the society purchases an amount of advertising space, the size and frequency of which depend on its budget and resources. Quite frequently members of the Press are also members of amateur societies and this helps to forge a link of good relations with the newspaper. There are two main requisites for a good story: (a) it must be concise and interesting, (b) great care should be taken to weed out extraneous material, and the style should be straightforward without flowery phrases which will probably meet the fate of a "blue-pencil". Most newspapers have a Diary of Fôrthcoming Events column. In this they publish information concerning dates of play openings. The Society columns will sometimes accept information as well. Their doing so is made a certainty when prominent local citizens, celebrities, well-known visitors to the city (town, village or hamlet) are involved. An example of this type of publicity might start as follows: "Mrs. Thomas Jones gave an informal after-rehearsal supper-party last night at the Welcome Café, Market Place. She entertained the cast of *Pygmalion*, in which her husband, Mr. Thomas Jones, the prominent local solicitor, will be seen as "Professor Higgins" when the Blank Drama Society presents the play later this month."

Make sure that the news copy, neatly typed, double-spaced, on quarto paper, reaches the local press several days before you would like it published. Material when hastily planned, untidy, and sometimes sent at the last minute, has less chance of being printed than well-organized copy.

Such publications as *Theatre World*, *Plays and Players*, *Drama*, and *The Amateur Stage*, may be prepared to carry announcements of forthcoming amateur productions. Addresses and publication dates of these periodicals can be found at the back of this book under "Theatrical Publications". Only when the society's production schedule is appointed far in advance can these monthly and quarterly magazines be utilized for publicity. Quite often local newspapers will send a photographer to a dress rehearsal in order to take several shots. These, together with selected news items and "stories", make excellent publicity immediately prior to the first night. If this cannot be arranged, it is a good notion to have the society's regular photographer (or better, a keen amateur photographer who happens to be a member of the group, or perhaps even a friend of a friend of a member) attend the dress rehearsal in order to photograph scenes from the play for publicity. It is, of course, quite useful to have a number of pictures taken as soon as some of the costumes are ready. They may then be used for display in newspapers incidentally publicizing actors who will take part.

At least one week before the first performance, two complimentary tickets should be sent to each of the drama critics of the local newspapers. When the village or town has only one local newspaper it is a good idea, if the accommodation in the hall is not too limited, to send two to the editor for his personal use, and two to the dramatic critic as well. If the dramatic critic happens to be the editor, it is as well to send four instead of two. Unless it is known just where these important folk prefer to sit in the auditorium, enquiries should be made. Many critics choose to sit on the side aisles; others prefer to be in the centre of the house, especially if there are centre aisles; some enjoy being well forward; others prefer to sit near the back. All critics must be placed where they will get an unobstructed view of the stage and where the "sight" lines are good, so that they can see the entire performance. There should be at least one member of the publicity committee whose special job it is to welcome the members of the press, give them complimentary programmes, see that they are served with refreshments at the interval, arrange that they meet the producer if they so desire. Above all they should not be asked what they think of the play. Whoever is in charge of press reception must have the soul of a true diplomat. It goes without saying that the critic must write what he truly thinks of both play and production, but courteous behaviour extended to him by the society's officers will help to create a favourable impression.

POSTERS AND HANDBILLS

We come to posters and handbills. The society's budget will determine the quantity to be ordered. Certain artists might be enrolled to turn out a number of posters for display at focal points, busy shopping districts, and other major positions in the town and surrounding districts. Once again it must be stressed that pictures or sketches must be eye-catching. A poster contest might be organized with great advantage, either among club members or among the community at large, with prizes in the form of season tickets given for the best displays. A large number of the posters submitted could be shown prominently. Usually shops, libraries, newsagents, even factories, offices and sometimes schools, will be only too delighted to co-operate in displaying advertising matter for an amateur production. It is wise to ask members who work in such places, to obtain permission to hang these advertisements.

Points to remember about the printing of posters and handbills are that: (a) it is more economical to have a large number of one layout printed than smaller numbers of several (the cost decreases as the number increases) and (b) changes in layout after the proofs are printed mean extra cost. All information on proofs should be carefully checked before being finally passed. Only a printer's error will be altered free of charge.

A bold and unusual, though simple poster design is desirable. Colour combinations like black background with red printing, or grey background with maroon printing, perhaps even soft cream background with scarlet printing, are sure to make people stop and look. Weak, wishy-washy pale colours do not attract inspection; garish, over-bright or clashing colour schemes make one yearn to close one's eyes. The latter may be all right for visiting circuses or funfairs, but will hardly endear the public to the drama society. Posters and playbills can be both tasteful and arresting after thought and prior consultation, before they are drawn up, with a member of the group versed in art.

The name of the play should be in prominent type, and important matter, such as date, theatre or hall, times of performance, prices of admission and where the tickets are on sale, should be legible. Some societies like to print cast names on the posters. In this case either all the names should be included or none. The billing of certain artists only, in large type, will lead to bad feeling; such, alas, is human nature! Name of society, author and producer (but the latter only if he is a professional), should be well displayed, and sometimes (but I do not think this is always a very sound idea) the name of the scenic artist. When all the society's membership—players as well as designers—are giving their services voluntarily, it is surely wrong to star one or two at the expense of the many. After all, those leading artists in an amateur dramatic society production are probably getting a great deal more out of their annual subscription as members of that society than the chaps who come on with the spears! They should not be compensated for their good fortune by being awarded star advertising as well as star roles.

Handbills should contain on the front leaf much the same information as the posters, but can always have on the back just sufficient of the plot to arouse interest and not give the "game" away. Interesting facts about the production, author, director, or cast may also be included. Handbills can be sent through the post to members and friends whose names members submit, to other dramatic or musical societies as well as schools, colleges, libraries, etc. If the community is not too large, they can be pushed into letterboxes by a group of members who spend an evening or two canvassing the town with handbills.

One enterprising group I knew even managed to persuade a friendly milkman to leave leaflets with the morning milk. Piles of handbills can be left on shop counters, and, of course, they must be handy and "get-at-able" in the box office or wherever tickets are being sold. Members of the publicity committee must always have a supply on hand to give to people they meet. In fact, many members of the society other than those specifically connected with publicity may be persuaded to carry several leaflets with them. Some societies prefer having cards printed rather than flimsy leaflets. They feel the latter may be too easily thrown out whereas a smaller thicker card may be placed on a mantelpiece and remembered.

The making and distribution of a number of permanent bill holders is a good idea, and certainly keeps the paper fresh and clean. Nothing gives a worse impression than torn, dirty, bedraggled posters. These bill holders can be easily constructed by members who are handy with a hammer, nails and saw. They can be backed with light wood or hardboard, with a slot left open at the top for removal and insertion of posters; alternatively they can be made with a removable back. Instead of using breakable glass, to front the holders, it is both practicable and inexpensive to use sheets of thick cellulose which can be obtained from any large stationery firm. These sheets are light in weight, fully transparent, and endure for years. Screws and wire for hanging the poster holder and folding braces can be affixed to the back, so that an obliging shop-owner may either hang or stand the playbill, whichever is most convenient to him, in a prominent position in his shop. Advertisements may also be displayed on hoardings, trams, buses and stations, but the space they occupy on such sites must be paid for, and again depends very largely on the size and budget of the society.

SPECIAL ACTIVITIES

Many members of the society may suggest new ideas, and it would be a good move to ask for publicity suggestions from the membership when it is circularized. These special activities will vary greatly in different communities—those in big cities being vastly different from those in tiny villages.

Window displays are good publicity. These may consist of an attractive layout of photographs, either of members of the forthcoming cast or past productions, scenes from the play, different settings, etc. In the latter case, care must be taken to publicize the present play prominently. In this way, the public will not think that the display is merely a pageant of past successes. A display of costumes or interesting properties will create interest as, indeed, will programmes of previous productions. The costumes might be shown in a department store's window or a draper's shop; while the programmes would be well displayed in the printer's windows or those of the local newspaper. If the production is a musical play, of which the score has already been published, and/or recorded, the music shops might well co-operate by featuring a window display of sheet music and records from the original production; they can, of course, by doing so, "push" the sale of same. Likewise, a bookshop might co-operate by displaying and selling copies of the play if it is published. Of course, the enterprising publicity manager must see that a large notice advertising the society's production is placed prominently in these windows, beside the music, records or books.

If the production is to take place in a theatre, glass slides may be purchased and theatre managements usually agree to display them during intervals in the current performances for the previous two or three weeks. The designs for slides should be simple but arresting, containing the briefest basic information.

Gummed strip posters giving the name of the play, date and place are sometimes used on car windows, on shop or even home windows. Canvas banners with the same information painted on them can often be strung between buildings in a main thoroughfare, high enough not to interfere with traffic. Local by-laws must be investigated before this is attempted. Souvenir programmes, complete with pictures, biographies, etc., may be printed in advance and sold in shops or at the box office to stimulate interest. Exchange of a certain number of complimentary tickets and programme advertising may be arranged with other dramatic or musical societies. Certainly the next play should be announced, if possible, in the programme of the current production.

If any member of the society, whether he is connected with the present production or not, achieves anything out of the ordinary in his job, wins a medal for athletic prowess, gets recognition for scientific discovery, writes a book, exhibits a prize-winning dog or cat, it should make a good "news" story for the local papers. Make quite certain it is mentioned that the prize-winning owner, or the scientific discoverer, is a member of your play society.

Social events, like dances, whist drives, parties, meetings, etc., sponsored by the society are useful for spreading publicity.

Contests for essays or poems on the theme, characters or locale of the play might be promoted among both children and adults of the community. Small cash prizes or tickets for the play can be given as prizes. Local newspapers will probably take an interest in such a project and may even print the entry forms. If not, they may be printed on the handbills. Winning entries could be read on the first night, perhaps printed in the programmes and/or published in the newspapers.

Sandwich men parading with colourful boards are often a good idea

during the week before the play opens. Those members of the society
with a good sense of humour can have, and create, a great deal of fun
with this sort of "stunt" publicity. He, or she, might be dressed in a
costume appropriate to the play. A gaily decorated, brightly lit car
or lorry driven slowly through the streets, or parked in a central position, can create great interest. If a loudspeaker system can be rigged
up in the vehicle, information might be broadcast regarding the production. People will, in the words of the late George Robey's famous song
"I stopped and I looked and I listened", indeed stop and look and
listen, and, if theatre members are nearby selling tickets, the public
might buy on the spot.

If any celebrities happen to live in the town, or are visiting it, they
should be asked to the opening night of the play, and press photo-
graphers should be tipped off to take pictures of them for publication.
Society columns will almost certainly mention them.

Quite frequently business clubs or ladies' guilds, sometimes the
local churches, are interested in having the society's producer, leading
actor or playwright (if he is a local person), come to speak about the
society and the present play at a meeting or luncheon. The publicity
manager should investigate this possibility.

A reading of the play might be arranged several weeks before it is
to be produced, either for an invited or public audience; this reading
will undoubtedly stimulate interest and speculation about the forthcoming production.

In the foyer, and even in the theatre itself, the publicity representative can arrange attractive displays through the publicity committee
of photographs of the cast and past productions, programmes, etc.,
which will prove of interest to audiences at the intervals.

If the clothes for a play are colourful and unusual a costume parade
might be arranged in a local department store, with a commentator
to give interesting notes on each costume. Permission will probably be
given by the store for the society to have a ticket-selling booth nearby.
A similar parade could be arranged at a garden-party or as part of the
social programme at various club meetings.

Depending upon the suitability of the play and availability of the
actors, excerpts might be given at school assemblies, in hospitals, in
factory or office canteens.

Broadcasting and television are excellent publicity mediums but at
the present time in Great Britain it is difficult to use these, particularly
for amateurs. However, if the possibility arises where the name of the
society or a forthcoming production may be mentioned, the publicity
manager should do his utmost to take advantage of such an opportunity.

It must be repeated that in most amateur societies the best publicity is personal contact by all members with their families, friends, and associates. Word-of-mouth publicity and personal recommendation sometimes sell more tickets than any poster, news-story or stunt. The wise publicity manager takes advantage of this by making sure that every member and associate member is kept completely up to date on activities. It will make his job easier and help to ensure "sell-out" houses. This will, in turn, allow the society to plan more ambitious productions and establish itself as a necessary and integral part of community life.

IX. STAGE MANAGEMENT

IN the pre-talking films, pre-television days when the professional theatre really flourished, stage management was a highly skilled occupation. Of more recent years this work has tended to be given to disappointed producers or not very skilled actors who are prepared to stage direct or stage manage, play a part, understudy another part and take on the duties of company manager on tour. For these manifold tasks the payment is a bit on top of the normal salary but nothing approaching the amount the management would have to pay four separate employees. This unsatisfactory method has been forced on promoters of plays due to the increasing difficulty of the Battle of the Budget. The costs of touring and taking over a West End theatre are increasing steadily and the audiences for live entertainment become more unreliable and capricious as their numbers dwindle. Therefore managements, even wealthy firms, use every means to keep their running costs at the lowest possible figure. Probably because the members of the stage management are not actually seen by the patrons their department has suffered most in the cutting down and doubling up process. The result is that scarcely any first-rate stage directors have been produced in recent years. Apart from the few redoubtable and constantly sought-after men—Osmund Wilson is an example—the present-day stage directors, having little background, are incapable of teaching the youngsters who will be the stage directors of the future. The situation worsens every year. I was fortunate in being trained for this side of the theatre, starting as a very young lad, under such folk as Harry Pringle, Charles Maynard, Herbert Vivian, William Abingdon and Danny O'Neil, among a host of men who were virtually captains of the big ship Backstage. Their orders were religiously observed, and they never hesitated to give them, because they themselves had a background of hard work and experience, which made their authority doubly imposing. Stage management, in those days, really meant what it said.

When I started producing and later became a manager-producer I searched in vain for the men who could completely control the stage and give my junior employees the same invaluable training and discipline which I received and for which I shall always be grateful.

In the United States, where it is forbidden that any member of the stage management shall do any job but his own, these posts are filled by wonderfully efficient and highly respected members of the theatrical profession.

I feel that enough cannot be said about the importance, to the success of a production, which lies in the functions of stage management. Too often, both in professional and amateur companies, these positions are given to people quite unfitted to hold them.

Many amateur societies operate with a stage manager and a prompter, plus an electrician, property man, carpenter, wardrobe mistress and stage crew. I think the professional method is preferable for the reason that some *one* person, with experience and authority controlling all activity on the stage, should be free from any specific duties so that he may oversee adequately all the various departments. That is, in effect, the role played by the stage director. He is in charge of, and directly responsible for, the entire staff backstage. He is the producer's right-hand man and is chosen almost as soon as the production is decided upon for his duties commence at once. Although the producer must be consulted, and agree with his choice, the stage director usually nominates his own staff—particularly the stage manager. It is important that he should be familiar with the abilities of the key people of his team and know that he can rely on them when the testing time comes. Under ideal conditions the personnel backstage in an amateur production should consist of:

The Stage Director;
The Stage Manager;
The Assistant Stage Manager (the A.S.M.);
The Electrician (sometimes several of them);
The Carpenter;
The Property Man;
The Wardrobe Mistress;
Dressers;
Scene Shifters;
Call Boy.

The people working backstage must be as well rehearsed and capable of doing their part in the production as the leading actor. Teamwork is as necessary to their functions as it is to the players, and they must work with speed, accuracy, precision and quietness.

The various facets of a production are knitted together by the producer to make a completed whole. In order to attain the result he is aiming towards, he must be able to depend on the correctness, sensitiveness and ability of the entire stage staff. If one member fails him, if the electrician misses or fumbles a lighting cue, if the stage manager fails to give a signal for music or for a "noise off", if the A.S.M. fails to manipulate the panatrope accurately and sensitively, if props are not put in the required spot—then the production has been let down. It

An amateur playhouse in the peaceful countryside—The Playhouse, Great Hucklow, Derbyshire.

An amateur playhouse on a busy city street—The Bradford Civic Playhouse, Bradford, Yorkshire.

A derelict shell . . .

. . . reconstructed into an amateur playhouse.

The Crescent Theatre, Birmingham, showing its playhouse before and after conversion in 1932. It is now further modernized.

doesn't matter how remarkable the acting is, how inspired the production, how enthralling the play itself—when any of these tremendously important points of production entrusted to members of the staff fail, the illusion is lost and the audience, often quite without knowing why, slacken their interest and the hard-won grip on them is lost.

The stage director must be a man of many parts. He must be sufficiently an artist to understand the producer's point of view, and to appreciate the play and what is being aimed at. But he must also be intensely practical so that he can organize with ease every department backstage and keep a tight, though friendly, rein on the actors and on the various people working under him. He will be in constant conclave with the producer through all the planning processes of the production and he should make a point of taking as much practical detailed work off the producer as possible. He must be absolutely reliable. When he is asked to do a specific thing he must make a written note of it and do it personally, or see that it is done, at the earliest possible moment. He should demand his own high standard of reliability from every member of his staff, and train them into the habit of working methodically, never putting off duties to a later date. The type of stage director and staff which consistently need to be checked by the producer, to ascertain if routine matters are going ahead on schedule, are worse than useless.

The stage director is present at certain of the early meetings between the producer, the scenic artist and the costume designer. Once their work passes beyond the design stage, and construction work is begun, it is the duty of the stage director to satisfy himself that it is progressing to schedule. If there are hold-ups or set-backs which might affect the production as planned, the producer should be informed at once in order that new decisions can be taken. Day-to-day difficulties, however, should be ironed out by the stage director without worrying the producer who will have his hands full with both casting and rehearsals.

When the date for the first auditions is settled the stage director, with the assistance of the stage manager, makes all arrangements. In the professional theatre the management presenting the play may decide all casting matters—sometimes with the collaboration of the producer, more often without. In amateur societies it may be the rule that casting shall be done by a committee, possibly the executive committee. Although the producer's opinion should carry the greatest possible weight it is wise not to leave the final decision in his hands or of any one person because, however scrupulously fair and impersonal he may be, he will not escape being labelled as biased by the disappointed candidates for parts.* Everyone connected with the auditions, whether

* This is applicable only to the producer in the Amateur Theatre.

H

deciding on casting or reading for parts, must be informed sufficiently far in advance of the date, the time, and the place. I have always disliked the mass auditions held in big theatres where actors—sometimes artists who are elderly and well established—are asked to parade on the stage in front of hundreds of their fellow artists, to be seen and heard by the three or four figures in front representing the management. It is a dreadful ordeal for actors and often they are scarcely treated with civility. I endeavour, when auditions are necessary, and I am responsible for casting, to see and hear people privately as much as possible. When many people have to be seen on one day I instruct my stage management to give all artists a definite appointment, with fifteen-minute intervals between each, and they are directed to one room as they arrive and ushered in individually by the stage management. In this way they are enabled to read the part with no outsiders present, except those people necessary to the conducting of an audition.

On these occasions the stage director organizes the proceedings. He keeps order in the room where the "aspirants" are gathered, and sees that no tough gate crashers manage to be heard before, or in place of, someone who has a specific appointment. As each artist is ushered in, the producer and the casting committee are told his or her name and the part being read. The producer will have chosen passages from the play beforehand which give the best opportunities for character depiction. These passages will have been typed—several copies of each—so that the producer and each member of the stage management have a copy as well as the members reading. Sometimes, if he has the ability, the stage manager, or perhaps the A.S.M., who is usually a girl, reads the other parts with the candidate for *the* part. One mustn't expect too much from the person who reads in for the other characters but it makes all the difference in the world if it is someone who knows the play and makes an attempt to act with the person who is being auditioned. On countless occasions I have turned up, as a young actor, with my heart in my boots, to read for a part I desperately wanted, only to find a sort of robot reading the big love scene with me and making it sound like a list of hotels in the A.B.C. A bright young thing once confided to me, "Oh dear, I am so nervous. I don't know anything about this play at all. I hope you don't mind!" I murmured, "Of course not—not at all," and thought, "Ah well, there goes that part."

When the casting is completed, the day of the first rehearsal is decided upon, and the stage director instructs his stage manager to notify the entire company by post and telephone, to attend, giving the time and place.

The stage management should arrive at all rehearsals fifteen minutes before the rest of the company in order to put the rehearsal room in readiness and mark the floor exactly to the shape and size of the set with tape or chalk. Furniture, approximate to that which will ultimately be used, should be set up in accurate positions. The rehearsal should be completely ready to begin at the time of the rehearsal call.

It is customary, at a first reading, for a row of chairs to be placed in a semi-circle for the cast. The producer sits at a table in front of them and, to one side, at another table, are the stage director, the stage manager and the assistant stage manager. The scenic artist and costume designer are also present at this first reading in case the producer wishes to confer with them. They, on their side, can familiarize themselves with the play and the artists taking part. The reading begins, and except for occasional interpolations by the producer, it continues to the end without interruption. At the end of the reading, after the producer has addressed the cast and has consulted the scenic artist and designer about any outstanding points, it is normal for the stage director to inform the cast regarding rehearsals, and to stress the importance of adhering strictly to the schedule laid down. In the professional theatre the latter stricture would be unnecessary. Discipline regarding rehearsals is strict in the extreme. If an actor is late for rehearsal he has committed a crime in the theatrical sense. It requires such detailed explanation that few professionals will risk such a position. It is noticeable in recent years that, when personalities with film, television or radio names, but little stage experience, have been given opportunities in the theatre, these rigid backstage rules are sometimes airily disregarded—often with no apology forthcoming—but never by real theatre people.

Actors *must* be in the theatre at a performance when the half-hour is called by the call-boy—half an hour, that is, to the rise of curtain. If there is a possibility that an actor may be late for rehearsal, or later than the half-hour at a performance, he must, at all costs, communicate with the stage director to inform him. Actors must be on the alert for their entrance cues. It is unforgivable, at a rehearsal, for an artist to be late for a cue and necessitate being called from a cosy chat in some distant corner of the stage. An actor missing an entrance, at a performance, by so much as a few seconds has committed a cardinal sin; there is no redress. One's fellow artists have been put in an impossible position, the audience has been let into the secret that something is amiss—a thing which must never happen. It is the business of the stage director and the stage manager, under him, to see that these foregoing rules are strictly obeyed.

When the readings of the play are completed, and there may be several, the stage director supervises the marking out of the rehearsal room to the exact measurements of the ground plan of the set which has been supplied by the scenic artist. It has been found most success-ful to use white tape for this purpose with drawing pins to hold it in place. The measurements must be accurate or the actors will be seriously confused when they finally get on the set and find themselves with much less space than they had during rehearsal. The assistant stage manager, known as the A.S.M., assists the stage manager in this marking out process, daily, before rehearsal.

The prompt book is the next all-important question to be considered, the marking of same, and the prompter. In the first place the stage director must understand this complicated business thoroughly and must make quite sure that he does not relax his supervision of the marking of the book until the stage manager and A.S.M. are absolutely competent to deal with it. When he is satisfied on this point, and has assured himself of the capabilities of the stage manager, he is at liberty to hand over the stage management duties to him and leave the rehearsal room in order to deal with the many other matters for which he is responsible. He must not do this however, until he is quite sure that the stage manager is maintaining absolute quiet during the re-hearsal and is not slow to reprimand anyone causing a distraction, or not on guard for entrance cues.

It is a good idea to make up two prompt scripts—one for use during the day-to-day rehearsals, and one to be kept in spick and span con-dition for use at all performances, and afterwards for record, and possibly publication purposes.

The method of putting a prompt book together is as follows: two quarto-sized hard-covered copy books should be purchased containing more pages than there are pages of the script. The pages of the play script should then be separated and each page pasted on the right hand pages of the copy book. Each left hand page of the book should have a line drawn from top to bottom dividing it in half. The directions for the actors should be written on the left hand side of the division and all lighting, music, and sound effect cues written on the right hand side of the division in capital letters. These three types of cues should be written in different coloured pencil—e.g.: music cues in green, lighting cues in red, and sound effect cues in blue. Apart from the actual cues to be given by the stage manager, a warning of all cues to be given should be written, in the appropriate colour, one full page in advance of the actual cue. Actors to be called in adequate time for their entrance cues are noted on the appropriate page, and the call boy sent off by the stage manager to warn the artists. On any page where a lighting, music or effects cue is to be given, a small red seal should be stuck in the centre of the top of the page and a line drawn from it to the point of dialogue or business at which the cue is actually given. Thus the stage manager is reminded, as he turns the page, that the cue must be given almost immediately.

It is essential that the stage manager should follow every moment of the rehearsal with the closest attention in order to be ready, at a second's notice, to prompt an actor or to correct an error in "business" —that is—an action or movement given to an actor at a previous rehearsal by the producer. As the producer decides on a piece of business, for example: "he crosses to left side of table right and on such and such a word he picks up the letter", these directions must be written in pencil in the space allotted for the purpose, opposite the speech or word on which the action takes place. Each piece of business should be numbered on the left hand page and the same number written beside the point in the script at which the action takes place. In this way the stage manager is never at a loss to prompt either dialogue or business immediately and accurately.

At the end of the day's rehearsal the stage manager should carefully peruse the business invented by the director, interpretations which have been decided upon, additions or deletions in dialogue, etc. The various moves and changes have, sometimes, to be written roughly and hastily for they come thick and fast when the producer really gets under way and have frequently to be altered before the effect is achieved; that is the reason for having a number one prompt script. When it is quite certain that the business and changes are finally "set" the stage manager should transfer all markings into the "pukka" number two copy so that, by the time the dress rehearsals commence, there is a perfectly marked, easily understood, up-to-date prompt script with every warning for sound effects, lights, warning actors, curtain etc., marked ready for use at the first performance. An accurately and clearly marked prompt script is one of the soundest safeguards against making catastrophic mistakes. I shall illustrate one page of the sort of marking I have suggested.

CALL BEGINNERS
  Miss Smith
  Miss Brown
  Miss Jones
  Mr. Lewis
	WARN: BARS
	       ELECTRICS
	       THEME MUSIC
	       CURTAIN
	       DOOR BELL
	       PHONE

(1) Potts enters, irritated. Brief business with cushion. D.L. to front door.	
(2) Ushers Raymonde towards study U.R.	GO: THEME MUSIC GO: ELECTRICS (House lights)
(3) Raymonde goes in, after looking around appraisingly.	GO: CURTAIN UP GO: ELECTRICS CUE (5 minute fade)
(4) Potts shuts study door and turns towards French window U.C. Telephone rings. She goes to it exasperatedly.	GO: DOOR BELL (a)
(5) Telephone in hand she bawls towards window.	
(6) Hugo enters in great irritation. Tries to take telephone from her as she is still talking into it.	GO: PHONE (b)
(7) Potts throws up her hands in despair. Goes towards kitchen. Remembers Raymonde. Returns and speaks loudly in middle of Hugo's conversation. She gestures towards study. He pays no attention except to wave her away.	

ACT ONE

At the rise of curtain the stage is empty. (a) *The door bell rings. Miss Potts enters.* (1) *She checks the room and goes to answer the front door.*

RAYMONDE: (*offstage*) Mr. Beddington, please. I have an appointment.

MISS POTTS: Oh, well you'd better come inside. (2) Would you mind waiting in the study, please. Mr. Beddington's outside. I'll call him.

RAYMONDE: Thank you. (3)

(4) *Miss Potts shuts study door again, crosses U.C. to French windows.* (b) *Telephone rings.*

MISS POTTS: Hello. Oh yes. Who wishes to speak to Mr. Beddington? Oh. Will you hold on a minute sir, and I'll call him? (*she calls*) Mr. Beddington! Mr. Beddington! (5)

HUGO: (*offstage. U.L.*) Yes.

MISS POTTS: Mr. Morris Benjamin wants you on the phone.

HUGO: (*offstage. U.L.*) Oh, my God . . .

MISS POTTS: Hello. Mr. Benjamin? (6) Mr. Beddington's just coming. If you wouldn't mind holding on.

Hugo enters and goes to phone.

HUGO: Hello, this is Hugo. (7)

MISS POTTS: Oh, by the way, there's a young lady by appointment in the study . . .

Prompting is an art. Few people possess it. At rehearsal when an actor has recently put his book down and is struggling valiantly, the prompter endures his worst period. If he prompts thinking the actor has "dried" but in reality is merely indulging in a new "dramatic pause", he is often made to feel most inept. But he must never be embarrassed by such situations for actors are notably nervy at this period of rehearsal, and notorious for explanations proving that they "didn't dry". However, the stage manager should be on his toes so that he does prompt when he is needed and does not interrupt the flow of a scene unnecessarily. This will not happen if he has followed all rehearsals intelligently and sensitively. He will learn the pauses and the actors' methods of delivery, and will quickly sense when they are in trouble. When an actor does "dry" and the line which is forgotten is, for instance, "Why did you burn the letter?" it is useless for the prompter to say "Why did you . . ." in a loud whisper. He must get to the words "burn" or "letter". They will convey the missing idea to the actor and he will pick up the thread immediately. Most important when prompting is never to take your attention, or your eyes, off the script and the stage, and the production as a whole, for so much as a second.

Early in rehearsal the stage manager must make a property plot. The majority of items required will be ascertained by reading the script carefully and noting every article as it is mentioned. Additional properties may be introduced by the producer throughout the rehearsal period. He may wish the leading lady, at a particular moment, to bring from a pocket "a red handkerchief". These extra props will be added to the existing list day by day. Under existing conditions most props are hired or bought. The A.S.M. is sent out during the rehearsal period to search for the items to be purchased, and the stage director makes arrangements that hired articles shall be ordered well in advance of the dress rehearsals. In the case of expensive articles they are sometimes loaned, providing a credit is given to the makers in the programme. If the amateur society has re-established the property man and his assistants *they* will collect the various items needed and will make many of them. This is the better way for the additional reason that the society will gradually amass a stock of useful props for succeeding productions. It is unnecessary to say that, although the property man is given a full and comprehensive list of props by the stage manager, he must steep himself thoroughly in the play, and know as much about its requirements as any member of the stage staff.

Properties are divided into three main categories:

1. Scene props—the dressings for the set, i.e., furniture, lamps, cur-

tains, flowers, shrubbery, bell pulls, pictures, mirrors, rugs, boxes, etc.

2. Hand props—items brought on and offstage by actors or handled by them on stage, i.e., cigarettes, walking sticks, food, papers, glasses, matches, letters, etc.

3. Sound and visual effects—any noise required offstage, i.e., rain, thunder, cars, horns, bells, etc., and effects seen by the audience, i.e., falling snow, rain, smoke, etc.

Under the direction of the stage director, the property man should instruct his assistants in setting all these articles upon the stage—or upon a property table offstage, in the case of hand props. Assistants placing props must be rehearsed minutely in making quick, accurate, silent and unobtrusive changes between scenes and acts. The success of a quick change depends on pre-planning with each individual knowing and understanding his specific duties.

After the first dress rehearsal, when the producer has passed each prop and piece of furniture and has decided its precise position on the stage, the property man should make a property plot showing the exact spot where each item is to be placed, and at which point of the play it is put into position. In the case of hand props the name of the character using them, the act and scene, should be written opposite the article. Any alterations made by the producer at later dress rehearsals should be carefully noted.

The stage manager has already been largely mentioned in this chapter but his duties extend into almost every department of stage management. His is the least enviable job in the unit. He does most of the actual work backstage, has a great deal of responsibility, and gets the blame when things go wrong. The good stage director delegates the carrying out of various responsibilities to the stage manager. It is the function of the stage director to organize and oversee—of the stage manager to put the plans into operation. During rehearsal he is in charge of the marking of the prompt script, as we have said. He should teach the A.S.M. the method of marking and, at periods, put him or her on the book to prompt. The stage manager and the A.S.M. share this responsibility of prompting after the first night. The stage manager is always on the book on the first night. It is his function to maintain complete discipline in the rehearsal room when the stage director is absent. He gives the cast their calls for rehearsal and notifies them in ample time if there are changes in the schedule. As the rehearsals continue and the actors put their books down and the production starts to shape, the producer will ask for props so that the players may become familiar with the objects they must handle. The stage manager will get from the property master—not necessarily the actual prop which will be used, but something approximating it. For instance, if an actress during one long speech must pour tea for six people, such a feat requires considerable rehearsal in order to time the business with the lines, and even an experienced actress would be nonplussed if she were presented with a full tea service for the first time at the dress rehearsal. These props must be carefully packed and stored by the stage manager and the A.S.M. after each rehearsal and brought ready for use at the following rehearsal.

When possible, if there is music within the action of the play, it should be rehearsed early on. There is little difficulty if the actor merely has to turn on the gramophone as the record can be used on-stage, but if the music comes from a radio it involves the use of a panatrope offstage. The A.S.M., as a rule, handles the panatrope. The producer chooses the records and the particular passages he desires. These are carefully marked and the records placed in order—that is, in the order in which they will be used. Such effects as these must be rehearsed to complete exactitude and the person in control of the panatrope must be sensitive and absolutely reliable. Most audiences are familiar with some of the more outstanding gaffs perpetrated by inefficient backstage staffs: the actress turns on the radio and her next line is, "I am playing you this tune because I want you to hear it before I tell you what happened. It will make you understand." but no music comes on!—or the actor who goes to the light switch saying, "We sit in the dark—all through our lives we're in the dark. For God sake let's have some light!" but no light comes on in answer to his touch. A tip here to all actors: if this happens on a light cue, glue yourself to the light switch, with your hand on it, until the light does come on. It may cause you to miss your next move and ruin the rest of your scene, but it will save you the derisive laugh from the audience —which is what the stage management deserve—but not you!

If the society is fortunate enough to have a costume designer with talent the productions will have a heightened attraction and beauty. But every designer must have a colleague, with talent and insight, to carry out those designs. We can call this person, who will be so valuable, the wardrobe mistress, or the costume mistress—it really doesn't matter. If the costumes are to be made within the society her ability and her energy must be enormous, and she must be greatly valued. If the costumes are hired the costume mistress is still essential. She should attend one of the initial rehearsals to take all the actors' measurements, or the actors are sent to her if there should be a room given up to the wardrobe. Complete measurements should be taken: the head, for wigs—the circumference, from the nape of the neck to the end of the hair line in front, over the top of the head from ear to ear. Full body measurements are taken—bust, hips, waist, full arm, arm bent, from shoulder to floor, shoulder to waist, shoulder to modern hemline, length of trouser leg, width of shoulders in men. The size of shoes, stockings and gloves should also be ascertained.

If the costumes are to be made, the stage director arranges the time of fittings with the costume mistress so that rehearsals are not broken into.

If costumes are hired, the stage director makes a full list of all necessary articles for each character and sends them with measurements, and a sketch if possible, to the costumier. Ample time should be allowed. If the ordering is left to the last moment a poor selection of costumes may be sent. Time should also be allowed for necessary alterations before the dress rehearsal.

The costume mistress must see that all costumes are ready and in order for the costume parade which takes place before the first dress rehearsal. She should attend with notebook and pencil in order to write down all changes and alterations desired by the producer. All alterations should be completed in time for the final dress rehearsal. The costume mistress is responsible for the care of all costumes during the run of the play. She should be prepared, at a moment's notice, to mend, patch, darn and clean costumes. She must always have an adequate supply of thread in various colours, needles, scissors, pins and an iron. This last is most important as all costumes should be inspected before each performance and creases ironed out if necessary. Washable costumes should be frequently laundered. Dirt and make-up should be removed from all costumes each time they are used.

Protectors should be sewn into the underarms of each costume. However fastidious an actor is he will perspire under hot lights, and costumes may be ruined unless proper precaution is taken.

Hangers should be provided for all costumes, and accessories either pinned to the garment or hung on the hanger.

Duplicate lists should be made of every article of clothing, accessories, shoes, wigs, etc., and a copy given to the actor concerned. When he returns the clothes to the wardrobe they may then be easily checked.

The costume mistress must insist that actors take adequate care of all garments while in their possession.

The building of the set is one of the main concerns in any production. It is to be hoped that competent members will be found inside the society who, under the guidance of one, perhaps professional, carpenter, will be able to do this important job. When the time comes for the "set up" the carpenter in charge should instruct the scene shifters, or stage hands, how to erect the set. At this important operation the stage director is in supreme command. He does not physically help with the setting up, nor does he ever move flats or furniture in a scene change. He stands with his back to the auditorium and instructs the various departments in their different jobs. He must have a complete and accurate mental picture of the scene, the furniture, the props, and immediately note when a mistake is being made or an article forgotten. If he takes part in the change himself he cannot give his complete attention to the overall picture. If he has organized well, every member of the stage staff will be fully occupied with clearly defined, specific jobs, which will be carried out with a maximum of speed and efficiency.

When there are a number of scene changes the problems are greatly increased. The first set must be erected with each stage-hand being assigned to specific tasks. It is then dismantled—again in a completely organized way—and the flats are stacked in a particular place as they are taken off the playing area. Every flat has its particular position offstage. The stage director must work out the change so that the flats on the P.S. of the set are stacked on that side of the stage and flats on the O.P. in their nearest adjacent position. The second set to be erected must have been stacked beforehand in the most convenient parts of the stage to get them into position with a maximum of speed. The taking down of one set and building of the next must be rehearsed over and over so that each movement of the various members of the stage crew goes like clockwork. Eight minutes is the maximum time allowed for clearing the furniture, taking down the first set, building the second and placing all furniture and props in their accurate positions. The public gives little thought to the tremendous labours that go on backstage while they are chatting in the interval, but when a scene change is done really well it is the result of expert organizing, long and patient rehearsal, and a tremendous effort at the actual time.

Sometimes it is necessary to change one scene while another is in progress, and this is an even more delicate operation because it must be done with no noise being apparent to the audience and be completed to a split second so that, as one scene finishes the next one can begin.

The stage staff is usually pretty tired by the end of the set up, but they can be allowed little rest because they are fighting the clock every minute of the time until the rise of curtain on the first performance. However, if the stage director has organized well he will have sufficient time in hand to send his weary men home for five or six hours before the lighting rehearsal commences.

It is for the stage director to appoint the hour of the lighting rehearsal and to do this with the approval of the producer. As the stage director has the responsibility of the actual marshalling of the backstage staff, their hours of work, the jobs specified to all the back room boys in turn, he is naturally the one who will have the best idea which is the earliest possible hour, convenient for all concerned, at which to embark upon the delicate, and consequently highly important business, of lighting the play.

Sometime prior to this rehearsal the producer will have worked out a provisional lighting plot naming the various colours he will require to express the different moods of the piece. From this plot the stage director instructs the electrician to assemble these colours which are referred to as "jellies" or "gelatines". I should perhaps mention that although this plot covers every phase of the play from a lighting point of view, it *is* provisional because the whole point of a lighting rehearsal is in fact trial and error, and lighting a stage, from the producer's point of view, is no more a cut and dried business than is another aspect of his production: the direction of the artists. The colours in the foot-lights (sometimes called the floats), the spot bar, the batten bars (of which there are several), the limes, perches and pageants are all, to some extent, unknown quantities until blended with the action of the play. Consequently, it is not unusual after the first dress rehearsal, for the producer to alter considerably his lighting plot in time for the second dress rehearsal. However, before the initial rehearsal, the electrician, following this provisional plot, will be changing the frosts in the floats to pinks or golds, while the A.S.M., who knows a bit about the job, is atop a high ladder doing likewise to the spot bar. The electrician will be careful to make a last-minute check of all colours in order to ensure that not only are the initial jellies in position, but the pinks and the golds, the frosts, the blues, midnights, steels, ambers and dark browns as well as sunny reds and surprise pinks are all stocked up ready for his changes. By the time the rehearsal is over almost all the colours used throughout the production will have been adjusted to their correct positions awaiting the rise of the curtain, and the various buttons or levers—depending upon the type of board—have only to be touched in order to get the rehearsed effect. If the "limes" are oper-ated from the front of house, and this frequently is the case when there is an upper circle, then the assistant electrician will change the jellies as required.

The first lighting rehearsal is run somewhat as follows: the producer is in front, moving around to various positions in the auditorium to see the effect from different angles, and calling out the numbers, which each colour must be known by. The reason that "gold", for example, is known by three different numbers, 51, 52, 53, is to save time and trouble. Take the producer who says, "Give me a light gold", or a "darker gold". In point of fact nobody on the stage can exactly decide which of the three golds he wants. But if he is able to say 53 instead of 51 the electrician will automatically know that he needs the most brilliant of the three. The business of lighting the stage is dependent upon the type of play embarked upon, as well as the method employed by the producer. The play may be a "mood play" in which the atmosphere created by constant and subtle light changes is necessary for the overall effect, although it may have only one setting and few characters. I have known such a production to take more time to light than a large-scale musical at the Palace Theatre.

Although the producer need know nothing about the electrical technicalities of lighting he should acquaint himself thoroughly with the various types of equipment which provide sources of light so that he will know exactly what to ask for. It is not enough to say, "I want it to look dark outside and light inside." He must know what equipment to use to get such an effect, and how to use it. To light a play effectively and dramatically is as much part of the producer's job as directing the actors.

At this first rehearsal every lighting cue throughout the play is patiently rehearsed until the producer is satisfied with the result. Each cue is numbered. The electrician makes a careful note on his plot of the number and the type of lighting change—whether, for instance, a light is switched on as an actor enters, whether there is a slow check, perhaps lasting for 20 minutes as night falls, a black-out, a fade-out, and so on. The stage manager carefully notes the numbers of the cues in the prompt script against the line or piece of business at which the lighting change is made, for he must give all signals for light cues to the electrician.

Finally the lighting rehearsal comes to an end—sometimes after ten or twelve hours—and the dress parade is called, and after that the first dress rehearsal begins. As we have noted in the chapter, "The New Society's First Production", this dress rehearsal is a great strain on everyone, but for the stage manager it is a sort of purgatory which must be lived through. So many things for which he is directly responsible go wrong that he wonders if anyone could be as inept as himself. His most arduous task, however, is controlling "the corner" as it is called, where the prompter sits, and where the board is located, through which signals are given for music cues, for entrances where actors come onto a silent stage and have no sight line to help them to gauge the exact moment of entrance, cues for offstage noises (some of which the stage manager handles himself, some of which must be done from various sound vantage positions on the stage). From this corner he warns the call-boy when to call actors from their dressing rooms to stand by for their entrances, he signals the front of house on a given line that the end of the act is approaching so the bar and refreshments will be ready for the audience streaming out, he signals the electrician for every lighting cue during the entire production, he signals the men on the curtain that the end of a scene or an act is approaching and gives them a further cue to drop the curtain. As it falls he signals the front of house lights to go on, and as the curtain is about to rise again, for the house lights to dim down and finally go out.

The play is timed during the final rehearsals and it is the duty of the stage manager to keep a record, at each performance, of the length of time of each scene, each act, and finally, the playing time of the entire piece. In a drama, the time should not vary from one performance to another. A comedy is variable. With a full house, and the resultant louder and longer laughs, the running time may lengthen by several minutes. This is a good sign but must be watched closely, because actors, loving audience reaction, are inclined to "milk" their laughs and slow up the production, to the detriment of the play.

The stage director always gives the signal for the rise of curtain and is there at the final drop of the curtain. He directs the curtain calls. If he has been a good stage director from the beginning there will be little else for him to do, except to lend his presence which represents discipline, and gives a feeling of reassurance to staff and actors alike.

Having discussed stage management generally I determined, in the next several chapters, to deal with each department separately and in detail. Many aspects I have written about myself, but for certain subjects I have asked specialists, most of them actively associated in past productions of mine, to contribute articles, some of which are highly technical. In this way I have been able to gather together expert detailed information which I hope will prove useful to amateurs who are just starting out, and to more experienced groups who are ready to "spread their wings".

X. DESIGN
by THEA NEU

I: SETTINGS

IN an amateur society the Designer should be a member who has
some skill, and preferably training and experience, in painting. In
very small groups the producer himself may undertake the task,
although this should be avoided if at all possible. In most communities
some person may be found who has made a hobby of painting and has
an eye for design. This is the person to be encouraged as a Set Designer.

He cannot begin the job until he has become thoroughly familiar
with the physical limitations and characteristics of the theatre, and has
spent some time studying the history of the visual side of drama from
earliest times to the present day. He should see as many plays as
possible and note the different styles and techniques used. Skill can
be developed by attending the various short courses and lectures
arranged by such organizations as the British Drama League, or by
County Drama Committees and educational authorities. Above all he
must get practical experience. All the theory, reading and observing in
the world will not make a good designer. He should try to work as an
assistant to a designer, or as an assistant stage manager, in order to
familiarize himself with the practical methods and the problems encountered in mounting and running a play. Amateur groups are in a
good position to encourage new designing talent by asking for volunteer
helpers from the art classes of local schools and colleges.

In the professional theatre the designer is chosen by either the producer or the management. As the producer must work closely with his
designer understanding between these two is essential. Quite often he
chooses a designer with whom he has worked before, because each
knows the other's methods of work.

It often happens that if a designer has a success with a particular
kind of setting he is asked to repeat this type in many different productions, and can become, like an actor, type cast. Although this is often
regrettable from the designer's point of view because it rather limits his
scope, one can understand a management's point of view. It may be
true to say that the theatre is the actor's stronghold, and that it depends
to a large extent on the actors and on the action whether the play

From a disused church . . .

. . . to a little theatre.
This building was converted from church to theatre by the Halifax Thespians, Halifax, Yorkshire.

A painted backdrop for Molière's *The Miser* at the Leicester Little Theatre, Leicestershire.

comes across and moves the audience. On the other hand, there is one moment when a designer can really make his big contribution—when the curtain goes up on "the place". A visual impression is a very immediate one, and in one moment a mood can be created which the play will subsequently develop further. There are also plays so light that an audience may not feel they are worthwhile seeing, unless the whole matter is treated like an exquisite luxury, with luscious sets and expensive clothes and furniture. Or a wretched back street hovel can convey its feeling of poverty and make an audience shiver before the first actor speaks. A setting also often gives an immediate key to the producer's approach to a play, particularly in classics like Shakespeare, where the material lends itself to a variety of interpretations in period and style.

There are, broadly speaking, two kinds of designers. One has a very personal style, and is often a highly individual easel-painter before being asked to design. He will probably only do shows in which he is allowed to express his personal ideas, and no matter what type of play is done his idiosyncrasies will be seen in the setting. Without referring to the programme an audience can murmur, "Ah! A James Jones set." The second kind of designer is a more adaptable craftsman, whose personality is not so definitely stamped upon his sets. He adapts his ideas to those of the producer and the play. If necessary he creates a setting out of whatever flats, etc. happen to be on hand. He is probably a more useful designer for a repertory company and for an amateur society than his more glamorous individualistic brother. But make no mistake—even the most glamorous designer must be, in the final analysis, a practical man of the theatre.

The designer's place in the theatre has become more prominent in the last fifty years. A distinctly modern innovation is the ripple of applause that often greets a setting when the curtain goes up. Sometimes a poor play takes on a certain aura and is assured of a fair run in the West End if its settings and costumes are brilliantly done. How often one has heard a member of the audience say as he left the theatre, "Well, I didn't think much of the play, but what an attractive house they lived in", or "Whatever it wasn't, it certainly was a colourful show." Cosmopolitan audiences have come to expect dazzling and unusual settings, and the musical comedy theatre in particular does its best not to disappoint them. There is a tendency among some companies today to get away from ornate decor, and back to the simplicity of curtains or even a bare stage projected into the audience. Sincere performances in these surroundings can be most effective, and take us back in time.

Let us look for a moment at the development of stage decor. It all

I

began with the story-teller, winding his spell with words and mime in the centre of a circle of friends. Perhaps he carried a stick to point his meanings, but he had no man-made setting . . . only the background of trees, grass and rocks. Eventually he "dressed up", putting on a crudely made mask to represent the animals, gods or elements he was portraying. Probably he was astute enough to arrange his story-telling at sunset, when the crimson natural light flooded his tale with romance, and caused his listeners to gasp as a modern audience does over a spectacular lighting effect.

Then the Greeks built their glorious outdoor amphitheatres whose seats stretched in a three-quarters circle, and their scene buildings from which actors could enter and exit on to the long platform which formed their stage in the centre of the amphitheatre. The first stage mechanisms were introduced including the crane that lowered the actors playing gods from their heaven on top of the scene building, and swept them away into hell if necessary. There were elaborate masks, made not only to disguise the actor, but to help him project his voice, working on the modified principle of a megaphone. Masks, high boots and flowing robes made the whole performance larger than life and theatricality was firmly established.

The Romans modified the Greek idea by providing an architectural façade with three openings. Two were to represent door openings and the third, in the centre, served as a side street.

In the medieval theatre in England mystery plays were presented on pageant cars . . . wagons which moved from place to place, setting up in any street or courtyard. These were often double-decked, the upper deck being used as the stage proper and the lower deck as hell, or as dressing-rooms for the actors. Simple costumes were introduced, but no painted scenery. Spectators stood in the street, and often the action moved out among them. On the Continent at this time a long platform stage, either straight or in a half circle, was developed, also outdoors and portable. Action moved along it. At one end was heaven, at the other hell. Grotesque masks and costumes were employed, and effects of smoke, flames and thunder frightened the simple audiences.

During the Renaissance formal architectural settings were developed in Italy. There were painted perspectives and vistas shown on a wall . . . much like a modern painted drop. The proscenium arch was developed to divide audience from actors.

In England the famous Elizabethan stage came into being. Round, roofless playhouses like the Globe were built, and the elements poured down upon the unfortunates standing in the centre (pit). Their wealthier compatriots sat in covered galleries built in a circle, and the forestage jutted out into the audience. Continuous action took place on this forestage, on the inner stage (a curtained recess behind and on the same level), and on the upper stage (above the inner stage). The upper stage was separated from the audience by a curtain and a low railing. Trapdoors were used, and a few scenic effects, but there was still no need for a scene designer. Acting, aided by costumes, was all.

Then came the Restoration stage, influenced by the Italian renaissance and the Elizabethan era. The proscenium arch was introduced to England, a full curtain divided audience from the stage, pictorial backgrounds were painted, and side wing pieces introduced. Most of the action was kept downstage, away from the setting. Sumptuous costumes were popular. The forestage was retained in modified form as the apron, in front of the curtain. Painted canvas flats were introduced, and scene changes were possible. Our picture frame stage had arrived, and so it has remained to this day. *10 45 11*

Until the latter part of the nineteenth century, only painted, unrealistic backdrops were required by way of decor, and often had little or no relation to the piece being performed. With the advent of realistic playwrights like Ibsen, and the formation of companies like the Moscow Arts Theatre, scenic design began to change. Realism in settings crept in. Painted trees were not enough. Real ones, or artificial ones made in three dimensions, stood on the stage. Interiors were faithful replicas of the parlours or kitchens of the day, even to cracks in the plaster and antimacassars on the chairs. A famous case of carrying Naturalism to the extreme occurred in 1912, when American producer David Belasco reconstructed Childs restaurant in detail on the stage for *The Governor's Lady*. Real steam arose from the pots and real food was cooked before the audience's eyes . . . a very aromatic and tantalizing experience!

With the coming of electricity, lighting effects began to influence staging. The German designer Adolphe Appia, in a revolt away from extreme Naturalism, made light seem three-dimensional, and his atmospheric lighted spaces introduced Symbolism as an attempt to make clear the inner meaning of the play. Gordon Craig, with his overpoweringly large flats and use of light, reduced the stature and importance of actors. His ideal theatre would make the scenery the most important means for conveying ideas, and would substitute puppets for actors. In Russia, Meyerhold introduced Constructivism, a style that utilized stairs, ramps, levels, scaffolds, girders and skeleton outlines of buildings, rooms, etc. His was the voice of the machine age.

The extremes introduced by these men are not followed completely today in most cases, but their influence is felt in nearly all settings, and they certainly established the importance of the Set Designer.

Perhaps the style most in use today is Selective Realism . . . a com-

STAGING THROUGH THE YEARS

Drawings by Michael Ford

(*Left to Right*)

1. Greek Open Air Amphi-theatre with Scene Building.

2. Roman Open Air Amphitheatre with Architectural Façade.

3. Italian Renaissance stage with Settings Painted in Perspective.

4. English Elizabethan Playhouse with Fore-stage.

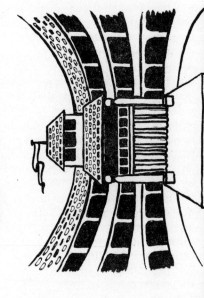

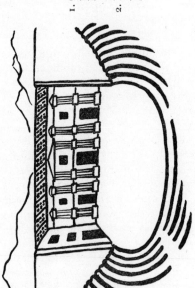

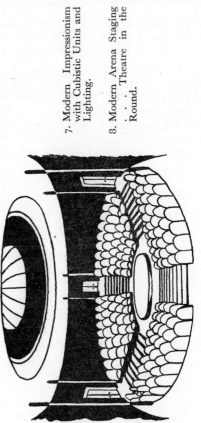

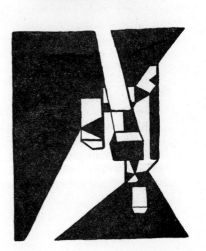

(*Left to Right*)

5. Georgian stage with Proscenium and Apron.

6. Modern Picture Frame Stage with Realistic Setting.

7. Modern Impressionism with Cubistic Units and Lighting.

8. Modern Arena Staging . . . Theatre in the Round.

promise, in which reality is suggested by selected details, but settings are not cluttered up with the paraphernalia of complete Naturalism.

One of the newest styles to find favour is Arena Staging, or as it is sometimes called, Theatre in the Round, where action takes place in a centre area with the audience seated in a circle around it. However, this style is not really new, but goes back again to the oldest dramatic form, with the modern aids of a covered auditorium and electric lights. Arena Staging is not yet widely practised in Britain, and the picture frame proscenium arch still rules the designer's task to a major degree. His magic projects itself to an audience of peepers looking through an imaginary fourth wall.

The amateur theatre should be able to experiment with various styles of staging. Not as limited financially as the commercial theatre, it could be, and in some cases is, the home of new ideas and techniques. An amateur designer could take the lead here, by introducing fresh ideas not only for new plays but with the proven classics. Good sets will help not only to sell a play but to make it an appreciated and remembered production.

PROCEDURES AND METHODS IN DESIGNING

Most designers have their own individual methods, adapted to their situation by experience, but there are certain general procedures that many designers follow; and which will apply in most amateur societies.

Research must begin as soon as the designer knows he is to do a play, and may start even before he has read the script if he knows the period of the play. In fact a general knowledge of the period will help him to visualize the settings as he reads. The script is read first for a general impression, and to place the story and characters in his mind. Next it is read for a more detailed mental picture of location, time, and style, if this latter is definitely indicated. Sometimes creative ideas come to a designer through his reading which, when conveyed to the producer, may alter the interpretation of the play or parts of it. When reading it is a good idea for the designer to imagine he is in the actual surroundings. He may think, for example, of what kind of ornaments an Italian immigrant in New York would place on her mantelpiece, what colour schemes she would prefer; or how a meticulous civil servant would place his furniture; or what kind of plants a lonely spinster might have in her window. Character analysis is as important for the designer as for the actor and producer.

After several careful readings, and when thoroughly familiar with the play, it is time for the designer to confer with the producer. This should take place some time before rehearsals begin. The producer tells the designer what approach he is using towards the production, the mood he wishes the settings to create, what style he would like used; and the designer adds any ideas he has on these points. There may be certain definite door, window, etc. positions which are vital to the action, and these the producer asks the designer to incorporate. Many producers leave the actual positioning of exits and entrances to the designer and plan actors' movements around these.

After this conference the designer makes the first rough sketches of the set. Often he does more detailed research at this stage. There are many sources of information. Local libraries have accurate books on historical data and often excellent collections of photographs. Museums are also very helpful. The Victoria and Albert Museum in London has a large and comprehensive Fine Arts Department, with photographs of homes, buildings and dress of all periods and countries. *Picture Post* magazine has a good photograph reference library, particularly for modern settings. Newspapers will loan reproductions of photographs. Factories, airports, military stations, manufacturing and engineering works, etc. are only a few of the places where information may be found. If a designer knows what he is looking for, and arranges appointments, such organizations will nearly always co-operate to the fullest in a search for data.

Sometimes the designer may feel a setting should be like a painting . . . a Rembrandt, a Van Gogh, etc. Then he will study paintings by these masters and try to get their feeling into the designs. An example of this was the setting I did recently for *Wedding in Paris*, which I thought should have the feeling of a painting by the French artist, Raoul Dufy, and I tried to get this mood into the designs. During the thirties there was a vogue for the reproduction of actual paintings, such as Hugh Stevenson's design for *The Gods Go a Begging* at Sadlers Wells, based on a Watteau. Rolf Gerard's design for *Love's Labour's Lost* at Stratford was also based on a Watteau.

It is a good idea for a designer to keep reference scrapbooks, into which he pastes photographs from magazines, newspapers, etc., on every conceivable subject and period. Information should be carefully indexed so that it is easy to find for ready reference. Amateur societies could compile wonderful scrapbooks by collecting material from their many members.

If the producer approves the first rough sketches, a coloured painting of the setting is then made. Unless the amateur designer is a skilled painter it might be wiser to dispense with this painting and to go ahead making a scale model, because the painting might delude. Often the general impression shown cannot be transferred exactly into the stage setting. Certain aspects may be read into the painting which cannot be reproduced in actuality. Finished drawings are a guide for colour and lighting however, and some designers produce these after the models have been completed and approved.

The making of models is very important in set designing, and they must be constructed to an accurate scale, usually $\frac{1}{2}$ inch–1 foot. The first step is to obtain the measurements of the stage to be used: width, depth, height of proscenium arch, wing space and flying space. If possible the designer should visit the theatre himself to actually see the space available. He must always keep scene changing in mind, and plan the scenery for minimum waits between scenes. He should move about the auditorium viewing the stage from every angle and every level, so that he knows what sight lines he must work to. This is, of course, checked again when the set is put up on the stage, but often forethought can prevent serious mistakes being made.

A cardboard model of the stage floor area and proscenium should be constructed, on to which are placed cardboard models of flats, door and window pieces, trees, ramps, levels, etc. . . . in fact all the scenery to be used. These may be moved into many positions, to try out various combinations, until the most pleasing arrangement is found. While planning and manipulating the models the designer must always think of the flats and other materials he has on hand to work with if he is adapting used scenery. As a general principle it is wise to keep the main shape of the set fairly low in height so that it will conform to the theatre's sight lines. Cardboard figures, also made to scale, representing actors should be used on the model stage to show how the human figure will look in proportion to the setting.

Models will save worry and confusion for both actors and producer. They give a far more accurate conception of the final setting than a sketch or drawing ever can. However, they are still not exactly like the finished work, and usually minor adjustments must be made even when models are accepted; but their value cannot be overemphasized. Once the general concept of the model has been accepted by the producer and management it may be painted to give an even better representation of the setting.

If he has not already done so the designer must find out next what stocks of scenery are already available for adaptation. These must be inspected and carefully measured, if there is not a detailed inventory. Societies would be well advised to keep such an up-to-date inventory. In most cases it is wise for the designer to check the actual scenery himself. It might cause delay and inconvenience if he depends for example on 4 flats measuring 10 ft. by 3 ft. and finds when work is begun that there are only 2 such flats, the others having been loaned out, mislaid or even destroyed.

It is important to know how much money has been budgeted for the scenery. This factor often determines the style and complexity of a set, and perhaps should be discovered before any plans are made.

The designer must know if and when a carpenter is available, or how many members will help to build, and whether they are experienced workers or novices.

He must find out where and when there is space for building. Some amateur organizations have workshops for this purpose, some build on the stage when rehearsals are not taking place, and many have to use a large room in a member's dwelling, an empty garage, or even do some construction outdoors—the latter being a rather poor arrangement in Britain's inclement climate! It should be remembered that water marks are almost impossible to remove from flats that have once become wet.

In the professional theatre, after the model has been approved it is sent out to a set-building firm for an estimate as to cost. Sometimes it goes to several firms and the one giving the most reasonable bid is given the contract. This is an unlikely happening in the amateur theatre, although if a carpenter is to be hired, especially for the first time, it might be wise to ask for estimates from several men.

Usually rehearsals begin before construction gets under way, and the designer should always be present at the first rehearsal. He should provide scale ground plans for the stage management, producer and carpenter. These are line drawings of the set outlines as seen from above, and are marked out on the floor at every rehearsal. It is important that the measurements be marked out correctly so that the actors are used to working in the exact space they will have on stage. This is the duty of the stage manager and his staff, but a wise designer will check the first time the plan is set out to make sure there are no misunderstandings about measurements. Even after rehearsals begin there may be changes made when movement is actually tried in the space allotted. For example, in a recent musical production which I designed, one of the rostrums, which seemed perfectly all right to everyone who saw the models, proved in use to be too small and had to be enlarged.

Once rehearsals have started the designer concentrates on construction, and in the professional theatre practically lives in a separate world from the rest of the company. In the amateur group it is more than likely he will be building the set himself, or at least helping. In any case he must be continually supervising to make sure his careful plans are carried out accurately. If he cannot always be present an experienced person should act as a liaison. Usually this will be the stage manager.

A detailed list of flats, rostrums, etc. required must be made, with exact measurements for each one. For complete clarity each piece should be drawn out, starting from say stage right and working round to the left. This is known as the Elevation Drawing. For inexperienced builders each detail should be drawn in, for example: position of stiles, hinges, cleats, etc. Flats on hand should be sorted out and exact drawings made showing how they must be altered. Designer and stage manager together must make lists of new materials required and the latter will see that these are ordered.

It is important to make lists of everything needed, including furniture, scenery, costumes and properties. These are compiled by the heads of departments involved, and probably added to as rehearsals progress. Whenever additions are made in scenery and furniture the designer should be informed. If the producer decides an extra chair is needed the stage manager must tell the designer so that he can arrange for this, and not find at the last minute that he didn't know about it. During the stress of preparing a production no one on the technical staff should trust to his memory. *Everything* should be written down. A little notebook and a pencil should be carried everywhere.

In the commercial theatre the people who build sets are skilled craftsmen, and their workmanship is highly important in the finished setting. They often have a greater knowledge of techniques and materials than the designer has, and may suggest alternatives in construction if there is difficulty in translating an idea into a practical object. Even in the amateur organization a designer should listen to an experienced carpenter if troubles arise, and be humble enough to submit to alterations if his design is too wildly impractical.

The designer is responsible for choosing the necessary furniture, window draperies and ornaments for the set. Sometimes the producer accompanies him to help choose these if they are being hired from a furniture store. Quite often he leaves the choice to the discretion of the designer, after basic requirements have been discussed. In amateur societies much furniture will be borrowed from members' homes, local shops etc. However, if the society has a little spare money it is a good investment to build up a basic furniture supply. Tours of second-hand shops will reveal surprising discoveries, and no matter how old, scratched and even broken, tables, chairs etc. may be, they can be reclaimed, painted and if carefully stored each time after use will serve the society for many years in many different plays. Quite often people have attics full of old furniture, clothes, ornaments, books etc., which they would like to get rid of, and will be only too pleased to let the drama club take away. A rich theatrical storehouse may be built up through drives on cobwebby attics.

If a society can't afford a really good full set, it is effective to use cut-out or unit pieces against black curtains, and concentrate on subtle lighting and colourful costumes. Badly built flats (set up with gaps between), walls that shake when doors are closed, doors and windows that don't open or close easily, and poor realistic painting will drive audiences away. A good impression of a play well done may be given by excellent costumes and little or no scenery, but never by a poor set, no matter how brilliant the acting and production.

A set of black velvet tabs (curtains) to surround the stage is a very valuable investment for an amateur society. Innumerable varied effects, periods, styles may be worked out against this neutral background. If these are too expensive a group may experiment with a set of black flats used in the same manner, but great care must be taken in building these so they fit together exactly, and good scene paint must be used to ensure a really rich black colour. Hessian curtains can be very effective with designs painted roughly on them in colourful slabs. The effect under lights is rich and thick, like a tapestry, and is particularly useful in Shakespearian and other historical plays. Grey tabs also take light very well and are next in preference to black.

A permanent formal set is a sound acquisition. This consists of flats, arches, pillars, rostrums and ramps painted in a neutral colour, which may be placed in different positions for different locations and dressed with colour and light. If such a set is contemplated it is really worthwhile to consult a professional designer.

Double-canvased flats are especially useful on small stages, and for limited budgets, as they save space and timber. They may be painted a different colour on each side and a new location obtained by merely turning the flats around. They are not very satisfactory for touring as the exposed side may well be badly scratched.

PAINTING

Once the set is constructed the designer begins to paint it. Even in the commercial theatre he sometimes paints his own set, and if not he closely supervises the work. In repertory theatres he nearly always does the painting. In the amateur society it is more than likely that the designer will also paint, with perhaps some help from members.

When the basic colour has been decided upon the designer should make a colour sample to decide what variations he will introduce. This can be done by painting a piece of paper in the required basic colour and pasting or pinning pieces of coloured material on to it to determine tone values. If costumes are being designed by another person he must collaborate at this stage to decide upon colours that will look well against the set. The British Colour Council at 13 Portman

Square, London, W.1, supplies excellent colour charts, which would prove most useful to amateur designers.

There should be a large stock of whiting on hand, along with stocks of powdered scene paint in all the primary colours. Good brushes in various sizes are also necessary. A large brush is used for "slapping on" the basic coats, medium brushes for painting in large designs, and small brushes for outlining, painting moulding, etc.

The mixing of paint is an art learned through practice. First a bucket of size must be cooked up. This is the ingredient that makes the colour stick to the canvas, and prevents it from rubbing off. Size must never be left out. It must be cooked carefully in a bucket placed inside another containing boiling water . . . the same principle as the double boiler. It must never be heated over a direct flame. Colour is then mixed with cold water and an equal proportion of size added. It is necessary to try out the colour on a piece of white paper and wait until it dries to see how it will appear on the flats. Colour always appears darker when wet. Further details on mixing paint will be found in the chapter on "Set Building".

New flats must have a priming coat before colour is applied. This is usually white with a larger than half amount of size added. If the flats are to be black of course a black priming coat may be used. Next a smooth coat of the basic colour is applied. This process is called "laying in". If a non-realistic effect is required the laying in may be roughly painted in a combination of several basic colours.

Flats should always be painted with vertical strokes from top to bottom, the brush picking up dribbles as it moves. Bold strokes are most effective. Finicky little strokes do not give such a smooth surface.

Two laying-in coats are usually put on, more care being taken with the second one. It is important to remember that rooms usually have darker shadows at the top, and a slightly darker shade of paint should be worked in during the laying-in process to show these shadows.

When painting an old flat it is more satisfactory to scrub off all the old paint with water, size the flat from the back to make the canvas taut again, and paint it as you would a new one. If there is a split in the canvas it should be mended from the back by pasting a patch of canvas over the opening, before the front is repainted. Painting over old coats of paint is rarely effective. The surface looks cracked and the flat becomes too heavy for easy scene shifting.

For interiors of wood or marble the surface should be brushed over with a layer of dark, then a layer of lighter paint, until a grained or mottled effect is acquired. For these effects the designer should carefully study the real thing or good colour photographs, then think up his own way of carrying it out. It is best to experiment on smaller surfaces before attempting the actual flat. For a final shiny surface a coat of size may be glazed over the finished painting, although this tends to make it brittle and will easily crack.

For dusty corners paint may be sprayed on over the basic coats.

It is very difficult to paint moulding that looks completely realistic. The best moulding is the wooden type which is nailed on to flats. However if it is not possible to have this, the painter must study real moulding closely to know just where the highlights and shadows come. He must determine where the source of light is in the setting, and then draw the moulding out in sections on the flats before attempting to paint it. Painting moulding is a very specialized technique and is only successful after long practice and careful observation.

Wallpaper designs may be done with a stencil cut out to the required shape and painted over with a stippling brush. The brush should be very dry to prevent the paint from running. A longer process, requiring great patience, but assuring a smart effect, is that of punching the outline of the design on a piece of cartridge paper, holding the paper against the flat, dusting black scene paint over the design, removing the paper, and painting in the design by hand around the outlines.

When painting landscapes it is wise to paint in light and shade while laying in, and to complete the shading in several coats rather than painting on separate highlights and shadows after the undercoats are finished. Everything should be added in stages, working from the darkest tones underneath up to the lightest on the top.

If the scenic artist or designer is not an experienced painter he will be wise to make stylized trees rather than badly painted realistic ones. Formalized shapes may be used, even in separate tree pieces, and are more effective than bad copies of reality. Felt and wire may be shaped into unusual plants and small trees. It is much better to suggest than to inexpertly copy great detail.

Backcloths and drops may be painted while the scenery is under construction. The ideal way to paint these is in a paint frame, but it is unlikely that many amateur groups will own these. Frames require a large building, which is at least twice the height of the cloth. Otherwise the cloth may be painted flat on the floor, if a large space is available, or hung on a batten on the stage and pulled higher by degrees as the painting progresses. It can be painted in sections, but this is often not satisfactory because the paint might change colour slightly while standing, as the painter waits for a painted section to dry. Paint also loses colour each time it is heated up. Heating is necessary because paint solidifies after standing any length of time. If no large floor space is available in the community for painting a cloth all at once, the designer should be prepared to paint it on the stage after rehearsals are over, staying up all night if necessary.

A stage cloth, for covering the stage floor, may have to be painted, depending upon the style of the play and whether or not carpets are used. It may even be necessary to paint a design on the cloth, and this is one of the jobs usually done at the last, just before the set goes up. Often the cloth must be touched up during the run in order to keep it fresh. A great deal of size must be added to the paint for a stage cloth.

THE SET-UP AND DRESS REHEARSALS

One of the most terrifying experiences the designer has is seeing his set on the stage for the first time. Any faults in design or painting show up glaringly. It requires great courage to look at these, and lots of imagination to know that the naked set, without furniture or lighting, will look well in the end. Ideas about how the setting could be bettered flash through one's mind, and these should be saved up for next time. The designer's panic mustn't show, and he must sensibly and practically supervise the dressing of the set, adding the furniture, curtains, ornaments, etc. He must know where everything should be placed, and check that the stage manager and property man also do. He must check everything to the last detail . . . even to the draping of the curtains. The designer has no direct authority over the stage staff and all requests for moving furniture, etc., should go through the stage director or stage manager.

After the play has been lit there may be minor bits of touching up to do on the painting, and covering up of scratches caused during the setting up. Although in most cases the producer does the actual lighting of a show, the designer should be familiar with the lighting process and certainly the effects of lighting colour upon his set. In some cases he may be asked to arrange the lighting. This is not usual in Britain, although it is often required in America, where lighting is considered part of the designer's job.

The designer must be present at all dress rehearsals as certain changes in furniture, colour, etc. may be needed when the actors are seen against the set. He will be present on opening night, and after that the job is finished. In the professional theatre he may be called in again to make alterations if the play transfers from one theatre to another, or goes out on tour, and this may possibly apply even to amateur groups.

A TOURING SET—"ANNA CHRISTIE"

A set designed for touring presents special problems, as it must be adaptable for many different stages. It might be useful here to set down in some detail how I proceeded with designing *Anna Christie*, which Peter Cotes produced for an Arts Council tour. The setting had to be practical for over thirty theatres and halls of various sizes.

It was decided to use a unit set inside black curtains. Above all, Mr. Cotes wanted a feeling of loneliness . . . a "lost" quality about the set. The black surround helped to create this mood. Three sets were required: a waterfront bar, the bridge of a coal barge, and the interior of the barge's cabin. I could learn about the waterfront bar from photographs and general research, but I knew nothing about barges. I paid a visit to the docks near London Bridge. There were no coal barges in sight, but there were a number of canal and channel barges tied up. There wasn't time to search for an authentic coal barge, so I decided to use the basic characteristics of a channel barge, and not reproduce complete naturalism. Instead the setting would be rather impressionistic, and as such could not be criticized for lack of exact detail.

I went aboard one of the Thames barges. It was ready to convey a load of apples to France, and the friendly co-operative crew showed me all over the boat, allowed me to make sketches and supplied me with refreshment.

Later I made a trip to the East India docks to find a ship's wheel. When a local ship's chandler was told about my purpose he loaned not only a wheel, but an anchor, ropes and other paraphernalia.

When the deck of the barge was completed it consisted of a rostrum, with certain selected details, like masts, the wheel, a capstan, ropes, etc. The suggestion of a bridge was there without too many cluttered objects. Dim lighting playing on the black surrounds gave an illusion of mist and fog, out of which came the faintly muffled, sad and eerie sound of a fog horn. The cabin interior and the bar were treated in the same slightly impressionistic manner.

For this particular production the models were taken to Salisbury and sets built there by an Arts Council repertory carpenter. I supervised the work and did the painting myself.

The tour opened in Cardiff and of course I had to be there for the dress rehearsals and opening night. After that the barge ploughed away from me through the theatres of Wales and Western England.

II: COSTUMES

To achieve a real unity in the stage picture it is often best to have costumes and settings designed by the same person. But on the other hand this may have disadvantages, as many clever designers haven't enough experience with materials and dressmaking to be able to translate their original ideas into actual clothes, so they find themselves very much at the mercy of their advisers. With many big productions, for example at Covent Garden, the designer may work together with a costume supervisor, who not only attends to organizing all the endless number of petticoats, stockings and odds and ends which need a lot of time and thought, but will also help with choosing the right kinds of materials and assist with fittings, etc. Costume supervisors themselves are often experienced designers.

If a society has two designers for one show . . . one for costumes and one for sets . . . the two should work very closely together, as well as with the producer. As a rule the costume designer should have an idea of the set his characters are going to live in before he finally works out his costumes. If the set has only one or two basic colours, for example, he might find it helpful to attach pieces of the materials he proposes to use on to a piece of board or paper painted in those colours, to see the effect produced.

The designer then completes sketches in colour which are seen by both producer and actors. Costumes are very important to actors, and must be comfortable as well as helpful to character interpretation. Sometimes a designer will think of a visual effect which he is sure is right for the play, but the producer and actor may feel that the costume, although it fits well into the general picture, is not right for the particular character. Here again it is important for the designer to think out the characters when reading the play, and to get the producer's and the actor's ideas before completing his designs. However, the designer may have ideas that will help the actor to achieve his character. The final design should be a fusion of ideas, and it must be remembered that an actor doesn't give his best performance in a costume he doesn't feel at home in.

The first sketches are suggestions, and will probably be revised. They show the general feeling the designer is trying to convey, and the colour scheme he would like to use. In stylized productions the designer's ideas will probably be completely accepted. However, as in many Shakespearian productions, when each character is a highly individual being, the actor's ideas should be incorporated providing they are practicable and meet with the producer's approval.

Basic architectural set for *Macbeth*, erected on the flat floor at one end of a large room, by the Great Hucklow Village Players, Derbyshire.

Research is an early phase of the costume designer's task, especially when period authenticity is required. Most libraries have volumes showing pictures of dress through the ages. Portraits and period paintings by the masters are invaluable not only for detail, but for mood and colour. Museums and art galleries are co-operative in a designer's search, and most will allow him to make sketches of articles like armour, headdresses, uniforms, etc. Second-hand bookshops are full of books containing authentic drawings of Victorian and Edwardian life, and often even earlier periods. Old volumes of magazines like *Punch* are a great aid to a designer, and inquiry in the community often unearths collections of such publications which people will gladly let a drama society use. Art schools will be sure to have information and plates of period costumes.

Scrapbooks may be compiled of pictures of dress in all periods, countries and styles, together with accoutrements used, like fans, parasols, jewellery, etc. Scrapbooks of materials in various textures and colours are also useful, especially in the making of colour charts for a production.

The designer should be familiar with the effect of stage lighting on various colours. He must know whether the scene is to be moonlight or bright sunlight, rainy and depressing or full of tropical glare, and whether any supernatural and eerie lighting is to be introduced. Colour value is learned through experience, but the following general principles may be observed:

Blue looks black under red, green and amber light; but is enriched by blue or purple light.

Red is rich under red light; but looks brownish under green light; dull under amber light; purplish under blue light; and slightly bluish under purple light.

Green looks blackish under red, blue and purple light; is enriched by green light; and tinged with yellow under amber light.

Yellow looks orange under red light; greenish under green light; brownish under blue light; greyish under purple light; and is enriched by amber light.

Flat White is not really good under any light, but is too stark. An off-white should be used.

Colour often expresses a mood or character at a glance, such as *red* for boldness and sex; *blue* for calm and peace; *purple* for royalty and *mauve* for decadence. However these are not rules, and opposite effects may be obtained by these colours, depending upon the style of the costume and the acting of its wearer.

The basic costumes of various periods illustrated in this book are only suggested as guides. Once the basic lines of a particular period are

K

established the designer is free to create his own variations in colour and decoration. Each designer will introduce his own particular flair in the finished garment.

Accessories, such as gloves, purses, belts, shoes, in some cases even stockings and petticoats, must be planned by the designer. Costume sketches should also include wigs. If these are particularly complicated separate drawings in detail should be made.

If the play is modern and all the clothes and accessories are being provided by the actors themselves, they should be checked well in advance. A dress parade is helpful if held just after rehearsals begin. Lists should be made of everything the actors can supply and everything the designer must find. The actual clothes must be worn at the dress parade so that colour tones and styles may be seen and accepted by designer and producer, and changes arranged if necessary.

The person who actually cuts and makes costumes is as important to the costume designer as the carpenter is to the scene designer. Sketches are only a beginning. The designer must be able to convey to the maker exactly what is required in a practical way, and should have a good knowledge of the difficulties involved in cutting and making. Some professional designers make costumes themselves as part of their business. In amateur societies the designer may very often have to make the clothes. If not, he must supervise continually and make sure that he has made his ideas clear enough in terms of materials. The cutter and sewer may be an artist too, and should be treated as a very important member of the company. Only when he becomes really interested can he give of his best. This can mean the difference between splendid and mediocre costumes.

If the same design were given to four different dressmakers the result would be four completely different costumes, each however being a close translation of the original design. Or if four different people were sent shopping for material for the same costume, they would probably return with four different types and shades. To get the exact effect he wants, the designer must have close personal supervision of each stage of the work.

He will probably wish to search for his own materials, as this is a fascinating business, especially now that there are so many kinds and colours to choose from, and materials can be found that he wouldn't think of unless he saw them in person. Before he begins shopping the designer must know what the costume budget is, and decide how much he can spend on buying materials. As a general rule I prefer to use plenty of cheap material rather than skimping with expensive cloth. Quite often lovely heavy fabrics will be found in drapery and curtain departments, and these are specially useful for many period costumes, but they don't have quite the firmness of weave of materials made particularly for dressmaking.

Cheap unbleached cotton is a good buy, and may be successfully dyed in almost any colour. If the budget is small it might be a good idea to make all the costumes out of the same kind of material, such as dyed cotton, and then paint patterns on them.

Rich effects are obtained by painting designs on cloth with textile paint, which takes a long time to dry but is washable. French enamel varnish may also be used, but great care is needed in its application because it is thin and has a tendency to run. If these paints are not available ordinary scene paint, mixed with a large quantity of size to prevent rubbing off, may be used. It is not as lasting and has to be retouched if a play runs any length of time.

Generally it is best to use large bold patterns, whether they are woven into the material or applied by hand. Small patterns tend to blur and become indistinct. The size of the theatre alters this to some extent, and the designer must take this into consideration. In a tiny playhouse smaller patterns may be more effective than overlarge ones, and vice versa.

Ingenuity and creativeness come into full play in the final decoration of costumes, and each designer will enjoy experimenting and working out his own ideas. Glitter, paper leaves and sequins may be effectively glued on to material. Vylene, a plastic material, may be cut out and painted for trimmings, and can be used like paper but has the advantage of not tearing as easily. Tubes of Bostik, a rubberized compound, may be squeezed out on to costumes in rolls and scrolls which stick to the material, dry hard, and may be painted in the desired colour. Copydex is a useful rubber adhesive which sticks material to material . . . for example, sticking on painted rope for braid on a uniform. Hat straw, bought by the yard, is interesting to work with, and felt, now so popular for women's skirts, makes up into inexpensive and rich-looking military uniforms.

If an amateur society made a drive for a collection of ladies' old hats there would be material and decoration aplenty for headgear in many plays of all periods. Fascinating styles can be concocted from old hats.

Sandals may be made from cheap felt or leather soles, on to which ties, jewels, etc. may be sewn.

If at all possible it is best to *make* costumes, which can be built up into a permanent wardrobe. The money spent on hiring would be better spent on buying materials, and if necessary paying a professional dressmaker. Hiring is always expensive, and rarely completely satisfactory as the costumes may be a mixture of designers' styles, conventions and colour schemes. Also, a society's own costumes may be altered, revamped, pulled apart and used again and again, which is a great saving in the long run. It is worth the effort to search the community for a designer who will make a kind of permanent hobby of this, or perhaps pay for an interested and talented member to take a course in design. In some cases it may be possible to pay for a professional designer to come in.

The costume designer will of course be present at all dress rehearsals, and if he hasn't made the clothes, will see that there is someone present who can make last-minute alterations if necessary. After the first night the designer's job is finished unless he is called in to design new costumes for the play for any reason.

CONCLUSION

In the designing, making and using of sets and costumes, as in every department of the theatre, one feels a wonderful sense of teamwork. Everyone is responsible for his own individual job, but all are working towards a common goal . . . the first night. Somehow all the worries, difficulties, frayed nerves etc., vanish when the team sees a well-mounted play come efficiently to life before a living audience. A thrill of accomplishment sweeps through one, if only for a brief moment, and all the struggles are worthwhile.

XI. SET BUILDING

by FRANK DRURY

GENERALLY speaking, there are two types of stage settings: a box interior or chamber set, and an open or exterior set.

The first should be made to look as solid as possible. It is made up of pieces of scenery known as "flats". The height of flats is generally 12, 14 or 18 feet, according to the height and requirements of the stage for which they are to be used. They can vary in width up to 8 feet, depending upon the requirements of the setting.

Flats are joined together edge to edge, but at different angles to one another to make up the setting. They are joined by a method known as "cleating". This is done from behind the flats. A line, attached to the edge of a flat about 18 inches from its top, is thrown over a cleat which is screwed to the next flat in a similar position. Looking at the flats from behind, the line is always on the left hand stile, and the cleat on the right hand one. The line is pulled tight and tied off on two screws, one on each flat, about 3 feet from the ground. Cleating is illustrated in Figure 1.

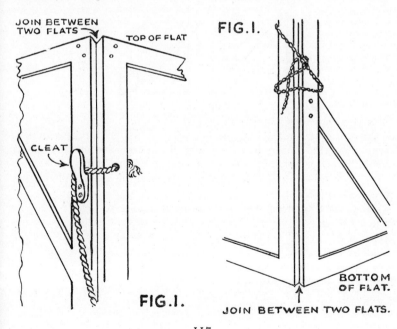

JOIN BETWEEN TWO FLATS

TOP OF FLAT

FIG. I.

CLEAT

FIG. I.

BOTTOM OF FLAT.

JOIN BETWEEN TWO FLATS.

Flats are braced at intervals, especially when they run in a straight line, or they would fall over. A "brace" is made of two pieces of wood joined telescopically and capable of being made rigid by the screwing up of a thumbscrew. One end of the brace has a hook in it, which is hooked through a screw eye in the back of the flat about 6 feet from the ground. The other end has a metal shoe on it, and on this a heavy metal weight is placed, as in Figure 2 (E and F)

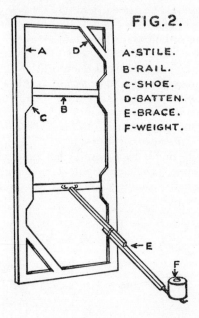

FIG. 2.

A-STILE.
B-RAIL.
C-SHOE.
D-BATTEN.
E-BRACE.
F-WEIGHT.

A flat is made of a wooden framework over which canvas is stretched, tacked and glued in the same manner as an artist prepares his canvas, except that the corners of the wooden framework are made rigid by mortising, or by halving. The size of the timber used in construction is 3 in. by 1 in. Figure 2 indicates the names of the various pieces that go to make up a flat.

When the framework of a flat has been made up, we are ready to stretch the canvas over it. Canvas may be bought in bales, already fireproofed, at widths of 36 in. or 72 in. The canvas is first laid over the wooden framework and then stretched and tacked down simultaneously. The tacks should be driven half in and should be on the inside edge of the wood right round the flat, about 4 inches apart. Next, glue is applied under the canvas which is pressed down firmly. The tacks are now driven home, and the glued part of the canvas swabbed with

rag and hot water. The canvas should be cut to meet the edge of the
wood, not overlap or be turned under. See Figure 3.

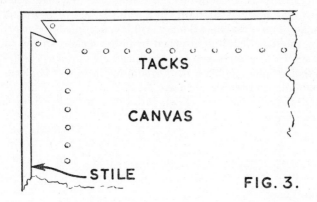

FIG. 3.

Once the glue is dry the flat is ready for painting. New canvas
should be primed first with a mixture of whitening, size and water.
Size in its crystal form is melted over hot water until it is of a fairly
thick consistency. It is then added to the whitening, and water added
until the mixture is right for applying with a brush. The size will give
the final stretch to the canvas, and
will prevent the whitening from
rubbing off. Scenic paint has to
be mixed with size for the same
reason.

TYPES OF FLATS

A flat with an unbroken surface
is known as a plain flat. A flat
with a door aperture is a door
flat; one with a window, a window flat; fireplace, a fireplace
flat, etc. In the parlance of
the theatre the word "flat" is
omitted, and the width and description of the flat is all that is
necessary. A six-foot door and a
five-foot French window are
therefore flats of that description.

Doors and windows are re-
cessed or "revealed". A "reveal"

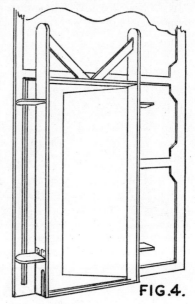

FIG.4.

is generally a piece of 6 in. by 1 in. running on its edge right round the door or window (Figure 4).

A door or French window or fireplace flat has a piece of iron an inch wide screwed across its bottom edge. This is known as a "sill iron" (Figure 4). The reveal on a door or window flat should be made separate from the flat itself, and attached by either a cleat line on each side or by a special type of hinged wedge (Figure 4). A door or French window reveal should also have a sill iron along its base. The front edges of doors and windows should have an architrave or moulding as one finds round actual doors and windows. For the stage they may be either painted on the canvas of the flat, or solidly built. Painting is not really satisfactory and always *looks* "painted". Mouldings should be the real thing. They may be either screwed or bolted to the front edge of the door or window. The whole piece, reveal and moulding combined, is then pushed through its respective door or window opening from the front of the flat, and cleated or wedged from behind as mentioned previously.

The height of flats to be used in a set is governed by the height of the proscenium opening, whether or not the theatre has a gallery, and if so, how high it is. These factors incur what is known as the "sight line". The other sight lines to be taken into consideration are from the side seats in the front row of the stalls either side, and the lower box seats, if there are any. These lines of sight determine how much of the acting area of the stage the audience can see, and how scenery must be

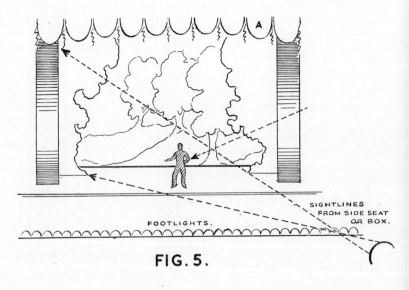

SIGHTLINES
FROM SIDE SEAT
OR BOX.

FOOTLIGHTS.

FIG. 5.

arranged so that spectators shall not be able to see any part of "behind the scenes" (Figure 5).

The width of a flat is generally governed by the size of railway trucks or lorries in which the scenery is to be conveyed, and also by the size of the scene dock doors of the theatre or theatres used for the production; 8 feet is usually the maximum. As it always looks better on stage not to see the join between two flats, it is possible to hinge two flats together and glue a strip of canvas down the centre over the hinges, slightly overlapping the flats either side. When travelling, the flat folds face to face. This is a very good way of "travelling" flats, as plain flats are often scratched when moved from place to place. A hinged flat is known as a "book flat".

If a play in production has more than one set, a change of scenery between acts or scenes is necessary. This will entail moving the scenery on and offstage by hand, and more than likely the pieces that run parallel to the footlights will be "flown". This means they will be hoisted out of sight by means of a set of three lines fixed high over the stage out of sight of the audience. Part of the new set may be dropped in simultaneously. These sets of lines pass through pulley blocks in a huge framework built high over the stage and called the "grid". The lines are then led down to a platform which is above stage level, and to one side of it. This is known as the "fly rail". Backcloths are flown on lines in the same way as flats.

A "backcloth" is a large expanse of canvas, the lengths of canvas being sewn together vertically with the seam at the back. The front is primed in the same way as a new flat and painted to represent either sky (for a sky cloth), or trees, roof tops, etc. In a box set, for example, we might want to see a garden through a window, in which case we should only need a small backcloth hung behind the window opening. For an exterior set, however, the backcloth may have to run the full width of the stage, being 40 feet or even longer. Along the top and bottom edge of the cloth are wooden battens, usually consisting of two lengths of 3 in. by 1 in. screwed and glued together, with the bottom edge of the canvas sandwiched between. A cloth, when hanging in position, should be just off the stage in order to keep the canvas taut.

In an exterior set the backcloth should be "masked in" at the sides by "wings" or "book flats" known as "book wings". These are flats painted to represent the sides and foreground of the scene. If the scene, for example, was a forest, the onstage edge of these flats should have a "profile" of plywood which should be canvased over, and cut away in places to represent the edge of tree trunks, smaller branches and leaves. To mask in the top of the backcloth and wings, canvas "borders", painted in the same manner, are hung parallel to the backcloth, and a few feet downstage of it so that people in the front seats cannot see up into the flies. One would probably need three borders hung at 6-foot intervals to successfully mask in the tops of cloth and wing flats hung 20 feet upstage of the setting line. Figure 6 is a rough indication of what an audience should see.

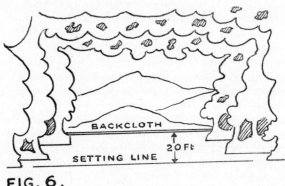

FIG. 6.

To mask in the top of the flats used in a box set, one does not use borders, but a "ceiling", which is dropped in and rests on the top of the flats. This provides a complete covering, as in a room. The ceiling used in a stage setting is made in a similar way to a backcloth, but it is stretched out over a wooden framework, and hung from the grid, lying face down, on two sets of lines, one upstage and one downstage. Then both sets are lifted together, taking the ceiling with them.

TYPES OF CLOTHS

Before erecting a set the stage should be covered with a "stage cloth". This is a very large expanse of the toughest canvas, and should be bound very strongly round the edge with 2-in. webbing. The cloth is stretched over the stage from the "setting line" (usually a line about 6 feet upstage of, and parallel to, the footlights). It is tacked down with half-inch tacks placed at intervals of about two feet. The stage cloth is painted to represent the type of floor the setting would have.

Apart from backcloths, there are "cut cloths" and "gauze cloths". A cut cloth has part of its canvas cut away, possibly to represent the gaps between trees and leaves. This gives an added depth to a set. When a canvas has been cut away between the painted leaves or branches, the gap left should be filled in with gauze glued on the back of the canvas. When the cloth is lit properly the gauze is barely visible. If there is a very large section cut away, for example between trees, and an actor has to walk between them, the gap is left open (Figure 7).

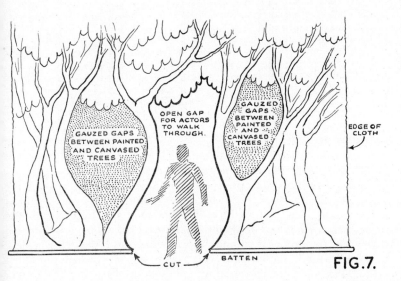

FIG.7.

A gauze cloth is a cloth made entirely of gauze, and is very effective for producing the effect of mist. If a backcloth is lowered a few feet behind the gauze cloth, and the scene painted on the backcloth very faintly lit with possibly a flood either side, and a ground row (compart-ments of lights lying along the foot of the cloth), the audience will see the scene as though they were looking at it through a mist. One may also paint a scene on a gauze cloth, and light it from the front. It will be clearly visible. Then by bringing up lights behind it and partly fading the lights from the front, the scene on the gauze cloth will disap-pear and the audience will see through the gauze. It will be seen that this is an effective way to fade from one scene to another.

GROUND ROWS

A ground row is built rather like a flat lying on its edge, with a profile on its top edge, and possibly on the ends (Figure 8).

Ground rows are usually built and painted to represent either a low hedge or rocks and boulders.

FIG. 8. GROUND ROW FROM BEHIND.

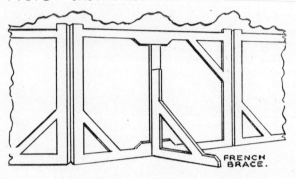

FRENCH BRACE.

ROSTRUMS

A "rostrum" is any section of the stage that is raised above the level of the stage floor. For example, it could be a staircase with a landing beyond, or possibly a dais projecting from under an archway on to the stage. A rostrum consists of two parts: the framework, which is built to the required length, breadth and depth out of 3 in. by 1 in.; and the top, which is made out of planks of 6 in. by 1 in. These are battened together with two pieces of 3 in. by 1 in. The top is padded with felt, to deaden sound, and covered with canvas which is tacked and glued down. The top is then screwed into position on the base. The framework is so constructed that it will fold for travelling. Rostrums may be made with either a curved "face" (the part seen by the audience), or a flat face. In either case the facing is done with plywood, canvased over. Wood of any description when used as a surface, should be canvased on one side. This is a requirement of all local fire prevention authorities.

A "boat truck" is virtually a rostrum on wheels. It is built in exactly the same way as a rostrum, the wheels being screwed underneath on lengths of 6 in. by 1 in. timber, which are "pin hinged" to the main framework. See Figure 9.

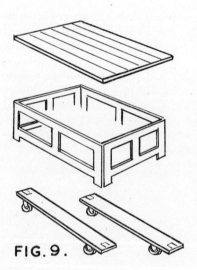

FIG. 9.

This figure illustrates the construction of a small rostrum with boat truck wheels and top separate.

BACKINGS

All doorways, and even smaller windows, must have backings. These are small flats, usually book flats, placed outside the door or window opening to mask backstage from the audience.

ARCHWAYS

An archway is constructed in the same way as a door frame, with two uprights and a piece across the top. If the arch has to have a curved apex, this is usually filled in with a piece of plywood which can be easily bent to give the required curve to the arch. The ply is then nailed in position and canvased (Figure 10).

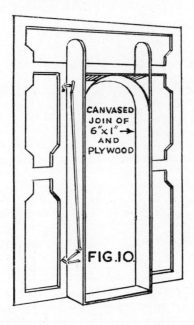

CANVASED
JOIN OF
6"× 1" →
AND
PLYWOOD

FIG. 10.

PRACTICAL BALCONIES

A practical balcony is a balcony on to which people actually walk. It is built in exactly the same way as a rostrum, to whatever size required. A balcony that projects from a window off the ground through the front side of a flat, will have to be supported by a pillar or pillars underneath, or if this is impractical, a special method of bracing from behind the flat has to be devised in order to support the balcony. In addition, there will have to be a rostrum offstage, behind the window, and a ladder to enable the actors to climb to and from the balcony from behind (Figure 11).

FIG. II.

BALUSTRADES

A balustrade can either be as simple as a park railing, or as compli cated as a carved stone balustrade from a palace garden. Usually the

FIG. 12.

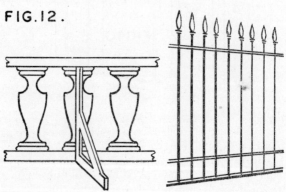

are made in profile. In other words, the shape seen by the audience is cut out in plywood, or in the case of a railing, it could be made out of 1 in. by 1 in. timber. The wood is then canvased. Figure 12 shows two types of balustrades.

COLUMNS

Columns, whether they have flat surfaces, or are rounded, fluted or tapering, are all made in the same way. They are built in sections to the height required. The whole is then covered with plywood to make up the surface of the column. If the column is fluted, the shape of the fluting is then built on to the plywood, with half-round moulding or 1 in. by 1 in. as may be required. After the building is complete, the whole is canvased. Figure 13 shows two types of columns in construction.

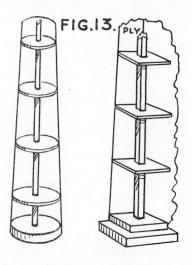

FIG. 13.

TREES

Built tree pieces, as opposed to trees painted on a backcloth, are made up in exactly the same way as columns, only they are obviously not of a uniform width from base to apex as a column is. Therefore, plywood is not normally used for the face. Instead, the inside sectional pieces are covered with chicken wire. This is then manipulated with the hands until the required shape is obtained, then the whole is covered with canvas. A good simulation of tree bark can be obtained by gluing strips of felt down the length of the tree, or papier mâché may be applied. But if a smooth tree is required, this is not done. The larger branches are built on to the main trunk in the same way, but the tops of trees are very seldom "practically" built owing to the intricacy of construction. Therefore, the tops are usually masked in with borders painted to look like tree leaves. Tree stumps and rocks are built in a similar manner, their rough shape being built out of timber to meet the needs and shape required, and then covered with chicken wire and canvas in the same manner as a tree. A rough section of a rock is shown in Figure 14.

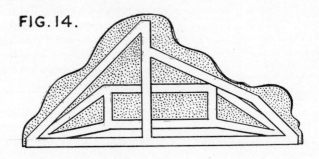

FIG. 14.

WOODEN PANELLING

Wooden panelling is normally painted on a flat, as actual panelling built on to the frame of a flat is too heavy. If necessary, of course, it may be built on, in which case the wooden frame of the flat is covered with three-ply wood instead of canvas. Then the moulding, in the various shapes and sizes of the panelling required, is screwed and glued onto the face of the flat. The whole of the face is then canvased and painted in the usual way.

BORDERS

Strictly speaking, there are two types of borders: a framed border, and a draped or cloth border. A framed border is really a flat hung from lines from the flies in the manner mentioned before, with one edge downwards. It is, however, considerably longer than a normal flat, perhaps upwards of forty feet. An ordinary cloth border is tied with laces on to a wooden batten, again hung from the flies. The best type of border is made of velvet, which looks very rich. A cloth border may also be made of canvas and painted to match the setting. A leaf border, painted with leaves, could mask in the tops of built trees or trees painted on a backcloth. Borders are usually in the region of 6 ft. or 9 ft. deep, depending on the depth required for masking.

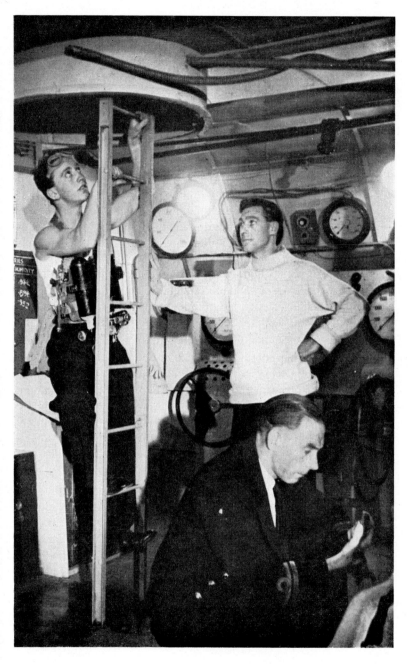

Realistic set—Interior, for Kenneth Woolard's *Morning Departure*, presented by
The Talisman Players, Kenilworth, Warwickshire.

Movable screens, rearranged for various scenes—in this case a street scene, from *The Face of Violence*, by J. Bronowski, at the Tavistock Repertory Theatre, London

WINDOWS

Stage windows are constructed in exactly the same way as real ones, except that the timber used seldom exceeds 3 in. by 1 in. Glass, of course, is not used. One or two thicknesses of gauze stretched over the outside of a window frame can be very effective, and windows can be made to look dirty by spraying the gauze with scenic paint. French windows, as well as sash windows, can be made to open in the same way as their "real life" counterparts.

FRENCH BRACES

A "French" brace is used when a normal type of brace is not available, and consists of a triangle of wood hinged to the back of a flat. When the flat is in position on stage, a stage weight is placed on the back of the brace to counter-balance the weight of the flat. The size of the brace to be used depends on the size of the flat it has to support. French braces are normally used to support ground rows. One is shown in Figure 8.

TYPES OF JOINTS

1. *Butt:* A butt joint is used in the building of scenery when the joint is reinforced by a triangular plywood plate which covers the joint and is glued in position and nailed with 1-in. nails (Figure 15).

FIG. 15.

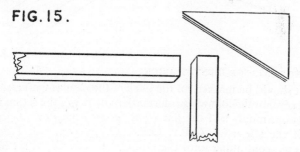

2. *Mitre:* A mitre joint is seldom used in building scenery. If used, it would have to be reinforced as for the butt joint. The ends of the timber to be joined are cut off at an angle of 45 degrees (as in the construction of a picture frame), glued together end to end, and plated as for the butt joint.

3. *Scarf:* A scarf joint is the joining together of two pieces of wood, end to end. The two ends of wood are cut away at a very fine angle, and then glued together as in Figure 16.

L

FIG. 16.

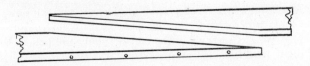

4. *Mortice and Tenon:* This is the type of joint one finds at the corner of flats when they have been made by a scenic craftsman. It is made by cutting a slot at the end of one of the pieces of wood and a tongue at the end of the other. These are then slotted together and fastened by inserting two wooden pegs through the joint, and then cutting them off flush.

5. *Halved:* A halved joint is self-explanatory in its name; the two ends of the timber are cut in half and lapped, then screwed and glued (Figure 17).

FIG. 17.

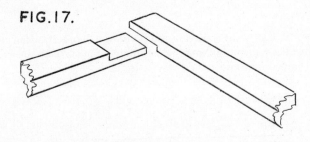

MARKING FLATS FOR IDENTIFICATION

A set should be marked on the back of the canvas with a stencil and should contain the following information: owner of the set, name of the production, number of the flat (numbering from downstage on both sides of the stage, i.e. O.P.1, O.P.2, O.P.3, etc., and P.S.1, P.S.2, P.S.3, etc., continuing until the numbers meet). If the set has a continuous back wall, this could be marked "back wall".

FIREPROOFING

A mixture of salts for fireproofing can be bought at most dispensing chemists. It is then dissolved in water to the strength prescribed and either sprayed or applied to the canvas part of the scenery with a brush. A recipe for home-made fireproofing mixture is given in the Appendix under "Useful Information".

MIXING PAINT AND GLUE

Size is bought in crystals, and melted over hot water to a medium consistency, and then used as required to add to paint. Scenic paint is mixed with size in order to make it adhere to the canvas. Scenic paint is obtainable from special colourmen who usually only stock this type of paint. It is usually in powder form, but is also obtainable as a pulp. The powder is mixed up with water until there are no lumps remaining, and the size in its liquid form is added in the proportion, usually, of one-eighth of a bucket of size to a bucket of paint. The thickness of the paint is something that can only be gauged by experience, but it is better to start off with a thicker mixture than a thinner one.

Glue used for scenery is the normal kind of Scotch glue, melted over hot water to the required thickness. A very good substitute is a mixture of strong size.

PIN-HINGING

A useful method of temporarily fixing two pieces of timber together is known as "pin-hinging". A back flap hinge has the pin that joins its two halves filed away, and a nail or piece of wire put in the pin's place. Figure 18 shows a section of a rostrum about to be joined together in this way. It is useful for quick scene changes.

FIG. 18.

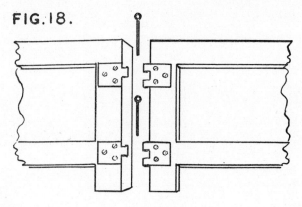

BASIC TOOLS

Essential tools for a scenic workshop are:

Saw
Hammer
Large and Small Screwdriver
Plane

Brace and various sizes of "bit"

3-ft. rule

Carpenter's pencil

$\frac{1}{2}$-in. blue tacks

1-in., $\frac{1}{2}$-in., $\frac{3}{4}$-in., $1\frac{1}{2}$-in. screws of the gauge one feels best able to operate, probably "tens"

2-in. back flap hinges

Hot plate, or some other means of heating paint, etc.

A power-driven saw may be a luxury, but is a wonderful investment, and cuts down working hours and effort considerably.

XII. PROPERTIES AND SOUND EFFECTS

IN big musicals in the professional theatre there is still a property man attached to the production, who has sole charge of the numerous props used during the performance. Sometimes on tour you come across a resident property man. But for the most part this interesting work has been taken over by members of the stage management staff. The tightening of the financial belt is the reason the property man has been dropped from the backstage personnel, and his absence is felt by all who saw and used the wonderful things he made and cared for, from "jewel"-encrusted crowns made from cardboard and coloured glass, to sumptuous-looking artificial meals.

Speaking of stage food reminds me of an incident in my production of *Come Back Little Sheba*. It was necessary that "Lola" should have bacon for "Doc's" breakfast, and that she put slice after slice into the frying pan as she excitedly told him a story. Real bacon was purchased, and each night one slice stuck to the other and could not be slapped into the pan in the careless, happy way which was essential. The problem was solved by my carpenter, an ex-property man of the old school, who came to the theatre one night with a pound of succulent bacon—not streaky bacon, but the best back—made from felt!

I believe that many amateur companies have reinstated the property man, which is a very good thing indeed. In his rightful position his work is of great importance. He comes under the direct authority of the stage director, and his manifold duties are discussed fully in the chapter dealing with Stage Management.

The following includes some methods for acquiring and/or making certain properties and sound and visual effects.

SCENE PROPS

Furniture may be hired from stores which specialize in theatrical stocks. These are usually located only in large cities and the cost of shipping furniture to small out-of-the-way places is high. A search round, and an appeal in towns and villages will often bring wonderful results from private parlours, attics and shops. Shops will often gladly lend pieces in return for a credit in the programme. As furniture has been further discussed in the chapter on Design, it is not necessary to go into it more fully here. Suffice it to say that an imaginative property staff can do wonders with re-upholstering, repainting and redecoration.

Pictures should have glass removed as this reflects the light. If they do not have to be changed during the play, or if the flat on which they are hung is replaced by another, pictures may be fixed, by wiring them through the canvas and fastening the wire to the wooden stile behind.

Mirrors must always be dulled with a solution of size, or soap, or whitening, rubbed on to prevent glaring reflections being thrown in to the audience. Care must be taken to prevent the surface from appearing streaky. Fake mirrors may be made by applying aluminium paint or tinfoil to a piece of plywood or cardboard in a frame.

Windows should be backed with fine gauze, tightly stretched and tacked to the back of the frame all around. This gives an illusion of glass. Of course if the window is to be broken during the play gauze cannot be used. The best effect for window breaking is a well-synchronized noise offstage to correspond to the action onstage. A sack containing pieces of broken glass when dropped on the floor sounds very realistic. If the producer is not satisfied with this effect, and real glass is in the window, it must be covered with very fine wire netting to prevent pieces flying out and injuring the actors. A plastic material, which looks like glass, but does not cut, is available, but extremely expensive. Real glass is *dangerous* at the best of times, and should not be used unless absolutely necessary.

Flowers. Real flowers may be used if available cheaply, and the run is short. They must be freshly watered each night by the props staff, and stored in a cool place until performance time. Artificial flowers are usually used, and may be made by members of the society who enjoy doing so. There is someone in every community who makes flowers for a hobby. If they are made, all the materials must be fireproofed before being used. Beautiful fireproofed artificial flowers are sold by stage property suppliers. They are expensive, but may be used for many years if carefully handled. All artificial flowers should be covered after each performance to prevent dust gathering on them. Onstage they should always be set in sand or earth in a vase. This makes them stand better, and by weighting the vase makes it less likely to fall over if brushed accidentally by an actor.

Fruit. Again if the run is short, or of course if it must be eaten on stage, real fruit is used. Wax fruit is frowned upon by fire authorities as being highly inflammable. Very colourful and realistic fruit may be made from papier mâché, the process for which is described on the next page.

Steps and Rostrums may be the responsibility of the property department, especially if they are small. This must be clarified with the stage manager. It is not likely that "props" will have to construct them, but they may have to set, change and store them.

Small trees, shrubbery and grass. Small real trees, set in tubs of earth, are effective. Shrubs may be made by sticking canvas unevenly on a wooden frame, so that it has a rough, bumpy appearance, then painting it green; or pieces of fireproofed green crepe paper may be stuck on. Artificial grass may be bought by the yard, or made by sticking fine strips of green wool, raffia or crepe paper on to brown canvas. When made with paper it will not last for a long run. Grass that is trodden upon on the stage floor or on ramps, should be well tacked down all around to prevent embarrassing and painful accidents.

Papier Mâché. Wonderfully real articles may be made with papier mâché, which has the advantage of being cheap, light in weight, and with a surface that takes brilliant colouring. Succulent joints of meat, ripe juicy bunches of fruit, masks, rough bark on trees, decoration on pillars and furniture etc., all may be successfully made in papier mâché.

The first step is to make a clay model of the article required. The model should be well greased over the whole surface, and on to this plaster of paris poured, which is easily lifted off when dry. The plaster should be about an inch thick. Papier mâché is applied to the plaster model by two methods, the first requiring less skill than the second.

1. Soak newspaper or other soft paper in water for several hours. Tear off small strips, dip them in flour paste (to which may be added a little warm glue for added strength), and stick them all over the greased plaster model, each piece slightly overlapping. Let this layer dry, then apply three or four more layers in a similar manner. It is a good idea to make the last layer of white paper, or those parts of a newspaper not covered with printing. For extra strength a covering of buckrum or coarse muslin may be pushed into the last layer of paper while it is still wet. When the paper is dry the object will lift off easily.

2. Boil the paper with water, stirring until it is soft and pulpy. Drain the pulp and mix with hot flour paste to which a little hot glue has been added. Stir the mixture until it is a thick sticky mass, then press it a quarter of an inch thick into the inside of the plaster mould, which has been well greased. Buckrum or muslin may again be pressed in. When the papier mâché dries it can be lifted out, and should be the exact shape of the mould. Pulp boiled in this way may be used to build out shapes on furniture, and will stick to the wood; or to spread on wire netting covering trees, to make bark; or may be applied directly to canvas-covered rocks etc., for jagged effects.

Vases may be made on a plaster model, or by covering a greased milk-bottle or jar with papier mâché. When dry the paper must be cut down the centre all around so that it comes away in two halves, which may then be easily glued together and painted. These vases are purely for decoration and will not hold water. For a practical vase, do not cut the paper away from the glass bottle, which will then hold water and have a decorated exterior.

For a shiny finish to any object, clear varnish should be applied over paint.

Ornaments. Unless ornaments are to be moved or lifted during the action of a play, they should be wired securely with fine wire on to shelves, bookcases, mantelpieces, etc. If the scene is to be changed there is no necessity to remove the ornaments from their positions during the change.

Ornaments which must be broken during action on stage may be made from plaster of paris, which is less expensive than buying a series of real ornaments, and is highly successful.

Clocks. Real clocks are usually used, but unless the action demands, should not be wound up, because moving hands, ticks, chimes, etc. are distracting to the audience. Alarm clocks must be carefully checked to make sure that the bell is not set to go off. Glass clock faces should also be dulled.

Books. Shelves completely full of real books are very heavy to move, and are not generally used. Cardboard fronts, painted to simulate book covers may be inserted on shelves and tacked down. Care should be taken to make these appear as realistic as possible unless the play is stylized. Sometimes it is possible to use a collection of real book covers from which the pages have been removed. These are glued together into a block of "books". Real books, if used, should have several strands of thin invisible wire strung in front of them to prevent their falling out during a change.

HAND PROPS

Some of these will be pre-set on stage and some brought on by actors. In the case of articles like walking sticks, umbrellas, cigarette cases, holders and cigarettes, spectacles, etc., which are part of the personal accoutrements of a character, the actor concerned should be responsible for looking after them. However, this must never be left to chance, and it is the props staff's duty to check with every actor before a performance, and before his entrance, to see that he has his personal props. In many cases actors prefer to leave these on the prop table where they may be picked up when needed.

Ashtrays and matches. Ashtrays should be placed on every suitable piece of furniture, mantelpieces, window seats, etc., so that actors may always have a place to deposit ash or stub out cigarettes. This is a safety precaution not to be ignored. Safety matches should be used, and several left sticking out of the box to prevent the actors from fumbling when taking a match. It is wise to scatter boxes of matches about the set as well.

Letters, documents and telegrams. If the play is a period piece, it is important to find out the style of these items in use at the time. Some actors like to have the actual wording written down for them on the paper, others prefer to use their memories. In any case the paper should not be left blank, for the discerning eye of the galleryite to behold. Envelopes should not be stuck down too well, because opening them might hold up the action. If a pile of letters must be in a particular order they should be numbered to avoid confusion. If a picture or other special document is to be pulled out, this should be marked on the outside so the actor knows at a glance which is the "right" envelope. Telegraph and cable forms may be obtained from any post office.

Newspapers. In a period play it is important to find or make books, periodicals and newspapers the same size and set-up as the originals. For a modern newspaper from which an actor must read, a copy should be used which does not have too definite spectacular headlines, as the audience in the first few rows, and those with opera glasses, will immediately recognize them and reality will be spoiled. When special headlines are required they may be painted on soft cheap paper and pasted over the real ones.

Fire-arms. Most fire-arms may only be used with a police certificate, and this should be thoroughly investigated (see the Appendix, under Useful Information). Swords, daggers, etc. should be well blunted to prevent accidents.

Torches. Flaming torches may not be carried on stage, but a realistic effect is obtained by making hollow cylinders of tin or heavy cardboard tapering to a point, and inserting a small battery and red bulb at the open end, covered with red gelatine in a conical shape like a flame. A wire may be run down the inside, attached to a push button at the base of the torch. When the actor pushes the button the torch lights up.

Candles. Naked candles are dangerous, and if they are not to be blown out, a cardboard tube with a small light bulb on the end, controlled by either a battery or electricity, may be used. If a naked candle must be used, it should be firmly set in a fireproof holder, and kept well away from costumes and scenery.

Meals, if eaten, must be freshly prepared backstage by the property staff. There is a hotplate available in most theatres and halls, which will be invaluable for the props department. Vacuum flasks are useful for keeping liquids hot. Tea and coffee, either freshly made or from a vacuum flask, should be served with sweet milk. I have had cold tea with curdled milk on stage, and can assure anyone it is an experience to make one feel murderous. Alcoholic and other cold drinks are usually made with water and food colouring or burnt sugar, the latter available at most chemists' shops. It is necessary to experiment with colouring until the correct shade is obtained. There is a kind of cider sold in champagne-style bottles, which looks like the real thing, even to forcing the cork to pop.

Food provided should be of a soft variety, easily swallowed by the actors. Chocolate is very bad, often causing a tickle in the throat, and may be substituted by raisins. Pieces of apple or banana may be substituted for meat. Scrambled eggs are easy to eat. Sandwiches should have the crusts cut off, unless there is a specific reason in the plot for not doing so, and they should always be filled with soft moist fillings.

Cleanliness is of utmost importance in preparing and serving stage food. All dishes should be washed in hot soapy water, and dried with clean cloths. I once knew an actor who became desperately ill through drinking from a dirty glass on stage. No chances should be taken. Dishes, glasses, etc., left out on the prop table overnight should always be covered.

Animals. Live animals are most unpredictable, and should be kept under strict control. In large centres it is possible to get animals specially trained for stage work, but it will be unlikely that many amateur groups can easily obtain these. Dogs should be kept on a lead and cats firmly held by someone with whom they are familiar, even if it means the animal living with the actor for some time before the performance. The strong stage lights and audience reaction are apt to make animals panic. So actors must keep a strong grip on them, and be ready to soothe them. They should be taken right away from the stage when not being used so that they do not dash on in the wrong place. It is a wise precaution to see that any pets the actors may have brought along (and this should be discouraged even though professional actresses are prone to bringing poodles into their dressing rooms!) are firmly tied up, and that the stage door is guarded from strays wandering in. One of the funniest episodes I have been told about concerned a little mongrel puppy, which had eluded the stage hands and wandered on stage during the tea scene between "Gwendoline" and "Cecily" in a country production of *The Importance of Being Earnest.* Needless to say, his performance and natural curiosity roused more audience response than the witticisms of those two elegant young ladies. He finally galloped off when "Gwendoline" threw a piece of cake into the wings, where he was quickly caught and carried outside squealing. Amusing as such isolated incidents may be, they cannot become a regular feature of play production.

Very "realistic" dead animals, fowl and fish may be made by the props department, by stuffing and painting cloth, and when necessary firmly gluing on and colouring chicken feathers gathered from a farm. Stuffed real birds may be hired, but must be carefully handled.

When actors are representing animals the costumes may be hired, or made by the costume department. However, props may be called upon to make papier mâché masks for the heads, and these can be extremely effective.

SOUND AND VISUAL EFFECTS

These must be devised, set up and operated by the property staff, sometimes with help from the electrics department. Most sound effects may be obtained on records, and are successful if there is not too much hum on the gramophone or panatrope. If the machine does not have a mechanical device for placing the sound, each record should be carefully marked with chalk on the groove where the needle is to be placed. A cue sheet is required for the panatrope operator.

Bells. These are the most frequently used sound effects, i.e. doorbells, telephone bells, gongs, church bells, etc. A set of electric or battery-operated bells fastened to a piece of board is very useful. They may then be operated by a single person, who is either following the script or being cued by the prompter. It is best for the bell operator to be in a position to see the action, for synchronization. If this is not possible he must carefully learn the exact line cues. It is best, if possible, to fix practical bells for those which have to be pressed on stage.

An old-fashioned door or servant's bell may be found by rummaging round second-hand shops, and can be rung by hand at the correct moment. There is nothing that quite duplicates this sound.

Real gongs can usually be found. Iron pipes hanging free, when struck by a padded stick give bell-like sounds, and are particularly effective for the sound of clocks striking. The sound varies with the length and width of the pipe and the type of stick used to strike it. Clock chimes may also be imitated by striking a musician's triangle. Records can be bought for nearly all bell sounds.

Thunder is transmitted from a thundersheet, which is a rectangular sheet of thin metal or plywood hung free in the wings at a height where the bottom may be grasped by the operator. By shaking this sheet, rolls of thunder may be produced. However, good thunder requires practice and getting used to the particular thundersheet, so it should be well rehearsed. Thunder will rumble off into the distance if drums are faded off after the thundersheet. Thunder drums may be made by stretching wet cowhide over the open end of a square wooden box or frame. The hide must be tightly tacked down all around, and heated slightly, say by a light bulb from underneath, just before being used.

It may be beaten with two padded sticks or the bare hands, and also requires practice.

Wind. The wind machine is perhaps the best known of all effects machines. It is a wooden-slatted hollow cylinder set in a framework, with an axle running through the centre, terminating in a handle which rotates the cylinder. A piece of canvas or heavy silk the same width as the cylinder is tacked on to a cross-bar beside the cylinder and parallel to the top of it. This covering is then thrown over the cylinder, and when the handle is turned the rubbing of the cloth on wood creates a howl and shriek like the wind. The faster the cylinder is turned the more fierce the storm.

Electric fans played from the wings are usually used for the visual effect of wind on stage. It should be very controlled, merely causing curtains to billow slightly. For wild tempests it is best for the actors to mime the gusts.

Rain. A rain machine may be constructed in a similar manner to a wind machine. On to the inside of a hollow cylinder or drum (complete with centre axle and handle), strips of wood 1 in. by 1 in. should be nailed at 6-inch intervals. The ends should be enclosed, leaving a small hinged door at one end. The cylinder is then mounted on a frame to turn freely, and a handful of dried peas inserted through the door. As the drum revolves the wooden strips lift the peas and drop them when they reach the top. The effect sounds like rain. Larger beans or shot may be used for the sound of hail. The speed of turning determines the strength of the rain, etc.

When actors enter from a rainy exterior their clothes must show some evidence of this. One of the props staff should stand by with a pail of water to sprinkle shoulders, hats, etc., unless actors prefer to do this themselves. If so, props should check to make sure it is done. A little varnish may be applied to umbrellas, coats, etc., for a permanent wet effect, if these articles are of no further value.

Rain on stage is difficult to show successfully. Rice grains falling from holes in a trough hung above the stage and gently rocked by a rope, may be used, but over a long period of action this creates a mess and a slippery hazard on the floor. Miming by the cast is more successful.

Rain may be projected on a backcloth by an effects machine by the electrics staff. If it is to be seen through a window, a pipe perforated at intervals may be fixed above the window, and water fed into it from a hose. A trough must be placed on the floor to catch the water.

Snow. A snow scene can be most effective if well lit, with flakes gently falling. This is done by the rocking of a suspended trough, called a "cradle", hung in the flies. In this case the cradle is filled with small pieces of white paper. To prevent odd flakes falling in the wrong scene, it is wise to keep a canvas cover over the cradle until it is required. Snow may also be effectively projected on to a backcloth.

Lightning is best created by electricity, as described in the chapter on Lighting in this book. Flash powders are dangerous and should not be used unless in the hands of an expert.

Stars. Very delightful stars are made by tying sequins at intervals along lengths of thread. The threads are then tied at intervals along a batten in front of the skycloth, and when light is played on them they twinkle as realistically as real stars. Each thread should have a little canvas bag into which it is rolled (round a piece of cardboard), and stored when not in use, to prevent tangling. Stars may also be electrically projected.

Shots offstage may be effected by the actual firing of blank cartridges, with permission from the authorities; or may be heard from records. If neither are available, two narrow planks placed on the floor and weighted down at one end, may be lifted and dropped, either singly, or in rapid succession for machine-gun fire. This method is rather primitive and requires luck as well as practice.

Explosions. Very loud explosions may be created by firing blank cartridges into an empty metal dustbin, or by placing wired maroons in the bin and setting them off electrically. In both cases the cast must be warned to stand very clear, and barriers erected if necessary. Maroons should not be used by inexperienced people, as they can be very dangerous.

Crashes. A crashbox filled with broken glass or bits of iron and other metal may be used by pouring the rubble from one box to another.

Avalanches and similar noises can be conveyed by rolling large stones, pieces of concrete etc., down a long steep wooden trough, if space is available for this.

Door Sounds. For the opening and closing of doors offstage, a miniature door in a frame can be easily erected. This is usually called a "doorslam". If it is fitted with a lock and key, these noises may also be effected offstage. Experiments may be tried to give the effect of metal or sliding doors, such as those in lifts, but usually records are best for these.

Horses' hooves may be imitated by beating two half coconut shells rhythmically on a hard surface.

Cars, carriages, trains and airplanes must nearly always be heard through records, although hand horns and whistles may be easily operated and add to the general effect. An airplane sound may be tried by fixing leather thongs to an electric motor which revolves like an electric fan.

A drum or piece of wood is placed so that the thongs hit it as they turn.

Rumbling traffic. A wagon fitted with uneven or octagonal wooden wheels, when filled with heavy pieces of rock and iron and drawn across the stage behind the scenery, sounds like traffic passing. If there is not much room, records are better.

Animal noises, if not on disc, can very often be successfully imitated by humans, as can bird calls. There are whistles available for bird song, but they are not very effective.

Smoke may be created with specially prepared powder available from theatrical suppliers. It is best to use this rather than home-made kinds, which will usually choke both cast and audience.

Coloured fire may be bought in tins and set alight for weird effects, but it must be very carefully handled, and always stored in closed tins, as it is highly combustible.

Pepper's Ghost is an effect used to show ghosts on stage, and consists of placing a sheet of plate glass, at a 45 degree angle to the audience, in front of the space where the ghost is to appear. The person representing the ghost stands or sits in the wings and his hollow reflection is thrown out to the audience. The edge of the glass must be masked by a door, archway, drapes etc., and the actor playing the ghost strongly lit in a dark background. One amateur group reports using this effect successfully for "Banquo's Ghost" in *Macbeth*, when the glass was supported by the canopy of a chair, and the actor, concealed by hanging draperies, lay on his back under the chair.

Trick doors, cupboards and ornaments. Doors and cupboards may appear to open and close mysteriously of their own accord either by being pushed with a stick from behind, or pulled by thin invisible wires. Wired ornaments, pictures, etc., may be manipulated by passing the wire through tiny holes in the canvas flats.

Moving boats. Although these will probably be constructed by the stage carpenter, it may fall upon the props staff to maintain and operate them. They are wooden platforms on wheels, with the front built up to look like a boat, and are pulled across the stage, with the ropes and mechanics well hidden by scenery. In the play *Colombe* the secrets of moving boats were given away during the last act, when the scene was set as though the audience was sitting backstage behind the scenery, facing the footlights. Two actors, representing stage hands, pulled a jerky boat across in full view of the audience. A very amusing scene, and one which always comes to mind now when I see Gilbert and Sullivan's 'Gondoliers' glide on stage.

Practical taps. A bucket or tank of water should be placed up high behind the flat in which the taps are situated, and a rubber hose led from the tank to the back pipe of the taps. These protrude through the flat or sink unit. A pail should be placed under the sink to catch water as it runs away.

CONCLUSION

There are many more property effects, construction ideas, etc., which may be tried. The personal inventiveness of the property master and his staff is invaluable to a society. Good property touches can often lift a play from the commonplace to the unusual, and the props department deserves a lot more gratitude and applause for hard work than it usually gets. Many amateurs consider "doing props" a hard and thankless task. That may be, but if entered into with a spirit of experiment and adventure, it can prove to be as satisfying and exciting as any theatrical department.

XIII. LIGHTING THE STAGE
by Peter Mullings

NORMALLY in an article like this the reader can turn to the end and consult the Glossary. I intend, however, that the Glossary for this chapter shall be more of a preface, so that the attention will not be distracted by having to turn to the end to find the meaning of unknown terms and theatrical expressions. So, with apologies to those who are already familiar with these terms, here is a short list of:

ELECTRICAL TERMS AND THEATRICAL LIGHTING EXPRESSIONS

A.C. Abb. for Alternating Current. The general form of electricity supplied in Britain. Normally with a cycle of 50 frequencies per second.

Acting Area. Type of lighting lantern. Abbreviations: A.A. and Ack-Ack.

Amp. Abb. for Ampere. The standard measurement of electrical current.

Arc-lamp. D.C. (q.v.) lantern where the light source is obtained from the burning of carbon electrodes. Usually used in F.O.H. positions. The term "Lime" is generally extended to cover arcs. (Lime is a word that has stayed in use in the theatre since the days of gas lighting, when a block of lime was heated, in a lantern, by a flame of gas mixed with oxygen.)

Barn door. Type of shutter used in spots to mask the shape of the beam. Also used on floods to narrow down the beam.

Batten. Strip length of compartment lights.

Black light. Slang term for Ultra-Violet (q.v.) lighting.

Black out. Switching off a series of lights on cue. When involving all stage lighting is referred to as Dead Black Out. Abbs.: B.O. and D.B.O.

Board. Abb. for Switchboard.

Boom. Abb. for Boomerang. Length of barrel piping (usually 2-inch diameter) rising vertically from the stage, to which spots (or floods) are clamped.

Check. Position to which lights are dimmed on circuits, e.g. Half check, Quarter check. (More often spoken of as Half-in and Threequarters-in respectively.)

Clamp. Metal clamps for fixing lighting apparatus to barrels and booms. Obtainable in various sizes and in adjustable types.

Colour master. Switch on board for controlling all lights belonging to the same colour grouping. (Boards are usually split into three colour groupings.) Can also refer to the Colour Master Wheel.

Colour medium. Material used in lanterns for colouring the light thrown by them. Usually of gelatine or a cellulose acetate base. (Referred to by name of colour or by their reference number.)

Connecter. Means of joining one electrical cable to another.

Cyclorama. Sky backing to the stage; may be of material or plaster. Abb.: Cyc.

D.C. Abb. for Direct Current. With this form of electricity one side of the circuit is always positive and the other negative.

Deck. Slang term for stage level.

Dimmer. Resistance used for controlling the amount of light emitted by lighting equipment.

Dip trap. Small metal trap in the stage floor containing electric plugs, in which lighting equipment may be plugged.

Fade out. To dim lights down to out.

Floats. Slang name for footlights; has remained in use in the theatre since the day when they were candles "floating" on water (for safety precautions).

Footlights. Batten type lengths of lighting compartments used at stage level outside the proscenium arch. Abb.: Foots. (see also Floats).

Kilowatt. Unit of electrical consumption, equal to 1,000 watts. Lanterns above the value of 1,000 watts are referred to by their kilowatt values, e.g. 2 K, 5 K.

Length. Number of electric lamps set on a casing. Sometimes called "strips".

Limes. See Arc.

Pageant. Type of lantern with no lens. See text.

Pre-focus. Type of lamp cap allowing the lamp to be inserted in the special pre-focus holder in such a position that the filament of the lamp is in the correct focal point in the optical system of the lantern without adjustment.

Spotlight. Type of lantern for throwing a controllable beam of light, Abb.: Spot.

Ultra-Violet. Light in the invisible end of the spectrum. Used for special effects to activate various substances to fluorescence.

Volts. The pressure at which electrical current is available.

Watts. Units of electrical energy, arrived at by multiplying Amps by Watts. (1,000 watts burning for one hour are said to consume one "unit" of electricity. This is the measurement by which electricity is charged for in this country.)

M

Way. A switchboard is said to be of a certain number of "ways", meaning the number of circuits available on it for various equipment.

ELECTRIC LAMPS

The spotlight lamps come in three different classes, A.1; B.1; and T. A.1 is shown below on the left, B.1 on the right.

The class A.1 lamp has the greater intensity owing to the more compact filament. Lamps of this class should not be burnt in a position greater than $22\frac{1}{2}$ degrees out of the vertical. They have a short "life", the average being 50 hours. They do not "burn out" completely at the end of this time, but the amount of light that is emitted is greatly reduced. In the class B.1 lamp, which has a life of about 800 hours, the filament is not as compact as in the class A.1. A spherical glass bulb permits the lamp to be tilted to a greater degree (Figure 1 explains this more clearly).

The class T lamp, life 200 hours, has the benefit of a class A.1 lamp filament housed within the class B.1 bulb, which gives a most useful compromise in concentration, life and tilt.

The class A.1 and B.1 lamps are available with a pre-focus cap which permits the lamp to be fitted into the holder in one position only, and that is such that the filament is automatically brought into the best optical position in the lantern. The other form of cap for these lamps is the Goliath Edison Screw (G.E.S.). The 250w class B.1 lamp for Baby Spots is not obtainable with the G.E.S. cap, but with the Edison Screw (E.S.) and pre-focus for the Baby Mirror Spot.

For Floodlights the General Service Lamps are used, with the G.E.S. cap. Battens and Footlights use the General Service Lamps with the E.S. cap.

LIGHTING EQUIPMENT

Equipment used in lighting the stage can be broadly classified under the following terms: Spotlights, Floodlights and Compartment Batten Lights. Though under each general term there are many variations, it will be unnecessary to deal with them all for the purposes of this chapter. As long as the reader grasps the general function of each group of equipment he will be able to choose the best lantern that is available for his purpose.

There are several manufacturers marketing lighting equipment in Britain, but I intend to deal with the equipment made by the Strand Electric and Engineering Company Limited, a name justly respected in the realm of stage lighting.

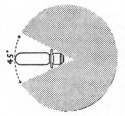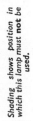

45° Shading shows position in which this lamp must not be used. 90°

FIGURE I.

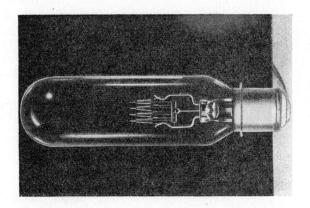

1. SPOTLIGHTS

The spot is the type of equipment that has the capability of focusing the light from a lamp into a beam of variable diversity (that is the conical angle). The maximum angle is usually in the neighbourhood of 30 to 45 degrees; the minimum angle about 10 degrees.

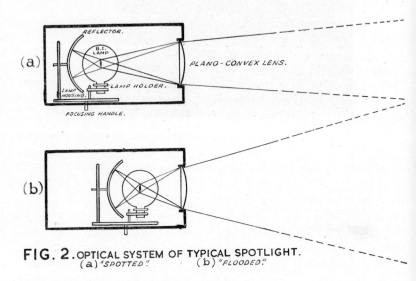

FIG. 2. OPTICAL SYSTEM OF TYPICAL SPOTLIGHT.
(a) "SPOTTED."   (b) "FLOODED."

The optical system of the spotlight is very simple. Behind the lens is a reflector, and in front a plano-convex lens. The diversity of the beam angle is obtained by moving the lamp nearer to the lens for beam spreading (normally called "flooding"); or away from the lens for beam tightening (normally called "spotting"). In each case the reflector moves with the lamp, being an integral part of the lamp housing. This is necessary because the reflector is so placed that the rays of light from the filament are reflected back through the lens, thus increasing efficiency (see Figure 2).

A. *Small Spotlights*. These may be used where space is limited, e.g. when a spot has to be placed in the footlights to accentuate a dramatic effect.

i. *Float Spotlight*

This spotlight takes a 100w or 250w Class B.1 lamp (E.S.); effective throw up to 15 feet. Maximum measurements: height 7 inches, width 9¼ inches, depth 6½ inches. This is a very useful lantern for lighting

FIGURE 3.

from the footlight position, hence its name; also useful in a fireplace opening for throwing "firelight".

ii. *Baby Mirror Spotlight*

This lantern is belittled by its name, as it is a veritable "giant" in all but its size. It burns a 250w or 500w pre-focus Class B.1 or T lamp and can give three different maximum beam angles. These angles are obtained by varying the lens combinations, and are 11, 22 and 37 degrees. In the case of the 11 degree angle a special lens tube with a slightly larger lens is substituted. The effective throw of this spot is governed by the beam angle owing to the dispersal of light. Throws are: 11 degrees—up to 65 feet; 22 degrees—up to 45 feet; 37 degrees—up to 30 feet. These are the distances given by the manufacturers, but from my experience I think it is quite fair to say that a third can be added to the dis-

FIGURE 4.

tance in each case and there will still be a good intensity spot at the end of the throw.

This spot has the advantage of an optical system such that the shape of the light beam is controllable by an adjustable shutter inside the lantern, giving a hard edged square or rectangular beam. This can be softened by throwing the beam out of focus. A circular spot can be obtained by using diaphragm masks (four different sizes are supplied with the spot), or by using the variable iris diaphragm.

The tremendous power of illumination this lantern is capable of giving comes from the revolutionary optical system. The lamp is surrounded, as near as possible, by a spherical reflector, with the result that most of the light emitted from the filament is collected and put to good use. This light is lost in ordinary spotlights. The Baby Mirror Spot is extremely good as a front of house spot in the little theatre, and apart from its power it is an extremely handsome piece of equipment. The maximum sizes are: height 1 foot, width 11 inches, depth 1 foot 1 inch.

B. *Large Spotlights.* I have decided to place the 500w spot in this class, although it can hardly be considered as a "large" spot, except on the "small" stage.

i. *Baby Spotlight*

This burns a 500w class B.1 lamp (G.E.S.) and is of use up to a 35-foot throw. It is very useful on the spot bar in the "small" theatre, and in the "larger" theatre can be used in the special "pin-pointing" that invariably crops up.

ii. 1,000w *Stage Spotlight*

This is the general purpose spot for lighting acting areas. It has a throw of up to 45 feet and uses the class B.1 lamp. The throw can be increased by using the class A.1 lamp. This lantern is the backbone of "straight" theatre lighting in the large and medium-sized theatres.

iii. *Pre-focus Mirror Spotlight*

This burns a 1,000w class A.1 or T lamp and has an effective throw of 70 feet. Like the Baby Mirror Spot the shape of the beam can be

FIGURE 5.

altered with the adjustable shutter, and so can be used to pick out irregularly shaped objects or to give a hard cut-off, clear of backcloth upstage and orchestra pit downstage. The lantern is therefore particularly useful for front of house work, but can be used anywhere on the stage. The lamp is carried in a large pre-focus holder which is tilted back at an angle of $7\frac{1}{2}$ degrees. This helps to compensate for the forward tilt of the lantern when using class A.1 lamps, the maximum tilt being increased to 30 degrees. With the class T lamp the tilt can be as much as 90 degrees.

iv. *Long Range Spotlight*

A "big brother" to the Baby Mirror Spot, this light takes a 1,000w class A.1 lamp with the large pre-focus cap. The effective throw is 100 feet. It is very useful as a following spot, comparable to but more convenient than a small arc.

2. FLOODLIGHTS

After spotlights the next most important section of theatre lighting equipment consists of floodlights. These, as their name suggests, have the power to cover a large area with light and so are used for lighting window backings, cycloramas, door backings, general stage lighting (especially in ballet, revue and variety), and all cases where a large area needs even illumination.

General Floodlight

There are several sizes of floodlights available, ranging from the Small Flood, capable of taking a 60w, 100w or 150w E.S. lamp. This can be obtained with two different reflectors, which is the case with most floods, and is a fact worth remembering. It is an advantage to keep a spare reflector of the different angle handy, so that the flood can be adapted in a few moments to the best possible coverage for the job in hand. Next to the Small Flood comes the floodlight for the 500w

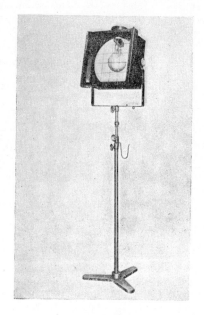

FIGURE 6.

lamp, and after that the 1,000w sizes. It is not necessary to describe these lanterns in detail as the general design is the same for all sizes.

Acting Area Floodlight

This takes a 1,000w class B.1 lamp (G.E.S.), with its base towards the front of the lantern, situated in a parabolic reflector. The small movement possible to the lamp in its holder will enable the beam to vary between 25 and 50 degrees. The general use of this lantern is that of a vertical throw down as it is mainly designed for lighting the "acting area" of the stage. I have used this lantern purely as a spot, and

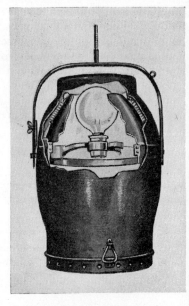

FIGURE 7.

FIGURE 8.

am inclined to think of it in this category rather than as a flood. As there is no lens to reduce the amount of light it is a very powerful spot and can be used on areas such as settees, tables and as sunlight falling down through windows. One of the great advantages of the A.A. is that it can be used to light areas close to the cyclorama or to a skycloth because there is no appreciable spill of light from it.

3. PAGEANTS

The Pageant lantern should really come under the heading of spots, although it has no lens. For this reason I have given it a section of its own.

Pageant

The pageant burns a 1,000w class A.1 or B.1 lamp. A narrow angle beam, between 11 and 17 degrees, is obtained by moving the lamp to or away from the 10-inch parabolic reflector. The beam is soft edged and is very intense, especially useful for sunlight through windows or from the wings in an exterior setting. It is also useful as a front of house spot as its throw is up to 100 feet. The model illustrated is a new one fitted with a masking disc directly in front of the filament to cut off any stray light. In an older model, still very much in use, circular "spill rings" are fitted for the same purpose.

4. BATTENS

Battens are lamps 60w, 100w or 150w strong, spaced at 9-inch intervals in separate "compartments", so that the "length" can be split up into different circuits (usually three or four), and a separate colour medium used in front of each circuit.

FIGURE 9.

The battens are usually a little longer than the proscenium opening, situated behind the borders, and are used to give a general overall illumination. Their use in a straight play is very limited as they tend to destroy any effective light pattern that may have been built up from the spot bar. They are the answer to lighting the cyclorama in the small to largish theatre. In the large theatre, and I am thinking of Covent Garden, they have to use a batten made up of 1,000w floods, with a total of 200 of these for cyclorama lighting alone. Battens are invaluable in lighting opera, ballet and variety.

5. FOOTLIGHTS

Footlights are made up the same as battens, although they are made for standing instead of hanging, and with a slightly different angle of lamp and reflector. In the theatres of old the footlights were always a permanent fixture, but nowadays they are falling more and more from grace because the light thrown from them always has the disadvantage of throwing shadows of the actors up and on to the scenery. The general trend now is to light from the front of house. This is a principle in which I strongly believe, although there are certain occasions when the only way of getting an effect is by using the footlights.

These are also more or less indispensable in the realms of opera, ballet, revue and variety.

It is possible to get footlights which will turn over and be housed under the stage when not actually needed in a production.

6. DIMMERS

Having dealt with the main types of lighting equipment I must now explain the various methods of controlling them.

Electronic and console boards are beyond the scope of most societies and small theatres, although they are the ideal means of control because the board can be remote from the actual dimmers, thus giving the operator the possibility of a full view of the stage from the front of house.

FIGURE 10.

There are two other main types of dimmers. First, and most widely used, is the Wire Wound Resistance Type. This consists of a wire resistance wound in such a manner that contact may be made with it in various positions, so that the amount of current flowing to the lantern can be varied. These dimmers can take many forms. They may be of a Slider type, as here illustrated, firstly with protective cover, and secondly without the cover.

In this type the wire is wound round two slate formers; and the contact made by copper brushes in a carriage which slides up and down a central pillar between the formers. These dimmers are obtainable in sizes ranging from 60w to 3,000w. Over 3,000w their bulk would become a hindrance. It is possible to get such dimmers wound so that they are capable of handling a load of one-third over or under the rated value, e.g. a dimmer rated at 1,500w will satisfactorily handle loads between 1,000w and 2,000w.

Then there are wire resistance dimmers which work by means of a radial arm which makes contact with brass studs connected to various positions on the resistance wire. I think it unnecessary here to discuss this type further, but the reader who wishes to learn more about it and other more complex dimmers may refer to the books in the bibliography at the end of this book.

The second type of dimmer I wish to mention is the Variable Transformer Dimmer, in which the current comes from the second coil of a variable transformer. The advantage of this dimmer is that no matter what the load of the lantern, the dimmer will operate in the same ratio of light emitted to the dimmer position. At the quarter position, for example, the lamp will be at quarter the maximum intensity whether it is a 60w or a 1,000w lamp. It is possible to get these dimmers capable of handling very heavy loads. One handling 54K was installed in 1933 in an Opera House in the South of England. The main beauty of this dimmer is that it can be installed as a "master dimmer" to the whole switchboard. A very large board could have, say, one dimmer for each colour group. Then no matter what the amount of equipment being used, the board could be made to do a general fade, or with selective switching, a fade on certain equipment only, with a perfectly smooth action.

7. SWITCHBOARDS

Of the actual design of switchboards it is impossible to give much idea in the space available. I have decided to describe only one type, which is the simplest. This is the Slider Board for the small theatre.

When using the word "small" I have in mind the stage which is not larger than 18 to 20 feet deep, with a proscenium opening of 20 to 28 feet.

For the purposes of such a stage a very useful switchboard can be made using Slider Dimmers. The following description is of a board I have designed for amateur companies or small repertory theatres, using 12 slider dimmers. This will handle all but very ambitious lighting schemes, and will make a good attempt at these.

To each dimmer I have given two plug sockets, two sets of fuses, and two three-position switches. By these switches the plugs can be made to take the current through the dimmer straight from the mains, or to

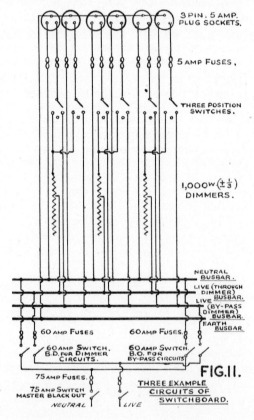

3 PIN . 5 AMP.
PLUG SOCKETS.

5 AMP FUSES .

THREE POSITION
SWITCHES.

1,000W ($\pm\frac{1}{3}$)
DIMMERS .

NEUTRAL
BUSBAR .
LIVE (THROUGH
DIMMER)
BUSBAR.
LIVE
(BY-PASS
DIMMER)
BUSBAR.
EARTH
BUSBAR.
60 AMP FUSES   60 AMP FUSES.
60 AMP SWITCH.   60 AMP SWITCH.
B.D. FOR DIMMER   B.O. FOR
CIRCUITS .   BY-PASS CIRCUITS

75 AMP FUSES .   FIG. II.
75 AMP SWITCH   THREE EXAMPLE
MASTER BLACK OUT   CIRCUITS OF
NEUTRAL   LIVE   SWITCHBOARD.

receive no current at all. This allows for two pieces of equipment to share the same dimmer and to be controlled independently. One lantern can be "full" or "out", whilst the other is at "check". Or both can be at the same "check". As the equipment is not permanently allocated to a given dimmer it is possible to arrange the "plugging up" of equipment so that lanterns requiring the same degree of "check" can share the same dimmer.

On each dimmer circuit it is possible to dim one lantern to "out" whilst the lantern that shares the dimmer is at "full" (in the by-pass position). When the first lantern is "out" it can be switched "off" and the dimmer returned to the "full up" position and the second lantern switched through to it. This second lantern can then be "checked" to any desired position.

Figure 11 shows three example circuits of this switchboard.

By this means it is possible to control 24 lanterns of 500w rating. In practice it will probably be found that some equipment rated at 1,000w will be needed for certain effects. When this is so it will have to be allocated to a dimmer of its own. (Unless it is "full up" or "out" only, when it can be controlled on the "by-pass" switch, and the "through dimmer circuit" used for another piece of equipment.)

This dimmer does not contain facilities for dimming the house lights, as they are usually a greater load than 1,000w; and a larger dimmer on the board itself would be awkward in the handling of the slider dimmers, which is always a tricky operation. A separate dimmer for the house light load can be mounted on the wall beside the board.

This switchboard requires a supply of 60 amps, though 75 amps would be better, in case any of the circuits have a load greater than 1,000 watts. (It is a good rough guide to say that 1,000w is equal to 5 amps at 230 volts.)

If instead of one "Master" switch, three are used (one as a "Grand Master", one for the "by-pass" section and the other for the "through-dimmer" section), it will be possible to black out part of the stage while leaving certain equipment still lit. For instance, all the "artificial" lighting in a room could be out and the "fire" and exterior lighting still up.

The foregoing sketch is a suggested layout for this board, but the mechanical design can be varied to suit the needs of the particular stage in question.

SCHEDULE OF EQUIPMENT

For a stage 20 feet wide and 18 feet deep, with a board as I have described, the following list of equipment will meet the needs of most productions:

Spotlights: Four Baby Mirror Spots, F.O.H. (two each side). Six 500w Spots forming a No. 1 "spot bar".
Floodlights: Two 500w Floods (Portable).
Footlights: None.
Battens: 18 ft. length for cyclorama top lighting (three circuits). 18 ft. length for cyclorama ground row lighting (three circuits).
Pageants: One Portable.

If all these were lit at one time thirteen dimmers would be required, but it is doubtful that this would occur, and should be planned against.

COLOURING THE LIGHT

When lighting the stage, colour is of the utmost importance. Lighting a show is not just a matter of putting light where it will illuminate the actors and scenery.

We all know that in everyday life daylight is "colourless". This is not strictly true, but may be accepted for our purposes. By the process of absorption reflected light takes a definite hue from the reflecting surface. Although this does apply to stage lighting as well as normal light, there is not enough colour to make the stage appear as "compelling" as it must be. The theatre is "larger than life", hence its great and lasting attraction. Lighting must comply with the "larger" quality required.

The Lighting Designer has not only "rose-coloured spectacles", but a range of about fifty colours to choose from when planning the lighting. It is in his power to turn a faded dress into a superb model; a modest old piece of furniture into an "antique" everyone would like to own. But, if he can do all this, he can also (more easily) ruin the show. The "model" can become "rags", and the genuine Chippendale can look like a glorified soap box. The man or woman who holds the "colour chart" must use great care in choosing hues and tints, considering not only the scenery but the clothes worn by the artists, the upholstery, the curtains, and to a lesser extent the make-up. (Artists can usually be prevailed upon to adapt their make-up to the lighting.)

Earlier in this chapter I stated that the two forms of colour mediums available were gelatine and a cellulose acetate base. There are two or three firms from which colour mediums may be obtained, but again I shall devote my remarks to the Strand Electric mediums. The reference numbers are used by all the firms in this country and are constant, within a shade or two.

COLOUR MEDIUMS

"Strand" mediums are available in two grades, "Gelatine" and "Cinemoid". ("Cinemoid" is the Strand Electric trade name for the cellulose acetate medium.) They are obtainable in the following colours:

1. Yellow	5. Orange	8. Deep Salmon
2. Light Amber	5A. Deep Orange	9. Light Salmon
3. Straw	6. Red (Primary)	10. Middle Rose
4. Medium Amber	7. Light Rose	11. Dark Pink

12. Deep Rose
13. Magenta
14. Ruby
15. Peacock Blue
16. Blue-green
17. Steel Blue
21. Pea Green
22. Moss Green
23. Light Green
24. Dark Green
25. Purple
26. Mauve

29. Heavy Frost
30. Clear
31. Light Frost
32. Medium Blue
33. Deep Amber
34. Golden Amber
35. Deep Golden Amber
36. Pale Lavender
38. Pale Green
41. Bright Blue
42. Pale Violet
43. Pale Navy Blue

48. Bright Rose
49. Canary
50. Pale Yellow
51. Gold Tint
52. Pale Gold
53. Pale Salmon
54. Pale Rose
*55. Chocolate Tint
*56. Pale Chocolate
*60. Pale Grey

* Available in Gelatine only.

Of these two grades of mediums, Cinemoid is much thicker than Gelatine and consequently much stronger. Although Cinemoid is more expensive in the initial outlay, it is cheaper in the long run for colours that will be used a lot. There may be occasions when a single hue is wanted that may not be needed again for years. In this case Gelatine will be more practicable.

It is also possible to get a lacquer for coating lamps with a transparent covering. At present it is available from Strand Electric in colours approximating Numbers 1 to 26 inclusive, and 32, 33, and 39. These "Lamp Dips" are extremely useful for dipping lamps for strips to light door backings, and for lamps used in practical table lamps etc.

Unfortunately colour mediums fade when used for a long time. Some colours fade more than others, blue being the worst. Fading depends upon three factors: intensity of the light, the time and heat to which it is exposed, and the angle of tilt applied to the lantern. (The tilt factor applies mainly to mediums used in floodlights.) Because heat rises, a medium in position above a lamp will get more heat and fade more quickly than one level with, or below, the lamp. Cyclorama ground row lighting mediums consequently have to be changed fairly frequently.

When the medium fades it is said to be "burnt out", and should be replaced as soon as any sign of fading is noticeable. If this is neglected the colour balance of the lighting scheme will suffer. Burnt out jellies (as colour mediums are usually called) should not be merely thrown out. If an assortment is kept on hand it may be found that several are useful for a special effect. I have found burnt out Number 8 (Deep Salmon) extremely useful.

It is impossible to give any hard and fast rules for lighting. It is an art as well as a craft, and depends upon the creativeness of the lighting technician as well as the producer. Lighting should always be the servant of the play, governed by the production, and not merely a series of pretty pictures with no relation to the production. It is largely a matter of personal preference, experience, and trial and error. The more trials, the fewer errors will appear. A lighting technician never stops learning, and by analysing lighting in other productions, can learn a great deal. He can decide why and how certain lighting was successful or vice versa, and what he would have done in the same situation.

Only through personal experiment will the lighting technician understand colour. He should try throwing coloured light on to various types of surfaces and colours, watching the effect of blues on red, reds on green etc.

I hope the following remarks on colour mixing and special effects will help in experiments. But it must be remembered that these are only suggestions as a start to experimentation. Time spent on this will diminish as knowledge of the behaviour of mediums in various lanterns grows.

COLOUR MIXING

Colour mixing with paint pigments is entirely different from colour mixing with light. In painting the Subtractive process is used, in lighting the Additive process is used.

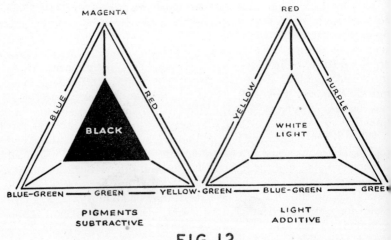

FIG. 12.

In the Subtractive process the Primary colours are Magenta, Blue-Green and Yellow (sometimes less accurately named Red, Blue and Yellow). From these three colours it is possible, by judicious mixing, to obtain all other colours. In the Additive process the three Primary colours are Red, Blue and Green, and similarly all other colours may be obtained by mixing these. From the seven colours of the spectrum (red, orange, yellow, green, blue, indigo and violet), three can be selected, termed the Three Primary Monochromatic Colours, and from these three it is possible to obtain all other colours, including "white light". The two colour triangles in Figure 12 will help to explain the mixing of colours in the two systems.

The two superimposed triangles in Figure 13 will give some guide to the effect of the primary light colours in illuminating objects of the same three colour groups.

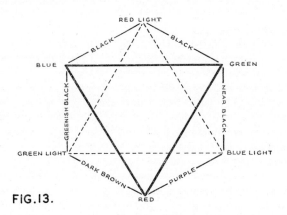

FIG.13.

The greatest use of mixing properties will be found in lighting the cyc. From the Primary colours it is possible to vary hues through all possibilities to white light.

SKY LIGHTING

Night. Blue light is very widely used for lighting the "night sky", but in my opinion this produces a very unreal effect. For a night sky through a window I prefer to use an "absence of light". This is not always possible because, for example, the spill of the stage lights may throw shadows of the windows on to the cyc or window backing. In this case some light will be necessary to wash out the shadows. If it is possible to cover the sky with black velvet the effect will be most satisfactory.

N

Day. For the day sky the time of year has to be taken into consideration. The winter sky usually has a cold appearance. One suggestion
for this is a combination of Numbers 17 (Steel Blue), 19 (Dark Blue),
36 (Pale Lavender) and 7 (Light Rose); another combination might be:
Numbers 17 (Steel Blue), 19 (Dark Blue), 34 (Golden Amber), and
53 (Pale Salmon).

Stylized. With stylized productions the lighting must follow suit,
especially with the sky. Blues, yellows and pinks are good possibilities.
I have found that a cyc lit entirely with Number 41 (Bright Blue), forms
a very pleasant background, especially for Shakespeare. The different
times of day can be suggested by varying the intensity of the light and
disregarding the colour change. Two thicknesses of Number 41 (Bright
Blue) used together give a breathtaking effect on the cyc. Used on the
cyc this colour gives a peculiar blue "rim-glow" effect to actors lit
with a pink range of colours, and can be used to advantage for special
effects.

If floodlights can be spared they will be found very useful to augment
cyclorama lighting. Floods with Numbers 51 (Gold Tint) or 53 (Pale
Salmon) are good for a summer sky, and with Numbers 17 (Steel Blue)
or 3 (Straw) for winter.

Dawn. For sunrise, from the lighting point of view, "rise" is the
operative word. The light should start growing from the ground row
equipment. As a rough guide the following explanation of the steps I
took recently when designing a Dawn effect, may help as a basis for
thought on this rather tricky subject.

The colours in the equipment were the primary ones. A spot was
placed on the floor between the cyc and the ground row and set to
throw a soft edged beam across the cyc but not directly hitting it. The
medium in this spot was specially made from scrap cuttings, using bits
of Numbers 3 (Straw), 17 (Steel Blue), and 54 (Pale Rose), with an
overall covering of 31 (Light Frost). The scene opened with the Blues
up to about one quarter. The first step in the Dawn sequence was just
"touching in" the red in the ground row lighting to suggest that dawn
was near. Then the special spot, mentioned above, was touched in,
which caused the base of the cyc to lighten slightly. Next the greens in
the top lighting were touched in, followed by a little green in the ground
row. This cycle was repeated slowly until the end of the scene. It is
most important when rehearsing the lighting to keep a list of the
sequence of steps taken so they may be rigidly adhered to in performance. Otherwise effects might be disappointing for the lighting designer
and embarrassing for the audience.

Sunset. For sunsets the procedure is the same as for sunrises, but in
reverse. Again a spot striking across the sky is useful, and should be

one-third up, the full visible height of the sky. A reddish medium, such as Numbers 7, 8, 9, 10 or 11, may be used very effectively to "break up" the sky area for a realistic sunset. With practice an artificial-looking sunset may also become a thing of beauty, but one must avoid being too lurid in the mixing, for this might distract too much attention from the play.

Rain. I shall not deal with actual rain drops. These may be obtained by a variety of methods, including optical projection. My remarks are concerned only with the appearance of the sky.

Light rain can be suggested by a general fade of the exterior lighting, with a corresponding check of the onstage lighting. The approach of a heavy storm can be effectively shown by the use of a cold colour, such as Number 17 (Steel Blue) or a mixture of Numbers 36 (Pale Lavender) and 50 (Pale Yellow). These may be used in a floodlight and this super-imposed on the cyc lighting which must also be dimmed. For an actual storm Number 55 (Chocolate Tint) superimposed in the same manner, gives a good impression.

Moonlight. Moonlight may be of two types, overall and directional. Overall moonlight is the most difficult to obtain. The best method I have discovered is to use a wide-angle floodlight from a reasonably high position. This gives a good overall coverage and some sense of direction without being too obvious. Moonlight from two definite sources would be as unacceptable to the eye as two sources of sunlight.

For directional moonlight (e.g. through windows), pageant lanterns are the most useful, although this depends upon the effect desired. In some cases a flood might be better. Again this is a matter of experiment.

The blue range is used for colouring mediums. Number 17 (Steel Blue) is excellent if used in double thickness in the same colour frame. Used singly it is too weak. Other blues which may be used are: Numbers 18 (Light Blue), 40 (Pale Blue), 41 (Bright Blue), 43 (Pale Navy Blue). One mixture I have found particularly pleasing is made from Numbers 8 (Deep Salmon) and 16 (Blue-green).

Sunlight. For sunlight through windows, pageants are again the best form of lantern to use, although light pooling down from an acting area flood is very effective. Colour mediums depend upon the time of day and year. Suggestions are: Numbers 3 (Straw), 51 (Gold Tint), 52 (Pale Gold), 53 (Pale Salmon) and 54 (Pale Rose).

Mist and Fog. Apart from lighting these effects may be obtained from the use of steam and smoke. The disadvantages of these methods are (*a*) that the steam pipes are liable to "rain" condensed steam, and (*b*) that the smoke will tend to choke both actors and audience, the latter because the draught in most theatres is from the stage to the auditorium.

A method I have found effective is to cross the beams of light from A.A.'s on stage, using a Number 55 (Chocolate Tint) in them. It is tremendously effective to sweep the stage just before the scene so that dust particles are seen in the light. This is about the only time that dust is a lighting designer's friend!

Lightning. The best method I know for getting a lightning flash is to use a photo-flood lamp in a small flood, controlling the current with a push button. For fork lightning it is necessary to use an effects projector. The old method of touching a carbon stick to a file, with a D.C. current between them, has been superseded by these much safer methods.

Fires. The best way to suggest a burning building is to tint the sky with 5A (Deep Orange) thrown on to the cyc from a flood. If a gauze is hung about three feet in front of the cyc, in front of the normal cyc lighting, and the orange glow thrown obliquely on to it, the effect will be heightened. It is important not to let the glow reach down to the bottom of the sky. Sound effects offstage will further implement the feeling of a fire.

Household fires onstage are usually coal or log types. The danger in coal fires is to make them too red. For the simulation of burning coals I have found it effective to mould the shape of the coals out of Windowlite. This is a translucent material with wire mesh running through it in one-eighth inch squares. The unburnt part of the fire may be painted out with an opaque matt black paint, and the burning coals painted in with stained glass paints in red and amber. A lamp is then placed beneath the Windowlite, and I prefer a 6ow Pale Amber lamp.

For firelight thrown into a room a float spot using Numbers 5A (Deep Orange) plus 55 (Chocolate Tint) is very effective. A realistic effect may be achieved by hanging a series of fireproofed strips of silk about four inches in front of the light beam and directing a small electric fan on them.

Log fires may also be made from Windowlite, and the light thrown by a float spot. One suggestion for colour mediums is Numbers 5 (Orange) plus 55 (Chocolate Tint).

OIL LAMPS

The bulb used in an oil lamp should be slightly tinted. I have found a Number 3 (Straw) effective, whether used as a tube of medium round the lamp or as lamp lacquer for actually dipping the bulb. For the covering light onstage various mediums may be used. I have found a very burnt out piece of Number 8 (Deep Salmon) particularly useful, as well as a Number 3 (Straw) or a combination of Numbers 9 (Light Salmon) and 49 (Canary).

If the lamp must be lit or turned up and down, it is necessary to have the dimmer circuit loaded so it will handle the small load of the pygmy light in the oil lamp. It is best, if possible, to feed the oil lamp from the same dimmer as the spot covering it. If this is not possible a spare piece of equipment should be wired in to the circuit in parallel.

CANDLES

The most frequently used form of stage candle is made from a tube of cardboard containing a torch battery. The bulb, in a holder at the top of the tube, is covered with a wisp of tissue paper slightly tinted with water-colour paint. The "candle" is lit or extinguished by a slight turn of the actual bulb.

Light covering candlelight should not be too cold, for it has been referred to through the ages as romantic. Again I favour a piece of burnt-out Number 8 (Deep salmon) as a medium. Other suggestions are Number 52 (Pale Gold) or Numbers 50 (Pale Yellow) plus 53 (Pale Salmon).

GASLIGHT

Suggestions for the covering light are: Numbers 3 (Straw), plus 17 (Steel Blue), 50 (Pale Yellow) plus 51 (Gold Tint).

JUNGLE LIGHTING

This type of lighting is not often called for, but is worthy of mention. The impression to aim for is that of humid heat. The main light in a jungle has to filter through trees and undergrowth with the result that the predominant tint is green. One may experiment in mediums with Numbers 21 (Pea Green), 38 (Pale Green), 17 (Steel Blue) plus 50 (Pale Yellow). Green must not be used entirely, but mixed with several warmer mediums such as: Numbers 7 (Light Rose), 8 (Deep Salmon), 9 (Light Salmon), 10 (Middle Rose) and 42 (Pale Violet).

A very effective jungle light was developed by George von Kuh and Richard Wadleigh for Peter Cotes's production of *Home of the Brave* (the Arthur Laurents play, also played under the title *The Way Back*). They attached a biscuit tin (with the bottom cut out) to the colour frame of a 500w flood, making sure that no light escaped. The tin was arranged so that a colour frame fitted on to the end, and carried a medium made from two thin sheets of asbestos card with about twenty irregularly placed holes, each about the size of a half-crown, punched in them. In front of each hole was stuck a piece of medium, sandwiched between the asbestos cards. Each colour frame had a variety of about eight colours, selected from such mediums as: Numbers 5 (Orange), 7 (Light Rose), 8 (Deep Salmon), 10 (Middle Rose), 11 (Dark Pink),

15 (Peacock Blue), 16 (Blue-green), 21 (Pea Green), 22 (Moss Green), 26 (Mauve), 36 (Pale Lavender), 53 (Pale Salmon). About four such floods were used, placed in a low position and angled to cover the scene. They produced the effect of sunlight filtered through trees and tropical flowers in a remarkable manner.

GHOSTS

Ghosts nearly always seem to be associated with green light. I have never discovered why, but it appears to be quite effective. The strength of the medium used depends upon the ghostly quality desired. For example, "Elvira" in *Blithe Spirit* would come off quite happily with Number 38 (Pale Green), whereas the "Ghost of Hamlet's Father" would call for Number 22 (Moss Green) or 21 (Pea Green).

Ultra-violet light can be used most effectively for ghosts if the apparitions appear in a position onstage where no ordinary light is called for. Using this method the "Hamlet" ghost could appear in a rostrum apart from "Hamlet", "Horatio", etc., who would be in their own pools of light. The ghost's costume would need to be treated with special U.V. dope, and the actor wear special U.V. make-up. The ghost would then have a luminosity of its own, and compared with the other figures on the stage would really look like something "out of this world". It would be necessary to switch on the U.V. light about five minutes before required in order to let the lamps warm up.

PROJECTED EFFECTS

Some effects can only be obtained by projection on to the cyclorama or backcloth. Among the effects available from Strand Electric are: Fleecy Cloud, Storm Clouds, Rain, Snow, Waterfall, Running Water, Smoke, Flames, Dissolving Colours, Water Ripple, Forked Lightning. It is impossible to describe all these effects here, but further information may be obtained from the manufacturers.

FROSTING

Although Number 29 (Heavy Frost) and Number 31 (Light Frost) are listed as "colour" mediums, they do not colour the light. Their purpose is to diffuse and should not be overlooked. (Another in this group is Number 30 (Clear).)

One of the main uses is to remove any unwanted sharp edges of spot beams, especially on the scenery, e.g. around doors. They may be used also to avoid any "hot spots" which floods may cause on the cyc. If it is essential to use footlights Light Frost in the compartments together with the colour mediums will help to cut down float shadows.

Windowlite may also be used very effectively. Its powers of diffusion are less than those of Light Frost, and in certain cases this can be a distinct advantage.

The purpose of Number 30 (Clear) is to keep the dust out of battens, floods and footlights that are required to be open, i.e. with no colouring medium.

CARE OF EQUIPMENT

I cannot stress too greatly the importance of keeping equipment clean. Theatres are notorious for collecting dust, and dust is the greatest enemy of lighting. The efficiency of a spot can be lowered by between 10 and 20 per cent by the dust that collects on the reflector, lens, and lamp itself. Not only does dust absorb the light, it diffuses light, causing a large amount of spill lighting onstage. The interior and exterior of all lanterns should be well cleaned regularly.

It is wise to keep several spare fuses already wired-up, near the switchboard, as well as a roll of insulating tape and a small screwdriver.

Every three or six months (depending on the amount of use), all switchboard connections should be checked, resistance wires cleaned, and slides slightly greased. All plugs should be unscrewed to make sure that every connection is firm, and all cables inspected for wear.

DON'TS

Don't try to put out any fire near electrical equipment with water. Use sand or the special type of extinguisher.

Don't try to use too much equipment on one circuit.

Don't mend a fuse with anything but the correct value fuse wire.

Don't burn a lamp over its "average life".

Don't try to mend any equipment that is "live".

Don't say "I think so", but always make sure equipment is switched off.

XIV. MAKE-UP

FROM earliest times men have used some form of disguise when portraying a theatrical character, whether it be as part of a primitive ritual, when daubs of coloured and white clay or vegetable dyes were smeared over the face and body, or as part of a more formal drama when masks were employed. Face painting has always been an integral part of the Oriental theatre. The medieval theatre in the western world specialized in "horror" masks and make-ups, which gave way in Elizabethan times to more simple cosmetics, wigs and beards. Then for many years, in fact up until the middle of the last century, actors played any type of part in the same make-up, for example David Garrick, who wore the white Court wig of George III for nearly every role he played.

Lighting, up to the discovery of electricity, was at best a crude affair, and guttering candles or smoky oil lamps threw no violent light upon sketchy make-up. Some performers like Eleanor Duse used no make-up at all. However, with the powerful coloured light used today, make-up is necessary so that the features will not disappear completely, and the audience be confronted with round, flat white discs.

Today make-up is as highly individual an Art as Acting. No two people achieve exactly the same make-up, just as no two actors, however physically similar, give the same performance in the same part. There are a number of general rules, there are hints and suggestions as to how to make oneself look "aged", "bucolic", etc., but in practical application the actor must create his own individual make-up according to his interpretation of the character he is portraying.

Make-up is an external aid but cannot create a character. It can help an actor to express himself to the audience, and may even make him feel that he looks like another person, but it cannot be relied on completely. True characterization always comes from within. A few daubs of red on a nose will not convince an audience that a man is a drunkard unless his actions, voice and inner feelings also convince them. Lines painted on and a grey wig cannot make a crippled old lady out of a girl whose dancing gait and swinging arms belie her appearance.

Great care must be taken not to over-exaggerate make-up, unless weird and supernatural effects are required. There is a great tendency among beginners and amateurs to use too much make-up. The result is often grotesque, when it is supposed to be natural.

It is often very amusing to see young beginning actors with enormous, elaborate make-up boxes containing every conceivable shade of grease-paint, while in the same show the "old pros" carry a few well-used sticks in a tiny cardboard box. The latter have learned through years of experience that it is not quantity that counts. Make-up carefully applied from treasured stumps of paint may be far more effective than liberally smeared coatings, badly done, from brand new sticks. Experience teaches the actor that economy of application is not only easier on the purse, but gives better results.

The golden rule for applying make-up is highlight and shadow, and never, never stark superimposed lines. A careful study of facial bone structure under strong light will show where the natural highlights and shadows occur. Make-up should be built up around these.

Practice is essential in perfecting the art of make-up. It is not enough to put on paint for the first time at a dress rehearsal, particularly if one is playing a difficult character. Make-up should be tried over and over again. Adjustments may have to be made after it is seen by the producer under stage lighting. He may suggest using more or less, or a slightly different shade to blend in with the light, but usually the basic conception will remain the same.

The size of the playhouse determines how much make-up should be used, much less being needed in a tiny auditorium than in a vast theatre. Altering make-up to meet such changing conditions only comes with experience.

An actor should always leave plenty of time before a performance to complete his make-up. A rushed last-minute job is rarely satisfactory. Part of the joy of doing make-up is in a growing feeling of taking on the "skin" of a part as the greasepaint is applied. A good actor begins to feel his stage character replacing his own as he changes his face.

Broadly speaking there are two basic categories of make-up—"straight" and "character". The first consists of highlighting the face so that it will appear on stage as it does in real life in the same age group as the actor. The second involves changing the face to resemble a character not like the actor himself. The character may be older, of different facial structure, plumper, thinner, or his inner feelings may be so different from the actor's own that they must be shown in the face. It is "character" make-up which is so often badly done, and requires most practice.

Each actor should acquire his own make-up materials, although in some cases a society may build up a good supply and loan pieces out or sell them for various shows. Everybody's make-up supplies will differ somewhat depending on age, types of parts usually played, etc. The following are the materials used in straight and character work:

Cream for cleansing the skin and removing greasepaint. Theatrical suppliers make this cream in various types, but if the manufactured article cannot be obtained, any pure oil or grease may be used instead. I have known actors who used lard, paraffin oil, olive oil, vaseline, or vegetable shortening. Some skins are very sensitive, and the actor will have to experiment until he finds a cream to suit him.

Cleansing cloths or tissues. Some actors use a soft cloth or towel for wiping off cream and make-up, but it is more sanitary to use either paper tissues or pieces of cotton wool, which are destroyed after use.

Greasepaints. These are made in sticks or tubes, in many flesh tints and colours, and may be bought at many chemists' or ordered from suppliers. There is a fashion nowadays, particularly among young people, of doing "straight" make-ups with a pancake type of make-up for base coats. This may seem quicker to apply, but gives a mask-like finish, on to which it is difficult to apply highlights and shadows. A fluorescent cream make-up is made in various shades for use under ultra-violet lighting, when the make-up glows brightly. Under ordinary lighting it appears quite normal.

Liners are thinner sticks of greasepaint in darker colours used for highlight and shadow, making up the eyes, and special effects.

Rouge comes in cream or dry form, and can be dispensed with if red sticks or liners are used for colouring instead. With pancake make-ups dry rouge is usually used, and is useful for touching up after make-up has been powdered.

Eyeshadow is a cream only necessary for glamorous women's make-ups, or exotic or weird effects round the eyes, and is made in a great many shades of blue, grey, purple, green, brown, silver and gold. It should be used very sparingly in normal make-ups, if used at all.

Eyebrow pencils are sticks of hard black or brown paint, made with paper wrappers or inside wooden protectors, like pencils, and are used for eyebrows and eye outlining.

Mascara is a dry paint, which must be dampened and applied to the eyelashes with a brush. It comes in black, brown, blue and green.

Heating cosmetic is a greasepaint originally intended for streaking the hair, but is also used for "beading" eyelashes to create a glamorous or "over made up" effect. It may be bought in black, brown, blue, silver, gold and white.

Powder is used to set make-up, and the special "blending" type made by stage make-up firms is more absorbent and clings better than ordinary face powder. It comes in a wide variety of shades to match bases, but is transparent so that it does not alter make-up colours. A "finishing" powder is also made, for application to arms, shoulders, neck and body to give a matt finish when no foundation is used. Hair powder is used for minor colour changes, or heightening the existing colour, and is available in white, black, grey, brown, blonde and reddish shades. Tinsel powder, in gold and silver, may be dusted on to the hair for a sparkling effect.

Powder puffs may be used to apply powder, although many actors prefer to use pieces of cotton wool. It is best to use a large puff or piece of cotton.

Complexion brushes or soft baby brushes are useful for gently removing excess powder.

Liquid make-up is used for body colouring. It comes in a great variety of tan and racial skin shades.

Crepe hair is a vegetable fibre braided into plaits and sold by footage for making beards, moustaches, hair pieces, etc.

Spirit gum is a gum arabic solution used for sticking crepe hair to the face, etc.

Rubbing alcohol is used to remove spirit gum.

Glitter powder, made in various colours, may be applied to eyelids, etc., if a unique sparkling effect is desired. It sticks quite well to grease-paint, although a little spirit gum will make it more secure.

Astringent lotion is refreshing when applied to the face after removing make-up.

Nose putty comes in sticks and may be moulded and stuck to the nose or other parts of the face for structural changes.

Tooth enamel is a liquid available in black, white and ivory, and its use will be explained later.

Congealed or liquid blood is manufactured by leading suppliers and is extremely realistic.

Make-up boxes with divided compartments for individual sticks are sold by stage make-up houses, but may be made inexpensively by dividing off cigar or other wooden boxes.

A good mirror, soap, and towels are primary requisites for any make-up.

MAKE-UP PROCEDURE

Light. The first step is to make sure there is a good supply of light. Specially constructed theatrical make-up tables have mirrors surrounded by light bulbs so the face is lit from all angles. Too often actors must depend on a hanging light from above, which casts shadows below the features and the face itself. If this is the only light available, it is important to examine make-up in a mirror from all angles around the light before finishing it.

Cleansing. The face should be thoroughly washed, dried, a thin coat of cream applied, and all surplus cream wiped off so the skin is not oily. Astringent lotion may be patted on as well if the skin is naturally very greasy.

Base Coat. The required basic colour is then applied. There are various ways of doing this, each actor having his own preference. Some dot greasepaint all over the face, some apply strokes of colour, some mix daubs of different colours on the back of the hand until the required shade is found, then work it on to the face with the fingertips. Whichever method is used, the paint must be smoothly blended to completely cover the face, ears, and any part of the neck which will be exposed. Covering the neck is of utmost importance. How often an otherwise good make-up is spoiled by a white neck showing under a tanned face! A well-powdered neck make-up will not spoil costumes to any great extent, and in any case the paint is easily removed from cloth by cleaning fluid or washing with soap and water. If even greater care is necessary, a lining of cotton can be sewn under the edges of collars, necklines, cuffs, etc.

There are no rigid rules about which colours should be used for certain parts or types of characters. This is largely a matter of individual skin tones and experimentation. Most often the base will be a blend of two or three colours. The colour chart of Messrs. Leichner's greasepaints will give some guidance, and any colour numbers referred to here will be found in this chart.

For a "straight" young woman, usually 2, 2½, Peach or a combination of these is used. For a "straight" young man, a mixture of 3 or 3½ with a little 4 or 9 may be used. For an aging part, 6 and 6½ may be blended in. Oriental parts may use 8 and 8b; Spanish, or similar types—10; African natives—11; Mulattoes—7.

Highlight and Shadow. Even young straight make-ups must have the features highlighted to bring out the desired contours of the face, otherwise a flat appearance will result under lights. This is where careful study of the bone structure is necessary, and a knowledge of which features are to be specially stressed. The principle of highlighting is that a lighter colour applied to any part of the face will make that part larger or more prominent; while shadowing means that a darker shade will make the part recede or appear sunken. Thus if one wants to make cheekbones prominent with a thinning of the face below the cheeks, a lighter shade than the base is applied to the cheeks, and a darker one to the hollows below the cheeks. These are carefully blended into each other, with no definite line of division. A small nose may be made to appear longer and straighter if a streak of light colour or white is painted along the top, and a darker shade blended from the top down each side. The reverse procedure will make a large nose appear smaller. Quite fascinating suggestions of change in nose structure may be worked out through practice.

"In age" or "character" make-up, highlights and shadows are of utmost importance. The most popular and misused colours for this are white and lake liners. Both are very useful but must be used carefully. Lake should be applied with a brush or the fingertips to the places where hollows are desired. These should then always be outlined with white, and the edges of the colours carefully blended, so that they disappear into one another. It must be remembered that wherever there is a shadow, there must be a highlight as well. If frown and wrinkle lines are applied around the eyes, or beside the nose running down to the mouth, they must again be a combination of Lake lined with white and softly blended. Better no lines than a hard criss-cross puzzle on the face. Age shows in the deepening circles on the neck, and these must not be forgotten. Too often one sees an "old" head on a "young" neck.

The best rule for a young person applying older make-up is observation. He should study his older fellow men, and remember where hollows, lines and circles appear; then try to recreate the effect.

Rouge should be applied to the cheekbone in a small patch, then worked out towards the temples where it is faded into the base coat. In male make-ups Number 9 is often used instead of rouge.

The Eyes. The lids should first be shadowed with a shade darker greasepaint than the base coat, fading up to meet the eyebrows. Then colour may be applied in a shade to match the eyes for a naturalistic make-up, or in any desired shade for exaggerated effects. It should be remembered that an actor with naturally deep-set eyes does not need as dark an eye shadow as one with normal or protruding eyes. To make the eye appear older or sunken, Lake may be applied below and above, blending into a highlight of white or a light shade of greasepaint.

To outline the eyes a thin line should be drawn with a fine brush or a sharpened matchstick along the upper and lower lashes, meeting and extending slightly beyond the outer corners of the eye. Colour from a black or brown liner or eyebrow pencil may be used for this. To make the eye appear larger a space may be left between the lower lashes and the outline, and this space filled in with white.

Eyebrows may be shaped with an eyebrow pencil, using short strokes rather than one long line. If very large bushy eyebrows are required, pieces of crepe hair may be stuck on with spirit gum. A faintly bushy effect is given if eyebrows are brushed backwards, towards the nose, with the desired colour.

For exaggerated or glamorous effects glitter powder in various shades may be applied to eyelids, or coloured sequins stuck on with spirit gum.

Age or fatigue lines, commonly called "crow's feet", may be drawn at the outer corners, or below the eyes, with a highlight line between each one. Again, these must be slightly blended and not too stark. Powdering down helps to soften these lines as well.

Lips. Most women are experts at applying lipstick or carmine grease-paint, and know which shade suits them best for "straight" make-ups, and which will blend best with their costumes. Men need very little carmine on the lips in straight roles . . . just a faint suggestion smoothly brushed on. For a definite lipline, particularly in female make-ups, a faint highlight applied above the upper lip is effective. For old age the lips may be left colourless or brushed with the base coat colour. A thin line of Lake drawn horizontally down the centre of the closed lips gives a tight-lipped quality. A cracked withered appearance is shown by fine Lake lines drawn with a matchstick in some of the natural vertical lines of the lips, taking care not to over-exaggerate. Short lines drawn down from the corners of the mouth suggest severity or sadness, while upward lines suggest jollity and happiness. The mouth can be a very expressive feature, and care should be taken to make it express exactly the mood and character desired. Too often it is ignored.

Powder. Every make-up must be finished off with powder in order to set it and give a matt finish to the face and neck. Powder should be dusted on liberally and pressed into the paint with a large clean puff or piece of cotton wool, then the excess gently dusted off with a soft brush or more cotton wool. Some actors pat cold water on to their faces after make-up is completed, but this requires skill in order not to spoil the painting. However, it does help to set make-up and is refreshing to the actor.

Eyelashes. These are usually made up after powdering is completed, mascara being applied with a brush in various colours. Heating cosmetic gives a lustrous beaded effect for glamour make-ups, and is applied to each lash with a matchstick from a supply heated in a spoon over a match, lighter or other flame. False eyelashes may also be glued on. Make-up should be examined throughout the performance, and touched up if necessary, as perspiration may cause it to run slightly, or colour may be unavoidably rubbed off. Most actors find too that they must apply further powder as the play progresses.

Body Make-up. Exposed parts of the body must be made up. In nearly all roles the hands are seen, and must match the base colour of the face. Only the top of the hand is coloured; and if it must be made to look older, thin lines of Lake, with accompanying highlights, should be drawn along the natural veins and crevices. Knuckles should be lined in a similar manner. Powdering hand make-up is essential.

For colouring arms, legs and the torso a liquid body make-up, often referred to as "wetwhite", is used. It is applied with a sponge or cotton wool, and washes off easily with soap and water.

Hair. Dressing the hair is of vital importance to make-up. If a hair style does not fit into the conception of a character, even the most brilliant application of facial paint will not make the character live. Even in a straightforward modern part, hair should be changed to fit the part . . . whether it be sleek for a dapper character, unruly for a farm worker, etc. Even the changing of a parting from side to centre or vice versa, will make a difference.

The two main problems encountered in hair dressing for the stage are: 1. Application of false hair, either as a wig or beard, and 2. The greying or tinting of hair to another colour.

1. (*a*) *Wigs.* If the play is a period piece wigs are almost always necessary. They may be rented from a costumier, and if it is at all possible the actor should visit the shop for a fitting. If this is not practicable, exact head measurements should be sent when ordering. Well-made wigs fit securely on to the head, but if there is any doubt they should be secured with hairpins. Many wigs have a narrow piece of gauze extending out along the edge over the forehead. This should be stuck to the skin with spirit gum, and coloured to blend into the facial base coat.

If a "piece" is worn to simulate a bald head, the base coat colour must be worked into the skull piece so that it looks like one naturalistic piece of skin.

For plays where a very ragged, shapeless head of hair is needed, and perhaps there isn't enough natural hair for the effect, wigs may be made by gluing or sewing crepe hair on to a gauze or buckram base cut to fit the head, or even onto the crown of an old felt hat. This must be painstakingly done for a naturalistic result. If a close-fitting hat is to be worn throughout a play, pieces of crepe hair sewn just inside, and showing below the hat, may be used, as long as the hat is so secure that no accident can knock it off and reveal the actor's real hair.

Many actresses own a switch or two or false hair the same colour as their own, which may be added as "buns" or hanging curls. These may be made of real hair, which is rather expensive, or of an artificial hair which looks very real. The latter is within the reach of most pockets, and an active amateur actress would do well to procure a switch. They may be combed and curled into almost any style. Smaller pieces for individual curls, front pieces, etc. are also sold or rented out by costumiers.

(*b*) *Beards and Moustaches.* Except for melodramas, the hook-on type of beard should never be used. Beards and moustaches, mounted on gauze are available for hire at costumiers, and are stuck to the face with spirit gum. When applying any false hair it is important that the skin be free of make-up, because the gum will not stick to greasepaint.

Effective beards are made from crepe hair. A section of the braided hair is cut off, the binding string removed, and the hair stretched out. It will appear tightly curled, and should be pressed out under a damp cloth with a warm iron before being used. Pieces are then cut roughly to the desired shape and stuck to the face with spirit gum. The fingers should be slightly dampened before pressing the hair down, or they will become sticky and may pull strands away. A damp cloth may be held against the hair until it is firm. For a small beard at least four pieces of hair should be applied; one on each side of the face, one on the chin, and one under the chin. A full beard requires six pieces. These should slightly overlap and be trimmed when the beard is secure.

Moustaches may be shaped from crepe hair and stuck on to gauze, which is then glued to the face. In this way the moustache pieces may be used more than once. Or the hair may be applied directly to the skin. In either case it is important not to cover the indentation which runs from the middle of the upper lip to the nose. This is not only uncomfortable, but detracts from the mobility of the face.

Short pieces of crepe hair make excellent sideburns.

Crepe hair is removed by applying rubbing alcohol under the edges and gently pulling the hair while working the alcohol along the face.

2. *Greying and Colouring Hair.* A young actor trying to look grey must practise his technique a great deal before opening night. There are various ways of greying. Specially manufactured hair powder may be applied and combed into the hair, or if this is not available cornflour is a good substitute. The difficulty with powder is that it dulls the hair, and if not carefully combed in and viewed from all angles in a mirror, may appear patchy and very unreal. White or silver greasepaint or heating cosmetic may be streaked into the temples for a slight touch of grey, but must be carefully dragged and faded into the hair.

Hair powder in various shades from black to brown, red and blonde, is sold by costumiers and make-up firms, for dusting into the hair and slightly changing the colour. It is easily brushed out. For a deeper effect the powder may be mixed with oil and brushed into the hair with an old toothbrush. In this case it must be shampooed out. Some actors darken the hair slightly with mascara, which is effective as long as it doesn't become wet, even through perspiration, when it will trickle down the face in dark rivulets.

Metallic powders in the hair should be used with great caution, and washed out as soon as possible, as they are often irritating to the skin and may cause the outbreak of a rash. However, ordinary hair powders and greasepaints are harmless to any skin but the super-sensitive.

Plastic Changes. Actual plastic changes in the shape of features or parts of the face may be effected by using nose putty, which, as its name implies, is used mainly on that feature. It comes in a very hard stick form, and must be worked with the fingers until it becomes soft and pliable. It may be slightly heated to help the softening process. Then it is kneaded into the desired shape and pressed on to the skin which must be free from greasepaint or cream. It is wise to apply putty before beginning to make up. If there is difficulty in making it stick securely, a little spirit gum may be used. The shape should be worked until it is very thin at the edges and fades into the skin. Then it must be covered with base coat, highlighted and shadowed, until it appears to be a natural part of the face.

Teeth. These may be brushed with tooth enamel, in black or ivory. Black blocks out the teeth and gives the effect of gaps, while ivory covers discoloration. Teeth should be dried before the enamel is applied, and the mouth held open until it dries, which is only a matter of a minute. Enamel is removed easily by wiping the teeth with a tissue or cloth, and should be examined from time to time to make sure none has rubbed off during performance. It is not recommended if an actor has to eat onstage, as it is liable to come off with the chewing of food.

Racial Types. Study of photographs, or if possible a real person of the required race, is the best guide for racial make-up, where bone structure, shape of the eyes, etc. must be changed. The Leichner company has a series of make-up charts for various racial types, showing how to apply colour, and these are sold for a few pence each. This same firm offers a free advisory service on any make-up problems, with a sample make-up done by an expert, to both professionals and amateurs. Appointments should be arranged in advance by contacting their London Make-up Studio at 44A Cranbourn Street, W.C.2.

Conclusion. For greatest effectiveness make-up should be applied sparingly and carefully, with a full knowledge of the character to be portrayed, the theatre to be used, and the general lighting scheme. In make-up as in almost every phase of the theatre, only "practice makes perfect".

O

XV. DANCES IN PLAYS
by FELICITY GRAY

IT is a very different thing to produce dances for a play than for a ballet or a musical show, and much the same rules hold good for both amateur and professional plays.

The dances in plays are not self-contained; they grow out of the plot as part of the whole, often without even calling for extra characters to be introduced. "Bring on the dancing girls" does not figure in every script which calls for dances within its length. This means that often it is actors who are asked to dance. Oddly enough, even where there is a legitimate reason for real dancers to be used, as in *Le Malade Imaginaire*, it is advisable to choose people who have a sense of character, or they are inclined to stand out as denizens of another world. In plays dancers enter an atmosphere and style different from that of ballet, therefore their own style must be modified to suit that of the play. If they do not understand this, their performance, however brilliant in itself, is liable to unbalance the entire scene.

The dance producer for a play is hemmed in by many restrictions and conditions, most of which hold good for any kind or period of play. First there is the fact that actors are seldom dancers, and dancers seldom actors. Then there is usually very little space on a "legitimate" set, and what there is is likely to be dotted with odd chairs and tables, carpets and lamp standards. Costumes suitable for acting in are often impossible to dance in, even quite discreetly. Music is a difficulty about which I will speak later.

The question of dancers for a play is always difficult, especially where they are also required to act. In the case of plays such as *A Midsummer Night's Dream*, it is well worth approaching the local dancing schools, but if this is done it should be made quite clear from the beginning that the producer has the final word on everything, including asking for the dances to be cut or altered.

Whoever produces the dances themselves must have a considerable talent for compromise. He should be in on all discussions of the scenes concerning him, otherwise the dances may appear to "stick on to" the production as extras, instead of being an integral part of it.

He should also be the one to choose the music, subject of course to the approval of the producer. The music right through any play should hold together in style and period. It is no good starting off with a little Beethoven, going on to a choice piece of Debussy, trying some Stravinsky for contrast, and ending up with a charming Chopin, however well each of those individual pieces seems to fit the mood of isolated scenes in the play. The music chosen for the actual dances for a play must defer as well to the limitations of those expected to perform to it; complicated rhythms and subtle phrasing put an undue strain on untrained dancers, especially if dialogue has to be introduced into the dances. When the tongue starts the feet usually stop!

In producing dances for plays there are several "do's" and "don'ts" which can help to hide deficiencies and highlight the good points. First for the "don'ts":

1. *Don't* use girls as boys unless it is quite unavoidable. For inexperienced dancers to get away with this is impossible.

2. *Don't* dress dancers in revealing costumes, such as all-over tights or severely plain bodices with no sleeve or shoulder decoration; the way the shoulders are held and move can reveal the non-dancer at once. The line of the classical ballet tu-tu is another that only dancers can wear convincingly.

3. *Don't* try to put over dances suitable to stand on their own merits apart from their position in the play. The first requisite is that the dances should be suitable to the play; that they should be striking or brilliant in themselves is only a secondary objective and very seldom attained.

4. *Don't* bring up flat front-of-house lighting in a mistaken effort to brighten the scene. It will only reveal the points better hidden.

5. *Don't* give actors a lot of steps to learn.

6. *Don't* give them a number of steps on one spot only.

7. *Don't* give them so much at once that they become obviously and loudly breathless.

8. *Don't* use solos unless unavoidable.

9. Don't overfill the music with movements.

None of these "don'ts" apply if you have professional dancers, except the last; but where actors, professional or amateur, have to dance they do apply.

Now for the "do's":

1. Dress actors as far as possible in long skirts or soft draperies; keep the body line clear but soften the shoulders and arms.

2. Have them dancing in and out of shafts or pools of light, and if there are certain moments of value to the play dramatically, these should be planned so that they take place in the necessary light. Following spots are not the answer because, except in very particular cases, they cut across the atmosphere very badly.

3. Use a few simple steps only, and vary the patterns and timing of them, as well as the use of the arms and body.

4. Steps which travel over the ground are best, as the attention is not then focused on the execution of the step itself, but on the flow of movement.

5. Give plenty of time for breathing spaces; this can best be managed by using your dancers in "answering" phrases. For instance, if you have three couples, let each one work in turn, whilst the others are still, or nearly so. In music, of the usual sixteen-bar phrase, four bars go to each couple, and the last four bars are taken by all three couples together.

6. Make sure that both at the beginning and the end the dance is skilfully tailored into the play. It must always respect the convention of the "fourth wall", if the play itself does so. Unwisely won applause for a dance that should be part of a scene, can destroy that scene.

7. Use floor patterns and entrances and exits so that the attention is held by a pleasing or interesting flow of movement rather than by the individual execution of set steps.

I have left the question of floor patterns to the last because it requires some elaboration. The patterns do not have to be symmetrical; far better not, unless the situation demands it and the setting allows it. In *A Midsummer Night's Dream* the fairies' scenes are spoilt if given symmetrical patterns, but where formality is needed, or where a dance is presented as entertainment for the characters in the play in a ballroom-type of set, then the symmetrical pattern can be very effective.

Patterns of folk dances are a most useful source of ideas; there are many to be found in the publications of the Cecil Sharpe house. In period plays it helps a great deal to preserve the style if the dances are based on the appropriate patterns, even if the actual steps and movements cannot be absolutely correct.

A piece of music is written in a certain key, and however many changes of key it goes through there is still its home key in the background, in which it starts and finishes. The same theory applies to the steps and floor patterns of a dance. A dance can be based on diagonal lines across the stage, or square box-like patterns, or a circle or a serpentine pattern, or straight lines up and down stage, or on a certain step. However many variations on the chosen pattern or step are used, it should recur and round off the dance at the end. Above all, there should be a logical flow to the pattern of the entire dance. The laws of design apply to dances, as well as the other phases of theatrical production.

Patterns also carry within themselves dramatic qualities. Broadly speaking, circles and curves express the softer, lighter feelings, also those of wariness, waiting, and attraction; straight lines and boxes are strong, and can have a resolute, harsh feeling, or one of youth and attack; whilst the diagonals give an impression of swiftness, purpose or hopeless quests, pursuit, or menacing approach. There are no rigid rules about these things, but only suggestions to help dance producers start thinking for themselves in the light of their own special problems.

To make patterns with your dancers does not mean that you have to have many people. There are numerous attractive variations on the simplest patterns to be made by three or four people. The art of using them lies in the timing of the movements of each dancer in relation to the others, and in the angle of their bodies and heads to each other during those movements.

Take the simplest of all; two people circling round each other. Even that can be done in several ways, as illustrated here:

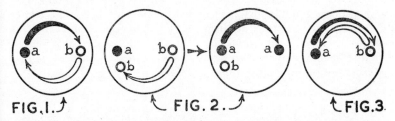

FIG. 1.   FIG. 2.   FIG. 3.

Figure 1 is the diagram of the plainest way; Figure 2 is a rather coy variation, as "a" is always moving away from "b", having first let him join her; in Figure 3 each does his full circle but going in the opposite direction. The latter figure shows a watchful quality of taking someone's measure, particularly if the dancers slide past one another face to face. If they pass unperturbed, each going his own way, you have a feeling of pride, disdain or something quite impersonal. More variations in feeling can be made by altering the speed at which certain parts of the pattern are covered; this does not mean altering the tempo of the music, of course, but merely doing the steps at double the speed of the music, or at half speed—of taking four bars to do a step or pattern, instead of eight. Pauses at certain points, the attitude with which the dancers pass one another, their eyes meeting or avoiding contact, form the punctuation as it were, and can give the same effect as any question mark, comma, exclamation mark, dash or asterisk. Providing the bodies and heads are well held, and the arms and hands used attractively without fuss, such variations on simple patterns carry one through most dances in plays.

If your dancers are actors then make use of every trick to give them a feeling of real characterization in the dance itself, to detract from the awful fact that they are actually dancing; but if they are amateur or inexperienced dancers and not actors, subtract from the acting within the dance as far as possible. An actor will dance better if he feels himself in a character still, whilst an amateur dancer is better if allowed to dance to the best of his ability without worrying about acting.

There are, of course, plays where it is impossible to avoid striving for the effect of real dancing, such as *Tobias and the Angel*. Again pattern is the first requirement, but as well as pattern on the floor, there is pattern in the air, that is, the designs made by the lines of the dancers' bodies in groups, and as they move past one another—the picture that they make. Frieze designs are very useful here, and comparatively simple to do, though they often take an unexpected amount of rehearsal. This is because most non-dancers and amateurs find it very difficult to feel exactly where their arms are, unless they are actually looking at them. They do not realize whether an arm is bent or straight, just above or below shoulder height; whether the palm of the hand is facing the floor or the ceiling or the front; unless they turn their heads and look at the limb in question. In friezes, where each dancer fills a definite line of a picture, such details are very important, because it is the exactness of the positions that gives the effect.

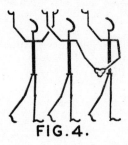 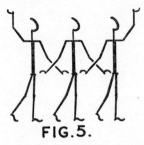

FIG. 4.   FIG. 5.

Figures 4 and 5 show a grouping possible for a frieze in a play with an eastern complexion. It is easy to see that if the angles at wrist and elbow, and the points of contact between the three sets of arms, were inaccurate the group would look quite accidental.

Once in a frieze position, dancers can move horizontally across the stage, arms in the same position all the time, using some definite rhythm of "up and down" in the feet, and even a complete turn of the hips to travel back a couple of steps in the direction from which they came. The head may also move, turning from side to side, or looking up and down.

Figure 6 shows a ground plan of a possible breakaway from such a formal style of group or movement. Having got your dancers down the sides, let them hold a position, but keep a rhythm going with their feet, then one by one they can move to the centre and build up a group, each dancer adding his own position. When all are in place, if a climax is needed for the end of the dance, the entire group can alter their poses together. Such a formation takes up a reasonable amount of music, is usually very effective, and need not strain slender capabilities.

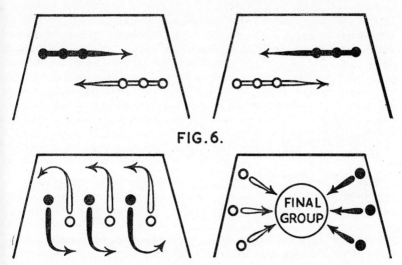

FIG. 6.

It is always a help for inexperienced dancers to make some kind of physical contact during a dance; this acts as a means of ensuring fairly accurate spacing in the floor pattern. Holding hands, holding waists, linking arms, or just having to touch someone on shoulder, arm or waist at a given spot, are great helps.

The most difficult dance to deal with in a play, that I have ever met, is that in *Back to Methuselah*, Part 5. Alas, it is practically impossible to find a collection of young men and women who look like Shaw's description, let alone who can dance according to his directions . . . "A dance of youths and maidens is in progress. They move with perfect balance and remarkable grace, racing through a figure like a farandole; they neither romp nor hug in our manner." Luckily that description is never repeated by any of the characters in the play so the audience is not made forcibly aware of the present-day physical shortcomings compared with the brave future.

The way I found round it was a sort of folk dance measure, holding hands and dancing fast in circles and lines, always going opposite ways or crossing one another; so that the effect was kaleidoscopic and no one settled anywhere long enough for the audience to see them critically.

A play which has dance movement all the way through, yet very little set dancing, is *The Insect Play*. Here there can be a continuous problem if the producer decides to accent the fantastic and play down the human side. In such a case the dance producer can be a great help. The movements of all the Insects all the way through need to be stylized and slightly fantastic, and each Insect must have his own, individual kind of movement; otherwise the ill-co-ordinated efforts of a large cast to behave as Beetles, Ants, Grasshoppers, etc., are liable to end up looking strangely monotonous and unconvincing. The Beetles should have a different kind of walk and run and body stance from the Ants, and Butterflies must not have the same movements as Grasshoppers or Moths. A dance producer can save a lot of time for everyone by sorting out the type of movement each is to do. The producer will almost certainly know what he wants, but he will get it more quickly through someone whose language is movement and who can therefore show the actors what movements are wanted, and also better explain how to do them.

When it comes to the battle of the Ants, you have what is really a choreographic scene. Although the shouted orders and tense "news bulletins" never stop, the scene cries aloud for music. In staging such a scene, one has to be most careful not to set movements obviously to the music. Nor can one simply arrange a series of warlike incidents and tell everyone to get on with it, hoping that they will all be over at roughly the same time as the music finishes, with the result that the scene occurs whilst the music is playing but has no relation to it. This distracts the attention of the audience by making them watch anxiously for that non-existent bond between music and scene which they know instinctively should be there. So one must not use steps at all, only running and stalking "character" movements, suitable to Ants in battle, worked out in many floor patterns with entrances and exits throughout, and without following the chosen music in detail as one does for a dance. One must try to parallel visually the swelling and fading of the musical phrases and all their climaxes, with battle incidents, struggles, falls, etc. That is the only way of binding together the music and the movement so that the content of the play is undisturbed by their addition, and the atmosphere is heightened.

The music for dances in a play is a great difficulty. Usually it must be taken from a record. Perhaps that sounds like a perfect idea—no variation of tempos, no complications re engaging pianists for rehearsals, and no worries about the quality of the piano in the pit. But there are several drawbacks; the music must be chosen from commercial records, which means that though you may know the exact piece you want, it is probably not available recorded by a suitable collection of instruments or voices; if you do find it, it is probably too short or too long, and the search must begin again. One cannot repeat a phrase from the middle of a record, and cutting is dangerous as so often the few chords of the bit before are heard, or one comes in a couple of bars late, an accident from which the dancers are not likely to recover!

When you finally discover a suitable record, the question of reproduction appears. A good gramophone with a good microphone and loudspeaker to the front of house is essential. If the one installed is old and tinny, then hire another. Nothing destroys the atmosphere of a scene more quickly than the sudden introduction of badly "canned" music. Listen to the rustle and whisper that goes round the house when this happens. It can also destroy the sense of reality among most amateur actors, indeed it takes a very good professional company to hold the audience and their own characters, in the face of bad mechanics. On the other hand, if the reproduction is good and the record well chosen, the music is a valuable help to both actors and audience.

The same thing applies if "live" music is to be used. If the piano is a bad one, hire a good one. If you are hoping to use strings and the players are poor, don't have them. Get a good pianist instead, or even records.

Incidentally, there are many amateur musicians in the country who have considerable talent and experience, and if "live" music is indicated it is well worth enquiring among the local music and operatic societies and clubs. Very many highly trained musicians give up their profession on marriage, or turn to some more reliable source than music for their bread and butter, but keep up their art as a satisfying hobby. The help and enthusiasm that an amateur production receives from such musicians is well worth the small effort of finding them. Because they are not always actively interested in acting they have to be sought out, probably talked into helping to begin with.

Without expecting rows of fully trained ballet dancers to spring from nowhere, there are certain graces which one can hope for in actors who must dance in plays, and in those who want to take part in the dances to be found in plays. And there are certain small skills which are useful for any actor to have if there is the slightest chance of his ever having to "foot it fleetly" in a role. The following remarks may be a guide to those who wish to fit themselves for such accidents as roles that require dancing, and also those who have to choose their dancers from among the comparatively untrained.

Actors should have an ability to waltz with a partner and alone, including the reverse turn, and to do this either smoothly or with a strong "down, up, up" beat. They should have an ability to polka, with or without a partner, and both ways round. Ballroom dancing is always useful, as in this way they learn to distinguish one foot from another, and also a little of the principles of "opposition", that is, the use of opposite foot and shoulder or arm. Greek dancing can be an excellent help to those who wish to learn quickly to be intelligent movers. It uses strong opposition and is excellent training for the sense of line. It does make people conscious of exactly where their hands and arms are placed.

Folk dancing is a most acceptable background, as it gives light feet, and a sense of pattern and individual placement in the pattern in relation to everyone else. A little study of Spanish dancing helps towards a proud carriage, attack, mobile hands, and a great sense of rhythm, with its clapping, snapping fingers, and stamping feet. There are many different styles of Spanish dancing, from various areas of Spain, and in some cases it is a very complicated and difficult art; nevertheless it has a lot to give enthusiasts even in the early stages.

Ballet itself I put last, as it is such a highly specialized form of technique, which in its early stages is actually inclined to restrict the ability of a person to move freely or with character; though nothing could be better if sufficient training can be, or has been, taken.

Personally, I think it an excellent idea for actors to be able to dance a little with conviction and style; and for dancers to be able to act, even though without words.

If an amateur society embarks on a production calling for dances, and they are within reach of an amateur ballet club, I am sure they would find a collaboration valuable, either for finding suitable dancers, or in a case where it is the actors who must dance, for finding a dance producer ready to work with the producer of the play. It is by such means that the standard of amateur work can gradually be raised and help to increase the influence of the movement in every direction.

XVI. THE AMATEUR MUSICAL THEATRE
by ERIC MASCHWITZ

NO country in the world has an Amateur Operatic movement comparable with that which flourishes in Great Britain today. And "flourishes" is not too extravagant a word; more than 800 operatic societies are now registered with N.O.D.A. (National Operatic and Dramatic Association) which, although all-powerful, is by no means all-embracing. In this "nation of shopkeepers" it is estimated that almost 100,000 British people each year give up their spare time to the rehearsal and performance of musical works, ranging from revue, through musical comedy and operetta, to grand opera. And musically-minded emigrants are carrying on the good work overseas, with ever-increasing activity, in Australia, South Africa and New Zealand.

In this country the older societies, some of them founded over sixty years ago, began in what might be termed a more serious vein, with the performance of light opera and *opéra bouffe* (Gilbert and Sullivan, German, Planchette, etc.). Some of these still hold to their original tradition; others, together with most of the younger societies, have already ventured far into the field of musical comedy.

I am often asked why, in view of my professional activities, I give so much of my time to the "amateurs". The answer to this question is two-fold; in the first place my own musical plays are often given a much better performance in this field, particularly from the musical angle; in the second place I am passionately interested in, and proud of, the movement as a whole (it has a vitality and gusto which seem to be vanishing from the professional theatre).

My own close acquaintance with the "amateurs" began twenty years ago when *Good Night, Vienna,* until then a radio and film story, was adapted for amateur stage performance. Attending productions of this play in different parts of the country, I had many good times and made many good friends; it seemed to me then to be a matter of national importance that singers, young and old, should be finding expression for their love of music, and gaining practical experience of the theatre, in this way.

The war, of course, "put paid" to a great deal of this activity, but within a few months of VJ Day the majority of societies were back in harness with ambitious plans for the future and I promised myself that as long as I was in business as a writer and producer of musical plays I would give a proportion of my time every year to writing for them and assisting them in any other ways possible.

Since 1946 I have adapted for amateur performance six of my own professional productions: *Balalaika*, *Magyar Melody*, *Waltz without End*, *Belinda Fair*, *Carissima*, and *Zip goes a Million!* In addition I have prepared amateur versions of four other musical comedy classics: *Die Fledermaus*, *The Dubarry*, *Night in Venice*, and (most recently) *Three Waltzes*.

Authors setting out to write or adapt for the amateur theatre would be well-advised to study the amateur operatic societies' requirements. In the first place the pride and glory of most societies, especially in Wales and the North of England, are their choruses. We of the professional theatre, who are, for reasons of expense, generally confined to choruses of twenty-four voices or less, listen with envy and admiration to the ensembles of fifty or more voices put forward by the "amateurs" as well as to the precise and beautiful quality of their singing. The average operatic society looks upon its chorus not only as its main support but as a principal attraction to audiences—and it is therefore almost essential, if a musical play is to be successful in this field, that its vocal score should provide liberally for chorus work. In the case of *Pink Champagne* (*Die Fledermaus*) my partner, Bernard Grun and I introduced chorus songs in Acts One and Three which are non-existent in the famous original.

Many societies today have the assistance of a local dancing troupe and, this being so, it is advisable to introduce an element of ballet into the score (though this should be, if possible, optional, since certain societies, principally the smaller ones, cannot call upon dancers). It is generally best to keep ballet, as far as choreography is concerned, as simple as possible—though I have been astonished at some of the performances given of the rather elaborate and modernistic "Reflections Ballet" which is an important feature of *Balalaika*!

I said a word above about the "smaller" societies. These do not always receive the publicity awarded to those larger groups in the big provincial centres which have the advantage of playing upon well-equipped stages in theatres and cinemas. But the Little Brothers are important all the same; their work is the backbone of the movement. For their purposes a play demanding heavy scenery, with many "changes", is practically impossible. Equally a play that requires many and elaborate costumes may well be beyond their reach financially. For this reason a writer designing a production for amateur presentation on the widest possible scale will be well-advised to reduce scene changes to a minimum and provide for a simple costume-plot. Recently in the cast of *Three Waltzes*, my own ingenuity was taxed to find a means of reducing an original scene-plot of ten changes to three full-stage settings, together with three small "insets" based upon a rearrangement of the same set of screens. One must remember that much amateur operatic production takes place upon the tiny stages of church halls, working men's institutes and so on. And it should not be forgotten, either, in the matter of taste, that certain plots, situations, lines and lyrics, acceptable in the West End theatre, may excite adverse criticism elsewhere.

It is interesting to note that as far as the amateur operatic stage is concerned, acting, as apart from singing, has improved immeasurably since the war. This is, in part certainly, a reflection of a similar trend in the professional theatre; the modern type of musical play, especially that imported from U.S.A., presents a more "real-life" set of characters than those of the old-time operettas, in which the ability to "stand up and sing" was usually the most required of Our Hero and Our Heroine. The upper voices, high soprano and tenor, very seldom go with acting ability; this being so, there is a tendency today to write leading singing parts within the average soprano and baritone ranges.

The principal source of play material for the amateur operatic stage must almost inevitably be the West End theatre. A long London run alone provides the national publicity necessary to make an amateur production "sure-fire box office". Audiences all over the country want to see their friends performing in plays they know of (even if they may never have seen them before) and singing music that comes regularly over the radio. I found this out to my cost when George Posford and I wrote *Masquerade* specially for amateur production; societies performing it (and many of them still do so every year) admit to having enjoyed the play immensely, found it musically effective and easy to present, but a number of them complained that the fact that it has no "West End name" slows up the sale of tickets! And that sale of tickets is all-important to all but a few wealthy groups, for with the inevitable increase in production costs, and the retention of the iniquitous entertainment tax, "sold out" notices are almost essential.

Unfortunately for the movement the West End has not of recent years provided the mine of material necessary to keep the pot boiling. The Theatre of years ago handed on such cast-iron favourites as the Savoy operas, *The Arcadians*, *Rose Marie*, *The Desert Song*, *The Student Prince*, etc., in the footsteps of which followed Ivor Novello with a fine handful of operettas with stirring popular scores. Today alas, the picture is quite otherwise! The societies in general prefer a score of the operetta type, with "big" choral opportunities, to the "song and dance" type of show. Nowadays most of the big shows seem to reach London from America, and all but a few of these have neither the singing opportunities nor the story setting which the amateurs require. Some years ago now *Annie, Get your Gun*, when first released for amateur production achieved many productions in its first season, then in succeeding years began to pass out of the repertoire. More recently *Oklahoma* has swept the country in a similar way, but one wonders if it will last. Such shows, great though they may be, contain too little choral work and too difficult dancing for the amateurs, while the American accent is not greatly favoured away from the big provincial cities.

The situation would be simpler if the demand of the societies for new shows was not insatiable. In the old days it was possible for them to attract regular audiences with the intermittent re-revival of the great "old ones", but this is no longer the case. Thirty years ago, when the public was comparatively starved of musical entertainment, the annual outing to the local amateur show was an event eagerly looked forward to. Today, thanks to radio, television, gramophone and talkies, we are almost literally drenched with popular music, and, this being so, amateur societies' productions, to bring in the audience, must have an element of novelty and adventure. A most important member of the committee is the Publicity Man; he wants a "story" for the local press —and the revival of *Iolanthe* does not, in most cases, constitute a "story"!

Until the London theatre spawns a new shoal of musical plays suitable for amateur production, where is the material for amateur production to come from? That is a question which anxious secretaries, as well as the publishers of musical plays, are asking themselves. It was with this problem in mind that I went in search of old favourites which had not yet been made available for amateurs, and came up with *The Dubarry*, etc. *Three Waltzes*, in which Evelyn Laye made a big success during the war, has been my latest effort in this direction, though I have gone back to the original and more spectacular Austrian version of the play for my adaptation. I have other similar projects in mind; also two new plays due for professional production, which should provide, if they are successful, the sort of material the societies are looking for. For new material must be found; the movement is increasing yearly in numbers as well as ambition.

I have seen amateur musical productions in every part of the country, in miners' institutes and on improvised stages in aerodrome hangars, as well as in the largest theatres and cinemas (where the "amateurs" in many cases afford the manager his most profitable week of the year!). In general the standards of both singing and acting are first-class (I would guarantee to recruit from the movement as a whole at least half a dozen composite companies, principals and chorus, with a perfectly professional polish). I have taken many experienced actors and producers for their first visit to an "amateur show" and noticed with sheer delight, though not with surprise, their amazement at the standard of singing, acting and presentation alike.

I have spoken often to the big executives of sound radio and television, urging them to publicize the Amateur Operatic Movement, and at the same time interest the vast body of its supporters, by broadcasting a series of classic musical plays performed by societies from various parts of the kingdom. Unfortunately my plea has so far fallen upon deaf ears. A sad waste of material, but understandable perhaps in view of present unemployment among professional actors and actresses; Actor's Equity is making a brave fight for its members, challenging any invasion of the field of paid entertainment by "part-timers".

The further you get away from the big cities, the more vital the movement becomes; in the smaller centres the activities of the local operatic society are throughout the year an important integral part of the life of the community; performers and audience alike follow with the closest interest the progress of the annual production. First the committee, with its producer and musical director, meets to discuss the choice of play. This is primarily a practical matter. Can we afford the cost of royalties, the expenses for scenery and costumes? Will there be enough work to keep our chorus and dancers busy and interested through the long months of rehearsal? Can we cast the principal parts with suitable actors? Are our stage facilities adequate? Has the play been recently produced in the immediate neighbourhood? Many, and often acrimonious, are the meetings before a vote can be finally taken and a choice made.

Next comes the casting problem. Certain societies are content to rely upon established local stars for the leading parts; the same popular and often accomplished figures appear on the bills year after year. I am glad to say, however, that of recent years I have noticed a healthy change in this procedure; today more societies than ever are encouraging newcomers—a departure which can only be a stimulus to the rank and file, leading to the discovery of hidden talent. Many amateur producers nowadays insist upon holding auditions for every principal role. This is to be commended.

The period of rehearsal varies considerably with local conditions; in outlying centres where, particularly during the winter evenings, there are comparatively few rival activities, rehearsal may be spread over six months; in the larger towns, they are often concentrated within a far shorter period. Music practice usually comes first; vocal scores in hand, chorus and principals under the baton of the musical director, familiarize themselves with the music until such time as they are able to "do without the book". After this the principals are concentrated upon their acting and singing scenes, to be joined in the final stages by the chorus and dancers for the slow and patient building-up of the ensembles.

During all this time the "back-room boys" are as busy as beavers. Estimates are sought for the hire of scenery and costumes. The producer prepares his dress-plot, the wardrobe mistress goes into the matter of measurements. The stage manager, having received the ground-plan of the scenery, marks out the floor at rehearsals so that his actors may become familiar with the area at their disposal, the positioning of exits and so on. The ticket secretary plans his sales campaign and canvasses advertisements for the programme. The publicity brigade is working on the local press. The prompter is studying his script. And a band of willing helpers are seeing to such mundane details as the matter of refreshments at rehearsals and after-hours transport for the cast.

This is the real Show Business—unpaid replica of life behind the scenes in the professional theatre—the stage slang, the etiquette, even the superstitions of Shaftesbury Avenue. And then comes the Great Day—the flowers, the telegrams, the "first-night nerves", the curtain calls, the speeches, the successes and failures of the Real Theatre (which, believe me, is no more real than this in its enthusiasm and hard work). For a succession of magical evenings Miss Smith becomes Evelyn Laye, Mr. Smith a Bruce Trent or a Norman Wisdom. There are the dressing-room parties and dressing-room gossip, the eager scanning of the newspapers for "notices", the regretful farewells at the "end of the run". The day after that exciting last night Miss Smith is once more the stenographer, Mr. Jones the cashier at the bank.

It should be plain, even to the moguls of Westminster (who occasionally appear to know very little of the life of the country they govern), that such activities are of the very greatest benefit to the social and artistic life of the country, and should not, therefore, be hampered, even made impossible, by the retention of Entertainment Tax, the enforced payment of which in the majority of cases makes the difference between profit and loss to the operatic societies. The movement, headed by N.O.D.A. and supported by a small body of understanding Members of Parliament, has for years fought for the abolition of this tax; up to the time of writing the struggle has proved unsuccessful.

Since the sad death of Ivor Novello the professional stage has provided little for the amateurs in the way of spectacular operetta featuring a large chorus with plenty of work to do. Apart from *Song of Norway*, few recent importations from Broadway have catered for the societies that look to London for their material. Messrs. Rodgers and Hammerstein in their series of remarkable successes have seldom given any great opportunity for choral singing, while the ballets which have been a feature of their productions demand a modernistic, acrobatic technique which is beyond the reach of all but a few amateur ballerinas. Of their rivals the least purely American is Irving Berlin, though neither *Annie, Get your Gun* nor *Call me Madam*, his two biggest post-war hits, affords really enough for amateur choruses. The rest—*Kiss Me Kate, Guys and Dolls, Wonderful Town*, etc.—have been frankly high-speed, rowdy song-and-dance shows which, even supposing they were to be made available for amateur production, would hardly attract a following.

When will the pendulum swing back again? It is to be hoped soon, for the amateur stage, increasing in strength and numbers every season, is greedy for new material! There is this to be said, however, for the London impresarios who seem to be starving us by their importation of American wares, that the cost of staging musical plays professionally, which has increased almost threefold since before the war, makes experiment in this field extremely costly. A "straight" play with one or two simple settings and a cast of a dozen characters can be "tried out" at the cost of a few thousand pounds, but there is no way of testing a musical show except by investing in a large cast, elaborate costumes, scenery, orchestrations, etc., at a cost of between £15,000 and £40,000. For this reason the London theatre-men prefer to "play safe" by bringing over from Broadway shows which by a process of trial-and-error have already proved their worth as entertainment.

Who, then, is to come to the rescue of the amateur movement with new material? Possibly the overlords of commercial television? There has not so far been an outstanding musical production on T.V. When it does come, it will be certain of an enthusiastic press and a nation-wide audience, both essential if a play is eventually to prove "box office" for the amateurs. I have had personal experience of the power of broadcasting to create amateur interest in a musical play that had never seen the light of day in the theatre; *Good Night, Vienna*, still, after twenty years a top-liner in the amateur repertory, was a radio operetta before everything.

To conclude this short essay may I return to my original premise: why am I, after nearly thirty years' battle in the professional field, so die-hard an enthusiast for the amateur movement? The answer is, because those who give their spare time, sometimes their lives, to it are both artists and enthusiasts; they are keeping alive a tradition of singing which in the professional theatre, with the aid of the ubiquitous microphone, has been reduced to either wailing or chirruping; their motto is "Make your own entertainment"—and that in a world where the rest of the people are seemingly content to absorb their entertainment at second hand.

Some years ago I was invited to a mining valley in South Wales to

P

witness a revival of one of my plays in the local Miners' Institute. I drove precariously from Neath through a blanket of fog, expecting from the description "Miners' Institute" to find myself in some sort of converted Nissen hut. As it turned out, the institute contained a two-tier theatre with room for 800 people; the switchboard was ultra-modern, an orchestra pit accommodated a band of over twenty musicians. When I went backstage at the end of the evening the local secretary apologized for cutting some twenty minutes out of the script. "I am sorry, man," he said, "but we have to finish in good time: most of the men, you see, have to go down the pits on the night shift!" And there in the dressing-room were our actors, skinning out of eighteenth-century doublets into their miners' overalls. Had I ever doubted the value of the amateur operatic movement, my doubts would have been then and there dispelled. And, believe it or not, there were tears in my eyes!

XVII. AMATEURS AND CHILDREN'S THEATRE

by Lois McLean

CHILDREN'S Theatre is a field in which amateurs can do excellent work, and a field that is as yet largely unexplored. There are a few good professional companies which tour Britain, playing in schools, halls and theatres, but there are not nearly enough to go round. They are usually able to play in a community only once or twice a year. Many remote villages and even certain sections of cities are not included on their busy schedules, and thus many many children never have the chance to see a play written and produced exclusively for them.

An annual outing to a pantomime is the only theatre experience countless British children have. And only those living in or near large centres have the dubious privilege of attending these shows which in so many cases are merely glorified adult revues, in which music-hall artistes and crooners do their "turn" which has no connection with the story supposedly being told. I suppose the child derives a certain pleasure from the garish colours, the lighting effects and the tricks employed in pantos, but how his favourite stories are mutilated beyond recognition! I shall always remember a wee Scots boy asking me at the end of a Glasgow panto, "But what happened tae Aladdin? I canna remember." Small wonder! Poor Aladdin was lost in a conglomeration of modern ballads, kilt parades, dance spectacles, acrobatics and bad shady jokes. Let the grown-ups go to the pantos, and let the children have a theatre of their very own.

This is where amateurs who are willing to work and experiment will find the most exciting audiences in the world. I count acting and producing for children, and sitting in an auditorium or outdoors watching their faces as a play mounted in excitement, among my most exhilarating and often moving theatre experiences.

There are varying conceptions as to just what children's theatre is. My own, and that of many others, is that it means plays specially written and acted *for* children but not *by* them. When children act their own plays we enter the realm of creative child drama, which very important field is outside this present chapter. Nevertheless good children's theatre should give youngsters an impetus towards creating their own plays, and although they are not onstage they should feel a part of the production as a whole.

Amateurs are in a splendid position to create children's theatre. They haven't the large financial problems which beset professional groups; they have more time at their disposal for study, rehearsal and preparation; they often have a permanent organization which will ensure the continuation of a programme over the years; many little theatres have their own playhouses in which to play to children; through living in a community, amateurs best know the particular needs of the young people and the conditions under which they will have to play; local societies can often enlist the aid of allied organizations, clubs, business people, educational authorities, etc., more easily than strangers who visit the community only occasionally; and perhaps most important of all, amateurs may be the parents and relatives of their audiences and thus the first to recognize the worth of children's theatre to their children and themselves.

Many amateur groups present annual Christmas plays for children, which are highly commendable, but too isolated. A once-a-year production is only a consolation prize. Regular monthly plays are of far greater value. Of course the number will depend upon the size of the community and society. It may be possible to produce only three plays a year, but by touring these to various parts of the city or to neighbouring towns and villages, a large number of children will be reached. It is hard, exhausting work, and not suitable for the faint-hearted or the slipshod. But then no theatre activity is suitable for these.

I believe that a children's theatre scheme would attract amateur societies' younger members, whose zeal, when aroused, knows no bounds. Too often young members in their late teens and early twenties find themselves almost outcasts in a little theatre. They would like to work in the theatre, but don't fit into the casts of many adult plays. They need experience, but classes and lectures, with occasional performances to "members only" audiences, don't give them the practical experience they would get playing to lively children. Teenagers are full of fresh ideas, and so close to childhood themselves that they know almost instinctively how to "come across" to their audiences, and what children like or dislike. Many established old stagers could learn a lot watching young adults play to children. At the end of this article I will give in detail a report of just such a children's theatre, composed of young people between fifteen and twenty years of age.

Children's theatre should not ignore completely the older actors, technicians, etc. They are most necessary for a correct balance. There is no better medicine than a child audience for an experienced player who has fallen into lazy mannerisms and technical tricks. He will soon find that he must start to think anew, really believe in the part he is playing, polish up his diction and movement, and generally revitalize his approach to acting. For you cannot fool the children. They are as sharp as the wisest critics and twice as loud in their criticism as well as their praise.

Before attempting a children's play it is wise for the actors, especially the inexperienced, to undergo a period of training and practice. Older members of the society may guide this training, and it might be a good idea to have a professional instructor, preferably someone with experience in playing for children. The training should be aimed at developing Concentration, Improvisation and Sincerity. An appreciation of these qualities is a *must* for the greatest effect in acting for children. No matter what happens in the audience or around him, the actor should be so used to *concentrating* on the job in hand that he keeps on playing even though little Willie in his excitement tosses his hat in the air and it lands at the actor's feet. The actor should be able to *improvise* upon any occasion, and in children's theatre there should be no sign of a prompter. If lines are forgotten they should be improvised until the story continues in the usual way. If the audience reaction is so strong that dialogue must cease the actor must be able to improvise action, never once dropping out of character. And above all, the children's actor must be *sincere*. He must never play down to his audience. He must accept them as seriously as they do him. Only when he creates a sense of "oneness" between the children and himself will he succeed in his purpose.

The training programme should also include work in Speech and Movement. Children must hear the actors clearly or they will become restless. Polished movement heightens both characterization and the action of the story.

Once training is well under way it is time to think of choosing a play, and this will be difficult for there are few plays now written that are suitable for children. Too many are too full of words. Children like action, and ruthless cutting of extraneous talk is recommended for most children's plays. Writers are scarce who really understand the child mind and can write words and actions that children will understand and enjoy. They need a character with whom they can identify themselves, a problem for him to solve, and complications arising on the way to the solution. Children should not be preached to. Any morals involved must come out of the story, not be merely superimposed rules of conduct.

It is often best to make up a play from a well-known story. Children never tire of their favourite tales, and love to recognize "Little Red Riding Hood", "Jack the Giant Killer" or "Hansel and Gretel" coming to life upon the stage.

Different age levels require different material. The five- to seven-year-olds like to see nursery rhyme characters in simple gay scenes, with a minimum of dialogue, and action that is neither too swift for them to comprehend nor characters too violent for their tiny feelings.

From eight to eleven years more lusty tales are appreciated, with plenty of action and again not too much dialogue. This age group likes adventurous fairy tales and stories of exploration and simple scientific wonders. They are very impressed by a few tricks, like cupboards that pop open without a visible cause, objects that float on stage supported by invisible strings, etc.

When children are between twelve and fifteen they begin to develop more sophisticated tastes, and this is perhaps the most difficult age group of all to play and write for. They are past fairy tales, can see through a good many tricks, and although they still like action, they want something more in the way of words and ideas. They will accept serious material as well as the humorous. Carefully adapted excerpts from classics like *Treasure Island, Ivanhoe* and *Tom Sawyer* may be tried. This is the right time to introduce Shakespeare, with scenes from comedies like *A Midsummer Night's Dream, The Tempest*, and *As You Like It*. Given a bright, active and understanding production young people may be persuaded to enjoy Shakespeare from the very first, instead of finding him boring because of tedious lengthy readings in a class-room.

Once the play is chosen or written it should be carefully rehearsed, and I believe that the actors should also have a hand in preparing the sets, costumes, properties, etc. This gives them a sense of the importance of every department, and an understanding of the difficulties, problems and techniques involved. It is particularly valuable for the training of young children's theatre actors.

Every aspect of the staging should be aimed at making the *story* a vivid memory. Only the basic essentials of a setting are needed. Too much furniture, shrubbery, etc., and too many properties are merely confusing and lead attention away from the main theme and characters. Colour should be of prime importance throughout. Gay costumes are an absolute necessity, even if the settings are plain curtains. Lighting is useful as long as it does not dominate and cause the effects to be more memorable than the story.

Audience participation is greatly to be encouraged throughout the play. This is most successful if the actors are on the same floor level as the children, and action flows out among them. Characters in the play may address the children, asking them to mime certain actions or to help the hero by calling out a certain word or name at a given signal. They may be asked a question at a crucial moment in the plot—the classic example of this being in *Peter Pan*, when, in order to save Tinkerbell's life, Peter calls out "Do you believe in fairies?" The children always answer "Yes!", and by thus saving the situation they have a real sense of belonging to the play.

Children love a simple tune, and if it is sung several times during the play they will go home humming it. They may even be encouraged to join in at certain points in the play. Because it catches the attention immediately, music is invaluable for beginning a performance. Talking and giggling will stop immediately music starts, but it should not be played too long before the curtain rises or restlessness will occur.

In all phases of the production it is important that nothing continue too long, or it becomes monotonous. Certainly the performance as a whole must not last too long. I recently saw an excellent professional children's theatre company play in a school near London, and my only quarrel with a beautiful production was its length. Cut by half an hour it would have been almost perfect, but in that extra time the children grew tired of sitting, and their minds were taking in just those few too many ideas. They were polite to the end, but I felt they would have enjoyed it all so much more had the play been shorter. Time varies with age groups, but I would say very young children should not be played to longer than one hour, this hour to include an interval of say ten minutes, during which they are allowed to stand, stretch, walk about. The twelve- to fifteen-year-olds can take a longer play, say one and a half to two hours with one or two intervals.

It would be a great step ahead if children could look forward to attending regular Saturday morning or early evening performances in their own local little theatres, halls or even in their schools by arrangement with the educational authorities. A stage is not necessary—only floor space, for wonderfully satisfying results are obtained by playing in the middle of a circle of children, or at one side of a room with the audience in a semi-circle.

Outdoor performances are a wonderful experience too, and very useful if no other accommodation is available. It seems to me that many British school and community playgrounds could be put to good use for children's theatre during summer holidays. There are certain grim grounds I know in London's Paddington and Camden Town, Glasgow's Bridgeton and Gorbals, and Dublin's Coombe, to mention only a few, which could well be brightened up by outdoor plays and wide-eyed audiences. But it is not the playground that is important— it is the children who live roundabout, many of whom spend their entire holiday playing in the streets, up and down the open closes, or on the grimy banks of a canal. Children's theatre couldn't take them away physically, but it might transport them in imagination to far-away lands, and turn them all into princesses and adventurous wanderers for a little while. The effects would linger afterwards and enter their own play in their own streets.

I would now like to tell about a two-month children's theatre season with which I was associated in Edmonton, Canada. A few years ago this city of some 160,000 formed a civic Recreation Commission whose main occupation was the promotion of sport, until a small group of six interested people, representing local teachers, members of the amateur Community Theatre and drama lecturers, got together and persuaded the Commission to sponsor a children's theatre. This sponsorship entailed a sum of money (approximately £20) given for sets and costumes; use of a van for transport; use of the Commission's premises for rehearsals and its playgrounds throughout the city for performances. The directors and instructors (the six people mentioned above) donated their services, and the actors were young people between fifteen and twenty years of age recruited from the city's high schools, shops and offices.

The young actors created their own theatre. The boards of the stage were blades of springy green grass, the auditorium was the whole outdoors, a gigantic spotlight was provided by the setting sun, and the audience sat on the earth before the players. The only concession to orthodox theatricality was a background of folding screens which withheld the surprises of the production from the audience until the proper time. These screens, together with a make-believe tree, a large wooden box, a table, two chairs, a few props and colourful costumes, formed the entire equipment of the travelling company.

Despite one of the rainiest summers in many years it was not necessary to cancel any performances, although several had to be postponed and presented on later, sunny days. Twelve performances were given in all, to an average audience of 200.

For a period of three months before the season began the group met once a week for classes in acting, speech and stagecrafts. Early in June, two short plays were cast and put into rehearsal. They were *Little Black Sambo*, based on the well-known story and incorporating characters and dialogue improvised by the cast; and *Circus Day*, written and produced by one of the group's directors. Sets and properties were made by the casts aided by members of the Community Theatre's technical staff. Costumes were designed by a high school drama teacher and sewn by members of the company.

By June 30th everything was ready for the first performance. Each week from then until the end of August saw at least one, often two, performances. Rehearsals were continued throughout the summer because each play was double cast to accommodate holidays and jobs.

Distractions for the actors were many. At various times there were low-flying aeroplanes, baseball games on the same grounds, breezes that threatened to blow away the braced screens and the props, barking dogs who enjoyed fighting with the "tigers" in "Sambo", a pipe band practising in a neighbouring field, a loudspeaker blaring advertising from a travelling van, the chug, chug of trains in a round-house a few hundred feet away, the threat of rain, the music of a merry-go-round very near, and, of course, the continual hum of traffic on nearby roads. That summer was a fine lesson for the players in concentration and bright, vivid playing to keep audience attention.

Perhaps one might best visualize a performance by following through the schedule of a typical evening. About 5.30 p.m. a van pulls up on to a playground, and from it are unloaded the aforementioned equipment. Soon the players appear from all corners of the city, by bicycle, bus, and on foot. Busy hands set up the screens on a good patch of grass, at an angle to prevent the sun from shining directly into the eyes of actors and audience. Costumes are unpacked from the gay red and yellow box marked "HI" in big letters. This box doubles as a property in *Circus Day* later on. While costumes are being ironed in the small playground equipment hut, make-up is being applied by the actors. Within an hour of the first arrival most of the cast is in costume, practising lines, munching sandwiches or just relaxing until . . . well it can't be called "curtain" time for there is no curtain . . . until performance time.

Soon groups of small, medium and large children, many of whom have brought parents along, begin to assemble on the grounds. They are seated by the Playground Supervisor and volunteer assistants, in front of the screens. Excitement mounts as the play time, usually 7 o'clock, draws near. "What are we going to see?" "Is it a film?" "Will there be really truly tigers?" "When are the clowns coming?" "Gosh, I wish it would hurry and start!"

In the hut the actors take a few deep breaths before going out. Although most have played the same roles several times, they always feel a little nervous before facing their audience. They know they will be playing to uninhibited critics who instinctively know a good performance and can be vociferous about a bad one.

Now it's time. A Barker strolls jauntily out front, while the rest of the cast steals quietly behind the screens. "Hurry, hurry, hurry, boys and girls! Get set! The Children's Theatre is here . . . ready to make you roll on the grass with its fun! Ready there, little lady? Comfortable, young man? Then, we're off!" Cane flashing, jumping from here to there, the Barker introduces the characters in the first play. Then off he goes as Black Mumbo shuffles on to begin *Little Black Sambo*.

The children are transported to Sambo's jungle garden, suggested by a lone tree which is accepted as thick foliage in their imaginations. Excitement builds as Sambo is left alone in his bright new clothes and is accosted by ferocious tigers of various sizes and shapes, each with a distinctly different personality and way of speaking. One by one they threaten to eat him, and little by little he gives away articles of clothing to save himself. One tiger with a 6-foot-long tail wraps it around Sambo and dances with him. Another goes to sleep and Sambo trips over him. At each new incident audience participation grows. One very small girl forgets herself completely and shouts, "Watch out, Mr. Tiger!", as Sambo backs towards the sleeping one. Eventually the tigers, each in a piece of Sambo's finery, become angry with one another as rivalry mounts over who is the handsomest tiger in the jungle. They begin to fight, chasing each other behind the screens. Yellow slabs (of dyed gauze) come floating over the top, and everyone knows that the tigers have fought themselves into butter. Everything is put to rights when Black Jumbo, coming home from work, discovers the butter, gathers it up, and Black Mumbo promises to make pancakes with it for supper.

Great sighs come from the audience as *Black Sambo* is finished, and the Barker reappears with the advice, "Stand up and stretch a while . . . a mile high if you want to . . . but be sure to be back in your places after the scene is changed for *Circus Day*."

Quickly the stage crew brings out brightly painted circus pictures, which when fastened on to the screens form a semi-circular background of gay clowns, elephants, and bareback riders. The table, chairs and the "HI" box are carried on. In the hut actors hurriedly slip out of tiger suits or rub off dark brown make-up and climb into clown suits, tramp clothes or tights, for most of the players appear in both plays. After a ten-minute break the show is ready to start again.

Out comes the Barker, down sit the children, and on comes *Circus Day*. The Barker explains, "Now we're going into a circus clown's tent to find out what happens to a little girl . . . just like some of you . . . who wants to join the circus."

For the next half hour the children watch in varying stages of hilarity, suspense and wonder as they view the adventures of Lorie and her Grandmother (who likes to tell tall stories about when she was in the circus). Lorie steals into his tent when Hi, the Happy Tramp Clown, isn't looking, hides in his big box, and gradually reaches out to take all the sweets from a bag placed near the box. Hi, amazed by the sudden disappearance of his sweets, finally, with the aid of Betsy, a Bareback Rider, discovers Lorie in his box. He lets her watch as he puts on his clown make-up. Then two other clowns, Biff and Buff, come in to practise their new trick. This is a mimed fight with oversize wooden swords, during which they are continually losing one another. Buff finally runs his sword between Biff's arm and body, and Biff falls "dead". After mourning a little and wringing tears from a large handkerchief over Biff's body, Buff decides to hide the body in Hi's box. There follow a series of hilarious stunts by the body in the box, to the complete puzzlement of Buff. The whole trick ends with Lorie and Hi's applause combined with that of the young audience.

The clown trick is aided by helpful comments from the spectators, such as, "He's in the box." "Look over there . . . behind you." "Don't cry, he's not *really* dead." or "Oh Buff, don't hurt Biff!"

To round the play off, Lorie learns some of Hi's stunts, tries on a too-big tramp clown suit, and Gran is chased by a circus "horse" (with Biff and Buff inside it). Lorie and Hi, now called Hi and Lo, do a stunt involving tramp bundles, an oversize hotdog, and long, long strings of sausages. This convinces Gran that it will be all right for Lorie to join the circus for a week, providing that she too can stay to share in the excitement. All ends happily as Lorie leads the circus parade round the audience, beating a loud drum.

The Barker brings up the rear of the parade, and as it disappears behind the screens he pops back to say, "That's all, boys and girls. See you again next year!" The children's theatre performance is over.

Several children run "onstage" to examine the sausages, swords, and other props, but nobody takes anything away when it's explained that all is needed again for the next performance. One little girl asks, "Are you coming back next week?" A small boy says, "Do you need any boy actors? I've had experience in school concerts." Still another repeats Lorie's line, "Golly, I wish I was in the circus!" A parent remarks, "This was the first play my children have seen. They were thrilled, and so was I." Everyone says, "Come back again!"

Soon actors are out of costumes and make-up. All the scenery is packed on to the van ready to go. The playground is empty. It's getting dark. The last child can be heard shouting as he runs home, "I'm Biff . . . I'm Buff . . . I leap, I run! . . ." The last actor leaves, feeling tired but very satisfied. There's nothing left but a few scraps of programmes fluttering a little on the grass as the moon rises.

XVIII. DRAMA FESTIVALS
by C. B. PURDOM

THE idea of a Festival is part of the very nature of Drama. For the drama is a public and social not a private affair; it depends upon an occasion and an audience, and is an expression of general rejoicing. We are reminded of this fact in the drama festival, when teams of players meet to offer to an audience the results of their work, and to invite the audience to share their enjoyment in it. For that reason drama festivals have become regular events in social life throughout the British Isles, though in their present form they are no more than thirty years old.

In fact, the drama festival restores to drama its ancient meaning; for classical Greek drama, from which our modern drama originates, was festival drama and nothing else. To think of drama apart from festival would have been impossible in ancient Athens, and the drama festivals now held throughout Great Britain and in many other parts of the world, remind us of what drama essentially is.

Drama comprises play, actors and audience, and all three elements are essential. There can be no drama without the play, which is an imaginative presentation of human life in action. Drama consists of words, but not any words; only words that contain thought, express character and convey action. Therefore, drama is a particular kind of poetic writing, to be spoken by actors who represent what is said and done. Although plays are mostly written in what is called prose, their language is essentially poetic: speech charged with emotion. Therefore, drama depends upon actors, who must possess skill in speech and movement, who are able to convince an audience of the truth of the characters and situation presented to them, and can hold the attention of the audience. Therefore, drama requires an audience for whose sake everything is done, to whom the play is addressed, and for whom the actors speak and move.

All this is carried out under conditions of festival, a gathering of people who come together to participate in an experience, for the situation presented in the play by the actors concerns human experience, in the imaginative re-creation of which all are invited to share.

It will be seen that I put the drama festival in a very high place. Of course there are other elements, in particular there are fun and entertainment, but unless festivals are regarded as more socially important than mere amusement, they will be certain to miss the mark. I am all for approaching festivals in high spirits, with excitement and joy, and I am all against heaviness and gloom; but unless festivals are looked upon as expressions of social life, having meaning for all who take part in them, with meaning especially for their audiences, their value is largely lost. In the great days of Athens every citizen was expected to attend the drama festivals; and though there is no compulsion upon audiences today, everyone who can do so should attend, because the festival gives pleasure and a sense of life that are not found elsewhere.

Of course, at a drama festival teams of players come to show what they can do. Most of them do well, because they have prepared well beforehand. A few do not, because they have perhaps not worked hard enough. A festival, therefore, is a test, and the element of a test has always been present in drama festivals. It is part of the pleasure of the audience to share in the test, for the final result of all dramatic performances is judged by what happens to the audience. At a drama festival, therefore, the audience is not passive: it does not sit there merely waiting to receive. To the audience belongs the judgment, which it can exercise only by its active participation in the performance. I will explain what I mean by this later on.

FESTIVAL ORGANIZATION

It follows from what has been said that a drama festival should be organized as a social occasion. The particular way in which it is organized depends upon circumstances. It may be part of a national festival organized in England or Wales by the British Drama League, or in Scotland by the Scottish Community Drama Association. It may by organized by members of the Amateur Drama Council of Ireland; or it may be part of the Women's Institutes' or Townswomen's Guilds' national or regional festivals; or part of a federal festival by some other national body. In all these instances the organization will be governed by national or regional rules, and the conditions and methods are laid down for the organizers. But always the three elements of play, actors, and audience are the factors to which attention has to be given. If any one element is neglected the festival suffers, so that the mere fact of being part of a national festival will not ensure success for a particular festival. Solid work has to be put into the organization, nothing being left to chance, or the results will be disappointing.

The majority of drama festivals throughout England and Wales are organized locally. Among them are many well-established, admirably organized and highly esteemed festivals. They are mostly found in smallish towns, where they are given strong and regular public support. The drama festival week is an event to which people look forward, and there is no doubt that they make a valuable contribution to social life.

Why are these festivals so successful? The answer is that they are thoroughly well organized. Each festival has a committee of people and officers who give careful attention to every aspect of the work involved, and competently carry it out. Fundamentally, success is invariably due to good organization. All concerned think that what they set out to do is worth doing, and they spare no effort to do it well. Thus they gain the respect of competing teams and of the public. The teams know they will be well looked after when they come to the festival, and the public know that a really good festival of interesting plays, reasonably well performed, will be offered each evening.

The original drama festivals in this country consisted of one-act plays, or excerpts from longer plays. These one-act play festivals continue, but more and more festivals are devoted to full-length plays. The one-act play festival is especially useful for new societies or for the less experienced players of established societies. Many active societies, however, do not want to devote time to one-act plays, for which there may be little scope in their normal work. For that reason, among others, the inclusion of single acts from full-length plays should be allowed. Although the one-act play provides variety, for three or four different plays can be performed each evening by the same number of different teams, there can be no doubt that the most interesting programmes for a week's festival, providing opportunities for the best work, are offered by full-length play festivals.

The first requisite for a festival is a theatre or hall in which to hold it. Where a theatre with an equipped stage is available the festival is lucky. Where a good hall with an equipped stage can be got the festival is also lucky. Unfortunately, too few places have buildings of this kind, the lack of which is the greatest handicap that exists upon drama festivals. Only too often an improvised stage has to be put up in the best available building. This is a great obstacle to success.

The first question to think about is the composition of the festival committee. It should consist of people who are individually prepared to be active in the festival. It is useless merely having names. It is equally useless to have people who care only for their particular interests and nothing for the festival as a whole. Members of local dramatic societies should be on the committee, but if possible the majority should not be actively concerned with particular societies, but mainly interested in the festival as such. The officers, especially the secretary, must possess practical ability and enthusiasm. There is no need to detail what officers are required, beyond saying that a first-class stage manager is essential.

The rules of the festival must be carefully prepared, stating clearly the conditions under which the performances are to be done. The teams should not be tied down too rigidly. Maximum time limits for plays must be stated and adhered to, also the maximum time allowed for setting and striking scenes. But do not go to the length of showing the audience an empty stage, the committee having insisted upon the first team setting its scene within the time allowed, while the audience waits impatiently for the performance to start.

The selection of teams to take part has to be done bearing in mind the need to provide a programme that will interest the audience. When the festival is announced, six months or more beforehand, invitations to participate should be issued to dramatic societies in the neighbourhood, also possibly to those far away. In the invitations the nature of the festival, the facilities available, the expenses allowed, and the awards offered should be stated. Many festivals offer moderate money prizes, others do not; but arrangements should be made to meet the reasonable costs of competing teams by offering a fixed (usually low) sum to cover expenses.

An important duty of the committee is to select the teams to take part in the festival and the order in which they are to play. Well-established festivals invariably have many more applications than the number of teams they require, so that the committees concerned can select the ones they think will provide the best programme. The order in which the plays are given is sometimes decided by ballot, but the convenience of the teams and the attractive make-up of the programme are factors not to be neglected.

The provision of properties, curtains, lighting equipment, etc., are matters to which attention must be given, and full information provided to invited teams. The facilities for examination of the stage, and, if possible, rehearsal upon it, should also be made known.

The awards offered in the festival are matters of importance. In one-act plays there can be awards for various categories of plays, for original plays, for first performances, and so forth. The important thing is the award for the best performance, whatever the category of play. Some festivals have a large number of different awards. Probably the fewer the number of awards the better.

The date on which entries for the festival are to close; the entrance fee, if any; the penalty, if any, for withdrawing, are among the matters to be dealt with in the rules.

The system of marking for the awards must also be stated. Sometimes this is left to the adjudicator, but it is better to have it a rule, so that everyone knows what is to guide the adjudicator in making the awards. This brings us to one of the most important features of drama festivals, the adjudication, to which extended attention must be given.

ADJUDICATION

It belongs to the nature of drama festivals to be competitive. There are people who think that competition in such festivals is a mistake, but it is a fact that the greatest festivals in European history, which possessed a deeply religious character, were highly competitive. The Greek characteristic was moderation, yet their drama was always performed under competitive conditions. Therefore, there is no need for apology in making drama festivals competitive. Of course, there must be moderation in the competitive element, for it should not be paramount, but the vying with others in play and performance is a means of urging all concerned to do their best. It gives added importance as well as vitality and interest to the occasion.

Whether the festival is competitive or not an adjudication is required to make the festival complete. The adjudication is an examination of the work done and a judgment upon it. Therefore, the adjudication is a part of the festival on which much depends, for the teams perform to have their work examined and to get it judged. And much of the interest of the audience is in the adjudication, what the adjudicator has to say, and what his judgment is.

The adjudicator may be described in the words of an eminent judge as, "An impartial judge, a man of standing, secure in his position, who has nothing to fear, and no favour to get from the result, whatever it may be." Impartiality, standing, knowledge of the subject, and ability to express his judgment freely, are what are required in an adjudicator.

In the first place, the adjudicator approaches a drama festival as one of the audience. He sees the play, accepts it, and enters into it, as any other member of the audience, indeed, as the best of the audience. He should be looked upon as the ideal spectator for he represents the audience in an ideal capacity: that is to say, what he does this ideal audience should be able to do. Unless the adjudicator looks upon himself in this way he cannot begin to judge. If he were to come to the play as an outsider, keeping himself aloof, looking at it from a distance, not allowing himself to be appealed to by the players, unaffected by the emotions they seek to arouse, he would be unfitted to be a drama adjudicator. To accept the play as one of the audience is the adjudicator's first step.

In the second place he has to think about what he sees. He reacts to the performance as everyone who fully participates in it should, but in addition he thinks about his reactions. Criticism or judgment is not a description of what a critic or adjudicator *feels* about a performance, but the result of his *thought* about those feelings. This necessity for thought is what makes adjudication difficult. Many people, perhaps everybody, can say what they feel about what has been seen, but not everyone thinks about it, or thinks sufficiently, or thinks with knowledge. That is what an adjudicator has to do: he examines the work, and examines also his reactions to it, and offers in his adjudication the results of thought based upon knowledge of the subject.

No one is qualified to be an adjudicator who does not (1) have knowledge of the stage, the theatre and drama from practical experience and study, (2) is able to apply that knowledge to the performance he sees, and (3) has the skill to express the results of his thought.

Here the importance of a marking system comes in. Without a marking system the adjudicator can only judge as he thinks fit, taking account of any factors he pleases. A marking system causes the adjudicator to examine the performance in a certain way and disciplines his thinking about it. For example, were an adjudicator an expert in stage management, he would be inclined, left to himself, to judge the play mainly from the point of view of its staging, dressing, lighting, properties, and use of the stage by the players. These are all very important matters, and probably to the expert in them the most important; but the performance as a whole goes far beyond these technical stage details. The acting, the production, the play itself have techniques of their own, all related to one another, each to be distinguished and worthy of recognition, and an adjudicator has to take account of them all.

A marking system ensures that the adjudicator, if he uses it properly, takes account of everything that makes a performance, and gives due weight to each element. The marking system now generally recognized is as follows:

Presentation	10
Production	35
Acting	40
Enterprise and Achievement	15
	100

At one time it was usual to allow ten marks for choice of play, reducing production to thirty, and the last category to ten. There are still many festivals that retain the original system. The change was made because the grounds on which marks were awarded for choice of play were ambiguous, and because some adjudicators were too fond of saying that they "liked" or "disliked" particular plays. It is true that there is difficulty in allocating marks under this heading; but the difficulty is reduced if it is remembered that adjudicators are intended

Q

to recognize the team's knowledge, skill and taste in choosing the play, which means an estimate of the dramatic value of the piece chosen.

The value of this category of marks is that it enables the adjudicator to indicate his judgment upon the value of the choice.

However, as it is a fact that the quality of the play affects the performance as a whole (the best play offering the best opportunities to producer and players) the absence of separate marks for the play itself is not of great importance. The adjudicator must, however, keep in mind throughout his adjudication what the play has demanded of the players. An easy play demands little, a difficult play much; a play depending upon tricks of lighting or staging may demand much ability from lighting staff and producer, but ask much less of the players: these are factors the adjudicator has to recognize and to evaluate.

Presentation, that is to say, lighting, setting, properties, dressing, make-up, is allowed ten marks. In presentation amateurs can be as good as professionals. Often they are careless in these matters at drama festivals, because the difficulties of putting plays on on unfamiliar stages are too great for them. But by taking sufficient trouble those difficulties can largely, if not entirely, be overcome. Those teams who do take trouble deserve commendation, and in my own adjudicating I much more often give full marks under this heading than any other.

Production is concerned with the play as a whole. Good producers are rare because the number of people is small who can grasp the meaning of a play, the relation of the characters to each other, and how the actors should interpret their parts to bring out the dramatic value of the play. What I ask when I consider a production are three questions: (1) Do the members of the team show that they know what they have to do? (2) To what extent have they carried out what is required? (3) What is the dramatic value of what they have been required to do? These are all matters that concern the producer, and the answer to these questions provides an estimate of the value of the work of production. Of course, every production has faults; and even when a producer knows what is required he is often unable to get it done satisfactorily; but allowing for faults and failures in details, it is possible by applying the three questions I have formulated, to arrive at a sound judgment upon a production. Other adjudicators have different methods, but the aim is to judge the production as such, that is to say, the performance as a whole.

The largest number of marks are allocated to acting, which means that acting is the most important element. These marks are the most difficult to award because to judge the acting of a play as a whole requires great concentration on the part of the adjudicator, as well as much knowledge of the art of acting. Furthermore, amateurs have less opportunity of acquiring that art than any other of the techniques of the stage. In judging amateur acting one has to remember that many people have natural acting gifts. It is always very agreeable to see such actors, and what they do deserves to be praised. What must be remembered, however, is that the display of natural gifts is being observed, and not the work of an artist. Many leading players have started on the amateur stage, and indicated their natural abilities there, but as amateurs they were potential embryo actors, no more. To be able to detect this potential ability is extremely difficult, and few persons have the ability. It is easy to be deceived by an excess of natural powers. What I am leading up to is that adjudicators have to beware of over-praising acting at festivals. I can say with confidence that no responsible adjudicator ever says publicly of any amateur player that he or she should go upon the professional stage, or gives such praise as to indicate that that is his opinion. The reasons for this need hardly be stated. The stage is a greatly overcrowded profession, especially for women. A player excessively praised is almost invariably a girl. No more need be said.

What is looked for in the amateur actor is ability to speak well, to move well, to show that he or she understands the character, and, above all, indication of the use of imagination. All these are valuable qualities, and amateur playing serves a useful purpose in developing them. To know how to use the voice, how to stand, sit, and walk, and to have good physical posture are all possible; and the players who show that they have given attention to these matters deserve praise. The real justification for the great amount of effort put into amateur playing, and especially into drama festivals, is that the performance of plays offers an opportunity not to be rivalled by any other means of getting imaginative experience. By acting, people get the chance of entering into other lives than their own, of creating in their imagination, characters, situations, and actions different from their ordinary lives; which is of the greatest possible cultural value. Acting is a way of transforming one's own life. It enables the audience that enters into what the actor is doing, to do the same. This seems to me to make the drama festival worthwhile.

All these things the adjudicator has to bear in mind. He has to examine competence, to enter into the mind and heart of each performance and the festival as a whole. He has not to simplify, make allowances, excuse faults, overlook deficiencies, say soft things, appear to be encouraging. To be insincere is the worst fault an adjudicator can have. He has to be sincere, candid, and have a genuine appreciation of what has been attempted. He can do this only if he loves the work and those who take part in it.

The final category of marks, Enterprise and Achievement, express a summing-up by the adjudicator of the effort and intelligence put into the performance by all concerned.

THE GUILD OF DRAMA ADJUDICATORS

Because of the growth of drama festivals and the demand for good adjudication, the Guild of Drama Adjudicators was formed in January 1947 by a number of experienced adjudicators. Their object was to maintain and improve the standards of adjudication, and so to help in the development of amateur drama. They had the further object of establishing a recognized standard of practice in the work of adjudication. The original membership of the Guild consisted of forty-six founder members, and additional members have since been admitted, bringing the total membership to just over two hundred. All candidates for membership are required to have professional and/or amateur stage experience (preferably both), and to possess a thorough knowledge of drama. Approved candidates are invited to attend an Entrance Conference held at a week-end twice yearly, for the purpose of instructing and testing candidates in the nature and method of adjudication. A report upon each candidate is then made to the Council of the Guild by an Approval Board, on which there is at least one person who is not an adjudicator. The Guild has found in practice that rather more than half the candidates for membership are successful. New members are normally admitted as associate members for a period of two years, when they may be admitted to full membership after not less than six adjudication engagements have been carried out. The responsibilities of associate members are the same as those of full members.

All members and associates of the Guild are required to observe certain minimum conditions of engagement, and are bound to abide by the rules of any festival at which they undertake to adjudicate. Disciplinary action may be taken against any member who fails to do so.

More than eighty per cent of the members of the Guild have had professional stage experience as actors, producers, or stage managers, and some are still engaged in the professional theatre; among these are highly distinguished members of the profession. All have experience of the amateur stage and of the conditions under which amateur plays are performed, and are interested in the furtherance of amateur drama. Many are engaged in some form of teaching the technique of the stage, voice production, etc.; for the ability to impart instruction is regarded as a necessary qualification for membership of the Guild, as well as sound judgment.

The Guild issues a Directory of Drama Adjudicators, with addresses

and particulars of the minimum fees payable; and with notes for
festival organizers on what adjudicators require to do their work
properly. A quarterly bulletin is also issued to members in which
matters of interest to adjudicators are discussed. The Guild is a small
but well-managed organization, the Chairman of which is Norman
Marshall.

XIX. SHAW AND THE AMATEUR

by BARBARA SMOKER

(A member of the Shaw Society)*

M ANY books have been written about Bernard Shaw, and many
more will be written, but the profile sketched in this chapter
shows him against the background of the amateur stage.

He had a vigorous enthusiasm for life, and appreciated this quality
in the theatre. One of his dramatic criticisms extols the lusty vitality
of a production—and of the audience—in Hoxton. And amateurs
bring to drama a breath of reality. Shaw's theatre criticisms, which
appeared each week in the *Saturday Review* from January 1895 to May
1898, dealt mainly with the professional theatre of the day, but he
sometimes devoted a whole article to the amateur theatre. Here is
an excerpt from one of these articles, bubbling with characteristic fun:

> "As to this performance of *Macbeth* at St. George's Hall, of course
> it was, from the ordinary professional standpoint, a very bad one.
> I say this because I well know what happens to a critic when he
> incautiously praises an amateur. He gets by the next post a letter
> in the following terms: 'Dear Sir,—I am perhaps transgressing the
> bounds of etiquette in writing privately to you; but I thought you
> might like to know that your kind notice of my performance as
> Guildenstern has encouraged me to take a step which I have long
> been meditating. I have resigned my position as Governor of the
> Bank of England with a view to adopting the stage as a profession,
> and trust that the result may justify your too favourable opinion of
> my humble powers.' Therefore I desire it to be distinctly understood
> that I do not recommend any members of the *Macbeth* cast to go on
> the stage."

After praising the witches, he says that Macduff was bad, but that "if
he feels himself driven to some artistic career by a radical aversion to
earning an honest livelihood, and is prepared for a hard apprentice-

* The Shaw Society was founded on Shaw's eighty-fifth birthday, 26 July 1941, and
seeks to promote a wider and clearer understanding of Bernard Shaw's life and work,
but its lectures and discussions cover a wide range of interests—to provide in Shaw's
own words: "a rallying point for the co-operation and education of kindred spirits and
a forum for their irreconcilable controversies". It is in close touch with the Shaw Society
of America. Both societies publish journals available to all members in the British
Isles and overseas. The English society holds its meetings on the beautiful premises of
the National Book League, and full particulars may be obtained from its secretary,
Eric J. Batson, 45 Steeplestone Close, London, N.18.

ship of twenty years in mastering the art of the stage, he could become an actor." Shaw then goes on, "As to Lady Macbeth, she, too, was bad; but it is clear to me that unless she at once resolutely marries some rich gentleman who disapproves of the theatre on principle, she will not be able to keep herself off the stage."

This Lady Macbeth was Lillah McCarthy, who not only turned professional but became one of the foremost Shavian actresses, especially at the Royal Court Theatre.

Three years after the article which thus "discovered" Lillah Mc-Carthy, Shaw turns his attention to another amateur production:

"It is characteristic of the authorities at Oxford that they should consider a month too little for the preparation of a boat race, and grudge three weeks to the rehearsals of one of Shakespeare's plays. The performance of *Romeo and Juliet* by the Oxford University Dramatic Society naturally did not, under these circumstances, approach the level of skill attained on the Thames."

He goes on to say that "the best amateur performances are more instructive than the most elaborate professional ones" because the one advantage that amateurs have over professionals is the possibility of unlimited rehearsal, and he advises the O.U.D.S. to practise reading Elizabethan plays in order to acquire technical skill and vocal power, without which to play Shakespeare "is, frankly, to make an ass of oneself". He continues:

"If the performers had been able to handle their vowels and consonants as bats and balls and sculls are handled at Oxford in the racket-courts and cricket-fields and on the river, then, whether they were able to act or not, the performance would have been full of technical interest; the gallery would have seethed with youthful hero-worship; and the performers doing something that every undergraduate would like to do if he could, would now be holding their heads high even among the athletes. On no other lines is there the smallest chance of a dramatic club becoming a really vital organ of an English University, or forcing the authorities, by sheer weight of public opinion, to build a University theatre as an indispensable part of their educational equipment."

The importance of diction is stressed in many of Shaw's writings, and his dramatic criticisms contain the following favourable comment on amateur play-readings:

"I have seen the suburban amateurs of the Shakespeare Reading Society, seated like Christy minstrels on the platform of the lecture hall at the London Institution, produce, at a moderate computation, about sixty-six times as much effect by reading straight through *Much Ado About Nothing* as Mr. Irving with his expensively mounted and superlatively dull Lyceum version."

It will be noticed that Shaw often chose Shakespeare when sampling amateur productions. So much for the popular notion that he disliked Shakespeare. Certainly, he considered that from the intellectual, psychological and philosophical standpoints Shakespeare falls far below Ibsen and himself, but he said he pitied the man who could not enjoy the magic of Shakespeare's poetry and his gift for telling a story, and he regarded himself as "an ardent Shakespearian". His anti-Shakespearian campaign was aimed not at Shakespeare himself but at the "bardolaters" who enthused over him without understanding his work and endowed him with qualities he lacked. Worse, their reverence for the past impeded the coming of the new Ibsenite drama of ideas, which he had constantly boosted in his theatre criticisms, thus preparing the way for his own plays. These, with their unconventional philosophy, wit, intellectual brilliance, violent changes of tempo, flowing speeches and sparkling dialogue, were to revolutionize the moribund British theatre.

To the more intelligent playgoers G.B.S. came like rain to a thirsty land, but for many years the doors of the commercial theatre in this country were locked to him. The London managers, accustomed to "well-made" plays with their conventional sentiment, stale situations and denouements, would not look at the freak offerings of Mr. Shaw. Why, they were not plays at all, they said! So it was left to the little coterie theatre societies to launch the new era of drama, and most of Shaw's early plays were given their "world premieres" by the Independent Theatre Society or the Stage Society. The actors were generally professionals, but in a sense they were taking a busman's holiday, for the performances were usually confined to Sunday evenings and Monday matinees in order to allow the actors to work in the commercial theatre during the week.

Although the Sunday performances were discreetly called "meetings", since playgoing was unheard of on a Sunday, theatre lessees were nervous of allowing them to take place in their theatres—even on the understanding that there should be no publicity, the audience being restricted to members. There was an additional cause for nervousness in the case of Shaw's third play, *Mrs. Warren's Profession*, for the Censor had refused it a public licence. Time and time again the date and place of a performance were fixed and the tickets printed, only to be cancelled because yet another theatre lessee had taken fright at the last minute, despite the fact that the Censor had no jurisdiction over private per-formances. The ban on this play was not lifted until 1924!

The first world productions of some of Shaw's plays were actually done by amateurs. *Caesar and Cleopatra* was performed "for the first time on any stage" by an amateur company in the Fine Arts Building in Chicago, over five years before the first professional production by Forbes-Robertson. Shaw's little-known playlet, *The Fascinating Found-ling*, was originally written for the daughter of the then Prime Minister, Asquith, and was given its first world production by her amateur theatre group for charity, nearly twenty years before it was ever done profes-sionally. The humorous one-act play *O'Flaherty, V.C.*, sub-titled *A Recruiting Pamphlet*, also made its debut at the hands of non-professionals, being first performed by a unit of the British Army on the Allied Western Front in 1917, over three years before its first professional production. And amateurs were responsible for the first American (though not world) productions of *Candida*, *The Man of Destiny*, *You Never can Tell*, *Passion, Poison and Petrifaction*, and *Augustus Does his Bit*.

It was Shaw's belief that the ideal producer of a play is its author. During the famous Vedrenne-Barker partnership at the Royal Court Theatre from 1904 to 1907—which owed its success, financial as well as artistic, to the plays of Shaw—he was responsible for the production of all his own plays, and he gives his unique assistance to all subsequent producers of them, for in their published form they are more or less "acting editions". The unusually long stage-directions, though pri-marily intended for the general reader, are a godsend to producers, and it is a fact that when a producer chooses to ignore them in some par-ticular he often regrets it later.

It has been suggested that all Shaw's writings on play-production and acting should be collected in one volume. Apart from articles for publication he wrote innumerable letters on these subjects and the interpretation of his own plays. One long letter to a boyhood friend, Edward McNulty, who was taking up amateur production, was later published as a guide to amateurs in the *Arts League of Service Annual*, 1921–2, and was reprinted by Samuel French in New York as a pamph-let under the title "The Art of Rehearsal", for giving away to their clients.

When Shaw was informed there were about 100,000 amateur groups in the United States, he said, quite unimpressed, "So there should be."

From 1911 to 1942 he was an enthusiastic member of the Council of the Royal Academy of Dramatic Art, and it was at his instigation that the Academy appealed in 1921 against the official ruling that acting could not be recognized in law as a fine art. After a long and com-plicated legal tussle, the case was finally won, with Shaw's able help.

He supported the establishment of a Diploma in Dramatic Art by the University of London, and was delighted when the R.A.D.A. was granted L.C.C. and other scholarships, which his presence on the governing body of the Academy had no doubt helped to secure.

Although Shaw took such a keen practical interest in theatre students and amateurs, when the British Drama League was launched in 1919 he refused to have anything to do with the project, which he deemed impossibly Utopian. Three years later, however, seeing that the League was miraculously surviving, he modestly submitted the usual application form for membership together with a guinea for his first annual subscription—a far greater compliment, of course, than any gesture of generosity or patronage would have been at the start. After that he used to attend the annual meetings of the League in London, and in 1933 he consented to journey to Edinburgh to address the B.D.L. Conference there on "Some Aspects of the British Drama". Actually he made the occasion the opportunity for raising the question of playwrights' fees to amateurs.

Realizing that the usual fixed charge of five guineas for not more than three consecutive amateur performances of a full-length play was not an economic proposition for many of the smaller amateur dramatic groups, which the new amateur movement (largely promoted by the B.D.L. itself) had brought into being, Shaw had for some time been campaigning for amateur companies to be treated as professionals and charged a percentage on takings. For most amateur companies this works out much cheaper than five guineas. Shaw himself had already started allowing this concession to certain amateur companies which had contracted to plough any profits they made back into the theatre and give nothing to charity. In order not to confuse his agents, Shaw dealt direct with these privileged companies, which included the Birmingham Municipal Players—who later built the Crescent Theatre out of their funds—and the Hedgerow Theatre of Movlan-Rose Valley, near Philadelphia, U.S.A.

Now he moved a resolution to the B.D.L. Conference, "as the humble delegate of the Welwyn Garden City Theatre Society", that the percentage arrangement should become standard. He read out the formal resolution thus:

"That this Conference urges the extreme importance as disinterested nurseries of drama and the art of acting of small dramatic enterprises started spontaneously by local residents—this takes a lot of breath—in villages and towns outside the commercial touring circuits, and calls the attention of playwrights—I am a playwright—to the wisdom of reserving to themselves personally the duty of licensing performances of their works by such enthusiasts on terms reasonably within their means though possibly not worth collecting commercially by their professional agents."

His speech, which is reported verbatim in the December 1933 issue of *Drama*, ended as follows:

"Remember that Richard Wagner, the composer, said, quite truly, 'Music is kept alive not in our great opera houses and in our concert rooms, but on the cottage piano of the amateur.' I tell you—and this is my last word—that the drama in this country and in every country is not kept alive by the great theatres, although they do something for the highest departments of the art of acting, but by the love of the people for the drama and the attempts they make themselves, when they are starved by the professional circuits, to give performances in the places the professional circuits do not reach. The object of the resolution which I now formally move is to make that as easy and as cheap as possible."

Thereafter he extended his percentage arrangement to all companies, and Shaw's secretary, Miss Blanche Patch, indicates in her biography of G.B.S. how much it benefited the very small amateur groups. "Several", she says, "sent him only half a crown, and once we found a single shilling in the post. Shaw was quite satisfied. It was not the money he wanted: his aim was to build up amateur theatre societies everywhere."

On the other hand, except in the case of home or classroom performances, he would never allow his plays to be performed without a fee at all. That, he said, would be "blacklegging". When Rugby School invited him to see an abridged and unauthorized production of *Captain Brassbound's Conversion* he wrote back: "To tell an author about an unauthorized performance, on a card headed with the emblem of piracy, is audacious. To allow him to witness a mutilated version of his play is to invite murder."

A happier correspondence with Rugby took place when some senior boys of the School House who had formed a play-reading society wrote and asked Shaw to reveal "the secret in the poet's heart" mentioned at the end of *Candida*. Instead of giving a direct answer, Shaw replied on a postcard asking them to try and guess the answer first. He received seven guesses from them, all wide of the mark, and in reply wrote a long letter in which he called them "sentimental blighters" and explained that in his opinion—though "everybody who buys the book may fit it with an ending to suit his own taste"—his poet no longer wanted "the small beer of domestic comfort".

In the last two decades of his life, when the high-standard amateur repertory companies were beginning to take root, Shaw frequently declared that his chief hope for drama lay in the amateur movement. In December 1936 the New York *Herald-Tribune* published an interview with G.B.S., quoting him as saying, "I am interested in the repertory theatre. That's where the whole thing is kept alive, in such theatres as the Malvern Theatre, or in the Hedgerow Theatre in the United States." Hedgerow, which is run as a communal enterprise—the resident members receiving free board and lodging, clothes, medical treatment, and so on, but no salaries—is one of the most persistently Shavian theatres in the world. Its first production, in 1923, was *Candida*, and Shaw has been prominent in its repertory ever since.

Since his death in 1950 a slight eclipse of Shaw has been noticeable in this country—a not unusual occurrence in the period between the death of a great man and the final assessment of his work—but this has not been so on the other side of the Atlantic. The Shaw Society, based in London, now has almost as many members in the United States as in all the other countries of the world put together—in spite of the fact that there is also a separate American body, The Shaw Society of America, Inc.

However, the Shavian eclipse is certainly not a total one, even in Britain. There was a large audience for "An Evening with Bernard Shaw" presented in November 1954, appropriately enough in St. Pancras Town Hall, by the St. Pancras Public Libraries Committee in association with the British Drama League. The programme began with a performance by the Richmond Shakespeare Society of *Overruled*, followed by a "reading" of scenes from *Pygmalion* by a professional quartette, who later took part in a discussion on the influence of G.B.S. on drama.

A perusal of the annual reports of The Little Theatre Guild of Great Britain, which comprises twenty-two of the best amateur companies, shows that, in spite of the slight drop in the number of Shaw productions put on by these companies since 1951, Shaw still comes second only to Shakespeare.

The general experience of amateur companies is that he is invariably "good box-office", and many financially precarious groups rely on him to help make ends meet, just as the Royal Court Theatre did fifty years ago.

XX. ORGANIZATIONS WHICH AID AMATEURS

THE BRITISH DRAMA LEAGUE

THE British Drama League is a unique organization in that its members, its work and its sphere of influence cover both the amateur and the professional theatre. Its aim is to "assist the development of the Art of the Theatre and its right relation to the life of the community". Thus it matters not whether the League is called upon for advice or information by a tiny society in the Hebrides or a wealthy West End management. Both are interested in the theatre, and so the League will come to their assistance.

In 1919, Geoffrey Whitworth had the idea that the theatre could be greatly helped by a central organization, through which information and services could be channelled. Being a practical man, as well as a man of vision, he set about establishing the British Drama League. Its first Chairman was that fine producer, Harley Granville-Barker, and its Honorary Treasurer Alec L. Rea, a prominent London Manager, with the late Lord Howard de Walden its first President. E. Martin-Browne succeeded Geoffrey Whitworth as Director in 1948.

Originally the League had a one-roomed office, but now owns two Georgian houses at 9 and 10 Fitzroy Square, London, W.1, and has a membership of six thousand. Three-quarters of these members are groups, so the total number of people associated with the League runs into hundreds of thousands. Among these groups are West End managements, provincial repertory companies, thousands of amateur societies, and a large number of schools and youth clubs. Hospitals, mental institutions and prisons are given service. Individual members vary from distinguished professionals, scholars, and teachers, to interested country vicars, miners and housewives. Members join both to assist the League in furthering its work and to get help they need for their own work in the theatre. The annual subscription for both individual members and organizations is two guineas per year; a life subscription may be taken out for twelve guineas.

Recognizing the fact that amateur leaders, actors and staff often need training in order to raise standards, the League has pioneered the teaching of drama to adults and children. It was mainly responsible for the Board of Education's official Report on "Drama in Adult Education" (1926), which did so much to encourage the teaching of drama to adults; and largely because of its work for the parallel development in schools the Training Department of the League is now grant-aided by the Ministry of Education. The first Theatre Conference ever held in Britain was convened by the League at Stratford-on-Avon in 1919, and it has held one annually ever since. The principal Theatre Exhibitions from 1922 onwards have been promoted or assisted by it. Schemes for the National Theatre (1929) and Civic Theatres (1943) were prepared by distinguished committees and submitted to the Prime Minister, and the informed public opinion created by the League has played a large part in the acceptance by Parliament of both of these ideas.

A highly qualified full-time staff of thirty-nine at the League's head-quarters is available to answer queries, look up information, etc., on nearly any question arising in connection with the theatre. Members need only ring, call, or write a letter for this service. In their work of organizing, teaching and adjudicating, staff members travel great distances—not only in the British Isles, but abroad. The Principal of the Training Department has recently returned from a four-month lecture and training tour in New Zealand.

There are branches of the British Drama League in Australia and New Zealand, and close contact is kept with similar organizations in Canada, the U.S.A., India, Ceylon, East Africa and the West Indies.

THE LIBRARY

Certainly the largest Drama Library in Britain, the B.D.L. Library is an invaluable help to members. It contains over a hundred thousand volumes. During the summer of 1954, with the financial aid of the Pilgrim Trust and private donors, the library was enlarged, completely renovated, and an attractive Reference Reading Room added. It was formally reopened by the Lord Chamberlain in the presence of distinguished theatre people and patrons.

The library's catalogue, "The Player's Library" (1950), is a volume of over 1,100 pages, to which supplements are added every two years. These volumes provide, not only a guide to the library, but an exhaustive annotated list of published plays and theatre books. The list, in itself, is an excellent source of information for all who work in or are merely interested in the theatre.

The reference library includes many unique books, including the William Archer Collection and loans from Gordon Graig, the executors of Nigel Playfair, and others. Hundreds of queries are handled each week by the library staff, from the copyright of the latest London release to the design of the ancient Greek stage, or the choice of play for a village gala, or the uniform of a policeman in the eighteenth century.

The library contains, in addition to printed volumes and plays in manuscript, files of theatrical periodicals and newspapers, programmes, photographs, music for plays, and theatrical design. In volumes of press cuttings there are dramatic criticisms of most productions of this century and the latter part of the last century.

Members may borrow three books at a time free of charge for a fortnight. Societies must appoint a representative to be responsible for the books borrowed on behalf of the society. Members of affiliated societies are entitled to use the Reading Room, but if desiring to borrow books for their personal use must join the League individually. Sets of plays (one copy of the play for each character up to twelve) may be hired for the fee of 3s. 6d. each set for the first week, and 1s. 6d. per week thereafter up to a maximum of twelve weeks. No society or individual member may hire more than two sets at a time for the subscription of two guineas, but for every guinea subscribed over and above the first, members have the right to borrow three further books and hire one further set. The library is open daily from ten to five; Wednesdays, ten to nine; Saturdays, ten to twelve-thirty.

The value of the borrowing service alone can be seen by the number of volumes that go out each year—approximately thirty thousand books and twenty thousand sets.

THE BOOKSHOP

The Bookshop sells both English and foreign books and magazines to members and non-members. A small stock of interesting theatre books is kept at headquarters, and at the Annual Theatre Week there is a special display.

THE TRAINING DEPARTMENT

This Department is of vital importance in fulfilling the B.D.L.'s aim of higher standards in all phases of the amateur theatre. Its staff are highly qualified and experienced professionals. There are two main categories of the training programme: Regular Annual Courses, and Instruction by Travelling Staff Tutors.

Regular Annual Courses

These include:
1. A ten-week full-time course, January to March, or April to June, annually.
2. Autumn and spring week-end courses in London.
3. Residential summer schools in holiday resorts.

1. The Ten-week Course, held in the practice theatre at the League's headquarters, is a very comprehensive one, planned primarily for pro-

ducers, tutors and instructors, and is the only course in England devoted entirely to the study of play production. Practical instruction is given by the B.D.L. Training Department staff, and visiting lectures by eminent professional producers. Candidates for the course should be over eighteen and under forty-five years of age, and are selected by means of a questionnaire, by recommendation of an employer, and if possible, by interview. The number of students must necessarily be limited, so preference is given to those recommended by Local Education Authorities, Universities, Institutes of Education and Training Colleges. Local Education Authorities often give financial aid to students from their area. Students are expected to have a fairly wide knowledge of theatre background, and a list of suggested books for pre-reading is sent to accepted candidates before the course begins. Subjects covered include:

Production, in which students are given individual practice in producing scenes with their fellow students as actors, and criticism by the instructors upon their work as well as lectures on all the phases of the producer's task.

The Teaching of Production, which instructs students in lecturing and holding week-end or one-day schools.

The Teaching of Acting which includes classes in interpretation, improvisation, mime, speech, movement, etc.

Stagecraft, including setting, lighting, make-up, costume and stage management.

Adjudication, in which students are given practice and criticism as well as studying classification marking and a general approach to this important, and often very difficult, phase of theatre work.

At the end of the course, students are given individual reports and B.D.L. certificates if their work is of a sufficiently high standard. Students may also take the examination set by the Drama Board whose certificate, "Associate of the Drama Board" (A.D.B.), serves as a special qualification for teachers of non-professional drama.

The tuition fee for this full-time course is fifteen pounds. The Drama Board Examination fee is five guineas per candidate.

2. Autumn and Spring Week-end Courses include Production, Acting and Playwriting. Lectures and practical work are given by B.D.L. instructors and guest lecturers. For Production and Acting, students are asked to study scenes so that discussions and rehearsal practice may be carried out. For Playwriting, students may submit an unpublished play of their own for criticism which must be accompanied by a reading fee of fifteen shillings for a full-length play, or ten shillings for a one-act play. They are sometimes asked to arrange to see a particular play running in the West End, for discussion purposes; and to submit a

written exercise set by the lecturer before the course begins. A recommended reading list is sent to students well in advance.

A postal course in play-writing is also offered. It consists of twelve lessons dealing with such fundamental matters as the Construction of a Play, Character-drawing, Dialogue, etc. Questions and exercises are appended to each lesson, and the answers examined, criticized and corrected by the Director of Studies. At the end of the course students are encouraged to submit an original play for written criticism. This course is available only to members of the B.D.L. A short course is also offered, with the same material, but fewer exercises.

Fees for the above courses are usually as follows:

	B.D.L.			Members of Affiliated Societies			Non-members		
	£	s.	d.	£	s.	d.	£	s.	d.
Production and Acting	1	0	0	1	2	6	1	5	0
Playwriting	1	0	0	1	2	6	1	5	0
MSS Reading Fee—									
3-Act		15	0		15	0		15	0
1-Act		10	0		10	0		10	0
Postal Playwriting	7	7	0						
Short Postal Playwriting	4	4	0						

3. Two Residential Summer Schools are held annually, usually during the first fortnight in August and the first week in September, at some attractive holiday centre. The courses are open to anyone interested whether members of the B.D.L. or not, but members are entitled to a substantial reduction in fees.

The syllabus is on similar lines to that of the full-time course though in a modified form, and there is as much emphasis on acting as on production.

About 100 students usually attend the August course and rather fewer the shorter course in September.

Guest lecturers in the past have included such people as Tyrone Guthrie, John Fernald, John Burrell, Michael MacOwen, André van Gyseghem, Peter Potter, and Norman Marshall.

Instruction by Travelling Staff Tutors

The travelling staff consists of fully qualified professional theatre producers and specialists with a wide knowledge of amateur drama, who are ready to undertake work throughout the year wherever it may be requested. Expenses of lecturers may be shared by various organiza-

R

tions if a series of engagements are arranged within the same area. Services offered include: Adjudication, One-day or Week-end Courses, Productions, and in London only courses of Weekly Lectures and Classes. Much the same material is covered as in the full-time and week-end courses mentioned previously. However, in addition, detailed study is offered in Costume, Making and Improvising a Basic Wardrobe, Masques, Pageants, Class Room Drama, Playmaking, Arena Production, Property-making, Period Dress, Manners and Dance. The great advantage of these courses is that more people are able to attend when the lectures are given in their own local areas. Short courses may be arranged for a group of amateur producers, a dramatic society, a group of actors, school classes, a youth organization, etc., and the lectures and practical demonstrations are planned with the special needs of the particular group in mind.

Terms for this instruction vary greatly, and are made by arrangement with the central office.

FESTIVALS

The National Festival of Community Drama. Started in 1927, this is the only nation-wide eliminating contest for one-act plays in performance. Through it, amateur theatre groups may meet in a series of festivals starting in their own localities and culminating in the National Final in London, usually held at the Scala Theatre, London, in June.

The Festival in England and Wales is directed by the League's National Committee for Community Drama, assisted by a special Joint Festival Committee of the League and the Standing Conference of Drama Associations. There are two separate stages in the Festival. Stage 1 (through which all companies must enter) comprises all preliminary festivals, up to and including the county finals. Stage 2, arranged directly by the League, consists of the Divisional, Area, and National Finals. For the purposes of administration there are three English areas—Eastern, Northern and Western, plus a Welsh area, and a separate Scottish Festival administered by the Scottish Community Drama Association. The National Final Festival is made up of a representative from each of these areas, chosen through the local festivals, making a final programme of five plays.

The Festival is open to all amateur dramatic societies affiliated to the B.D.L., and although all members of the company must be amateur, a professional producer may be employed. Material presented may be either a one-act play or an excerpt from a longer play, and must not exceed a running time of forty minutes. It must be duly licensed by the Lord Chamberlain and contain not less than three speaking parts.

In all Stage 2 Festivals, the B.D.L. provides the theatre and its stage lighting, the necessary organization, and one set of stage curtains, to which the individual companies may add doors, windows, and their own furniture, properties, etc. Box sets are not permissible.

Entry fees for B.D.L. member teams are one guinea per company, and for those coming to Stage 2 from an associated festival, five shillings in addition to the local entrance fee. Royalties (up to one guinea per play) and reasonable travelling expenses (for not more than twelve persons) are paid by the League.

A public adjudication, including constructive criticism, is given for all plays and private discussions arranged between adjudicator and the companies concerned. Finalists from Stage 1 proceed to Stage 2, and from among the latter, five teams are chosen, who compete for a national trophy, the Howard de Walden Cup which is given for the best production in the Final Festival. To encourage the writing of new plays, two new awards have been announced by the B.D.L. for the best original unpublished one-act play presented during the entire Festival. The author is given a prize of ten guineas and to the society presenting the play, the Geoffrey Whitworth Cup to be held for one year. A typewritten manuscript of the play, together with a reading fee of ten shillings, must be sent to the League for the play to qualify in this competition.

The Festival of Original Full-length Plays. This Festival was inaugurated during the 1953-4 season, and is an important step ahead in the encouragement of production of new plays.

A judge appointed by the B.D.L. visits entrant societies in their own halls or theatres, and views the new plays in performance. The Festival period is usually from the end of November to the end of May, and at the end of this time the judge selects the best production of the best new play he has seen. The play must never have been performed before on stage, television or radio. Entrance fee is 5s., plus 15s. if a written adjudicator's report is required. Societies must also pay the adjudicator's fee and travelling expenses, as well as providing accommodation. A script of the play must be sent to the adjudicator two weeks before the performance.

Believing that the right way to assist new authors is by finding a market for their plays, and by increasing among both players and public, interest in new writing for the theatre, the League makes its awards in this festival to the winning company rather than to the author of the play. All authors whose plays are shown in the festival have the immediate benefits of a stage performance, enlightened and constructive criticism and, ultimately, a wider interest in and demand for their work.

The winning company receives an award of £25 given by an eminent author, and an invitation to present its production at the League's annual Theatre Week. In addition any play entered and considered of sufficient merit by the judge, will be held in the League's Library and, together with the winner, will be brought to the notice of suitable theatrical publishers and/or managers.

PUBLICATIONS

Drama is the League's quarterly theatre magazine, and has been published continuously since 1919. It contains articles on every aspect of the theatre by well-known authorities; reports of current plays running in the West End; reviews of new theatrical books and newly published plays; and news of the activities of the League, its members and associates throughout the world.

Besides "The Player's Library", already mentioned, the League has published a number of theatre books, some of which are listed in the bibliography at the back of this book.

RECORDS

As an invaluable aid to actors, producers and teachers, the B.D.L. has had made twelve double-sided records of dialects of the British Isles. These are the result of an extensive survey and the speakers chosen are natives of the districts represented. Each record starts with the same "Standard Passage", which contains all the sounds in the phonetic alphabet. It would be impossible to record all the dialect variants of Britain, but those chosen are the chief ones, and include:

1.	(a) Cornwall	7.	(a) Lincolnshire
	(b) Devon		(b) Norfolk
2.	(a) Somerset	8.	(a) Cockney
	(b) Dorset		(b) Sussex
3.	(a) Gloucestershire	9.	(a) Scottish border
	(b) Oxfordshire		(b) Ayrshire
4.	(a) Shropshire	10.	(a) Fife
	(b) Lancashire		(b) Aberdeen
5.	(a) Westmorland	11.	(a) North Wales
	(b) Northumberland		(b) South Wales
6.	(a) Yorkshire: East Riding	12.	(a) Ulster
	(b) Yorkshire: West Riding		(b) Eire

In addition to these, there are four records of American Speech variants by Ruth Draper and Arthur Klein. The British records are 7s. 6d. each, the American 9s. each. A booklet of the phonetic script for the standard passage is available for 3s. and a booklet for use with the American records is 1s.

THEATREGOERS' CLUB

This club recently formed by the B.D.L. is open to all members of affiliated societies, or individual members. The club arranges monthly theatre parties to see various professional plays, with supper afterwards to which are invited the producers and actors from the play seen. Quite often concession rates on tickets are obtained. An annual subscription fee of 7s. 6d. is charged. Although the Theatregoers' Club was first formed in London, the idea has now spread to other large centres. The League feels the club is a real opportunity for the development of friendship between professionals and amateurs, and that it helps to create the basis for wider contact between the League and its membership. It is also a practical means of assisting the theatre by the provision of audiences at a time when they are most needed (over 2,250 theatre tickets are sold in a season).

The scheme has met with wide approval within the theatrical profession, and many famous personalities have joined in the after-theatre suppers. Paul Rogers, Old Vic actor and member of the League's Council, is the club's patron and shows great interest in it.

THE OVERSEAS SERVICE

Although contact has always been maintained with organizations and individuals overseas, the B.D.L. has recently formed a new service, through which overseas correspondents receive *Drama* and each one is entitled to write personally for advice and assistance to members of the League's staff, and is welcome to visit the League's headquarters and activities should he be in London. Annual subscriptions for this service are ten shillings per individual and one pound per society. This includes cost of the Bulletin sent by surface mail.

THE JUNIOR DRAMA LEAGUE

The formation of a Junior Branch of the B.D.L. is now under way. The League has long felt that children, the audiences and artists of tomorrow, should be further encouraged in their theatrical interests by an organization and services of their own. During the Christmas Season 1952–3 and 1953–4 a series of lectures and demonstrations of acting, costuming, make-up, etc., were given by professional actors specially for children, in a London theatre. There have also been classes for the children themselves during the Christmas and Easter holidays. So great was the interest shown by the children attending, that the Junior League seemed an immediate step forward. It will include a special children's branch of the library, a club room, classes in various aspects of the theatre, discussion of problems arising out of their school productions, criticisms of their own plays and other special activities. The subscription to this newest B.D.L. venture, which should be of great interest to young theatre lovers, will be 10s. 6d. per year.

THE ANNUAL THEATRE WEEK

Each summer the League holds a Theatre Week in London or at a provincial holiday centre, during which professionals and amateurs have a chance to meet together. Productions by both professional and amateur companies are seen, and discussed on the lines of a special theme chosen for the week. In 1955 the theme was "The Theatre in Contemporary Life". Lectures have been given by outstanding producers, actors, and critics on such varied subjects as "The Producer's Approach to Shakespeare" and "The Critic and the Producer". Often members of overseas organizations attend and bring a fresh outlook to the British theatrical scene.

Theatre Weekends are held in provincial cities from time to time on the same lines.

To conclude, it would seem that the British Drama League is perhaps the most important and extensive organization of its kind in the world today. It is a veritable gold mine of information; its training programme is a powerful educative force and a great step towards higher standards; its conferences and festivals provide the impetus for meetings, discussions, and exchange of views, as well as a measuring stick for good production and fine performances. In its work with active professional and amateur theatre people, as well as with audiences, students and interested spectators of the art, it is in a position to promote understanding and goodwill among these varied spheres, which is most necessary for healthy and flourishing theatre as a whole.

THE NATIONAL OPERATIC AND DRAMATIC ASSOCIATION

The National Operatic and Dramatic Association, usually spoken of as NODA, was formed in 1899, and is the oldest organization of its kind in the world. It was started not by one individual, but by a group of societies that felt they needed a central body to help in their many business, production and other problems, and to assist in the exchange of ideas and encouragement of high standards. The contribution NODA has made in smoothing out questions of contracts, copyright, entertainment duty, hire charges, insurance, legal advice, performance, publicity, etc., has been invaluable to the amateur theatre movement.

From the small beginning of a nucleus of forty societies, NODA's membership has grown to over one thousand. There is also a flourishing individual membership of around five hundred, and newly acquired large offices at 1 Crestfield Street, London, W.C.1, house a permanent paid staff of eight.

Although on excellent terms with the professional theatre, NODA works exclusively for and with amateurs. In contrast with the stated aims of the B.D.L., NODA does not primarily try to influence the cultural standard of the works performed by its affiliated societies. Rather it tries to assist societies in every way possible to raise the standard of performance, and in all business negotiations.

The majority of the members are operatic societies, although there are also a few hundred "straight" dramatic groups. These members are not only in Great Britain, but in Africa, Australia, Canada, India, Malta, New Zealand and the Channel Islands.

As an organization of fine reputation and substance, a united force representing so many people, NODA is respected and recognized as a qualified national voice by government departments, the railway executive, performing rights owners, costumiers, scenery contractors, and public departments of all kinds. Part of its policy is to obtain concessions for its members, and to protect their interest in every way against the encroachment of those who might seek to impose injustice upon them.

One of the finest of NODA's works in this respect has been its campaign to exempt amateur organizations from entertainment duty. In 1949 its first petition was presented to the Chancellor of the Exchequer in this regard, and was supported by many Members of Parliament. However, it was not until 1953 that the constant urging of the Association bore fruit, and in the Finance Bill of that year, the Chancellor modified the stringency by permitting the employment of paid producers, instructors and managers. However, the employment of a paid conductor and/or musicians in the orchestra during performances is still not permitted. This is rather ironic when most of NODA's members, being operatic and musical groups, have to employ musicians. However, the relief has made a tremendous difference to straight dramatic groups, and the campaign to abolish completely the duty for all amateurs, without reservation, is still continuing.

ORGANIZATION

The main Council of NODA is comprised of a President, Vice-President, and ten Sectional Councillors, plus two Life Members. For the purpose of representation, Great Britain is divided into ten geographical sections. Each section has a Council elected by societies and individual members of the section. Each Sectional Council elects one representative to the Central Council.

An Annual General Meeting is held each year, usually in early October, during which discussions and exchange of ideas takes place. The meeting is open to all members of societies and to individual members. Regional conferences are held from time to time at convenient centres to enable sectional members to get together.

ADVANTAGES OF MEMBERSHIP

The Head Office sets out the advantages of belonging to NODA as follows:

1. Mutual support between affiliated societies and the moral and material strength of union.
2. Free Publications:
   (a) Year Book which is unique.
   (b) Fixture lists.
   (c) The Association Journal, the NODA Bulletin.
3. Free legal advice.
4. Competent critics and lecturers arranged for at small fees.
5. Special schemes of insurance for amateur societies at advantageous premiums.
6. Substitute players in cases of emergency.
7. Free use of the most comprehensive Operatic and Dramatic Libraries in the United Kingdom.
8. Protection against prohibitive charges.
9. Help in matters of taxation, etc.
10. Help in selection of operatic and dramatic works to perform.
11. Free publicity of forthcoming performances in the Association publications and resultant financial support from affiliated societies.
12. Interchange of ideas at meetings and conferences, and opportunities for social expansion.
13. Loan of musical scores, libretti, dramatic works, theatrical handbooks and marked stage books of musical works, some of them unobtainable elsewhere.
14. Hiring of vocal scores and sets of plays for readings and rehearsing purposes.
15. The provision of specimen rules to put societies on the soundest possible constitution.
16. Practical assistance in organizing drama festivals.
17. Advice readily, courteously and promptly given on all matters connected with the theatre and societies' activities no matter how great or small.

THE YEAR BOOK

Published once a year, this book is sent free of charge to members, and is full of useful information on all phases of business matters; details of NODA services; a sectional and an alphabetical list of all members, both group and individual; a list of marked stage books available in the library; a list of plays for which NODA Ltd. is agent for the performing rights; an Index of all operatic and dramatic works performed by societies, with a cross-reference to the various societies that have performed them. This service enables societies to exchange ideas, possibly costumes, sets, etc., and if a sudden replacement in cast is necessary, to contact quickly a group that has performed the piece in the hope that a member who already knows the part may be able to step in and save the performance for a fellow society. The Year Book also contains names and addresses of coaches, producers and musical directors; costumiers, music publishers, stage fitters and scenic artists; as well as performing right holders, agents, lighting experts, wig makers and make-up houses. It is truly a useful business "bible" for amateur societies.

THE BULLETIN

The NODA Bulletin is published thrice yearly, and also sent free to members. Besides news of general interest to societies, and regional reports, it contains "Fixture" lists which give the exact dates, titles and place of performance of member societies. Synopses of the latest London musicals are also given, and titles of recent musicals and plays released for amateurs. In each issue is a complete cast list (with types of voices required), synopsis of plot, outline of scenes and musical numbers, of one opera or musical comedy. Separate copies of these synopses, available for the most popular musical comedies and operas, can also be purchased from the head office for one shilling each, or a selection of twelve for ten shillings. This is of great assistance to societies in choosing productions.

THE LIBRARY

The Association's Library possesses some seventy thousand volumes, comprising marked stage books, vocal scores, libretti, dramatic works, pictorials and general literature of the stage. Many of the marked stage books, including the whole of the Gilbert and Sullivan series, have been revised by experienced coaches. The Association has made arrangements with the owners of musical comedies, of which only manuscript copies exist, to place a copy of such works in the library for reading purposes. Books and scores may be obtained on payment of suitable deposits and nominal hiring fees, as follows:

Single copies of vocal scores, libretti, dramatic works, pictorials and handbooks are loaned FREE for reading purposes for fourteen days. Hiring fees where books are required in quantities for a period for rehearsal purposes: Vocal Scores—one shilling per copy per month or portion thereof. Libretti—sixpence per copy per month or portion thereof. Dramatic works—sixpence per copy per month or portion thereof. Sets of most published plays can be hired for reading purposes for a period of ten days at threepence per copy.

In some cases where no vocal score has been published lithographed copies are available, exclusively for the Association.

ORCHESTRAL LIBRARY

For many years the Association managed on behalf of the Carnegie United Kingdom Trust a library of orchestral music. In 1937 the Trustees gave to the Association the whole of the contents of this library to continue, as originally intended, the service to amateur orchestras who can become members on payment of a moderate subscription. Thus, this music is available to all NODA members, and a free catalogue of the works in the library is supplied free on application.

LEGAL ADVICE

The Honorary Solicitors of the Association are prepared to advise societies, through the NODA Director, upon all legal matters in connection with productions and theatrical matters generally.

SCENERY AND COSTUME HIRE

Standard comprehensive contracts have been formulated which have been approved and agreed between the Theatrical Traders Association (Amateur Section) and NODA.

INSURANCE

The Association's official Insurance Broker is able to effect policies of Insurance for societies at advantageous rates protecting against Common Law Liability, and against losses arising from unforeseen circumstances such as fire, national calamity, destruction of theatre, etc., also loss of, or damage to, costumes or scenery, musical instruments, members' personal effects, etc.

OFFICIAL DEVICE, BADGE AND LONG-SERVICE MEDAL

There is an official device for affiliated societies to use on their notepaper and other publications; and an official badge, embodying the device, is supplied at moderate charge to societies for their members. It can also be produced in quantity bearing the name of the society, or can carry the various titles of officials . . . as "President", "Secretary", etc. A silver medal with ribbon is supplied for presentation by societies to those who have given service to a society without payment or reward for not less than twenty-five years. There are silver bars available for further periods of service over and above twenty-five years.

NODA LIMITED

This company conducts trading activities essential to the work of societies and controls the performing rights of a considerable number of operas, musical comedies, pantomimes and dramatic works. Special advantageous terms are reserved for affiliated societies in some cases. It also arranges for the services of professional producers, critics, and adjudicators. A few of the professional producers who work through NODA are able to make this their full-time career producing six or seven full productions per year.

OPERATIC SUMMER SCHOOL

This is the only course of tuition organized by NODA, in conjunction with the Advisory Committee on Amateur Opera. It is held annually for a period of eight days in the summer. Enrolment is about sixty, and highly qualified professional instructors are in charge. Several operas are chosen for study, and the students familiarize themselves with these works before the course begins. The operas are then cast, studied in detail, and performances given on the final day. There are also lectures on Acting, Stage Management, Make-up, and Operas in Schools. Tuition and work are also planned for those interested in Conducting, Producing and Accompanying.

MEMBERSHIP FEES

The membership fee for Operatic Societies is £5 5s. od. of which a rebate of £2 2s. od. is made if the yearly gross receipts do not exceed £100; and rebate of £1 1s. od. if they do exceed £100 but do not exceed £400. School Operatic Societies pay £2 2s. od. per year, while Dramatic Societies, Federations, or Festivals pay £1 11s. 6d. and Overseas Societies £2 2s. od. Entrance fees are also payable, except by School Societies, at the same rates. Operatic Societies newly joining, that have not yet given a performance, pay an initial fee of £3 3s. od. plus an entrance fee of £3 3s. od. with appropriate adjustments should the annual gross income exceed £100. Individual members pay a fee of £1 os. od. yearly.

Individual members are entitled to nominate Members of the

Council, vote at all general meetings, receive copies of the Bulletin and an abridged version of the Year Book, may apply for advice on all subjects connected with the theatre, and can have criticisms on original operatic and dramatic works. They may borrow single copies of all library books, with the exception of marked stage copies.

ANNUAL REPORTS

An Annual Report is issued to each member, giving a résumé of the Association's work during the year, and a report is published after each Annual General Meeting.

From the foregoing it can easily be seen how valuable an Association NODA is. It is a down-to-earth, practical, working organization, run by a knowledgeable and devoted staff, and its work has helped immeasurably to increase the business efficiency of operatic and dramatic societies, as well as to raise standards and promote exchange of ideas and goodwill among societies. Proof of the latter is that many societies hire a coach, travel all day, to see the production of a fellow company, and spend the night travelling back. Perhaps the watchwords of NODA should be Efficiency and Good Fellowship.

THE LITTLE THEATRE GUILD OF GREAT BRITAIN

The Little Theatre Guild has a limited membership of permanent independent amateur groups owning or controlling their own theatre. A high standard, not only of production but in choice of plays, is a requisite for membership.

The Guild was organized in 1946 by four groups that had already been exchanging information and views for some years. These founder members were The Questors, Ealing; The People's Theatre, Newcastle upon Tyne; The Highbury Little Theatre of Sutton Coldfield; and the Bradford Civic Playhouse. Representatives met together, drafted a constitution and invited several other established groups to join the first organization.

Theatres now apply for membership, and must be sponsored by two member theatres familiar with the applicant's work and programme. If there is any doubt as to the standard, representatives will attend performances and report to the Guild. Usual qualification is that the group must be exempt from Entertainments Duty as a partly educational organization not conducted or established for profit. New members are elected by a majority vote of the Guild.

Its objectives are to promote closer co-operation between Little

Theatres, to act as their co-ordinating and representative body, to maintain and further high standards, and to encourage the establishment of other Little Theatres. A representative of the Guild now serves on the Council of the British Drama League, and on the Executive Committee of the Standing Conference of Drama Associations. The Guild is also a member of the International Amateur Theatre Association.

There are no permanent headquarters and no paid staff, but The Questors of Ealing have acted as Secretary since the beginning because of their central location, so the Guild may always be contacted through that group. A membership fee of £5 5s. od. per year covers most expenses.

MEETINGS

Weekend meetings are arranged three or four times a year, during which representatives forgather at one of the member theatres for business and policy sessions, and informal discussions on varied aspects of production, organization, acting, etc., led by experienced theatre people. Delegates attend a production given by the host theatre on Saturday evening, on which a discussion is held the following day with producer, cast and other members of the company.

NEW PLAYS

One of the Guild's objectives is to encourage the production of worthwhile new plays. One year it commissioned a play, which was performed by several members and later published. Another year it ran its own new play competition. It co-operated with the Charles Henry Foyle Trust in establishing an annual New Play Award for the best play by a non-established dramatist produced each year by a list of specified theatres (including the Guild's members and those of the Council of Repertory Theatres—the latter being professional groups). Original plays are nominated for this Award by the theatres that have produced them.

The Guild circularizes its members with brief particulars of new or nearly new unpublished plays submitted, which are thought to be worthy of production. It advises groups not to be afraid to try a new play, and to leave the "tried and true" paths occasionally. More and more Little Theatres are realizing the importance of new works and the number of original plays produced by them is increasing. One theatre devoted an entire season recently to new plays.

GUILD LETTERS

Newsletters are sent to members throughout the year, exchanging production news and giving information on various topics of theatrical interest.

LIBRARY SERVICE

The Secretary of the Guild keeps a list of plays in the libraries of member theatres, through which they may obtain books and plays from one another.

CIRCULATING PHOTOGRAPHS

Photographs of members' productions are circulated by the Guild for display by the various groups.

EXCHANGE OF PRODUCTIONS

Some members are able to visit each other apart from the usual Guild Weekends, and to exchange productions. This is rather an expensive undertaking, but with enthusiasm and local hospitality these occasions have usually proved most successful. Guild members have entertained several travelling groups of American college players, and in one case a Guild member housed a Dutch Company, later returning the visit by taking an English production to Holland.

FESTIVALS

On the whole Guild members find their schedules too filled to allow them to partake in festivals, although sometimes their student groups are encouraged to enter. No festivals are organized within the Guild.

TRAINING PROGRAMMES

The majority of Guild members have their own student groups for training young people and newcomers to the theatre. Courses vary from one to two years, are usually given by senior members of the group concerned, and public student productions are given in the parent theatres. Students are often given preference when new working members are being recruited.

ANNUAL REPORT

Each year a report is sent to all members, telling of all activities during the year. This booklet also lists the names and addresses of all members together with lists of productions they have done during the year.

In summing up one might say that the Little Theatre Guild does not encourage dilettantism in the theatre. Its members are sufficiently keen on their work and organized to such a degree that they have procured their own theatres. In its continual seeking for higher standards the Guild can fulfil an important place in theatre today by encouraging new, exciting and experimental productions which are impossible to do in the professional commercial theatre. Through the work of sincerely interested men and women, who do not depend upon the hazards of making a living in the theatre, may come the fresh approach and new forms of presentation which will give an impetus to an art in a crippled state because of rising costs and rival forms of entertainment.

THE STANDING CONFERENCE OF DRAMA ASSOCIATIONS

The Standing Conference of Drama Associations is the national organization of County Drama Committees. These Committees exist to promote and encourage dramatic activities and to develop and co-ordinate practical schemes of dramatic education within their respective areas.

In 1927 the Carnegie United Kingdom Trust allocated a small sum for the further development of music and drama in the rural areas of England and Wales. This was administered by a Joint Committee of the National Federation of Women's Institutes, the British Drama League and the National Council of Social Service, and the grants were available through accepted County Committees.

In 1940 administration of music and drama was separated and the Joint Committee for Drama was set up with the help of the N.C.S.S. to administer the grants. In 1945 a much larger sum was allocated and a national drama adviser appointed. Offers of grant-aid were made to every county in the United Kingdom, as well as assistance towards the appointment of full-time professional advisers. In 1945, the National Council of Social Service, in its desire to further the work of the County Drama Committees and to safeguard their future and at their request, called the meeting which brought into being the Standing Conference of Drama Associations.

Its headquarters are at the National Council of Social Service, 26 Bedford Square, London, W.C.1, and this body provides the secretariat.

The Conference meets annually and elects an Executive Committee which appoints various sub-committees for specified purposes. The Executive Committee meets at least six times a year and the sub-committees as required.

ANNUAL MEETING

Delegates to this meeting are producers, actors, educationists and interested persons from the counties and national bodies who discuss the progress and problems of amateur drama. The meeting is usually held in London, and lasts three days. It generally takes the form of a number of speeches by experts in various fields and discussions in groups which subsequently present reports. From these reports conclusions are reached and often policy and plans for progress outlined. As an example, the subjects discussed at one recent general meeting included: Teaching Acting, Aesthetic Values, Adult Festivals, Needs and Hopes, and Shakespearian Production.

NEWSLETTER

A monthly Newsletter is sent to all Conference members, and contains details of county activities, information of general interest, conference business, a diary of forthcoming lectures, courses, local plays, etc., and reviews of new worthwhile theatre books and plays.

COUNTY DRAMA COMMITTEES

These are the members of the Standing Conference and they do excellent work throughout the country in aiding amateur drama. They arrange courses and lectures in all phases of theatre; issue bulletins of information and coming events; encourage and assist in planning new auditoriums; develop youth groups and youth festivals as well as adult festivals; some have collections of costumes, lighting and stage equipment which they hire out at very nominal rates to amateurs; their advisers are available to help amateur producers and to speak to groups on a variety of theatre subjects; some issue regular magazines full of theatrical news, photographs, advice, etc.; all are in close communication with educational authorities and are working towards greater drama activity in schools.

The Standing Conference does important work in furthering drama as an educative force. Its decentralized committees are able to give valuable aid to amateurs in their own localities because of their knowledge of local conditions.

THE SCOTTISH COMMUNITY DRAMA
ASSOCIATION

In 1926 a meeting of representatives of Scottish amateur societies was convened in Glasgow by the late D. Glen MacKemmie, in order to organize a Scottish area for the British Drama League's National Festival. From this meeting an Association was formed not only to deal with the Festival, but to encourage and assist amateur drama in Scotland in every way. Until 1932 the National One-Act Play Festival was run in conjunction with the B.D.L., but since that date the Scottish organization has undertaken all responsibility for it, with the final Scottish winner being free to enter the B.D.L. finals in London if the group so desires.

Many outstanding theatre personalities have been Honorary Presidents of the S.C.D.A. since its formation, including Sir James Barrie, Professor J. R. Allardyce Nicoll, Dr. Gordon Bottomley, Mr. James Bridie and Mr. Alistair Sim. Their aid has been invaluable to the work of the movement.

Membership has now grown to 850 amateur groups and 2,600 individual members, with a headquarters established at 19 Melville Street, Edinburgh. There are a permanent Secretary and several full-time professional Advisers, who travel throughout the country giving courses, adjudications and advice on the many aspects of drama.

The S.C.D.A. feels a special responsibility in encouraging the production and writing of Scottish plays, and although the playwriting competitions it organizes periodically are not limited to Scottish drama, special interest is shown in such work, and member groups are encouraged to try out new plays by native playwrights.

There seems to be a great deal of this original creative activity in Scotland, which might well be emulated by other parts of Great Britain.

For purposes of administration, the S.C.D.A. has five Divisional areas, each with a Divisional Secretary who acts as a liaison officer with the head office. Each Division sends three representatives to meetings of the General Council, which are held yearly. This Council directs general policy.

Annual rates of subscription are: Clubs 21s.; Individual Members 7s. 6d.; Youth Clubs 5s.

Services offered to members are as follows:

FESTIVALS

A National One-Act Play Festival of Community Drama is organized by the S.C.D.A. annually. It is held in three stages: Preliminary, Divisional and Scottish Final, and each is judged by expert adjudicators, who give teams both public and private criticism. Travelling expenses not exceeding £25 and royalties of teams participating are paid by the Association. The general rules are similar to those of the B.D.L. Festivals mentioned in greater detail previously. A special award, the D. Glen MacKemmie Trophy, is given for the best presentation of a play dealing with Scottish Life and Character.

Some full-length play festivals are held in Divisions, and it is hoped that these may also develop on a national scale.

S

Special Youth Drama Festivals are organized in many Divisions, and these are mainly non-competitive. Constructive adjudications are given, with the hope that this sympathetic advice will help to raise the standards and encourage young people, as well as giving them a chance of performing publicly with the help of a qualified stage staff. Most of the costs of presentation, with the exception of costuming, rehearsal and certain local expenses, are paid by the Association.

A season of amateur plays, which might almost be called a Festival within a Festival, was arranged annually for some years by the S.C.D.A. at the Edinburgh International Festival. A number of outstanding productions were presented and societies not only from Scotland, but from England, France, Canada and Norway were invited to take part. They often provided exciting plays not seen in the commercial professional theatre.

LIBRARIES

Believing that decentralization is a practical policy, the S.C.D.A. operates five separate Libraries, one in each Division, and if the books desired are not available in that particular library, it is arranged to procure them from another. Full catalogues are available for each library and a National Catalogue is planned to incorporate these. The libraries contain reference books and single copies of plays. These are loaned free to members, and there is a charge for sets. Assistance is given in choosing plays and textbooks.

DRAMA SCHOOLS AND COURSES

In 1929, the B.D.L. organized the first of the St. Andrews Summer Schools of Drama, in that Scottish centre, and in 1932 its administration was taken over wholly by the S.C.D.A. The school is held for two weeks every summer, and employs a large staff of professional experts who give two courses in Acting, one for beginners and one for more advanced actors; in addition to a course in Production, which includes instruction in all phases of play producing, there are additional classes in Mime, Speech and Make-up. Some students come back year after year, because each time new ideas are brought forward, there is a chance to meet and exchange views with fellow amateurs, and the setting of St. Andrews itself provides an ideal holiday. Scholarships are available for students who would otherwise be unable to attend.

An Autumn Drama School is also held for those who are not free in the Summer, on similar lines to the Summer School, but the location of this varies from year to year.

Another development, the Stratford Festival Drama Course, has recently been inaugurated. It is held for a week in a college near

Stratford-on-Avon. Students study and attend all the plays presented by the Stratford Memorial Theatre Company, and there are discussions and lectures given by experts. Special bus transportation is arranged from Scotland to Stratford for this course.

Another recent innovation is a School for Playwrights, which is arranged as a special week-end of lectures by experts and discussions on this subject. This is held in a large Scottish centre.

Many short-term and week-end courses are organized by the District Committees in various parts of the country at which use is often made of the Association's advisers to deal with many aspects of production and acting. Special interest is shown in courses for Youth Leaders and members of Youth Clubs. The Advisers travel throughout the country, not only giving lectures but practical assistance in producing plays, and answering queries that may arise on any phase of a society's activities. Advice is also given on the construction and equipment of halls used for dramatic performances.

PLAYWRITING COMPETITIONS

A One-Act Playwriting Competition is arranged periodically and besides a money prize being awarded, public performances are arranged for the three best plays and publication guaranteed to the winner. These are presented at a specially arranged Original Play Festival on a given evening, and a helpful public criticism provided at the finish by a qualified expert.

A Three-Act Play Competition was sponsored during Festival of Britain year by the S.C.D.A. in association with the Arts Council of Great Britain, and further work in this field is being planned. In 1955 the prize was £100, and inquiries were received from professional repertory companies regarding production of this prize-winning play.

PUBLICATIONS

The S.C.D.A. Bulletin is published thrice yearly, and issued free of charge to all members. It contains articles of theatrical interest, news of S.C.D.A. Festivals, Drama Schools and Competitions, as well as reports of members' activities, and lists of new Library books.

STAGE EQUIPMENT

A rather unique service offered by the S.C.D.A. to its members is the use of stores of scenery, curtains and lighting equipment, which are kept in each Division. These stores are continually being enlarged and hire charges are moderate.

In conclusion, the outstanding characteristics of the Scottish Community Drama Association seem to be: its special encouragement of the writing and production of plays about the Scottish scene, and its realization of the importance of trained Youth in the Amateur Theatre. Although highly independent and fiercely proud of its national heritage, the Association is fully co-operative with similar organizations throughout the British Isles. One feels that besides wanting higher standards, the S.C.D.A. fully subscribes to the policy of "getting on with the job" with little fuss, and applying the best tenets of "professionalism" to amateur production.

THE AMATEUR DRAMA COUNCIL OF IRELAND

This Council was formed in 1952, and is made up of representatives from twelve area drama festivals throughout Ireland. Its aims and objects are as follows:

(a) To foster, develop, promote and encourage amateur drama in Ireland.
(b) To co-ordinate the amateur drama movement in Ireland.
(c) To represent the interests of amateur drama in Ireland and to negotiate when necessary with departments of state or other interested bodies in matters concerning amateur drama.

FESTIVALS

The Council holds an annual All-Ireland Amateur Drama Festival in Athlone, which is at present the Council's headquarters. Inquiries may be addressed to the Honorary Secretary, 34 Beech Park, Athlone.

Unlike many festivals the Irish one caters for both one-act and three-act plays. The competitions are divided into five sections:

1. Two or more Acts (Open)—entry fee £5.
2. Two or more Acts (Rural)—entry fee £3.
3. One-Act (Open)—entry fee £2.
4. One-Act (Rural)—entry fee £1.
5. Verse. Short verse plays of one or two Acts, or excerpts of not less than thirty minutes' acting duration—entry fee £1.
   ("Rural" denotes places with a population under 1,000.)

To compete in the All-Ireland Festival a group must be nominated by a member festival of the Council, each festival nominating four of its winning teams as follows: one nomination to each of the sections 1, 2 and 5; and one nomination to either sections 3 or 4.

The remaining rules are similar to those of the British Drama League Festival, with travel grants of up to £12 being paid for a Three-Act play and £6 for a One-Act.

COURSES

The Council has organized several successful courses for producers at Athlone, Charleville, and Bundoran, conducted by professional theatre people. It is hoped to continue these courses in other centres.

LIBRARY

The nucleus of a library has been started, which, as it is built up, should prove very useful to individual groups.

GENERAL

The Council is hoping to build up a league for uniting all individual dramatic societies, but the area festivals, some of which are well established, have been assisting groups for a number of years in their many production and other problems. The Council's Honorary Secretary reports: "If we are to build up an organization on the lines of the B.D.L. it will come through regional groups being eventually brought into a central organization."

Although Ireland's Drama Council is a very new body, there is a great deal of enthusiasm for its success and development throughout the country, and it should not be too many years before the Council takes its place in achievements beside its older related organizations in England and Scotland.

THE RELIGIOUS DRAMA SOCIETY OF GREAT BRITAIN

The Religious Drama Society of Great Britain was formed in 1929 "to foster the art of drama as a means of religious expression and to assist the production of plays which explore and interpret the Christian view of life".

Interest in Religious Drama, from which grew the idea of a national body, was revived by Dr. Bell, Bishop of Chichester (then Dean of Canterbury) in 1927, when he inaugurated the Canterbury Festivals, for which a religious drama was commissioned to be written each year by a well-known author. With the aid of Dr. Bell, the R.D.S. was formed in 1929 by Sir Francis Younghusband, Mrs. Stevenson and E. Martin Browne. Their first temporary headquarters were in a hall near Ludgate Circus, London. All work was voluntary until 1945, when the first permanent office was established in the S.P.C.K. House, Northumberland Avenue, London, W.C.2. There is now a permanent staff of six trained experts in the head office.

Many distinguished plays have been commissioned for and produced in Cathedrals, Churches and other buildings throughout the country since the R.D.S. took over this work; including T. S. Eliot's *Murder in the Cathedral*, first done at Canterbury Cathedral in 1935; and Christopher Fry's *Thor with Angels* and *The Boy with a Cart*, presented at Canterbury Cathedral in 1949; as a special venture for the Festival of Britain Christopher Fry was commissioned to write *A Sleep of Prisoners*, which the Society presented in London and toured throughout the country. All these plays were later produced by the commercial theatre in Britain, America and other parts of the world. Though Dorothy Sayers' best-known play, *The Man Born to be King*, was written for broadcasting, it has also been performed in churches, and many of her plays were first written for Cathedral production.

The Society is interdenominational and ready to aid and advise any group or individual member on dramatic presentation of a religious nature. It works in close collaboration with the Society for Promoting Christian Knowledge, which aids the R.D.S. financially and publishes its plays and literature.

Annual subscriptions for groups or individuals is £1 1s. od., and individual Life Memberships are £15 15s. od. National bodies, Regional or Diocesan Committees may be affiliated to the Society for an annual subscription of £2 2s. od.

THE NEW PILGRIM PLAYERS

This is the Society's own Company of professional players who tour Britain with religious plays, and play at the invitation of church, industry and other organizations in halls, churches, even in factory canteens. Using only simple adaptable curtains, steps, units and costumes, they are able to play anywhere and their simplified production is an example to many amateur groups of effectiveness with a minimum of equipment and expense. The original Pilgrim Players group was formed by E. Martin Browne in 1939 but had to be disbanded during the War, in 1943. It was reorganized in 1952, under the direction of Pamela Keily, who has produced and travelled with the group ever since.

At one time the New Pilgrim's programme included stopping long enough in large centres for members to help local amateur groups to produce religious plays, and to give them lectures and demonstrations on various phases of theatre. For economic reasons this plan had to be discontinued, but it is hoped that some similar programme will be worked out for the future, with experts who are not members of the travelling players.

Other services provided are varied—from the Library and Play Hiring Service to the work of a Travelling Adviser, and are as follows:

THE LIBRARY

The R.D.S. Library is comprised of religious plays and reference books on the varied aspects of dramatic presentation. These may be borrowed by members for the charge of 2d. per one-act play; 3d. per three-act play (price 3s. 6d. or under); 4d. per play or volume (price over 3s. 6d.); and retained for a fortnight. Sets of plays are also available for hire, at the rate of 2s. 6d. for one week; 3s. 6d. for three weeks; 5s. for six weeks; 10s. for twelve weeks. These sets should be booked a fortnight in advance, and only one set may be hired at one time.

ADVISORY SERVICE

A full-time, fully qualified Travelling Adviser is available to give expert advice on all questions of organization, and on all aspects of production, acting, verse-speaking, costume, lighting, etc. There is also a panel of specialists available for consultation.

SCHOOLS AND COURSES

Under the guidance of the Travelling Adviser, a ten-day Summer School is held each year during which courses are given in various phases of drama, movement and music, by professional experts in these fields, culminating in student productions. Two chaplains are in attendance and regular services held. The object of this summer school is not merely to instruct in drama, but to imbue the participants with a clearer understanding of the part that Religious Drama can play in the world today, and to promote fellowship through Christian ideals. Week-end courses are also arranged at the request of groups in various centres throughout the country.

ANNUAL GENERAL MEETING

This is a one-day Conference held usually in London in November, at which reports are given of the year's activities, discussions are held, and sometimes a Brains Trust, followed by tea.

PUBLICATIONS

A quarterly journal, *Christian Drama*, is sent free of charge to all members. Non-members may buy it for one shilling per copy. It contains articles by experts on Religious Drama, its production, acting and writing; news of the New Pilgrim Players; Library notes, including brief reviews of new religious plays and theatre books; and in a section entitled "Far and Wide", news of religious drama groups in Great Britain and other parts of the world.

The R.D.S. also publishes, or has published through the S.P.C.K., plays of special merit and pamphlets on various aspects of religious drama.

ADVICE TO PLAYWRIGHTS

Plays may be submitted to R.D.S. readers for constructive criticism for fees of 7s. 6d. for a one-act play and 15s. for a longer play. Outstanding plays may be recommended for publication. Plays may be sent for consideration without a fee, but no criticism is supplied.

COSTUME

The Society will provide, upon request, a list of recommended firms from whom costumes may be hired.

BRANCHES

The Society encourages the formation of branches in various centres, here and abroad, which are comprised of local organizations affiliated to the R.D.S. These branches facilitate communication with the head office and act as centres for training, books, advice, etc.

To sum up, one might say that the Religious Drama Society of Great Britain is an organization that uses drama to promote the Christian Faith, but in doing so encourages a high standard of performance and production. Its sponsorship of new plays by playwrights including Eliot and Fry is important not only to religious enthusiasts, but to all lovers of the living theatre. And the zeal, artistry and ingenuity of its little band of strolling New Pilgrim Players could well be emulated by amateur groups everywhere. Whether or not one agrees fully with all its objectives, the R.D.S. is, nevertheless, a constructive and creative force in theatre today.

XXI. AMATEUR THEATRE IN GREAT BRITAIN
by Lois McLean

WIDESPREAD organized amateur theatre in Great Britain has developed enormously over the last fifty years. Amateur players have always existed, but before the Industrial Revolution acting for recreation was mainly confined to the aristocracy who had the money and leisure to indulge their hobby. As working hours decreased and wages increased, as books became available for all and most people learned to read, playmaking grew to be a popular recreation and means of self-expression for everyone who was interested.

The first attempts were not very skilled, and consisted mainly of skits performed in front parlours on special occasions, or at church concerts. The material was usually appalling and there was little or no direction; each actor giving his own individual interpretation.

Then numbers of individuals who loved the theatre and enjoyde acting as a serious hobby began to form together into permanent groups, with the purpose of presenting plays at regular intervals. Some were guided by ex-professionals living in the area, and in most cases the leaders had seen professional plays and based their productions upon these.

Today there are many thousands of amateur groups. Their membership in the British Drama League alone numbers around 4,500 and in the National Operatic and Dramatic Association around 1,000.

As interest grew so did the need for instruction, information and advice from professional specialists. From this need, central organizations like the B.D.L., N.O.D.A., S.C.D.A., etc., were formed. They instituted short courses, travelling advisers, summer schools, libraries, etc., as already discussed previously.

EDUCATIONAL DRAMA

Some thirty years ago educational authorities began to encourage a more widespread knowledge of drama by introducing evening classes for adults in many aspects of theatre, and by encouraging drama in schools. Although there are few formal courses in drama taught to school children, teachers are becoming increasingly conscious of the value of children's playmaking, either as a completely imaginative creative activity or as a stimulation of interest in other subjects.

Typical of the activity sponsored by Borough and County Councils is that of the London County Council's courses. These are held in the evenings from 6.30 to 8.30 throughout the week, and include such subjects as Modern Drama, Shakespeare, Stage Technique, and Poetry and Miming. The entire curriculum is available to anyone living in the London area for 15s. per year (three terms). The centre of activities is the City Literary Institute, which has a fully equipped modern theatre seating 250. Regular productions are given here, not only by those enrolled in classes, but by many London societies.

The classes produce at least one Shakespearian play each year, and an evening of scenes from Shakespeare, as well as two modern full-length plays and several programmes of one-acts. Audiences consist mainly of friends, relations and other students, although programmes are sometimes toured to hospitals, homes for old people, and during the war were taken to the forces.

Members of the cast pay towards the cost of production and usually maintain a costume fund. Much of the scenery and properties is made by the students. It is seldom possible to advertise on a large scale and members of the group are expected to sell most of the tickets.

Modern plays chosen are nearly always comedies, although farce is avoided as being too difficult for amateurs. Play choice is limited too by the predominance of women taking the courses. Some productions have included: *The Dover Road* by A. A. Milne, *Trelawny of the Wells* by Pinero, *Shadow and Substance* by Paul Vincent Carroll, etc.

FESTIVALS

The Festival movement in Britain began with the desire of societies to see the work of their neighbours, as well as a wish to show their productions to a wider audience, and to meet and exchange ideas with people from other parts of the country, whose interests were the same. The competitive element in these festivals has rather spoiled them in many cases, and a number of communities, regional theatre guilds, and county drama associations prefer to have small non-competitive festivals among themselves rather than enter the larger nation-wide events of the British Drama League, the Scottish Community Drama Association and the All Ireland Drama Council. There are scores of smaller festivals throughout the country, and they cater for both full-length and one-act plays.

PROFESSIONALS

Although the amateur theatre does not exist merely as a proving ground for professionals, a great many amateurs have turned professional and count as their earliest experience the work done with local societies. Some of the well-known theatrical personalities who were once amateurs include: Renee Asherson, Richard Attenborough, Alfie Bass, Helen Cherry, Alec Clunes, Rosalie Crutchley, Edith Evans, Vida Hope, Michael Hordern, David Kossoff, Benny Lee, Guy Middleton, Joan Miller, Cecil McGivern, Anna Neagle, John Neville, Peter Noble, Bill Owen, Wilfred Pickles, and Patricia Roc.

In addition to these are hundreds of excellent actors, actresses and technical people who are working in repertory companies throughout the country, playing supporting roles in the West End, making their mark in radio and television, and working in the theatre in other countries.

SOCIETIES

There are several different types of societies, including: 1. Those which are branches of the activities of social or commercial organizations; 2. Those which are organized to present a play only for special occasions; 3. Those attached to educational institutions, such as Universities; and 4. Permanent Groups whose main purpose is presenting a regular programme of plays. Most of the latter are known as Little Theatres.

1. The first category probably contains the largest number of amateur groups. These are formed and sponsored by Women's Institutes, Townswomen's Guilds, the Y.W.C.A., the Y.M.C.A., Boy Scouts, Church Associations and social settlements, office, transport, bank, factory, government, military, and countless other employees' organizations. Some of these societies take their work very seriously but many use drama only as a mild form of recreation, or as a money-making scheme for the parent organization. They are filled with enthusiasm, goodwill and good fellowship, and too often with self-satisfaction. They often lack trained producers and technicians, and good material. They know that friends will pay to see "good old 'Arry" in a bad script as long as there's a laugh in it. What many of them don't realize is that there would be twice as many laughs in a good play well produced.

2. Groups in the second category are usually citizens from all walks of life who are specially gathered together perhaps to present a pageant at a town's jubilee celebrations, or to commemorate some national event or holiday. They also include those who "get a play or a skit up" for local concerts, birthday parties, wedding anniversaries, etc.

3. Thirdly we have student societies, and from these many of our leading professional theatre people have come. Either they themselves discover through the society that theatre is their vocation, or they are "discovered" by some management in a student production. Societies like the famous OUDS at Oxford, and the Cambridge Footlights Dramatic Club are often training grounds for future professionals.

However, many young people (like the medical student hailed recently as a top-rate comedian in a Cambridge Revue) prefer to continue their studies, and turn down lucrative commercial theatre offers. The experience they have gained in student plays will, in many cases, make them valuable amateur community players when they go into their chosen professions.

4. Lastly there are a smaller number of little theatres, who take their work very seriously indeed. Their prime aim is good theatre and the promotion of high standards in play choice, acting and production. These are the zealots of the amateur theatre. Many of their members are professional in every aspect but payment for services rendered. They devote all their leisure time to their theatre.

In the following pages the origins, development and work of some of the little theatres is outlined. The list is by no means complete but is a fairly representative selection from the British Isles. The majority are those whose efforts have enabled them to own or control their own playhouses, and most are members of the Little Theatre Guild of Great Britain. They are not merely playing at play acting, but have a respected place in the theatrical scene, often presenting exciting new plays and styles of production not seen in the commercial theatre.

Their formation stretches over a period from 1902 to 1950, with the majority beginning between 1925 and 1935. Their originators have been for the most part groups of people interested in theatrical art, but a few theatres have resulted from the work of one individual. The rest have been formed by such widely diverse groups as civic employees, a newspaper staff, social settlements, past-pupils' unions, a Bible class, political parties and automobile factory employees. In all cases they have broken away ·from these bodies and become independent play-producing units.

Most of their playhouses, in which everyone has a justifiable pride, have been converted by their own members from old houses, churches, barns, warehouses, shells of buildings, a store, and the cupola of an abandoned mine, while others have been planned and constructed as new buildings. One has bought a proper theatre, and several play in cinemas. A number also have club-rooms and rehearsal space in other buildings. Several were bombed out during the war and have had to begin all over again.

Before they acquired their homes the little theatres played, as most other amateur societies do, in rooms, schools, dance studios, community centres, town halls, homes, hotels and in expensive hired theatres.

The majority are club theatres, which means that only members may buy tickets. Subscription membership varies from 100 to 2,000, while active working members range from 15 to 200. Annual subscriptions vary from 5s. to £2 2s. a year. For the larger amounts subscribers are usually given a seat for a certain number of shows per year, and enjoy use of club-rooms and canteens, as well as having lectures, discussions, concerts, films, social evenings, etc., arranged for them during the year. The subscription system assures the theatre that it will have some money available at the beginning of the year and makes budgeting rather easier. However, a few maintain public play-houses, tickets being bought by anyone for any performance.

The average number of productions done each year is six, but there is a range from two or three to twenty-eight per year. Usually plays run one week to ten days, although some run two to three weeks.

A small percentage of new plays are done, and most of the little theatres rely upon Shaw, Shakespeare, the Restoration writers, Maugham, Priestley, Ibsen, Synge, and Anouilh (the last-named being their most popular writer at the moment). With these are mixed light comedies by less important writers with box office appeal; and in some groups O'Neill, O'Casey, the Greeks, Strindberg, etc. In a number of cases plays written by members, officials and founders are performed, and some of these have been later played by professionals in the West End. Topical Christmas revues, written by members, are popular. Scottish groups have taken a good lead in encouraging new Scots writers.

On the whole the little theatres are very willing to co-operate with, and learn from, the professional theatre. For the most part too, they are interested and intelligent audiences for professional plays. One amateur group has actually launched a professional touring company which now operates independently; another hires a nucleus of profes-sional actors but runs all the business and publicity itself; yet another rents its theatre to a repertory company, but controls the management and plays alternate seasons with the professionals.

A few have organized courses of training for younger and more inexperienced members, and one has a playwrights' training course.

CONCLUSION

The British Amateur Theatre is in a healthy and flourishing state at the moment. There is more activity than ever, and more oppor-tunities for sincere endeavour. With the professional theatre in the doldrums because of rising costs and the infiltration of television, the amateurs are in a fine position to encourage audiences all over the country back into the living playhouses.

LITTLE THEATRES

THE ALTRINCHAM GARRICK SOCIETY

Garrick Playhouse, Barrington Road, Altrincham, Cheshire.

In 1912 six people interested in theatre formed the Garrick Society in Altrincham. The first production, *The Silver Box*, was staged in a schoolroom. Between regular productions playreadings were given. After the first World War, the Society grew and plays were presented in the biggest hall in the town. In the '20's the Society began to save and work for its own theatre. First it bought a plot of land in a good position, and in 1932 opened the Garrick Playhouse—built solely for its own use, and entirely by its own efforts. The building is not let for any purpose. Apart from the Society's own fourteen productions per year, each running for six to ten nights, other societies are invited to bring their plays from time to time . . . usually about three or four times each season.

During the last war the theatre was occupied by a professional repertory company, but the playhouse was still run by the Society.

Since the playhouse was opened the Garrick players have produced 200 plays, which have ranged from Frederick Lonsdale's *On Approval*, with a cast of four, to such major undertakings as Shakespeare's *Antony and Cleopatra* with a cast of forty, and Coward's *Cavalcade* with a cast of eighty, full orchestra and 400 costumes. The latter was a special Coronation production.

Membership has been fixed for many years at 2,100, of which about 200 are active workers. All pay a subscription of 21s. per year, and a collection is taken at each performance. The Society finds that this system is financially successful. For many years there has been a waiting list of would-be members.

The group is now working towards a new extension to the theatre, comprising another rehearsal room, a workshop below and an additional storeroom. This will free the present rehearsal room for a lounge and refreshment room. The auditorium seats 500 people, and the proscenium opening is 32 feet wide with a 24-foot depth.

Recently an old house next door to the playhouse was bought by the Society, and this has enlarged the car park, and given extra accommodation for the Library (containing 6,000 volumes) and for the Wardrobe and furniture store. The Garrick Society is self-sufficient in the matter of sets, costumes, lights and stage equipment.

With such full seasons, members are constantly at work. While one production runs, two are in rehearsal . . . one in a hired room nearby, and another in the rehearsal room. But in spite of its size and success the Society reiterates that it exists primarily to produce many plays of quality which might not be acceptable in the commercial theatre. They try to present a balanced programme of old and new, classic and experimental. Examples of these are: *Lady Precious Stream* by S. I. Hsiung (this was the first amateur production of this play, and had a Chinese producer. The author attended rehearsals); Shaw's *Caesar and Cleopatra* and Shakespeare's *Antony and Cleopatra* (both presented in the same season); *1066 and All That* by Reginald Arkell; Ibsen's *A Doll's House*; and such popular favourites as *Waters of the Moon* by N. C. Hunter; and Roger MacDougall's *Escapade*. Among "First" productions are *If Four Walls Told* by Edward Percy; and *Gallows Glorious* by Ronald Gow.

The Society employs a professional producer, scenic artist and stage carpenter, but all other work is voluntary. It has organized a Drama School, with ninety students. There are two classes for juniors, one for teenagers and one for advanced students, and they cover all branches of theatre.

THE BOLTON LITTLE THEATRE (L.T.G.)*
Hanover Street, Bolton, Lancashire.

Formed in 1933, this Little Theatre now plays in its own playhouse, seating 340, which is owned by the President. Members have always done most of the reconstruction work on the playhouse themselves, and recently reseated more than half the auditorium with new seats, and made many improvements backstage.

Six major productions are played per year, each running from one to one-and-a-half weeks. Professional producers are engaged for these, although all other staff is voluntary. Members make all costumes and sets; and lighting equipment is owned by the group.

Included among the many successful plays done over the years are: Shakespeare's *Macbeth* and *Midsummer Night's Dream*; and *Tinder Box* by Hans Andersen; as well as two original plays written by Alan Cullen, a member of the group, *Puppet Prince* and *The Story of Rahman*.

A junior group meets regularly for classes and lectures in all phases of the theatre, and they give occasional public performances of one or two nights.

Present membership stands at around 970. Members pay £1 each per year, giving them seats to the value of £1 1s. 0d. The box office is also open to the general public.

THE BRADFORD CIVIC PLAYHOUSE (L.T.G.)
Chapel Street, Leeds Road, Bradford, Yorkshire.

Bradford is a busy commercial city, set in the centre of industrial

* Member of the Little Theatre Guild of Great Britain.

England, and it wasn't until the beginning of this century that its inhabitants had the leisure or money to think much about the arts. Then a number of musical organizations sprang up, and church or chapel concerts were given, which included dramatic sketches, usually performed with great gusto and little skill. From these grew groups devoted only to drama, and one of these was the Bradford Civic Playhouse, established in 1929. It is now considered one of the most outstanding amateur organizations in the country.

The first impetus for its formation came from the larger neighbouring city of Leeds, which already had a flourishing Civic Playhouse, and for the first few years of its existence the Bradford group was a branch of the Leeds society.

The first meeting of the tentative Bradford Civic Playhouse was held in the home of J. B. Priestley, and he was appointed its first president, which position he held for a quarter of a century. His sister was the society's first secretary.

The first piece produced was the medieval morality play, *Everyman*, presented in a church with a mixed Leeds-and-Bradford cast. It ran for two successful weeks. For several years thereafter the casts were mixed, each production opening in Leeds and then transferring to Bradford or vice versa. This proved an exhausting routine, but did not dampen the ardour of the players.

At this time the group hired the Jowett Hall in Bradford, for performances, and operated as a "free" theatre, i.e. a silver collection was taken, but no admission charged. Annual subscriptions of five shillings guaranteed a reserved seat. The system of paying is described as follows: "The five-shilling subscribers took their places first, walking past the queue of those waiting for free seats and trying hard not to feel—or still worse, look—superior. Then, about five minutes before curtain-up, the doors were thrown open and those waiting filled the remaining seats. During the long interval, announcements were made in a gentle, almost casual manner. But this was slowly worked up into an impassioned speech and appeal prior to the taking of the collection. Neither the nobility of the cause nor the eloquence of the speakers prevented the society from accumulating the largest foreign-coin and button collection in the North of England. The money was sorted out and counted during the third act and dropped into the night safe at the bank. It usually made a pleasant thud." Thus these northern pioneers were not only making "art" but "brass" as well.

Upon secession from affiliation with Leeds, the Bradford group gave the former society a gift of £200 for goodwill. They quickly recouped this amount in their first independent season. Unlike the Leeds Company, which depended more or less upon the leadership of one brilliant man, and which eventually employed professional actors, the Bradford Civic Playhouse has always worked through democratic committees in all phases of development, and apart from professional producers and scenic designers, has invariably used voluntary artists and officers.

In its first independent season, James R. Gregson was employed as Director and Philip Robinson as Scenic Artist. These men guided the artistic policy and ensured a high standard for several years. Among the guest producers were such distinguished theatre people as Komisarjevsky, Elizabeth Craig and Esme Church.

Early in 1935 a fire gutted the Jowett Hall, and the society decided to try to buy the property on which it had stood, and to build their own theatre. A vigorous campaign for funds was led by its chairman, who was then Director of Education for Bradford. Plans were drawn up and construction began. A certain amount of money was found, but it fell considerably short of the required sum. Then a generous personal investment of £5,000 was made which enabled the new theatre to be completed. Several years later, and after a series of successful productions, the donor was repaid his £5,000, much to his astonishment.

During the building of the theatre performances continued in other halls, but they were not always financially successful. Then the Bradford Civic Playhouse Travelling Theatre was formed, which presented many plays on different improvised indoor and outdoor sites. Due to the enthusiasm of a much-rained-upon company, a creditable sum of money was raised.

The new theatre, seating 300, opened in 1936 with a world première of J. B. Priestley's *Bees on the Boat Deck*. With the acquisition of the new premises several of the society's activities were extended, and new ones introduced. The showing of "uncommercial" continental films was begun, and a Drama School was organized. The library was enlarged, and the café and lounge used for exhibitions of paintings and drawings. In 1948 the Bradford Civic Theatre became one of the founder members of the Little Theatre Guild of Great Britain.

During the last war production continued, under the full-time leadership of Esme Church. A magazine was published, and a Concert Party was sent to hospitals, gun-sites, etc. Miss Church first produced Shakespeare for the society. She organized a fee-paying, full-time school of drama for those intending to become professionals, under the ægis of the Playhouse. This organization instituted the Northern Children's Theatre. Later Miss Church took over ownership of the Theatre School and the Children's Theatre and gave her entire time to them. Her organizations now share facilities with the Bradford Civic Playhouse.

The Playhouse aims at a programme of mixed "popular" and classi-

T

cal fare, to appeal to catholic tastes, and all plays are accorded a high
production standard. Fourteen major productions are given each year,
running for seven to ten days, and among some of the most successful
are: Shakespeare's *The Tempest*; *When we are married* and *The Linden
Tree* by J. B. Priestley; Shaw's *The Doctor's Dilemma*; and *The Man who
came to Dinner* by Kaufman and Hart. Naturally most of Priestley's
plays have been performed, not only because of their quality, but
because of his very personal relationship with the Company.

Although it is no longer a "free" theatre, there are over a thousand
subscription members, who provide a regular audience. The Playhouse
is completely self-supporting, and depends for its income upon subscriptions and the box office. At present the only professional staff
engaged are a stage carpenter and a caretaker, the rest of the work being
undertaken by the large membership of faithful voluntary workers.

THE CAXTON PLAYERS (L.T.G.)

The Little Theatre, 120 Cleethorpe Road, Grimsby, Lincolnshire.

This society was founded by John L. Knowles and other members of
the staff of the Grimsby *Evening Telegraph* in 1941, "chiefly so that they
had something to do to while away the time while firewatching at the
Telegraph premises" during the war. Because numbers were limited
it was difficult to find a suitable play for production, so the founder
wrote a play to fit the cast. It was produced, proved successful, so the
same author wrote other three-act and one-act plays, which have been
presented not only by the Caxton Players, but by other amateur groups
as well as repertory companies.

Within a few years as the society grew and expanded it was severed
from the newspaper where it began, and membership opened to the
general public. It still operates as a private theatre, to which members
only may be admitted.

Up to 1948 most of the plays were presented in the St. Andrews
Church Hall, after which premises were rented in Cleethorpe Road and
converted into a Little Theatre, with a seating capacity of 120. Most
of the conversion work was done by members for a cost of £1,000.

During the war, and in the immediate post-war years, many performances were given at Army and R.A.F. camps all over Lincolnshire.
At the present time seven or eight plays are produced annually, each
running for seven nights. There is an Associate Membership of 2,000
and an Active Membership of 140. The latter do all the work connected with the theatre, from cleaning to building sets, from business
management to making costumes, and acting and producing. There is
no paid staff. The group also owns its own lighting equipment.

Among the most successful plays done are Priestley's *The Linden Tree*;

Farquhar's *The Beaux' Stratagem*; *The Holly and the Ivy* by Wynyard Browne; *Dear Evelyn*; and *Hogsblood and Hellebore*.

In 1954 a student group was formed for young people under the age of eighteen. They attend fortnightly classes of lectures, and present a play in public performance once a year. Members of this Junior Section who show promise are admitted as Full Members of the society upon reaching eighteen years.

THE CLONES DRAMATIC SOCIETY
Clones, Co. Monaghan, Ireland.

This society was formed in January 1951, with the object of presenting plays of merit as a regular feature of the cultural life of the community. Since its formation it has presented two three-act plays each year, running three nights in the autumn and the spring, and has had increasing interest and support from the public.

In 1952 the group entered its first festival, and since then has won many festival awards including first place in the All-Ireland Festival, 1954, and second in 1953 and 1955.

The Company is self-supporting on box-office receipts and owns a good selection of scenery and lighting equipment. It has on lease, for all rehearsals and performances, a large hall seating 350, with a well-equipped stage.

Active membership is small, not exceeding fifteen, which limits the choice of play.

Among the most successful plays done are: *Paul Twyning* by George Shiels; *Vacant Possession* and *Mungo's Mansions* by Walter Macken; *John Ferguson* by St. John Ervine; and *Two Dozen Red Roses*.

THE CRESCENT THEATRE PLAYERS (L.T.G.)
The Crescent Theatre, The Crescent, Birmingham 1, Warwickshire.

The story of this well-known little theatre began in 1924 when a dramatic society was formed among civic employees in the Birmingham Council House. It was originally intended to provide Christmas entertainment for the staff in the Canteen, but when a regular society grew out of this, and a constitution was drawn up, it received the name of "The Municipal Players". Its prime aim was stated as, "The cultivation of dramatic art by the production of plays in the Council House Canteen and elsewhere, and the encouragement of play-writing." For the first two years the Players performed on a makeshift stage, which had to be erected and dismantled for each production, and the audience was confined to staff members and their "immediate relatives". However it was soon realized that if improvement in standards and a bank balance were to be achieved, larger audiences were necessary. In 1926 the Canteen was abandoned and the first production was given in the Birmingham and Midland Institute. An associate membership system was inaugurated and a reputation for good theatre began to be built.

In 1931, while looking for storage space, Crescent members discovered a derelict old house at No. 18 The Crescent. It had been a fine Georgian building, built in 1788, had since served as a meeting place for the first group of local "Free-Thinkers", later as a warehouse and a factory. In 1931 its high walls were covered with crumbling plaster, its floor was rotten and its roof leaked. Nothing daunted, the Municipal Players took up a collection among their members and took a long-term lease on the building. In the evenings and at week-ends officials, clerks and school teachers took up the spade, the trowel and the saw and the brush, and under the leadership of the technically qualified became excavators, bricklayers, painters and carpenters.

In April 1932 the renovated theatre opened, with a production of Edmund Rostand's *The Romantics*. At that time the seats were converted tram seats, which have since been replaced by foam rubber cushioned ones. Nevertheless, crude as the accommodation might seem, it was a permanent home.

With the opening of the Crescent Theatre, the Players opened their staff and audience membership to all. It was no longer thought wise to limit the group to civic employees only.

At the beginning of the war the theatre was used for A.R.P. work for a short time, but later for free entertainment of troops in the city. A regular programme of plays, called Garrison Theatre, was presented both by theatre staff and visiting companies.

After the war normal full-time activities were resumed, and associate membership grew to 1,750, while the present active membership stands at 250. None of the staff members are paid, all scenery and costumes are made in the Crescent's workshops. A large lighting board and numerous lights are owned by the group. The auditorium has been redecorated and modernized since its first rehabilitation, and is now a comfortable modern playhouse, seating 188 patrons.

The Crescent Players consider a training programme of great importance to the building of ever higher standards, and believe in systematic training for all actors, artists and stage technicians. To this purpose the Crescent Theatre School of Acting and Stagecraft was established in 1948 for both members and outside students. It has received financial support from the Charles Henry Foyle Educational Trust and from a private source. Professional staff are employed to guide the training courses. This year it has proved necessary to limit the courses to theatre members only, but it is hoped to be able to extend these to outside students at a later date. Although the theatre feels this programme to

be valuable pioneer work for theatre generally, it is an expensive undertaking, and must proceed slowly towards its goal.

At present seven full-length productions, each playing for thirteen
performances, are done throughout the year. The theatre is administered by a Board of Management comprised of eight elected theatre
members, the Director, the Treasurer, and the General Secretary, plus
three Trustees elected by the Municipal Players and a representative
from the Birmingham Municipal Officers' Guild. New members are
enrolled as Temporary Staff Members and, subject to continued reliable
and regular service, may be recommended for admission to General
Staff Membership. All the work of the theatre is done through Executive Heads of Departments, Team Managers and Teams.

Through the years the Crescent Theatre Players have presented such
diverse works as Cocteau's *The Typewriter*; Dorothy L. Sayers' *The
Devil to Pay*; O'Neill's *In the Zone*; Toller's *Masses and Man*; and Gogol's
The Government Inspector; as well as many of the plays of Shakespeare,
Shaw, and other classical and modern authors. New plays by members
have been done occasionally, including *The Harvest of Faith*, and
Supremacy by T. C. Kemp; a new translation of Rostand's *The Romantics*
by Bladon Peake; and *Before the Dawn* by Norman Leaker. The plays
mentioned have been picked arbitrarily as examples of varied types.

I would like to quote from a Crescent Theatre booklet, a paragraph
which so well states the need for and purpose of groups such as their
own: "The daily experience and specialized training of the common
man can be brought within the framework of the stage, and this in
due time can bring about great and formative influences in the living
theatre. The limitations of the amateur will always remain, but given
freedom, and, most important, continuity in development, these associations of ordinary men and women will increasingly promote good
play-writing and good acting and good craftsmanship."

THE CROMPTON STAGE SOCIETY (L.T.G.)
The Playhouse, Gordon Street, Shaw, Lancashire.

The Crompton Stage Society was formed in 1934 by a group of drama
enthusiasts, and acquired the use of upper rooms in the local Odd-
fellows Institute. The first major production in October 1934 was
Jeffrey Farnol's *The Broad Highway*.

In 1938 notice to quit the premises was received. This proved to be
a blessing in disguise for a frantic search for premises led to the acquisition of the present playhouse, a disused Methodist church, bought for
£150. It was converted into a little theatre seating 181, by amateur
labour, and in September 1938 it was ready to open with Shakespeare's
Romeo and Juliet.

One hundred major productions and 160 one-act plays have been performed. Play selection has been broad, but strict standards have been set, and every important period and phase of drama has been covered. Such productions as the following have been most successful: Coward's *This Happy Breed*; *Distant Point* by Hubert Griffith; Irwin Shaw's *The Gentle People*; Shaw's *The Apple Cart*; and Van Druten's *The Voice of the Turtle*. First performances have been given of *The Rolling Stone* by Leonard Irwin; *The Guardian Angel Play*, by Dr. Max Mell; and *The Castiglione Brothers* by Alberto Colantuoni.

All work is voluntary and there is an Active Membership of 100, who pay a fee of 10s. annually. There are also 800 Subscribers, who pay 15s. annually, which entitles them to a free seat for five plays during the season.

Each play runs for ten days, and there are around six major productions per year.

The society recently celebrated its twenty-first birthday, and, as one member stated, "It is hoped, the celebrations over, that we can settle down to tackle the next two decades as seriously and illogically as ever, to the profit of numbers of the people." The *Oldham Press* recently said, "The Crompton Stage Society sets the standard for drama in this area."

THE DUNDEE DRAMATIC SOCIETY

The Little Theatre, 58 Victoria Road, Dundee, Angusshire, Scotland.

The Dundee Dramatic Society was formed in 1924 by a group of people interested in the theatre. At first only one-act plays were presented in the Training College Hall. The difficulty of finding suitable accommodation for rehearsals was solved in 1925 when the society rented premises for that purpose. Soon afterwards the first three-act plays were presented at the Palace Theatre. The society claims to have played in all the theatres which Dundee once possessed—Her Majesty's, The Queen's, The Broadway, The Palace, and The Victoria.

As one by one the theatres closed their doors to reopen as picture houses, it was imperative that the society should find its own theatre. Accordingly, in 1936 the members, both honorary and active, rallied together and an unpromising store was rented at the back of the Vic cinema. Most of the work of conversion was undertaken by the members, and later the Dundee Dramatic Society presented its first production in its own Little Theatre, which was for some time the only living theatre in Dundee. It is a well-equipped building, seating 195 people. The professional Dundee Repertory Company made its first appearance there until it moved to its own theatre.

The society has always taken a keen part in the work of the Scottish

Community Drama Association, and three Chairmen of this organization have come from the Dundee group. In 1932 the society gained
second place in the S.C.D.A.'s annual Festival with Thornton Wilder's
The Christmas Dinner, which was taken to the Old Vic in London to
represent Scotland in the British Drama League Festival.

During the war the society turned chiefly to Concert Party work and
toured many army camps as well as appearing at the Dundee Garrison
Theatre.

After the war normal activities were quickly resumed. In 1950 with
the generous help of its members as well as friends, the society became
the owner of the Little Theatre. This was a bold step to take, as the
cost of running and maintaining such a building was steadily rising.

Now the society presents annually four three-act plays, each running
seven nights, several one-acts and occasionally a revue. During the
season of 1954–5 a total of thirty-nine performances were given in the
Little Theatre, and two performances given as guests of societies in
other towns.

All staff, players, etc., are amateur, and they build all their own
scenery, own their own lights and some costumes. The Honorary
Membership stands at 286, while the Active Membership is seventy-six.

Among its most successful productions the society counts Thornton
Wilder's *Our Town*; Coward's *Peace in our Time*; *You Can't Take it With
You* by Kaufman and Hart; *The Story of Madelaine Smith* by Howard
Lockhart; and *As Long as They're Happy* by Vernon Sylvaine. Several
original plays by members of the society have been performed, including
Aubrey Writes a Book by Alex Robertson; and *Drumgarth, Grissell Jaffray*,
and *Temples of Paestum* all by Philip Blair. A number of plays by other
Scottish playwrights have been presented, which is encouraging for
native writers.

THE EVERYMAN THEATRE COMPANY
Spennymoor Settlement, King Street, Spennymoor, Co. Durham.

The Everyman Theatre Company was formed as part of the activities of the Spennymoor Settlement, and it is interesting to note the
beginning of this organization.

"The Spennymoor Settlement was established during the year 1931,
when the collieries were idle, or working short time, and some coal was
being drawn from a nearby drift. The township was but one little part
of the wreckage left on the verge of civilization's shore by the receding
tide of economic prosperity. Unemployment, with the resulting priva-
tion and despair, hung over the town like a cloud. The people's life
was a day-to-day struggle against forces they did not understand and
were most inadequately equipped to deal with."

A Warden was sent from Toynbee Hall, London, to extend the Settlement idea of community self-help amongst the workless miners and their families. This was financed by the Pilgrim Trust. During the Settlement's first years, classes were held in a small shop, a back room and outhouse, and as the years passed the acquisition of other adjoining shop premises was made to accommodate the growing numbers of members who attended the classes. Play-reading, local government, singing, history, women's classes, cobbling, woodwork, a sketching club, etc., were some of the subjects.

The Everyman Theatre Company was formed in the early years, and in 1938 plans were prepared for a Settlement Theatre Hall. From various donations received, the building, with a seating capacity of 160, was duly erected. Thus the company was able to present its plays in its own theatre, instead of using hired halls in the town, which had no theatrical equipment whatsoever. The theatre was equipped with a first-class switchboard, lights and dimmers. A box set and curtains were obtained and used in productions.

The Everyman Company, like the other classes, was under the direction of the Warden, who had had professional experience in the theatre, and many first-class productions were presented to the public. In the early years at least a year's rehearsal and planning was given to a play before its production.

The Everyman's theatre has been in constant use, not only for its own productions, but for visiting professionals and classes.

When large grants from the parent body ceased, the Durham County Council and the Spennymoor Urban District Council made it possible for the Settlement to continue, although the County Council's grant ceased several years ago, and it fell upon the Everyman group to endeavour to raise sufficient funds for the Settlement to carry on its work. The theatre did this by increasing the number of productions to four each year, with four performances of each play.

Unfortunately even this was not enough to maintain a full-time Warden, and now the work is carried on under the guidance of an Executive Committee and a part-time Warden. Classes still continue to be held, now organized by the Workers' Educational Association.

The Everyman's productions are left to the experienced members, who have received their training many years ago. Recent productions over the last year have played to increased audiences, showing a renewed interest, and houses are almost full for each performance, with membership steadily increasing.

Theatre membership is 15s. per year, and members number approximately 100, with forty of these being active in production, acting, etc.

Good plays of all periods and countries are presented, and among the most successful have been *They Came to a City* by J. B. Priestley; *Quinn's Secret* by G. Shiels; O'Casey's *Juno and the Paycock*; *The Holly and the Ivy* by Wynyard Browne; and *The Seven Sleepers* by R. Gittings. Other works chosen have included those by Ibsen, Strindberg, Synge, Maugham, and others, as well as several original plays by the Company's members.

THE EXPERIMENTAL THEATRE CLUB

7 Cheapside, Manchester, Lancashire.

This unusual club was formed in 1948 by R. Maxwell Taylor, and its aim is to experiment in the theatre . . . with new plays, new authors, and new techniques and approaches to established works.

In 1955 the group attained premises of its own, in a cellar which seats sixty people, where actors perform without a stage, at one end of the room, using the natural walls as background. An extract from the *Manchester Guardian* of 3 March, 1955, describes the impact of the first production in these surroundings:

"In a cellar in Cheapside, Manchester, last night the Experimental Theatre Club presented a genuine experiment in amateur dramatic entertainment and showed what can be done with a little courage. Without stage, curtains, or set, with no more space, in fact, than the corner not needed for the audience, they presented three fulsome plays . . . a pert piece of Grand Guignol, a garrulous Chekhov comedy and a Eugene O'Neill melodrama . . . each of which demanded acting in the grand manner. The enjoyment was contagious, caught by the audience and players alike, and suggesting that this is perhaps a wiser policy for true amateurs than the attempt to do however well what the professional can always do better. Amateur productions are seldom as much fun for the audience as for the actors, and yet if both are to be members of the theatre club then their pleasure should be equal. An intimate cellar appears to afford that equality."

For the first four years all productions were anonymous, the whole Company preferring this. However, press and public demanded names, so these have been given since.

Membership numbers around 150, with a solid working nucleus of sixty. Three major productions are given each year in the Lesser Free Trade Hall, the Queen's Hall, and in the Library Theatre (when the resident professional Company is not active). Tickets for these productions are not limited to the membership, but open to the public, and range from 6s. 6d. to 3s. Each play runs for a week. Many more special productions are given for members only, in the group's own small theatre.

The plays chosen vary greatly, and among the most successful produced have been Anouilh's *Thieves' Carnival* (which the group was invited to present at the British Drama League's Malvern Theatre Week in 1954, and was seen by a large international audience); Saroyan's *The Time of Your Life*; Elmer Rice's *Counsellor at Law*; *The Assassin* by Peter Yates; and *Dark of the Moon* by Richardson and Berney. Original plays presented include *We Dig for the Stars* by T. B. Morris; *The Mountain*, and *Great Uncle Pompeo* by Anthony Garwood. *We Dig for the Stars* made headlines when it was banned by the Lord Chamberlain, and a public performance was not allowed. However, after a postponement, the Experimental Theatre Club presented it to "members only" audiences, and count it among their finest productions.

Certain special pieces of scenery and costumes are made by the Club, but most of these are hired, as is lighting equipment.

THE GLASGOW JEWISH INSTITUTE PLAYERS
95 South Portland Street, Glasgow, C.5, Scotland.

In 1936 a group of people formed a drama section as one of the activities of the Glasgow Jewish Institute, which is a social and cultural centre for the Jewish community in Glasgow. There were no facilities for dramatic activity within the Institute building, and the first performance, of one-act plays, was on a specially erected temporary platform. However, encouraged by their successful reception even on a makeshift stage, the group continued to function, and through an appeal for funds was able to build a properly equipped stage which was opened in 1938. The auditorium seats 185 and has tip-up seats acquired through public and private subscription.

During the war years activities were stopped but some members continued to gain experience with the Glasgow Unity Theatre.

In 1944 the group began once more to present plays in their own premises, and now gives three full-length plays for seasons of two weeks each, throughout the year, in addition to preparing entries for various festivals.

A keen interest is shown in festival work, and awards have been won both in Scottish and B.D.L. finals.

A number of original one-act plays have been presented by the Company over the years, many written by members. Some of these include: Avrom Greenbaum's *The Bread of Affliction* (later published in J. W. Marriott's collection of *Best One-Act Plays of 1937*), and the same author's *Kultur, Children of Dreams*, and *Watch on the Clyde*; Michael Goldberg's *Hymn Without Praise* and *Down Track*.

Successful revues include Michael Goldberg's *Sweet and Sour*, and *Sweeter and Sourer*.

Among the most successful full-length plays produced the group counts: *Awake and Sing* by Clifford Odets; *Morning Star* by Sylvia Regan;

The Gentle People by Irwin Shaw; *The Dybbuk* by S. Ansky; and *Juno and the Paycock* by Sean O'Casey.

Membership is open to all members of the Jewish Institute but active participants in productions number roughly between twenty-five and forty-five. There is no separate fee for membership in the drama section, and the box-office is open to the general public. All profits go to help the parent body, but the drama group is free of rentals for performance and rehearsal space. Most rehearsals take place on the stage.

Recently alterations were made to the stage and lighting equipment so that the latter is now controlled from the back of the auditorium. The group owns its own lights, and some scenery and costumes, although hiring is necessary. The only professional help used is in the matter of scene designing.

The Players are ardent devotees of the "group theatre" system, and state: "We firmly believe in ample, systematic discussion of a work before, during and after the performance, and we don't tolerate the 'star' mentality."

THE GREAT HUCKLOW VILLAGE PLAYERS (L.T.G.)
The Playhouse, Great Hucklow, Derbyshire

Most of the little theatres dealt with in this book are centred in large cities or towns, but the Village Players, a group with a vast reputation, has its home in the tiny Peakland village of Great Hucklow in the hills of Derbyshire. It has perhaps two dozen houses and a hundred inhabitants, but its unique theatre attracts not only coachloads of spectators from large cities such as Manchester, Liverpool, Sheffield and Derby, and from centres as far as seventy or eighty miles away, but visitors from the Dominions, America, and other far-away countries, who have heard about the Players before they left their homelands. How has this come about? It is a fascinating story, and is told in picturesque detail in a book published in 1952, entitled *Twenty-five Years of Play Producing* by the Players' founder, L. du Garde Peach. It will only be possible here to pick out a few of the salient facts and features of the group.

Basically it is the result of the work, ingenuity, faith and finance of one man . . . L. du Garde Peach, who has always been and still is the Director. He has produced all the plays, acted in a number, written many (a great number of which have later been done in London and by repertory and amateur groups), and has turned his hand to theatre building, set construction, business management, in fact at one time or another to all the aspects of "getting a play on" at Great Hucklow.

He states the organization of the group as follows: "The Village

Players were different from the beginning. They have never been a Dramatic Society which anybody could join, and I sincerely hope they never will be. In this single fact lies much of their strength and staying power. No one pays or ever has paid any subscription to belong and no one is ever cast for a part unless they are capable of giving a reasonably good performance of it. But once anyone has played a part, however small, he or she becomes a Village Player for life, although that is no guarantee that they will ever get another part, and certainly confers no right to demand one." Players are recruited "for particular parts with a pretty good pre-knowledge of their capabilities. There is, of course, as there must be in any company with a continuous corporate existence, a hard core of reliable players, men and women who have parts in one production after another. But even they change, and it is not always the old hands who play the leads." Casting is always done by Mr. Peach, because he maintains that the producer should always cast the play. However, if there is any doubt the "old hands of the Company talk it over without prejudice. If no one suitable can be suggested by any of us, the play is dropped.

"It may be asked how the Company is held together at all, when there is no membership and the hope of parts so uncertain. The answer is the Village Players' Club, a body entirely separate from the Village Players as a play-producing team, but of which anyone who has played with us twice becomes automatically a member. We meet throughout the year in the theatre, when no productions are in the making." These meetings are usually social occasions, and such activities as games of darts are enjoyed as much as theatrical discussions.

The Players began in 1927 when Mr. Peach decided to do a production of Shakespeare's *The Merchant of Venice*. At an annual village party he put forth this idea and had completed the cast before the evening was over. He had at his disposal as a theatre, a large dayroom, 50 ft. by 20 ft. This was in a building called the Holiday Home, which had been erected through the efforts of Mr. Peach's father, a clergyman who began the idea of holidays for poor children from nearby Sheffield in the clean air of Great Hucklow. At first the children were housed with villagers, later in the Holiday Home. During the winter months the building was empty, and free for theatrical productions. Half of the dayroom's floor space was used for a "stage", the other half for the audience. From the beginning the founder insisted upon first-class productions. Although the early settings were simple curtains and units, etc., they were carefully planned, and just as carefully constructed, decorated and lit. No shoddy, makeshift scenery was allowed. Curtains were well hung and masked, the home-made costumes and properties accurate in detail. Insistence upon "quality" has earned the Great Hucklow Players their wide reputation. Even today they do only three or four productions a year, each running for three weeks, and this ensures the wholly amateur actors and backstage workers plenty of time for careful preparation in every aspect of presentation.

The first play was followed by Shakespeare's *Twelfth Night*; then Shaw's *Arms and the Man*; Shakespeare's *As You Like It*; Shaw's *Pygmalion*; and the medieval *Everyman*, and *The Shepherd's Play* . . . the list is too long to print every one. All the plays chosen are of a high standard, for as Mr. Peach states, "If the players are inexperienced the more need for a good play." A good adage for any and all amateur groups.

In 1933 the Players presented their first world première, *Clive of India* by W. P. Lipscomb, and this inaugurated a long series of "first" productions. This play was subsequently done in London with a professional cast, where it ran for over a year, and was later made into a film. Another Lipscomb première at Great Hucklow was *Ninety Sail*, which also ran in London afterwards.

Productions continued in the Holiday Home until March 1938, when it was taken over by people not sympathetic to winter amateur performances, and the Players looked round for another home. This they found in the stone "cupola" of an abandoned lead mine. They had been storing scenery in this shell of a building for some time, and in August 1938, began to reconstruct it into a theatre. The work was helped by a loan of £500 from the Sheffield Council, out of which £200 was paid for the building, and £100 for the land around it. All the work, from digging drains to building stone pillars, was done by players in their spare time. Even casual onlookers found a spade or a trowel in their hands.

In October 1938 the Playhouse opened with four one-act plays written by L. du Garde Peach. Apart from a twenty-month period in 1944, production has been continuous from that time, although during the war the number of performance nights had to be cut because of transportation difficulties. During this time, too, productions were taken to such centres as Buxton and Chesterfield.

The finished theatre contains 265 tip-up seats (most of which were obtained at a sale from an old hall in Sheffield for 1s. 9d. each), a well-equipped stage 28 feet wide and 30 feet deep, dressing-rooms and a Green Room under the stage, a workshop attached to the main building, a box-office, central heating, and even a car park with accommodation for 100 cars. Not all these conveniences were completed upon the first opening, but were gradually added. The Players now own a good stock of scenery, two sets of stage drapes, tapestries, a panatrope, lighting equipment and a number of costumes. When a set is being built, four Sundays are set aside for construction parties, to which all volunteers are welcome. Usually there are three weeks of rehearsals for each play.

All income is derived from the box-office, at which each seat is sold for 2s. 6d.

Among the most successful Village Players' productions Mr. Peach lists Shakespeare's *Othello* and *Macbeth*; Gogol's *The Government Inspector*; *Anastasia* by Marcelle Maurelle and Guy Bolton; and his own *The Path of Glory*, *The Town that would have a Pageant*, and *The White Sheep of the Family*. But these are only a small number of the memorable performances seen at Great Hucklow.

THE GREEN ROOM THEATRE

The Green Room Theatre, Cheapside, Manchester 2, Lancashire.

The original theatre was destroyed by bombing during the war, and the present one converted by members from a derelict basement. The result is a modern, well-equipped intimate little theatre seating ninety-eight. This post-war theatre was opened in 1946 with a production of Ronald Duncan's *This Way to the Tomb*, with music by Benjamin Britten.

The Green Room Theatre specializes in doing unusual, off-beat plays, and has presented a good number of world premières as well as "first" English and European productions. Among those performed for the first time on any stage are Lord Byron's *Cain*; *A Captain of Industry* by Robert Tarnacre; *Saraband for a Dynasty* by Lydia Ragosin; *Outrageous Fortune* by Parnell Bradbury; and *The Death of a Traitor* by Anthony Mervyn. The first European production of William Saroyan's *Jim Dandy* was given by this Company, as well as the first English presentations of such plays as *Tree of Heaven* by Mervin Mills; *Wrack* by Peader O'Donnell; *The Swedenhjelms* by Halmar Bergman; *Wife to a Famous Man* by Sierra; and *Right You Are* by Pirandello.

The theatre has 250 associate members, and 220 active members. All work is voluntary, and all sets and most costumes are made by members. Lighting equipment is owned by the Company.

Five productions are done per year, each playing eight nights.

The President of this theatre group is Dame Sybil Thorndike, and the Vice-Presidents are Sir Laurence Olivier and Sir Ralph Richardson.

THE HALIFAX THESPIANS (L.T.G.)

The Playhouse, King Cross Street, Halifax, Yorkshire.

This successful little theatre was first organized by a small group of Halifax citizens zealously interested in forming an amateur repertory company, as distinct from the half-hearted, casual dramatic societies in the community. In September 1927 a meeting was held at the White Swan Hotel, to which over 200 "Persons known to be interested" were invited by the small group. The result was the founding of the Halifax Thespians, with a constitution, a general committee, and appropriate sub-committees for finance, management, casting, stage, play-reading, music and play-writing. This same general structure is followed at the present time.

The society's first public activity was a series of nine play-readings given in a lecture hall, and included works by Shaw, Ibsen, Galsworthy, Yeats, Chesterton, Barrie and Synge.

Plays were first staged at the Y.M.C.A., and in 1928 a special matinee of Barrie's *Dear Brutus* was given at the Theatre Royal. Up to 1930 rehearsal rooms were hired, and in this year a Green Room Club was formed within the society, which has operated ever since. It prepares private monthly shows in which younger and less experienced actors, producers and technicians are given a chance to gain experience. Lectures, play-readings, discussions and classes in all phases of theatre are also part of the Green Room Club's programme.

In 1930 too an agreement was drawn up for the Thespians to take over tenancy of the Alexandra Hall.

The Halifax Permanent Building Society had plans for building a public hall, and were instead persuaded by the Thespians to convert the Alexandra Hall into a theatre. This was done, and the most modern cyclorama, lighting equipment and stage facilities installed. In 1931 the Hall was opened with a production of Capek's *Adam the Creator*.

Plays were presented here until 1939, and the Thespians built a reputation for advanced and modernistic production technique and lighting effects. However, the group still hoped for a building of their own, where high rents would be obliterated and shaky finances made more steady. In 1934 three club rooms were found, one of which was converted into a tiny theatre for Green Room shows, and where the Thespians could entertain visiting professional companies as well as have social evenings. The latter are now held at intervals throughout the year so that the newer members of the society may meet and mingle with the more established members.

In 1937 a Play Reading Circle was inaugurated which now meets every three weeks and presents rehearsed readings of plays unlikely to secure the necessary support if staged. Its activities have expanded to include musical evenings, lectures by theatre experts, unusual films and individual prose and poetry readings.

When the war came the Alexandra Hall was requisitioned by the military, and many of the Thespian's members left for the forces. However, the remaining members decided to carry on, and played in the hall of Heath Grammar School. During the war audiences increased and successful productions were staged of such plays as Shaw's *In Good King Charles's Golden Days*; *Thunder Rock* by Robert Ardrey; Priestley's *When we are Married*; and the first British production of Maxwell Anderson's *Wingless Victory*. Camp tours were also organized and in a week of special performances at the Grand Theatre £687 was raised for the Red Cross and St. John's War Organization.

At the end of the war, in 1946, with £1,300 on hand from their earnings, the Thespians took up the search for a home of their own. They found it in a disused Methodist chapel, which was lying almost derelict and filled with rubbish. The members themselves converted it into a modern playhouse with all amenities. The auditorium seats 298, there is an advanced lighting scheme with the latest equipment, dressing-rooms, wardrobe-room, scene shop, furniture store, kitchen and café, and a courtyard with flowers and shrubs.

The completed playhouse opened in September 1949 with *The Merry Wives of Windsor*, and since then nine public performances have been given every year, each running for ten nights. General membership stands at 1,000 and the active members carry out all construction of scenery, making of costumes, lighting, etc. The only paid staff includes a box-office clerk and a caretaker.

A variety of plays is presented, with the emphasis on comedies in order to encourage audience attendance, and among the most successful productions have been Emlyn Williams' *Spring 1600* and *Night Must Fall*; Anouilh's *Ring Round the Moon*; and a special Coronation show, *Theatre Cavalcade*, being excerpts from plays pre-Shakespeare to the present day with special narration by the society's president, Dr. Phyllis Bentley.

A Producer's Forum is now held at which producers meet and discuss the productions. This has been found to be very useful.

A scheme for reduced prices for school parties and old-age pensioners is in force. In order to help pay the amount still owing on the Playhouse, the building is let to other organizations for plays and concerts when the Thespians are not using it. A very active Canteen not only pays for itself but adds funds to the society.

THE HALL GREEN LITTLE THEATRE (L.T.G.)
Pemberley Road, Acocks Green, Birmingham 27, Warwickshire.

In 1950 this comparatively new little theatre decided to construct its own theatre building. A booklet entitled "Greasepaint and Girders" was published, containing the following lively description of its history and plans:

"The Hall Green Little Theatre does not only consist of bricks and mortar, of sand and cement. It is a force, created by a group of talented amateur artists and technicians of all ages who have pooled their resources, forgotten their differences and worked as a team."

Today the Hall Green Little Theatre is becoming well known and its path can be clearly seen. It has not always been so. Let us look back and see how it rose from the inevitable anti-climax which followed the Second World War.

One early feature of the return to peacetime conditions was the need for self-expression. Men and women, accustomed to the fast pace of the war years, found postwar living conditions dull and stifling. They sought an emotional outlet and many found it in the amateur theatre movement. The Hall Green Little Theatre, officially born in September 1943, flourished, in company with other similar groups throughout the country.

Several plays were presented in local halls and one or two spartans constructed scenery under deplorable conditions in a tiny shed, neither wind- nor rain-proof. The original idea of a theatre building was pursued by members of the Committee and application was made for a site in Fox Hollies Road.

To the general members, however, progress in this direction appeared slow and they soon became restive and unsettled in consequence. Between shows they rarely met and, before long, it became evident that a central meeting place was essential if the group was to survive.

Then came the news that one member had located a dilapidated repair garage which was to let. Its acquisition was to prove the turning point in the company's history. At last there was somewhere to rehearse, somewhere to construct scenery, make costumes and properties and, most important of all, somewhere to meet and "talk theatre".

They moved in. The job of refitting the garage was a colossal one. It involved raising the roof, putting in a new floor, repairing the walls, decorating, battling with rats and rain. In a surprisingly short time the job was done and the Hall Green Little Theatre had a home of its own.

Then individual talents came to light. Members revealed capabilities of which they were not even suspected. Exquisite work was produced by a young scenic artist. Others turned their attention to making electrical equipment, resulting in a stage lighting section of which any theatre might be proud. Costumes were designed and made—not haphazardly but with a strict regard for detail, colour and period. Each individual saw the others in a new light. The members had found themselves. Talking and quarrelling gave way to respect for craftsmanship, and responsibility of each for the whole was born.

Plans for the theatre building were discussed with renewed vigour. Temporary buildings were inspected, members travelling hundreds of

U

miles in the process. The idea of a permanent brick-built theatre, once little more than a dream, became nearer. It was suggested that an architect be approached. "Why do that?" asked one member. "I'll draw up some plans." Within a few weeks he had done so and they were submitted to the Authorities.

Minor technical difficulties necessitated revised drawings but the Corporation departments were ever helpful and early in 1950 the plans were finally approved. Immediately a building licence was applied for and secured on the grounds that no outside labour should be paid for.

Building began on 1 April 1950, and the theatre opened just one year and one week later, with a production of *The Circle of Chalk* by Alfred Henschke. Construction was carried out during the evenings, weekends and any spare time any members could give. It is still not completed, with enlargements to be made to the stage, auditorium, foyer and dressing-rooms. Building goes forward during the summer months when plays are not being performed. At present the theatre seats 163, but will accommodate 208 when finished. The acting area will be 25 feet wide and 31 feet deep plus a bow-shaped "apron". The proscenium will extend across the entire auditorium giving an unobstructed view of the whole stage from all parts of the house.

The Hall Green group has always presented a varied programme of plays, and count among the most successful, *The Golden Legend of Shults* by James Bridie; Thornton Wilder's *Our Town*; Shakespeare's *Twelfth Night*; the Capek brothers' *The Insect Play*; and *Beauty and the Beast*. At present five plays are given per year, each running for nine nights.

The theatre's active membership is about 100, with a subscription audience membership of 1,000. All work is voluntary and all sets, lighting and costumes are undertaken by members. A student group operates under a professional instructor.

The Hall Green Company has played host to interesting visitors from overseas, including in 1952 a Copenhagen University group who presented *Playboy of the Western World* by J. M. Synge; in 1953 the Denison Players from Ohio who gave a programme of one-act plays; and in 1954 the American College Players in *Papa is All* by Patterson Greene.

A film unit presents unusual foreign films for members at regular intervals.

In 1950 Sir Laurence Olivier accepted the Presidency of the Hall Green Little Theatre.

HIGHBURY LITTLE THEATRE (L.T.G.)
Sheffield Road, Sutton Coldfield, Warwickshire.

The Highbury Little Theatre is a tiny private-membership theatre primarily devoted to the presentation of plays that cannot normally be seen in the commercial theatre.

It was first formed by a group of progressive young people in 1924, and for the first year activities were confined to play readings. After that and for the next twelve years plays were given full stage production, but the group did not have a permanent home. In 1935 a building fund was opened, and in 1937 a site was purchased for £200. It was part of a garden of a private house. Because the Building Fund contained only £40 the players were forced to borrow money from each other to purchase the freehold. A member who was an engineer drew up plans and construction began. All available money was reserved for materials, and the labour was carried out completely by members in their spare time. During the winter nights they built by floodlight. It is interesting to note that during the wartime blackouts, work was carried on under a large canvas cover which went outside and over the new brick walls.

Five years later, in 1942, the first performance was given in the finished theatre. Sixty people had been engaged in the building at one time or another during the five years, but there were not more than thirty people at any one time; and the major part of the work fell to a small group of less than twenty. Three steps were planned in the building, and to date the first of these is completed. At present it seats 112 people, has a proscenium opening 15 ft. 6 in. wide by 11 ft. 6 in. high, with a stage depth of 21 feet. There are dressing-rooms, a Green Room, scene dock, storage rooms, full lighting equipment, etc., but it is hoped to add in the future a roof garden, more dressing-rooms, and enlarged auditorium and stage space.

Six or seven major productions are done every year. Each one is rehearsed for one month and runs for two weeks. Plays are chosen to fall loosely into four categories: 1. A new play . . . one that connects the theatre strongly with our own times. 2. An international classic . . . a first-class piece of theatre chosen from any place or time. 3. A play chosen for no other merit than that it is good theatre and seems particularly appropriate to the moment. 4. An English classic.

The programme for 1954–5 illustrates the choice of play policy:

A Penny for a Song, John Whiting.
You Never can Tell, G. B. Shaw.
Three Honourable Gentlemen (First English Presentation), Gunther Wisenborn (trans. by Michael Bullock).
Take Back Your Freedom, Winifred Holtby and Norman Ginsbury.
Lady Windermere's Fan, Oscar Wilde.
The Macropulos Secret, Karel Capek.

The theatre tries to encourage new writers, but although many scripts are received, few are of great enough merit to present. Some outstanding original plays which have been produced include: *Twilight Bar* by Arthur Koestler; *Love and Lunacy* by Peter Philp; *Therese* by Jean d'Esté, *The Laughing Stock* by Maurice Kurtz; and *Sweet Liberty* by B. and M. Jaeger.

Generally each play has to satisfy the requirement that it cannot readily be seen elsewhere by the theatre members, although some new method of treatment might justify production of a play comparatively well known. Professor Gilbert Murray's reconstruction of the Menander fragments, which he has called *The Rape of the Locks*, received its first performance at Highbury. *The Three Sisters* and *Le Bourgeois Gentilhomme* were performed with new translations; no record had been found of any other performance of Jonson's *The Devil is an Ass* since its original production in 1616; or of James Shirley's *Lady of Pleasure* since 1635.

All sets and costumes are designed and made by members and all lighting equipment is owned by the group. For several years a paid Staff and Productions Officer was employed, but this did not prove a satisfactory arrangement. Now no professional staff is engaged in any capacity.

Theatre membership (about 2,000) is open to the public for a registration fee of one guinea, or an annual payment of 1s. Tickets for each performance are 3s. Membership in the Operating Company is by audition (for acting), interview and invitation.

There is a Student Group limited to a maximum membership of fifty, who pay a subscription of one guinea, and receive general lectures, an acting or technical course, and courses in stage movement and speech training. These activities take up at least two evenings a week. Each year a number of public performances are arranged by the Student Group, including many one-act and experimental plays. Most of the courses are given by senior members of the Operating Company, but distinguished theatre people are often brought in for special lectures.

The Sunday Club organizes concerts, recitals and lectures in the theatre on Sundays, given by distinguished professional musicians, theatre people and other personalities. A subscription of 30s. is paid for eight programmes per year.

Among the many varied lecturers and musicians who have contributed to the Sunday Club are Noel Mewton-Wood, Dr. C. E. M. Joad, Val Gielgud, Sir Noel Curtis-Bennett, James Laver, Jeanne de Casalis, Cyril Smith, and many others.

The Film Group tries to show and study films not normally available in the commercial cinema. Unusual, experimental, and classic films from all over the world are shown and discussed. Subscription for a series of five film programmes is 10s. and for the Film Discussion Group, 5s.

At the end of each year a Theatre Conference is held for a week, during which there is a series of lectures and discussions on matters important to the theatre. Some distinguished leaders who have contributed to these Conferences include: Louis MacNeice, Michael MacOwan, Allardyce Nicoll, and many others. The conferences are primarily intended for members of the Highbury Operating Company, but delegates are invited from other groups doing similar work, from the University, Local Education Authorities and Senior Schools.

One of Highbury Little Theatre's most interesting contributions to theatre as a whole is its launching of the Arena Theatre Company. Although this is a professional group it should be mentioned here because it is unique in Britain to find an Amateur Theatre launching a professional company. Its formation is reported by Highbury as follows:

"After several years of experimenting with Apron stages and closer contact with the audience at Highbury Little Theatre, a small group of professional actors, artists and technicians was formed in 1947 called the Intimate Theatre Group.

" The Group's purpose was to study the present position of the living theatre in relation to its kindred arts, and to experiment with theatre form. After two years the name of the Group changed to the Arena Theatre Company, and the work done so far has led to the construction of an experimental Arena Theatre, in which problems and opportunities are being worked out under practical conditions of performance.

"Seasons of Arena Theatre have been given in Birmingham, Cardiff, Newcastle-on-Tyne, Stafford, Stoke-on-Trent, Walsall and Weston-super-Mare.

"Since its inception the Governing Director has been John English, and the General Manager, Alicia Randle, both Foundation Members of Highbury Little Theatre. Amongst members of the Council of the Arena Theatre Company are included Sir Barry Jackson, Mr. E. Martin Browne and Mr. Herbert Marshall.

" In its six years of operation the Arena Theatre Company work has developed considerably artistically, and information has been collected that will enable a permanent theatre of somewhat revolutionary form to be built when the opportunity arises.

"The Arena Theatre Company has also been studying the difficulties and problems of Children's Theatre, and now commissions special plays for this side of its work. It is now the largest Children's Theatre in Great Britain, and finds the Arena Form specially suitable for this work.

"The Company's work has become one of the most considerable experiments in theatre form in Great Britain."

THE LEICESTER DRAMA SOCIETY (L.T.G.)

The Little Theatre, Dover Street, Leicester, Leicestershire.

In April 1922 a group of Leicester people interested in the art of the theatre met to discuss the formation of a Dramatic Society. Miss Lena Ashwell was invited to address this gathering, and as the result of the meeting the Leicester Drama society came into being.

A permanent home was established in 1930 in the Little Theatre, which seats 367. Now twelve productions are given each year, running for seven performances.

Present membership of the theatre is 650. A stage carpenter and a scenic designer are employed by the society but all other work is voluntary. All sets and costumes are designed and made by the society, which owns its own lighting and stage equipment.

Early in 1955 a tragedy befell this group when a fire completely gutted the stage and part of the dressing-rooms. Fortunately the auditorium was unharmed. Within ten days of the fire a performance was given in the rehearsal room, by the undaunted players. It will, of course, take time and money to restore the stage, but with a fine record of persistence and high standards behind them it should not be long before a new and better stage rises from the ashes.

Among the many and varied plays given by the Leicester Drama Society since its inception it counts as most successful Bridie's *The Sleeping Clergyman*; André Obey's *Noah*; Anouilh's *Ring Round the Moon*; and Shaw's *Pygmalion*. Many Shaw and Shakespeare plays have been done, and these two are extremely popular playwrights with Leicester audiences. Among successful original plays produced are two by the President of the society, Geoffrey Mead, *Dust Among the Stars* and *Remember Sparta*; as well as R. Eric Pochin's *The Highway*.

THE LOFT THEATRE (L.T.G.)

Victoria Colonnade, Leamington Spa, Warwickshire.

The official name of the group which occupies the "Loft Theatre" is "The Leamington and Warwick Dramatic Study Club", but it is known far and wide by the shorter title. The study club originally began in a private house in Warwick in 1922, and early activities were mainly concerned with play readings and discussions on drama. At the end of the first year there was a membership of forty-seven, and a single performance of Galsworthy's *The Silver Box* had been presented on stage.

As time passed the performance of plays became the major activity, although readings are still popular and twelve are given each year.

In 1932 the society rented premises in Leamington consisting mainly of a "loft", after which the theatre was named. Plays were presented here regularly for nine years, during which a following and reputation were built up. The atmosphere was very intimate, the stage being only two steps high. Performances were private, no charge being made for seats but a collection taken, which realized an average of less than 6d. per head.

In 1941 these premises had to be vacated and for two years the Club was without a home, and performed one-act plays in various church halls plus plays with a box-office appeal in the Town Hall. A Little Theatre fund had been started some years before, and this was augmented during the homeless period, in addition to raising £400 for war and related charities. The fund was increased to £2,500 by donations, loans and box-office receipts, and in 1945 the Club bought a home in the Colonnade. It was a shell of a building, having been used as a circus, a cinema and a skating rink, while during the war a camouflage department occupied it.

Once in possession the members themselves built a stage, proscenium and auditorium seating 230. Shaw's *Fanny's First Play* opened the theatre on a temporary stage, while Ashley Duke's *The Man with a Load of Mischief* played a short time later on the new permanent stage.

Today membership stands at 1,100, and an annually elected Committee controls the management. The group is financed by subscriptions and box-office receipts. During a season, from September to June, usually eight plays are given, each running for eight performances extending over a period of three weeks. The programme is planned to try to satisfy the variety of members' tastes, and not only to provide good entertainment in a town that is without a professional theatre, but to present in each season at least one play which is rarely seen. On this basis of choice some of the most successful plays presented include: *Murder in the Cathedral* by T. S. Eliot; *Our Town* by Thornton Wilder; *The Winslow Boy* by Terence Rattigan; *Mungo's Mansion* by Walter Macken; and *Hassan* by J. E. Flecker.

Among successful original plays performed are: *The Prisoner Before You* by Brian Olver (one of the Club's producers); *They Fed the Fire* by Olive Popplewell; and *Poet's Corner* by Muriel Grant.

All set-building, lighting and costuming is carried out by members themselves, and the only paid staff member is the building caretaker.

The Club believes in concentrating all its resources on the plays produced in the theatre and avoiding external activities such as participation in competitive festivals, although groups of members some-times do enter these completely apart from their Loft activities.

THE MIDDLESBROUGH LITTLE THEATRE
Toft House, Orchard Road, Middlesbrough, Yorkshire.

This society was formed in 1930 when the one remaining legitimate theatre in Middlesbrough was converted into a cinema. Those people who had been responsible for local amateur performances in the district joined forces in order to present good plays, well acted and staged, under the direction of a professional producer, and with the eventual aim of building a theatre.

Initial funds were sufficient to convert the platform of a Church Hall into a stage 45 ft. wide by 40 ft. deep, leaving a seating capacity of 400 in the auditorium. Up to the end of 1954 the society had presented 121 plays in this hall. Six productions are given each year, running nine nights, and audiences are generally near capacity.

The first few years of the society's existence were a succession of financial crises, but gradually the merit of the productions began to attract more members and larger audiences. Improvements in the seating and auditorium were followed by the installation of excellent lighting equipment and a cyclorama. By the outbreak of war in 1939 the society was firmly established and though activities had to be greatly curtailed it still functioned throughout the period of the war years.

After the war a large house was bought for use as headquarters, with ample land adjoining for the site of the new theatre. The building fund was commenced in 1944 and boom audiences in the theatre in subsequent years enabled the Executive Committee to transfer large sums to the fund from revenue. The members, the general public and local firms gave generous support.

In 1950 an amalgamation with the old-established Cleveland Literary and Philosophical Society brought a large contribution to the building fund and considerably widened the activities of the society by means of lectures and a well-appointed reading room and library in the centre of the town.

By all these means a total of £31,000 had been subscribed to the fund by the time restrictions on building were removed, and plans for the theatre were drawn up by architects. In 1955 the Middlesbrough Town Council made a donation of £5,000, and £500 was received from the Arts Council of Great Britain.

The theatre is intended for the production of the society's own plays, but it is also hoped to present professional companies including Arts Council and Shakespearian productions, intimate opera and ballet, music recitals, lecturers of national repute and films which are not generally available in commercial cinemas. Actual building on the theatre was begun in 1956.

In their present quarters, the Little Theatre members build their own sets, and make some costumes. Full membership now stands at around 2,500.

Among the varied plays done by this group are successful productions of Fry's *The Lady's Not for Burning*; Anouilh's *Ring Round the Moon*; Priestley's *Johnson over Jordan*; Reginald Arkell's *1066 and All That*; and the old melodrama *East Lynne*.

A Studio Theatre meets at the Society's headquarters with the object of training new acting members, and presents experimental productions of non-commercial plays of merit.

A professional producer is employed, but all other work is carried out by amateur members. Mr. Tyrone Guthrie is the President of the Middlesbrough Little Theatre.

NEWPORT PLAYGOERS' SOCIETY (L.T.G.)
The Little Theatre, Dock Street, Newport, Monmouthshire.

In 1924 a small party of people met in the Central Y.M.C.A., and after some deliberation it was decided to form a Dramatic Society to unify amateur dramatic work in Newport. And so the Newport Playgoers' Society came into being.

Most of the society's early work consisted of play readings, but in the summer of 1925 an open-air production of *As You Like It* was performed; and the following year the society gave its first public performance, *Pygmalion*, at the Lyceum Theatre.

Various halls were used between this time and 1937, when the society acquired its own building. This was formerly a church and required eighteen months' planning, altering and equipping before it was opened with a week's highly successful run of *And So to Bed*.

Since then the Little Theatre has operated continuously, doing seven plays a year, each running for a week, except during the war, when the number of productions was necessarily curtailed. The theatre was in danger of being requisitioned, but a "gentleman's agreement" prevented this, under which it was used as much as possible for Services entertainment. This entertainment was given by the society and visiting concert parties. Since the end of the war membership has grown to 3,000, with a long waiting list. Further improvements are planned in rehearsal and storage space, new properties and stage fittings and structural alterations.

The Newport Playgoers set out three main principles in their policy, "Membership, voluntary work and co-operative management through committees and Council". Under the first only members are admitted to the plays. Six plays per year are seen without further charge. The seventh one is public, which members and public pay to see. Through this system the society feels that it need not depend for its existence on box-office takings, and knowing at the beginning of the season approximately what income to expect, can budget accordingly. The "voluntary" principle means that only those who have a real love for the work are engaged in the society's productions. No professional staff is employed in the artistic field, the only paid worker being a building caretaker. Work is all arranged through committees, which are often divided into sections of helpers. Representatives from these committees, together with Executive Officers, make up the Council. The Council determines the society's artistic policy for each year. This aims at a balanced programme of classic, standard and worthy modern plays; and the development of the art of acting. To aid the latter, classes, courses and individual lectures are arranged. Some of the courses are arranged by the society and some by the Monmouthshire Drama League. Professional instructors are engaged for many of these. The ideal towards which the society strives is "Dramatic education in its widest and best sense for audience and players".

There is a Youth Section, numbering about thirty young people, between sixteen and eighteen, who meet periodically throughout the year and study various phases of theatrical work. They give one production each season.

It is always difficult to choose the best productions, but among some of the memorable ones done by the Newport Playgoers' Society are: *The Ascent of F6* by Auden and Isherwood; Shakespeare's *Henry V*; *The Wind of Heaven* by Williams; and Carroll's *Alice in Wonderland*. This gives some idea too of the variety of choice in plays produced. Successful original plays done include *Bless this House* by Welsh playwright Eynon Evans; and *Change* by J. O. Francis.

THE NONENTITIES SOCIETY
The Playhouse, Kidderminster, Worcestershire.

This unique society in British Theatre was formed by Kenneth Rose in 1933, in order to arouse the theatrical interest of Kidderminster and district, to provide worthwhile well-presented drama and to perform his own plays, of which fifteen have been produced. In the beginning, the society met and performed in the New Meeting Hall and later in the Convent Hall and the Town Hall in Kidderminster, but there was always a desire to own a proper theatre of its own, and every year a certain proportion of the proceeds was set aside for this purpose. In 1945 the dream was realized when the Nonentities bought the Playhouse (known as the Opera House) for £6,000. This interesting build-ing is fifty years old, and comes of a long line of theatres on the same site. It is said that Sarah Siddons played there, and most certainly H. B. Irving, Mrs. Patrick Campbell, Vesta Tilley, Forbes-Robertson, Pavlova and Sir Frank Benson did.

With the advent of films, the Opera House became derelict, ending up as a wartime store.

When the Nonentities took possession an enormous amount of repair and rebuilding was required, which was completed in eighteen months, and the Playhouse, seating 650, was officially opened by Sir Barry Jackson in November 1946. In the five years following this, costs of rebuilding, equipment, etc., totalling £19,000 including the purchase price, were repaid, through Nonentities productions, grants from the Arts Council and the Town Council, public gifts, deeds of covenant and rentals.

The theatre is staffed and managed on a professional basis by paid employees, and the Nonentities alternate their amateur seasons with a resident professional repertory company, which rents the theatre from them. When the Playhouse first opened, the Arts Council's Midland Repertory Company was based there but has since had to move to Coventry for the practicability of a touring circuit.

Michael MacOwan wrote, when the theatre was opened: "It is the first time in the history of the theatre that amateur and professional have been housed under the same roof—a noble experiment."

In a Souvenir Booklet published in 1951, upon the occasion of the fifth anniversary of the opening of the Playhouse, the Nonentities put forth their "Place in the world of the theatre" as follows:

"The Playhouse remains the only theatre in Great Britain owned by an amateur dramatic society, which operates as a professional theatre all the year round. There has never been the slightest friction, although at times both sections have had to take turn-and-turn-about to occupy the stage for rehearsals.

"There are two musts to this co-operation. The time given to amateur performances must be strictly limited—in our case to seven weeks a year (this means seven productions), and the public must know which it is paying to see.

"We can best serve the stage as a society by shunning West End successes and concentrating on revivals, the classics, and experimental plays; and by training recruits to the profession. In the first place we have largely failed, owing to the imperative need to make money—often to cover losses on professional shows. In the second we have played a more worthy part."

At present the society reports that it is struggling against the onslaught on audience of TV. Attendance has fallen somewhat, but with such a courageous and lively past one feels that the Nonentities will manage to survive and thrive.

Among its most successful productions the company counts *Noah* by André Obey; *The Rose without a Thorn* by Clifford Bax; *The Marvellous History of St. Bernard* translated from the French by Sir Barry Jackson; *The Mask and the Face* by C. B. Fernald; and *Pinocchio* (a Christmas play with music) by Kenneth Rose. Among other original plays by Mr. Rose there have been successful productions in recent years of his *Gloriana* and *The King who Couldn't Laugh*. The resident repertory company which operates when the society is not using the theatre, also has a reputation for presenting new plays, and organizes a New Play Competition. Some of the amateur Nonentities actors have gone into this professional company or to others.

At present the Nonentities have fifty acting members and 1,650 subscribers, who pay one guinea per year. Sets are built and painted in the theatre by the resident professional scenic artist, costumes are mainly hired, but all stage and lighting equipment is owned by the society. The acting company is entirely amateur.

Occasional instruction courses are given, and regular play readings for trying out new members. In its early years the society entered and won a considerable number of drama festivals but has not time with its own Playhouse to carry on this work. However, the theatre is used for local festivals and the society encourages other amateur groups to enter. Talks on theatre and Sunday concerts by distinguished professional actors, musicians, etc., are arranged for the general public. Subscribers' nights are also arranged periodically, and include ballet, one-act plays and hearings of promising local artists in various fields.

Exhibitions of painting, etc., are held in the Circle Lounge, and One-man Exhibitions prove an encouragement to many young artists.

An appreciated service offered by the Playhouse is that of free transport, which is provided from doorstep to the theatre and back again, up to twenty-five miles, to any person or group or club arranging a party that entirely fills a coach. Reduced ticket prices are also in effect for such parties. These parties have enjoyed meeting the players in the lounge after the show over coffee and sandwiches.

The late James Bridie said of this society, "Best of luck to the Nonentities! I wish the Somebodies had one-tenth of their enterprise and public spirit."

THE NORWICH PLAYERS (L.T.G.)
The Maddermarket Theatre, Norwich, Norfolk.

No better words could introduce this famous theatre than those of its founder, Nugent Monck: "The Norwich Players were formed in 1911. Without a corporate existence, they had already produced a morality play . . . *The World and the Child*, and two morality plays, *The Annunciation* and *Flight into Egypt*; as well as a dialogue, *Holly and Ivy*, composed of medieval carols. All these were performed in my drawing-room before packed audiences; so packed, indeed, that they numbered seventy on each occasion. Three years later we moved into the Old Music Room, once the home of Isaac the Jew, where we could seat ninety-nine people. The first production was the Chester Cycle of mystery plays, then Molière's *Mock Doctor*; *The Merchant of Venice* and *Twelfth Night*.

"There followed the World War, and the Norwich Players dispersed to act their parts in very different theatres. Death, wounds, the changes of a post-war England broke up that 'fair company', but the idea and the ideal lived on, and the Norwich Players were reborn in September 1919, when *Much Ado About Nothing* was performed in the Old Musick House, and women were first admitted as Players. In 1921 we had to move again, and having launched out into the bold venture of buying a derelict building, and reconstructing it, the Maddermarket Theatre came into existence.

"We have performed 184 plays in these twenty-five years. We have painted our own scenery, designed and made our own costumes, and, for the first time since the days of Elizabeth, acted all the plays of Shakespeare under the conditions which ruled the theatre at that time."

The building, now converted into an Elizabethan playhouse seating 340, was successively a chapel of the Roman Catholic faith, then a general warehouse, and finally a citadel of the Salvation Army. It was empty and in bad repair when Nugent Monck discovered and bought it in 1921, and became an owner-producer-manager. It stands off an ancient square where country people used to bring to market the "Madder"—a plant from which dye was made to colour the woollen goods of the local looms. The atmosphere of the Middle Ages is still strong in this part of old Norwich, and seems to permeate the theatre building itself.

The stage is equipped to modern standards, and plays of all nations and periods are performed, from the medieval *Gammer Gurton's Needle* to Bernard Shaw's *Saint Joan*; from Browning's Victorian *Pippa Passes* to Sean O'Casey's *Within the Gates*; from Molière's *The Forced Marriage* to Pirandello's *Six Characters in Search of an Author*; from Euripides' *Electra* to Ibsen's *Hedda Gabler*; from Congreve's *The Way of the World* to Norman Ginsbury's *Viceroy Sarah*. Such unusual fare has been presented as the Indian play *Sakuntala* by Kalidasa; the Japanese *Kantan* by

Seami; and the Italian Commedia dell' Arte *The Magic Casement* (with dialogue by Nugent Monck); and all Shakespeare's plays.

Productions are geared to the ideal that the Play's not only the Thing, but Everything. Thus the author's words are not lost in a tangle of extravagant production tricks. Mr. Monck does not believe in "frills". No one is seated after the play begins, until the interval; there are no curtain calls and no names on the programmes. The Players do not attract the actor who acts only for personal glory. There isn't any in the Maddermarket Theatre. Its members work in the theatre, after the jobs in which they earn their livelihood are done for the day, because they love the theatre and not for personal acclamation.

Eleven plays are produced each year, for runs of nine days. Professional staff include the Producer, Stage Designer, Stage Manager and Wardrobe Mistress. There is no subscription membership; the only income coming from box-office receipts. Thus any member of the public may buy seats. Tickets vary in price from 6s. 6d. to 1s. 6d.

A Studio Theatre has recently been formed to provide lectures and instruction in dance, stage movement, make-up and speech. A yearly subscription of 5s. is paid by members of this group and they give quarterly productions of plays.

Nugent Monck recently retired as Director of the Maddermarket Theatre but it continues, under other directors to fulfil the ideas and ideals he began.

THE PEOPLE'S THEATRE (L.T.G.)
Rye Hill, Newcastle upon Tyne, Northumberland.

One of Great Britain's most distinguished amateur theatres is the People's Theatre, Newcastle upon Tyne, which began in 1911 as the Clarion Dramatic Society. It was then an offshoot of the British Socialist Party, created to make funds for that organization, but it very soon began to have an independent life of its own. *The Bishop's Candlesticks* by Norman McKinnel and *Pot Luck* by Gertrude Jennings were the first plays it produced, but it found these unsatisfactory and looked around for better material. *The Shewing-up of Blanco Posnet* by George Bernard Shaw was newly written at that time, and still under the censor's ban. The society presented it as a private performance, at the same time creating for itself a reputation for the unusual and within itself a taste for good things in drama. The plays of the first few seasons were nearly all those of Bernard Shaw. In fact, all of Shaw's plays have been performed by the People's Theatre, and most have been revived at various times. In 1921 Shaw visited the theatre to see *Man and Superman*, and again in 1936 he came to view his *Candida*. He was favourably impressed by the performances on both occasions.

When the Socialist Party began to question the society's choice of plays, the society, anxious to maintain freedom and independence of choice in its programmes, broke away from the Party, and opened its own premises.

The building had to be heavily mortgaged, and it was not until the later years of World War II that the mortgage was paid off. Through the publicity for this campaign for funds a steady regular audience began to attend, and has continued up to the present day. The theatre now presents twelve plays each year for seven nights, to near-capacity audiences, the theatre seating 310.

Chekhov was first introduced to Newcastle at the People's Theatre in 1916–17, and among many successful original plays done are: Norman Nicholson's *Prophesy to the Wind*; Peter Dennison's *Boy from Vienna* and *Twice upon a Time*; Eric Barber's *Tudor Murder*; and F. L. Lucas's *Land's End*.

The Founders of the theatre stated a general policy when they said, "If we are to murder any plays, let us for glory's sake murder only the best." This policy has always been adhered to through, to quote a member, "bad performances and audiences small in number,' through innumerable financial crises, through two world wars, and through the more insidious dangers of periods of comparative success". The group has attempted to present the best of the world's plays of every period in the best possible manner, and state that "the work has always been, and always will be, its own reward". Their programme is unique in the district which they serve, and has included such successful productions as Shaw's *St. Joan*, and *Back to Methuselah*; *Juno and the Paycock* by Sean O'Casey; *Our Town* by Thornton Wilder; Ibsen's *Peer Gynt*; and most of the plays of Shakespeare. The People's Theatre has never lowered its choice of play to pander to the so-called "popular taste" but rather has tried to present the great and the good plays in such a fine way as to make them "popular" fare.

The policy is to go where the commercial theatre, for economic reasons, thinks it cannot go, and put before the public the plays which have something to say as opposed to those with more entertainment value; plays which are the best of their period and kind; and plays which are seeking new forms of expression in the theatre. They say that the doubters would be very surprised at the very high entertainment value of such classical and experimental ventures. The People's stage is not a mere classroom or laboratory but an engrossing living theatre.

The group has ventured into the realm of opera several times, and presented with some success the first English production of Stravinsky's *Tale of the Soldier*; as well as Rutland Boughton's *Immortal Hour*, with the composer producing; and Villier Stanford's *The Critic*. A Music

Society is now affiliated with the theatre and engages (with some assistance from the Arts Council) musicians of a high standing.

A Film Society has been formed in recent years, which is very successful financially; and a magazine was published, which although eagerly read, ran at a loss and had to be abandoned.

The People's was one of the founders of the Little Theatre Guild and maintains a lively interest in that organization's work.

In 1951 the theatre was invited by the Scottish Community Drama Association to play for one week during the Edinburgh Festival and its production of Chekhov's *The Seagull* was highly praised there.

The theatre is financed wholly by box-office receipts, and there is an active working membership of 150. All work is voluntary, and all sets and most costumes are made by the group. Lighting equipment is also owned by the society.

There is no student group, although the theatre encourages new and younger members to join and partake fully in all activities.

Many famous visitors have attended performances at the People's Theatre, including J. B. Priestley on several occasions, Michael Redgrave, Sybil Thorndike, Edith Evans, Roger Livesey, S. I. Hsuing, Tyrone Guthrie and Thornton Wilder.

THE QUESTORS (L.T.G.)

The Questors Theatre, Mattock Lane, Ealing, W.5, Middlesex.

The Questors of Ealing have recently launched one of the most exciting building projects in British Theatre history, professional and amateur. Early in May 1955 at a crowded meeting in Ealing Town Hall, the Lord Mayor of Ealing, its Member of Parliament, and a number of distinguished theatre people, opened the building campaign, each speaking in glowing terms of this experimental but practical new theatre. The writer was present at that meeting, and left with a feeling of gratitude for a group of amateur players with the vision and imagination to plan such a building, where plays may be produced in many styles.

A special building committee was formed, whose members spent over a year in research for the new theatre. Theatre architecture of the past and present was thoroughly examined. Playhouses in Britain and on the Continent were visited and plans for the most modernistic North American theatres were closely examined. With this background, and a carefully compiled list of accommodation necessary for their own particular purposes, the Questors' building committee asked one of the group's members, who is an architect and who had upon several occasions designed sets for them, to draw up plans for the new theatre. The main requisite was that it should be as flexible as possible within practical limits. When the designs were completed it was found that by moving a series of panels and slightly rearranging the seating, plays could be presented in a picture frame set with or without forestage; on an extended forestage only, with the audience on three sides; in a complete "arena" style, with the audience on four sides; or in a "space" setting with scenes pin-pointed by light, using the whole width of the playhouse. A photograph of the model for this new theatre is shown elsewhere in this book.

The building will stand on the ground the group already owns, next to the present playhouse, which will continue to operate during the construction and then be demolished.

Great interest was shown throughout the planning by professional theatre producers, designers and actors, who formed an Advisory Panel.

As yet the theatre scheme is only beginning and it will probably take several years to complete . . . depending on the generosity of Questors' members and interested folk outside the group. Most of the construction work will be carried out by members in their spare time, and presents a real challenge. However, with a record of determination and success behind them one feels that Ealing's newest theatre building will soon rise high in Mattock Lane.

The Questors was founded in 1929 by a small band of enthusiasts who wanted to act. They did not much mind what they acted and had no particular policy, but soon decided to do only classical revivals and plays of high quality which their audiences would be unlikely to see elsewhere. In 1933 they started to reconstruct their own theatre in a disused chapel, which is the present theatre building. For the first five years they shared the tenancy with a Boy Scout Troop. The theatre now seats 183, and has a fully equipped stage with a special forestage.

During the war, productions were taken to gun sites, factories, hospitals, etc. Since the war, membership has increased, now stands at 1,350, and activities have been greatly broadened. Seven full-length plays, each running for ten performances, are produced every year; as well as a number of programmes of shorter plays.

It is a club theatre, meaning that only members may purchase tickets. Full Club Members pay £1 per year for which they are entitled to one free reserved seat for each production, and to buy tickets for friends, as well as to use all the theatre's facilities, attend meetings, discussions, and to vote at all General Meetings. An Associate Member pays 5s. per year, and is not entitled to free seats but enjoys all the other privileges of membership. Junior Members under eighteen years of age pay 10s. per year and have the same privileges as full Club Members. The Acting Membership is subject to audition.

X

Apart from a paid permanent Theatre Manager, all staff, producers, actors, designers, business and technical workers, are purely voluntary. All profits are devoted to furthering the theatre's aims. The direction of the Club is in the hands of a Committee of Management elected by the members. The theatre has its own workshops and wardrobe, and owns its own lighting equipment.

It is a founder member and secretary of the Little Theatre Guild of Great Britain, and provides a permanent address for that organization.

Worthwhile plays of all periods have been presented by the Questors, and among the most interesting productions they count Shakespeare's *King John*; *Clerambard* by Marcel Aymé; Pirandello's *Right You Are (If You Think So)*; Chekhov's *The Seagull*; and *The Merchant of Yonkers* by Thornton Wilder.

An important facet of the Questors' policy is the performance of new plays, and to celebrate their twenty-fifth birthday they presented in 1954–5 a Silver Jubilee Season of new works. Since its beginning the theatre has presented over twenty full-length original plays, and thirty-five new one-act plays. It is encouragement of this sort which should spur new playwrights to send their plays to such amateur groups, whose high standards ensure a good tryout of their work. Among original plays done by the Questors are *The Dark River* and *Diary of a Scoundrel* by Rodney Ackland; *A Jig for the Gipsy* by Canadian playwright Robertson Davies; a special translation from the Broad Scots tongue of *The World's Wonder* by Scottish playwright Alexander Reid; *The English Captain* by Lydia Ragosin; and *Fanfaronade* by Rodney Diak. The latter was awarded first place in the British Drama League's 1955 Festival of Original Full-Length Plays.

In order to encourage the writing of new plays a Playwright's Group was established four years ago, and meets regularly to read and discuss plays, and to hear lectures by experts in the field. Readings and private performances of plays written by members of this group are often given. It is the stated aim of the Group to develop a "Questors' School of Playwriting" but understandably this will take some time and much hard work.

The Questors run a two-year Theatre Student Training Course, under the auspices of the Middlesex County Council Education Committee. First-year students chosen by audition are limited to twenty, and of these twelve are admitted to the second year. Courses in Acting, Movement, Speech and Make-up are offered, and are primarily, but not exclusively, aimed at training actors and actresses for the main acting group of the Questors. Some instruction is also given in Stage Management and Design. Fees are £1 1s. per term. Practical work is done by Second-year Students in two full student productions in the

theatre each year.   At the end of the second year, students may
audition for admission into the theatre's regular acting company, if
they so wish.   Courses are led by senior Questors' members and other
qualified instructors.

Weekend courses are also arranged during the year for acting members.

A Young Questors' Club for young people over fifteen years of age
meets once a week for discussions and lectures on the theatre, led by
the Theatre Manager. It is hoped to introduce a Children's Theatre
programme in the not-too-distant future.

There is a theatrical library from which members may borrow
books.

Club Nights are held throughout the year when members hear lectures by theatrical authorities, see films, hear play readings, and enjoy
other programmes of general interest.

A magazine entitled *Forestage* is published regularly and contains
news of forthcoming productions and Questors' activities, reviews of
recently published theatre books and plays, and articles of general
interest by members.

Director of the Questors is business man Alfred E. J. Emmet, who is
one of the most active and enthusiastic workers in British Amateur
Theatre today.

THE RUNNERS DRAMATIC SOCIETY
Tullamore, Co. Offaly, Ireland.

"The Runners", founded in 1949 by a former Town Clerk of Tullamore, is a group whose name originally stood for people who were not
born and bred in the town, although the membership is not now
limited to these.

For the past three years the society has experimented with imaginative and unusual productions of Irish verse plays, particularly those of
W. B. Yeats, and has built a considerable reputation throughout the
Irish Amateur Theatre. For three years in succession "The Runners"
have won the Verse Drama Award in the All-Ireland Drama Festival,
with Donagh McDonagh's *Happy as Larry* (1954); Yeats' *The Dreaming
of the Bones* (1953), and *At the Hawks' Well* (1955).

Noel MacMahon, the Runners' producer, writes as follows: "The
productions of *At the Hawks' Well* and *The Dreaming of the Bones* have
caused much controversy inasmuch as they depart from the accepted
mode of presentation. We have tried, and we believe, succeeded, in
presenting these plays to a larger audience of a less sophisticated type
than was originally intended (by the author). We have sought to create
and increase the beautiful atmosphere of the plays' poetic content by

presenting them before abstract settings which were designed to deliberately heighten the effect of stillness and loneliness."

That the group has succeeded is shown in the remarks made by the adjudicators in the All-Ireland Festival: of *The Dreaming of the Bones*—"I cannot remember a presentation of this play in which mood as well as the meaning of the poet was as effectively presented to the audience. This production compared more than favourably with most of the professional productions which I have seen"; and of *At the Hawks' Well*—"We have seen magic on the stage." The latter adjudicator went on to say she thought dramatic history had been made that night, and that this was a group that should be representing Ireland in the Paris Festival as the very cream of Irish acting and production.

Reported in an Irish newspaper was the effect of *At the Hawks' Well* upon the Festival audience: "The crashing cymbal at the opening of the play brought a great hush over the audience and the muffled rumbling of drum beats heightened the dramatic effect so well that from the time the curtain went back until the final curtain hardly a ripple was heard in the auditorium. Lighting played a big part too. Here the task was made difficult by trying to create moods by effectual lighting on a set which was in the main abstract. This was contrived by the use of spots and floods of varying colour, each reflecting the different moods of Yeats' verse, and the overall unreality was accentuated by the blue-green aura which engulfed the stage. At the back was a symbol of the Hawk, set against an evening sky, and in whose eyes yet another symbolism helped the audience to unravel the mystery of what Yeats had written. This was achieved by lighting the eyes throughout the play, except when the Hawk took the form of a graceful bird-like woman who sought to beguile the young man."

Although they have not yet acquired a home of their own, it is likely that such an ambitious society will not be long in finding one. At present in Tullamore they play three times a year in a local cinema (which seats 600) for three nights. Active members of the group number twenty, and they make all their own scenery and costumes, as well as devising some of their own lighting equipment (the rest being hired or borrowed).

Another Runners' presentation which evinced much interest both in Tullamore and Dublin was the first production of *Eoin Gabha*, a play in Gaelic by Patrick Pearse.

THE SIZER-SIMPSON REPERTORY COMPANY (L.T.G.)
Hessle Road, Hull, Yorkshire.

The Sizer-Simpson Repertory Company is an amateur organization with a professional producer, and was founded in 1925 by the late

Isabel Sizer-Simpson, the principal of a local school of Music and Drama. In 1937 she retired from the Company and her daughter became Director and Producer.

In January 1955 this Company was forced to close its playhouse because of lack of funds, but plans are being made for future reopening, with the emphasis on arena-style production. Although operations are therefore suspended at present this group should be mentioned as one with an excellent record of achievement.

Until 1949 the group had no permanent home, and in order to plan a programme of worthwhile productions they began to search for a suitable building. They found a derelict Congregational church, and after the honorary architects had drawn up plans, work was begun by the members in their spare time. Outside recreations were forgotten as demolition and then construction were tackled. Before a stage could be built pews and choir stalls had to be removed, and all the floors levelled. After three months the entire site was clear and building started on the interior walls. In one transept went the dressing-rooms and in the other a Green Room, later to be fitted with a coffee bar. The stage covered an area of 1,000 square feet, and above this were a regulation grid, plus 40 feet of height for flying scenery. Drapes, and full lighting and dimming equipment were also installed. The auditorium seated 250.

Through difficulties in obtaining materials, the work which should have been finished in four months, dragged on for seven. For over a year the Company had been existing on capital, and it was very necessary to find some money to meet the heavy expenses to be paid before the next season started. Although tired after a winter of hard manual work, and although audiences are not so good in the warmer months, the Company decided to open the theatre in June 1950 with Maeterlinck's *The Blue Bird*, for which eighty-three costumes had already been designed and made. In just over a month the play, a large and complex production, was rehearsed and the sets built. Audiences came, and the play succeeded both artistically and financially.

Among other successful productions the Company has presented are: Ibsen's *Peer Gynt*; Rostand's *Cyrano de Bergerac*; *Our Town* by Thornton Wilder; *Dark of the Moon* by Richardson and Berney; and Shakespeare's *Othello*. An original play, *Fires on the Earth* by Kevin Carroll, a local writer, was also played.

Before the theatre's present closure, around eight productions were given every year, each with a run of a week. There were fifty Active Members (subscription one guinea per year), who were the actors and backstage workers, and attended Wednesday Club nights during the season to rehearse or watch plays in production, and during the other months of the year for play readings, lectures and various classes. There were also seventy Patrons, who paid one guinea per year, and were entitled to two weeks' advance booking, and free car park facilities; 300 Associate Members, paying 5s. per year, were entitled to one week's advance booking.

Classes were arranged for Active Members from time to time, in Movement, Speech, Mime, etc.

Throughout its history the Company has entered many Festivals and won a number of awards . . . mostly for individual performances, verse speaking and choral speaking.

THE ST. ANDREWS PLAY CLUB
The Byre Theatre, St. Andrews, Fifeshire, Scotland.

The founder members of the Byre Theatre were originally the leaders of a Bible Class Dramatic Society, and they started the enterprise as a development of the work they had begun under the auspices of the church. They were determined from the beginning to have a home of their own in which to present interesting plays. One day in 1933 they heard that an old byre (barn) belonging to a dairy farm in St. Andrews was vacant. The farm had been taken over by the town council and parts rented off to various merchants. The byre itself was filthy, filled with rubbish and the walls green with damp . . . but it was a building, and available for a rental of £10 per year. In December 1933 the Play Club was officially constituted and took over its new premises.

Then began the back-breaking work of conversion, all carried out by enthusiastic club members, who laid a wooden floor, whitewashed the walls, cleaned out the loft (where fodder had been stored) for dressing-rooms, built a stage 12 ft. by 12 ft., made lighting equipment and wired it in, and installed seating for seventy-three. The work was held up by lack of funds, and although performances were given in the meantime at the Town Hall, they did not bring much into the coffers because of high overheads. Members raised money by selling cakes and scones, making toffee, running a punch board, delivering lectures on drama, and organizing sales of work. A private donation came in from a lady who was impressed by the Play Club's Scottish Festival entry, *The Foreigner*, a play about Fife fisher life written by the club's president, A. B. Paterson.

In May 1935 the first plays were given in the Byre Theatre . . . an evening of one-acts, presented to an invited audience. Public performances were not begun until 1937, when the Byre was licensed as a public theatre, with construction and renovation completed.

During the summer months of that year a triple bill of one-act plays was presented regularly, which were fully attended by the tourists and visitors who came to the resort of St. Andrews. These summer seasons have continued successfully ever since then.

In the autumn of 1937 it was decided that in order to attain a higher standard of technical skill, club members should receive expert training. It was agreed that the club pay the expenses and tuition of one of the members for a two-year course of stage training at the Edinburgh School of Dramatic Art. In return this member visited St. Andrews every weekend to give the members instruction in stage movement and voice production. In order to meet these expenses a regular series of plays were presented during the winter months.

During the winter of 1938–9 members and the pupil-teacher had become proficient enough to give a series of lecture-demonstrations to British Legions and Women's Rural Institutes. These proved valuable not only as experience and propaganda, but gave an objective to those taking part in the training scheme. At these displays the club usually did a folk dance, elementary Greek dancing, mime, one or two poems, and prepared scenes.

When the trained member finished his course in Edinburgh with distinction he went on into the professional theatre, with the club's good wishes.

When the war began in 1939 most of the Byre's men were called away to the forces, etc., and the club was in a quandary as to how to continue. Curiously enough there had always been more men than women in the group, but now there were hardly any males left. At that time a professional repertory company was formed in nearby Dundee but was delayed in using its own theatre, so it came to St. Andrews and rented the Byre, playing there for a short season until its own theatre was ready. This gave the Play Club the idea of hiring a small professional nucleus of their own in order to carry out a full programme in spite of depleted amateur numbers because of the war.

The plan went into operation early in 1940, and has remained ever since. The Amateur Play Club retains control of the playhouse, and handles all business, publicity, box-office, etc., but hires a professional producer, and actors. These latter are in the main young people just graduated from drama colleges, who stay at the Byre for a maximum period of two years. The twenty amateur club members play parts when casts are larger than six, as well as assisting in the building of scenery and other technical work. Some of the amateurs are as experienced as the professionals, having played for months on end. Fifteen plays are done each year, running two weeks during the winter and three weeks during the summer.

Native playwriting is encouraged by doing fifty per cent Scottish plays every season. In the 1955 season the other fifty per cent were plays of other nations . . . France, United States, etc.

Among Byre's most successful productions through the years have been Shakespeare's *Macbeth* and *Twelfth Night*; Ibsen's *Peer Gynt*; Sophocles' *Oedipus Rex*; and Tennessee Williams' *Glass Menagerie*. From the long list of original plays, mostly by Scottish authors, they count as remembered presentations: *The Open* by A. B. Paterson; *The Sassunach Shuffle* by Lyon Todd; *Alas, Poor Goody* by Donald Craig; *Murder per se* by Charles Marford; and *Parsons and Posters* by George Grant.

ST. PHILOMENA'S DRAMA GROUP
c/o The Gate Club, Lawrence Street, Drogheda, Co. Louth, Ireland.

This group had its origin as a play-reading branch of the St. Philomena's Past Pupils' Union, which was formed early in 1939. At first there was no intention of staging plays, and it was not until 1941 that a one-act play, *Petticoats Preferred*, was presented in the Drill Hall of the Presentation Convent, where all productions were staged until 1944. These were all one-act plays.

The first three-act play, *Ladies in Retirement*, was presented in the Town Hall, where the group had to build its own proscenium, for a stage 26 feet wide, to leave an opening of 21 feet. Later, stage, proscenium, curtains and some of their equipment, on loan to another society, were destroyed by fire. The group now plays in a cinema, giving usually three productions per year, each running three nights.

They own two complete interior sets (which are rearranged and repainted as required) plus a certain amount of lighting equipment and costumes.

Present membership is forty-five, of which seventeen are acting members. All pay a nominal annual subscription but the group is financed mainly by box-office receipts.

This society has entered and won a number of Festivals, and count among their most successful productions and festival winners, Barrie's *Quality Street*; Coward's *Blithe Spirit*; Priestley's *The Long Mirror*; *Treasure Hunt* by Stewart Black; and *Tolka Row* by Maura Laverty. They also gave the last play as a broadcast.

THE STOCKPORT GARRICK SOCIETY (L.T.G.)
The Garrick Hall, Stockport, Cheshire.

The Stockport Garrick Society has been called the "father" of British Little Theatres, because it was the first of its kind to be formed. The impetus for its formation was given by the late Edwin T. Heys, a young engineer with a love for the theatre, who at the turn of the century ran a dramatic society in a local church. When a dispute arose between the elders of the church and the Society over the digging of a passage for crossing under the stage of the Sunday School Hall, Mr. Heys and his colleagues-in-drama decided to form an independent and undenominational group. Thus the Garrick Society was born in 1901, and its first production, *The Merchant of Venice*, took place in the Mechanics' Institute in March 1902.

Soon after this, the Garrick came under the influence of Charles Charrington, a professional manager who first introduced Ibsen and Shaw to the provinces. Members of the Garrick admired and even assisted in some of the Charrington productions in Manchester in 1904, and in the same year they themselves produced, for the first time outside London, Ibsen's *Pillars of Society*. So began the pioneer work of the Society in producing plays of the new "realistic" school of playwriting, a daring departure for an amateur group. When new upstairs rooms of their own were opened in 1904, the *Manchester Guardian* had this to say: "At the suggestion of Mr. Charles Charrington they have opened a theatre of their own, and commenced the season with a performance of Mr. George Bernard Shaw's *Candida*, to be followed, it was announced, by Ibsen's *Ghosts*, and other plays which, in the ordinary theatre, are not regarded as good commercial speculations. The enterprise is worthy of all admiration and praise. It gives the Society a real function, a place in the world, and in other people's lives, something to live for, if we may put it so, which cannot possibly be said for the best of ordinary amateur dramatic societies."

And so the first Little Theatre had its own premises, in Cobden Place, seating 130 people, up a rickety staircase on an upper floor, with a small stage one step up from the auditorium, and right in the middle was a pillar. On the floor above was a similar room used for rehearsals, scene making and painting.

It is interesting to note that in 1907, during the course of a correspondence between Shaw and the Society, he advised them, "Your Society must give up the cheap and obvious policy of depending on Shaw and nothing but Shaw. You must play Galsworthy, Housman, Masefield, Hankin, McEvoy, Bennett, Miss Mack, Conrad, Fox, Synge, Ibsen, Hauptmann, Sudemann, Brieux, Tolstoi, Strindberg, etc. etc." Taking this advice, plays by all but four of these playwrights were performed by the Garrick in the following years.

In those early days there was no admission price, but a silver collection was taken. If there was a balance from a play it went towards the expenses of the next or to a reserve fund started with the idea of building a theatre some day. Some productions were taken to neighbouring towns and villages, whose groups reciprocated with return visits. Soon a junior section was formed, as well as a dramatic circle, and a library and reading room. Well-known professional people like Granville Barker, B. Iden Payne and Miss Horniman came to see the Garrick's work, and the latter later told the Society it was their pioneer work that finally decided her to choose Manchester as the centre for her famous repertory work at the Gaiety Theatre.

During the First World War activities were curtailed somewhat, but Garrick concert parties entertained the wounded in war hospitals; and in 1917 the Garrick Magazine was started.

In 1920 a limited company was formed in order to purchase larger premises, the present Garrick Hall, which seats 350 people, and has a well-equipped stage. The Society's aim was to eventually buy out the non-member shareholders, and this was achieved finally in 1948. The Carnegie Trust aided this by a grant of £1,000, which they gave with two conditions: that no plays banned by the censor be performed, and that when the Society acquired the whole share capital of Garrick Limited the company should be converted into a non-profit-making trust. Both conditions have been fulfilled.

During the Second World War activities were curtailed for a short time, but later full programmes were carried out behind the blacked-out windows, and a considerable sum of money raised for war charities. In fact the last wartime season was the busiest, for in it were five full-length plays, eight one-acters, two operas, and a pantomime.

On the musical side, the Garrick Orchestra was formed in 1923 and has since provided entr'acte music for plays, and played for various opera productions. These latter productions have not been too successful artistically, although popular with audiences.

At the present time the Society presents an average of six full-length plays and several one-acts during the year, each production running for seven consecutive nights. There is a subscription membership of 1,200; 500 of these being active members. All sets and costumes are made by members, and the large wardrobe is now administered by a formal committee of its own, as is the library.

There are first and second year courses for young people, led by a professional instructor; and a special play-reading circle. Occasionally a professional producer is brought in for a special production, but in the main the producers are members of the Society.

The Society counts among its most successful productions: *Johnson Over Jordan* by Priestley; André Obey's *Noah*; Shaw's *The Apple Cart*; Ibsen's *Hedda Gabler*; and Fry's *Venus Observed*.

Although few new plays have been produced, there have been quite successful "first" productions of: *Fool's Bauble* by Martha Alexander; *Bess of Hardwick* by Margaret Dixon; and *The Lovers of Gudrun* by F. L. Lucas.

THE SUNDERLAND DRAMA CLUB
The Royalty Hall, Sunderland, Co. Durham.

In 1923 a small group of people banded together to present Maugham's *Jack Straw* in Sunderland's Victoria Hall for one of the town's charities. They called themselves the "Thespian Society". Encouraged by the interest shown upon this occasion, but very conscious that there was much to learn, the team occupied itself for two years with a number of one-act plays, performed in church halls, until in October 1925, with a membership then totalling thirty-six, they called a public meeting. As a result the Sunderland Drama Club was launched with an annual subscription of 10s. admitting subscribers to all productions.

The newly organized club's first play, *A Bill of Divorcement* by Clemence Dane, was presented in March 1926, and thereafter two or three full-length productions given until 1932, when the group, now 650 strong, acquired and converted a building into a Little Theatre seating 130. It had an adequate stage, good lighting, workshop and club rooms. From then onwards each season provided four public performances in the Victoria Hall and two for members only in the Little Theatre which was also used for one-act plays, experimental nights, play readings and discussions, week-end drama schools, etc.

For ten years this theatre operated, offering varied fare, among which were outstanding productions of plays like Shaw's *The Doctor's Dilemma*, *St. Joan* and *Candida*; Capek's *R.U.R.*; and Drinkwater's *Abraham Lincoln*. The membership increased to well over 1,000 and steady public support continued.

The war caused a curtailment of activity, with so many members joining the forces, dispersal of families, war-work, black-outs and other necessary restrictions. Productions were confined to the Little Theatre. In 1942 both the Victoria Hall and the Little Theatre were destroyed by enemy action.

The remaining nucleus of the active members remained in touch and at the request of the Town Authorities organized again in 1942–3, and during the next two seasons gave open-air performances in one of the town parks under the "Holidays-at-Home" scheme. The plays were Shakespeare's *The Tempest*, *The Taming of the Shrew* and *Twelfth Night*.

The problem was to find another home, and after several small halls had been used for occasional productions, the Club leased the Royalty Hall, formerly a church hall, which members converted into a theatre seating 278. It now has a well-equipped stage, comfortably seated auditorium, dressing-rooms and newly furnished Green Room used for small meetings and rehearsals.

Members own their own lighting equipment and make their own sets and most costumes. An electrician is employed but all other work is done by members. At present there is a total membership of 900, who pay a yearly subscription. Other income is derived from the box-office.

Six full-length and three one-act plays are performed every year, each programme running for four nights. Among the most successful plays performed have been: Sheridan's *The Rivals*; O'Neill's *Anna Christie*; Fry's *The Lady's not for Burning*; and the first performance of *Dog for Delmont* by Joseph Colton (this play was later done by a commercial management and played a successful West End run under the title *The Gay Dog*).

The world première of Fry's *The Firstborn* was given by the Sunderland group, with final rehearsals under the direction of the author. Another original play produced was *While of Unsound Mind* by Nan Richenberg.

British Drama League Festivals have been won by Sunderland productions of *Anna Christie* and *The Rivals*, while *Dog for Delmont* won a Harrogate Festival.

THE TALISMAN THEATRE PLAYERS (L.T.G.)
Talisman Theatre, Kenilworth, Warwickshire.

The beginnings of this Little Theatre are rather different from most. The Company, originally known as the Rover Players, established in 1941, consisted entirely of employees of the Rover Car Company. However, membership was thrown open to a wider public when a building was acquired in 1942. This was an old barn, which the players converted into a small playhouse seating 171 people. The owner of the building, who is the President of the group, allows them to use it rent free.

It is a club theatre, with audience membership of 3,500, who pay a subscription of 1s. per year. Tickets for all shows are 2s. 6d.

The Company occasionally hires costumes and lighting equipment, but mainly makes and owns its own. All sets are built by members. The only paid staff is a part-time cleaner, all other work, artistic, business, organization, etc., being voluntary.

Since its inception the Talisman Theatre has presented over 130 productions, among which have been two plays by Shakespeare; two by Shaw; and representative works by Priestley, Coward, Emlyn Williams, Tennessee Williams, Anouilh, Maugham, Rattigan, Fry, Guitry and Wynyard Browne. *The Perfect Woman* by Wallace Geoffrey and Basil Mitchell achieved a box-office record; and other successful plays, artistically and financially, include *Prunella* by Laurence Housman and Granville Barker; Berney and Richardson's *Dark of the Moon*; John Patrick's *The Hasty Heart*; and *Prison Without Bars* by Peggy Barwell.

An original pantomime is performed each year. Seven of these have been by Anthony Farmer, and three by other members of the Company. World premières of *The Light in the Storm* by Thomas Muschamp, and *The Tender Years* by A. P. Dearsley have been given; and the Company has produced its own translations of Chekhov's *The Seagull* and *The Three Sisters*. They report that they are always ready to consider new plays, but are rarely sent any to read. Authors might well take note of this fact.

It is interesting to note that the Kenilworth group found the size of its audiences reached a peak in 1951, since when there has been a steady though not yet alarming decline. Recently the players began to give seven performances of each play, instead of six, and to do fewer shows with more rehearsal time—thus now doing nine productions per year. The pantomime runs for two to four weeks instead of the usual one. So far there has been no increase in the total attendance per show, but the theatre intends to persevere with the new system in the hope that improved production standards will gradually lead to bigger audiences. At the moment audiences may be anything between 550 and 850 for any one production.

In choice of plays they try to do at least a few of the sort of plays not seen in the commercial theatre, but also do a number of the normal repertory choice which have popular audience appeal.

The full programme makes it difficult to enter for Festivals, but they have entered the Coventry Drama Festival four times, and in 1955 entered Tennessee Williams' *The Strangest Kind of Romance*.

An interesting observation about amateur theatre in the Kenilworth area is given by the Talisman's Business Manager: "Kenilworth, with a population of some 10,000, possesses two flourishing amateur theatres, which may be something of a rarity. Moreover, only five miles away, the Little Theatre Guild has another member in the Loft Theatre of Leamington Spa. There is a very large number of Societies in Coventry, though none has its own theatre (unless you count social clubs which have a stage). There is a good deal of coming and going of actors between all these groups, which is probably a good thing. On the other hand there are those who argue that a much higher standard would be achieved if there were fewer groups in the district." This last is a debatable point in any area, and an interesting problem for the amateur theatre as a whole.

THE TAVISTOCK REPERTORY COMPANY (L.T.G.)

Canonbury Tower, Islington, London, N.1.

The name of this well-known Little Theatre is familiar not only in this country but abroad. Such is the Tavistock's consistently high standard of production and efficient organization that it is often quite reasonably mistaken for a good professional repertory company. This is not the case. Apart from part-time office and box-office help, all arists, directors, and backstage staff are unpaid. Film directors and B.B.C. producers have voluntarily worked with the Tavistock from time to time which gives them a chance to experience legitimate theatre.

The group was founded in 1931 and since then has presented over 250 productions. Active members are all experienced in some branch or branches of the art, and new members are invited to join after an audition and/or interview. The Company is non-political, non-racial and classless, "Theatre" being its common interest; and consists of men and women from all walks of life. For the first eighteen years plays were presented in the Bloomsbury Playhouse which the Tavistock Company helped to found as a public theatre and which was attached to, and part of, the Mary Ward Settlement in Tavistock Place. In 1949, when renewal of the licence for the theatre was refused, the Company moved into temporary premises in an old school building attached to a church. The cramped surroundings and the tiny seventy-seat auditorium gave the Company little scope, however, for artistic development and the maintaining of the high standards of production which it had set itself, and in the autumn of 1952, a move was made to Canonbury and a very big venture undertaken. This involved the taking of a long lease of the beautiful premises composed of the Canonbury Tower (for 350 years the London home of the Marquess of Northampton and his ancestors) and a handsome hall attached to it and standing in the garden. It is this hall which "The Tavistock" converted into a fully equipped, modern Little Theatre, which was opened in February 1953.

Canonbury is a charming location for a theatre, and on a recent visit the writer was taken on a tour of the Tower after a performance. These tours are arranged each Friday and Saturday evening, and one feels a real sense of stepping back into time when climbing up the winding staircase to view the lovely panelled rooms, in which the carving dates back to the sixteenth century, and is beautifully preserved.

The history of the Tower is rather fascinating . . . it has been the home of many famous men, who would no doubt be filled with wonder to hear the sounds of hammer, saw, and declamation; and to smell the glue and greasepaint of the players. Built by Prior Bolton in 1509, the Tower (which is 66 feet high and reveals its period by the staircase which winds round a series of lofty cupboards up the centre; the cupboards now proving most useful for Tavistock storage) was part of the Manor granted by Edward the Sixth in 1547, to the Earl of Warwick. After the dissolution of the monasteries, Canonbury Tower was occupied by various court favourites. Among these were Thomas Cromwell, the Earl of Essex, John Dudley, Earl of Warwick and later Duke of Northumberland, and Thomas Lord Wentworth.

In 1570 Canonbury was acquired by Queen Elizabeth's wealthy Lord Mayor of London, Sir John Spencer. With the marriage—in 1599— of Sir John Spencer's daughter to Lord Compton (afterwards Lord Northampton), the Tower became part of the Northampton estate. Tradition says that the couple eloped—the daughter concealed in a baker's basket, and her lover disguised as a baker's boy.

Since then, Canonbury Tower has been the home of Sir Francis Bacon, Oliver Goldsmith and Washington Irving, and its many visitors have included Queen Elizabeth the First, Sir Walter Raleigh and Charles Lamb. The Bacon Society is now a sub-tenant of the Tavistock Company and permanently leases a room in the Tower.

So much for the past. In the present, the Company has equipped a buttery, rehearsal room, wardrobe, workshop and Warden's flat (permanently occupied by a member of the group). In the theatre building itself there are 182 seats, a 32-foot-wide stage with an apron, a lobby, cloakroom, coffee bar and box-office . . . all designed and executed by the members, with the aid of professional firms for the engineering, carpentry and electrical wiring. Backstage is a multi-dimmer switchboard, also designed by a member. Dressing-rooms are built off a passage joining the theatre to the Tower. Scenery and costumes are designed and executed by members.

Between the theatre and the Tower is a lovely garden, with a very old mulberry tree, a goldfish pond, lawns and a dovecote. Productions like Shakespeare's *A Midsummer Night's Dream* are often given outdoors in the garden when the weather is fine.

The Tavistock "Rep" gives thirteen or fourteen productions per year, each running two weeks, with three performances each week . . . i.e. six performances of every play. Among the most successful productions they count *The Country Wife* by Wycherley; O'Neill's *Anna Christie*; Thornton Wilder's *Our Town*; Fry's *The Lady's not for Burning*; and *The Moon in the Yellow River* by Denis Johnston.

Three times during the past few years the Tavistock has been selected to represent England in International Festivals of Drama. Early in 1952 the British Drama League sponsored a Tavistock team playing

Shaw's *Man of Destiny* to the International Festival of Amateur Theatre held in Brussels to establish the formation of an international body to link Amateur Theatres of European countries. A few months later the same Tavistock team represented England when Scottish and Welsh teams were also invited to a Festival at Aberdare. Finally, early in 1953, when the International One-Act Play Festival was held in London at the Institut Français, the Tavistock was again the English team—this time with a production of Fry's *A Phoenix too Frequent*.

The group is always on the lookout for worthwhile new plays, and has given notable productions of a number of these including *The Tree of Heaven* by Merryn Mills; *The Wintry Hour* by Leila Forde; *The Face of Violence* by J. Bronowski; and the first English production of André Obey's *The Hopeful Travellers*.

The Tavistock is a public theatre, which means that anyone may purchase tickets, even though not a member. However, there is a membership of both active workers and interested spectators; special clubrooms in the Tower are open only to those members. At present the Acting Members (30s. per year) total 130; Full Club Members (21s. per year) reach 85; and Theatre Club Members (5s. per year) total 350. Only members may attend Sunday performances.

There are no regular courses arranged by the theatre, but from time to time ex-professional members have given a series of classes on speech, movement, mime, etc. A school of dance and drama rents the theatre during the daytime, and two of its directors are Tavistock members. Members who wish tuition are encouraged to attend this school.

THE THEATRE CLUB, MOUNTVIEW (L.T.G.)
104 Crouch Hill, Hornsey, London, N.8.

Having a rather unusual beginning this club was formed in 1945 in Colombo by a group of young Englishmen in the forces. They presented several productions there with, and for the entertainment of, their friends and associates. Upon returning to London after the war they reorganized and played for a time in the Y.M.C.A.

Later they found an old house in London's Hornsey area, attached to which was a derelict hall. Members have converted the hall into a well-equipped intimate little theatre, on whose tiny stage excellent staging effects are achieved. The house provides club rooms and a flat for one of the theatre's directors.

It has one of the busiest schedules of all the Little Theatres, and is in fact a full-time spare-time occupation for its nucleus of working members. Twenty-eight productions are given each year, with each play running for six days. There are 1,300 members who pay an annual

A curtain set for *Nuit de Noces* by Frederick Witney, presented by the Unnamed Society, Manchester, Lancashire.

From the settled charm of Great Britain—The Byre Theatre, St. Andrews, Fifeshire, Scotland

. . . to the wilder beauty of the Canadian Rocky Mountains—The Student Chalets, at the Banff School of Fine Arts, Banff, Alberta, Canada.

subscription. The rest of the finance is obtained from the box-office. There is no paid staff in any capacity and members build their sets and make most costumes.

Among the most successful productions given, both artistically and financially, are *The Rose Without a Thorn* by Clifford Bax; O'Neill's *Ah, Wilderness!* and *Mourning Becomes Electra* (performed in its entirety on alternate nights); *The Witch* by John Masefield; and *The Happiest Days of Your Life* by John Dighton.

Among successful original productions given are: *Queen's Knave* by Frank Broadbridge; *The Waking Dream* by M. Mincher; and *Full Circle* by Mary Murray. The American playwrights Howard Richardson and William Berney attended a Mountview production of their play *Dark of the Moon* and declared they were very impressed by the high standard of presentation. They hope the group will do more of their plays, perhaps even before they are professionally produced.

THE UNNAMED SOCIETY (L.T.G.)

Whitworth Theatre, Whitworth Art Gallery, Oxford Road, Manchester 15, Lancashire.

The Director of this renowned group writes as follows: "The Unnamed Society was founded in the summer of 1915 by a group of artists, writers and musicians meeting in the garden of a large house in Hale, Cheshire, determined to talk of everything except the then prevailing war. At first their discussions ranged over the whole realm of art and they had no intention of founding a dramatic group or building a little theatre. Many of the members were interested in the theatre and unable to see the kind of plays they wished to see in the commercial theatre of the time, so they soon began to present plays themselves, costumed, designed and often written by the members.

Such a group needed a name, but being unable to find one suitable they decided to remain, "Unnamed".

What was known as "the new movement" in the theatre began soon after the formation of the group and the Society was soon taking an important part in this movement, which led to a renaissance of drama in England.

At first plays were presented in a large room in the Midland Hotel, Manchester, where the scenery consisted sometimes of no more than a ladder, a chair and a potted palm. Later a move was made to a dance studio, which certainly had a stage but where the chairs had to be cleared after each performance and taken down three flights of stairs to the basement. The Society felt in urgent need of premises of its own where it could continue its experimental work without interruption. Eventually an old warehouse in a slum district of Salford was dis-

Y

covered, and the members, by their own efforts, converted a portion of this into a well-equipped little theatre, which was opened in the autumn of 1923. Plays were presented here for seventeen years during which time the Society and its original work became known, not only in Manchester, but all over the English-speaking world. In 1940 the theatre and most of the surrounding district was destroyed by bombing; in half an hour the Society lost everything it possessed. Productions continued, however, almost without a break; rehearsals taking place in a member's flat and presented in a variety of hired halls often to the detriment of the work, until some kind of a permanent home could be found once more.

The opportunity to do this did not arise until September 1945, when the Director of the Whitworth Art Gallery, Manchester, was approached with a view to securing one of the unused galleries in the building for conversion to a small theatre. Terms were agreed and work began once more on a fresh theatre; a thing unique so far as is known for this must be the first time, at least in this country, that an active little theatre has been part of an art gallery. Members of all ages and conditions worked heroically until, in the autumn of 1946, the task of conversion was completed, and the theatre, seating 155, formally opened by the then President, William Armstrong, the well-known producer and former Director of the Liverpool Playhouse.

Through all the changes of homes and of membership the policy of the Society has continued as it was in its early days, which is to present plays either for the first time or plays of a definitely educational or experimental nature which have not been seen in the neighbourhood, or which the commercial theatre ignores for financial or other reasons. Six plays are done per year, each running for seven performances including a matinee.

Settings, costumes and properties are designed and made on the premises. There is no paid staff but the Director receives an honorarium.

The theatre is financed by membership subscriptions and box-office. Membership is of two kinds: (a) Full Membership—member is able to book one seat for each production without extra charge, attend general meetings and vote (£2 2s. od. per year); (b) Theatre Membership—member is advised of production and may book seats at 3s. each, but has no voting or other rights. The public cannot book seats or pay at the door as this is a private theatre.

Almost from the start of the Society until his death in January 1955, the Director of the Society was Frank Sladen-Smith, a producer, playwright and critic whose work was of considerable value to the amateur movement in all parts of Great Britain. On his death, George Nutkins, who had been his deputy for many years, was appointed to succeed him.

Since 1915, 218 plays have been presented, of which sixty-five were for the first time on any stage, and ten for the first time in England. Among the more outstanding productions have been: Goethe's *Faust, Part I*; O'Neill's *The Hairy Ape* (first time in Britain); *Versailles* by Emil Ludwig; *Roar China* by S. Tretiakov; *Orphée* by Jean Cocteau; *Murder in the Cathedral* and *The Family Reunion* by T. S. Eliot; Auden and Isherwood's *The Ascent of F6* (first performance . . . seven days before its London opening); *Out of the Picture* by Louis MacNeice; *The Old Man of the Mountains* by Norman Nicholson; *Top of the Ladder* by Tyrone Guthrie; and Anouilh's *Colombe*; as well as most of Ibsen and all of Chekhov. *Haunted House* by Geoffrey Whitworth was given a première as were Frank Sladen-Smith's *Wonderful Zoo, St. Simeon Stylites, The Man Who Wouldn't Go To Heaven* and many other plays written by him.

The future of the theatre, as a building, is in some jeopardy due to the pending take-over of the Whitworth Art Gallery by the University of Manchester, which may not be prepared to renew the lease when it comes up next year. The Society will however continue to present plays in accordance with the policy formulated by its founders.

THE UNITY THEATRE SOCIETY LIMITED

The Unity Theatre, Goldington Street, London, N.W.1.

Formed in 1936 this amateur group has added many distinguished productions to the London theatrical scene and many fine actors to the professional ranks. It is registered as a non-profit-making society, owning and controlling its own theatre.

The theatre is a converted building with a fully equipped stage and an auditorium seating 330. Six plays are given each year, and each has a run of from eight to ten weeks. The only paid staff member is a resident stage manager who also makes all the sets. All costumes are made by members, and modern lighting equipment is owned.

Finance comes mainly from the box-office, but there are 6,000 associate members who pay 2s. 6d. per year, as well as 650 active members, and 218 affiliated societies. These latter include trade unions, co-operative societies, drama groups, labour parties, etc.

Groups of first- and second-year students take classes in Voice, Movement, History and Theory of Drama. There are also weekly theoretical and practical talks, discussions, and demonstrations.

In the late thirties Unity won the British Drama League Final Festival with *Plant in the Sun* by Ben Bengal.

Among the most successful productions done they count: *Spanish Village*, a translation of Lope de Vega's *Fuente Ovejuna*; *The Ragged Trousered Philanthropists*, adapted from Tressel's novel; *The Russian*

Question by K. Simonov (translation from the Russian); *Babes in the Wood*, a pantomime by B. Fase and C. Parsons; and *Longitude 49* by Herb Tank. This last was first performed by Unity, as was Sean O'Casey's *The Star Turns Red*. (O'Casey is a popular playwright with this group, who have performed most of his plays.) Another original play performed was *Strangers in the Land* by Mona Beard.

XXII. AMATEUR THEATRE IN THE BRITISH COMMONWEALTH

AUSTRALIA
by NEVILLE TEEDE

THE Amateur Theatre in Australia, as in other Commonwealth countries, has played a somewhat different role from its counterpart in Britain. In both city and country there are groups performing plays at irregular intervals, purely as an expression of that group, and for no reason other than "to put on a play". These groups are amateur in the strict sense of the word, their productions are similar to their counterparts throughout the world, and need no further comment here. But there are also the large groups mainly centred in the cities, run on professional lines, presenting plays regularly, running in competition with the few professional productions and offering plays that commercial managements will not present. These groups, at times verging on the professional, have been the hard core of the Little Theatre Movement in Australia for some twenty years or more. The work done by them for the Theatre is important and for the purpose of this review, the most interesting of all in Australia. The accent falls heavily on them and their achievements.

The groups are not affiliated in a national body as the term "Little Theatre Movement" may suggest, the term deriving from the common purpose behind the bulk of the work presented by them. Structurally each society is different, policies varying from group to group, state to state, but they have in common the aim to keep alive interest in the serious drama and to re-establish the Theatre in Australia. This aim is not necessarily a constitutional one, most groups aiming to put on good plays as well as possible as often as possible, and they may not be aware of it as a statement. Nonetheless, viewed nationally, the purpose shows clearly. Indicative of the type of plays done by them is the final of the Jubilee Festival of 1951 when *Our Town*, *Murder in the Cathedral*, *Desert Highway*, *Much Ado About Nothing*, *Ladies in Retirement* and the *The Little Foxes* were presented before Mr. E. Martin Browne for judging. Few professional managements would attempt so varied a programme or so consistently high a standard of play, and the little theatres throughout Australia have some right to be proud of their contribution to the cultural life of the country.

Many of them have been established for forty years or more, others are fairly new. Some, having done valuable work, which is their monument, no longer exist. To name them all, and appraise the work done would be impossible, so at the risk of treading heavily on the sensitive extremities of the amateur theatre "world" in Australia, a typical group, arbitrarily chosen, but unnamed, must stand as an example for them all. Some have better organization, others are less fortunate, some have higher ideals, and others are excessively arty-crafty, pretentious in concept but noteworthy in presentation. To those deserving mention who do not get it, I beg pardon. The organization chosen has the advantage of forty years' continuous existence, a high standard of achievement in that time, and through a subsidy to build a theatre is assured of a future.

As one of the Repertory Club-type Theatres, this group depends largely on a subscription list for support. Membership of approximately one thousand is not all active in the production sense, but both active and audience members have the same privileges; the use of club premises, advance and party booking, and other benefits usual with club theatres. A management committee elected by the members, together with a full-time, paid secretary and an assistant, are responsible for the smooth running of the organization. This committee, with the professional Director of Productions advising, decides the policy for the season's productions, and selects the plays to be presented. Usually ten productions are planned annually, each play to be presented for a three-week season, but by having one opening night per month a successful production can be extended for a fourth week without upsetting the opening of the next production. The resident Director produces most of the season's plays, and for the remainder, invites outside producers who work for a nominal fee, or are unpaid. In the general running of the season, the Director is assisted by a resident Stage Director. With full-time direction both backstage and onstage a good standard of technical efficiency is maintained.

The ten plays selected aim at giving a balanced season, representing the various dramatic modes and forms, but as can be seen from a recent season, the accent falls more heavily on the lighter, more commercially successful type of play. A recent season comprised: *Our Town*, *The Old Ladies*, *See How They Run*, *The Cherry Orchard*, *Hay Fever*, *Ghosts*, *Twelfth Night*, *Shop at Sly Corner*, *Gaslight* and *The Corn is Green*.

The plays are cast mostly from club members, but in some cases actors are invited for specific plays from outside societies. The actors are always unpaid, but are not necessarily amateur, as many radio actors seeking something more theatrical than broadcasting, give their spare time "for love" to work with the group.

Except for the highly technical work of the resident Stage Director, all backstage work is unpaid. Scenic designers work voluntarily, and all construction and mounting is done by club members under the designers' supervision. A wardrobe mistress and staff are appointed from members for a whole season to control and supplement permanent stocks, but for each production a different wardrobe mistress is appointed to work with the permanent staff, and is responsible for the dressing of that production. Props masters and stage managers, staffed separately for each production, are supervised by the Stage Director, but are responsible for the running of the show to which they have been appointed. Advertising and advance booking are managed by the permanent Secretary and the assistant, while daily box-office and front-of-house are voluntary jobs run on a roster system of available club members.

A converted warehouse, seating about 300, serves as the theatre for this group. Well fitted-up it has its own dressing-rooms, wardrobe stores, prop stores, scene dock, club rooms and cafeteria, which surround the foyer and auditorium. Though cramped, accommodation is a unit allowing both freedom and control of presentation and rehearsal. With one show playing (except for the summer "off-season", when the theatre is closed from mid-December to mid-February) there are always two shows in rehearsal. This allows a maximum of eight weeks' rehearsal for each show, and is designed for amateur actors with full-time commitments outside the theatre rehearsal schedule. The full eight weeks are not always taken, the decision resting with the producer, who usually utilizes the full period. Although rehearsal space is limited, the forthcoming show is assured, in most cases, of rehearsing onstage for the final week of preparation.

With the structure of the society working at its best, this little theatre has been able to maintain, technically at least, a high standard of production for many years. Performances have varied with its actors, but the discipline of the organization has helped even the worst of them to overcome or cover some of the inadequacies. Indicative of the standard is the fact that the group has been able to pay its way by audience support for most of its existence without incurring too great a debt for too long at any given time . . . and debt is the bugbear of most of these groups tightly balancing on the "shoestring".

Not all societies throughout Australia are as fortunate as this one in having their own small theatre. They can't afford them. At most they can boast only permanent rehearsal and storage space. Nonetheless, they continue to offer drama to Australians in halls, converted churches, and out-of-doors. The best example of good work being done in an out-of-the-way place comes from the John Alden Company formed about six years ago. Alden started to present Shakespeare, mounted in a first-class manner, in a church hall in Sydney. Everyone was paid except the actors, who were mostly professional radio artists giving their services in their spare time. The work was highly respected throughout the city, and so much faith put in the project that a commercial offer started them on a nation-wide tour with several Shakespearian plays. It was recognition of a need that the professional theatre had previously ignored . . . a success for the "filling in" purpose of the Little Theatres. It is the "filling in" for the lack of, or restricted offering of, professional entertainment which dictates the policies of the various little theatre groups.

When the professional theatre was at its most brilliant, from 1870 to 1900, the amateur theatre in Australia was still largely playing at "play-acting", and was relegated to a very inferior position, playing whatever happened to strike the fancy of the group at the time, and supported on the "friends and relations" principle. But as the professional theatre declined (fascinating reading, but too lengthy to include here) and presented only the froth and bubble of the drama, the amateur groups developed, presenting consistently the more serious drama, to balance professional offerings. Later when there was almost no professional theatre of any kind in Australia other than musical comedy and variety, the policies of the little theatres were dictated by what other groups in the same area were presenting, rather than by the professional theatre. This resulted in groups being known for the type of play presented: one for classics, another for the *avant-garde* play, but with the wisest of them trying to maintain a balance. As always, though policies changed with the changing face of the professional theatre, the groups continued to keep serious drama alive, hoping to maintain its audience and enlarge it where possible, in preparation for the time when the professional theatre would rightly re-assume its position as leader in the Australian theatrical scene.

This constant aim, appearing as the essence of purpose behind the Little Theatre Movement, can be seen clearly in the light of Australian Theatre History, and in its hopes for the future. Historically, the Australian amateur theatre goes back a long way. On 4 June 1789, eighteen months after the First Fleet landed at Sydney Cove, settling the Colony of New South Wales with convicts and soldiery, Australia heard its first play. In a hut or barn decorated with a few yards of coloured paper and lit by a dozen farthing dips stuck about the walls, His Excellency the Governor and his officers saw, mounted behind oil-lamp footlights and played by a convict cast, Farquhar's brisk comedy, *The Recruiting Officer*. Little is known of this production, though the early chronicles valued at twenty pounds the box-office takings which were paid in rum, wine, tobacco, poultry, corn and wheat; numbered the audience at sixty; and noted that the occasion marked His Majesty's birthday. Captain Watkin Tench of the Royal Marines, present on this evening, writes in his journal, *Settlement at Port Jackson*: "Some of the actors acquitted themselves with great spirit, and received the praises of the audience: a prologue and epilogue written by one of the performers were also spoken on the occasion: which, although not worth inserting here, contained some tolerable allusions to the situation of the parties, and the novelty of a stage-presentation in New South Wales." A pity that the Captain was not more interested in this event for posterity, for knowing the nature of the cast and existing conditions, "the tolerable allusions" to the situation may have been well worth preserving. In any case, the choice of play shows considerable taste from what was truly a cast of "rogues and vagabonds". It is worth noting, though it will never be known what prompted this first entertainment, that in spite of difficulties (any good history of Australia will supply details of hardship in the early settlement), such a group of people under such adverse conditions should turn to drama for cultural activity. And if the drama did not stem from the conditions as a direct statement of the situation (although a quick glance at the text of this play will show that sections of the text relating to "pressing" and "trials" were relevant to the immediate situation), it must be remembered that these people were only recent exports from England and would naturally borrow from their native drama. In any case, eighteen months will not produce a new-world folk-lore.

Few will argue that the status of this production was amateur (except on the grounds of state sponsorship?), and like many other performances given in the early days when public entertainments were few (floggings soon lost their flavour), the amateur filled in for that shortage. This was the first time. The pattern recurred and continues to do so. Until the turn of the nineteenth century, the amateurs had it all their own way. From the limited drawing-room society of Sydney to the isolated Garrison at Norfolk Island amateur performances were drawn, the latter presenting a series of plays by permission of the Commandant. In 1800 the first professional performances were given. Again, *The Recruiting Officer* was the choice, and was followed almost immediately by *Henry IV, Part I*. A theatre had been built by convict labour provided by the Governor. It opened to a most enthusiastic reception. Unfortunately, the rowdy element of the Colony, delighting in the new-found pleasure, became too enthusiastic and the theatre was closed soon afterwards by order of the Governor. From that time until the 1830's when Barnett Levey opened a theatre in Sydney, the amateurs again had most of the running. From 1830 the professional theatre grew in importance, until it reached the purple of its career in the last twenty years of the century. This was the time of Sarah Bernhardt's visit, the Boucicault-Vanburgh Company, the première of a London Gaiety Show in Melbourne: the era that the older generation talk about as the great past (for the young this is infuriating: they can't argue with the facts). During that time, amateur performances are recorded, but the best of them were presented in the newly founded states, where the professional theatre had hardly touched. The most significant date in the history of the amateur movement during that time is 1889, one hundred years after the "first" play, and that is the founding of the Sydney University Dramatic Society. Its existence has not been continuous. Like so many undergraduate groups it had to depend on the enthusiasm and capabilities of the current group in the University's population, and so thrived and suffered accordingly. The significant events in the little theatre movement had to wait until later.

As the twentieth century gathered years, Australia settled down to a stable way of life. Gold rushes and the like were less frequent and life a trifle duller. Perhaps by reflection the professional theatre waned. The "moving pictures" became more than a rumour, and, very early, some of the fine old theatres became cinemas. The First World War closed many more, and finally, the Depression obliterated all but the most powerful of the commercial managements, who had to play safe with box-office successes in the few remaining theatres. During the 1930's there was a short revival, but the Second World War stopped the few timid gestures. With a few notable exceptions, Australia had seen little serious theatre from 1930 until the Old Vic toured in 1948 under the auspices of the British Council. This marked a new stage. Since then, the Old Vic have returned, Stratford Memorial Theatre companies have toured, and more commercial ventures are taking shape. Nonetheless, the commercial managements are playing safe with the assured box-office successes. Perhaps they will change at a later date.

Against this brief historical survey stands the amateur movement. In answer to the waning professional theatre the Adelaide Repertory Theatre was founded in 1908 to produce the *avant-garde* plays of the day. Founded with a membership of 100 it has grown into a major cultural force in Adelaide, with a membership of over 3,000 and a new theatre under way. Perth followed suit in 1911, but cut off from the rest of Australia by 1,500 miles of expensive travelling making theatrical touring there almost prohibitive, its aims were not quite as high as Adelaide's. Its taste is catholic, to say the least. Nonetheless, it has done extremely good work and now has a State subsidy to build a new theatre. During the 1920's, Gregan MacMahon in Melbourne and Duncan MacDougall in Sydney were actively campaigning for the serious theatre, and much notable work came from their productions.

In 1929 Doris Fitton, its leading producer, formed the Independent Theatre, and led a successful tour of the most "uncommercial" of plays, *Mourning Becomes Electra*, in three of the Australian States. In Sydney, the Metropolitan, under the guidance of May Hollingworth, and the Mercury have contributed greatly to the movement. In Melbourne, the principal groups have been the Arrow, the Little (which has produced a number of Australian plays and toured country areas), the Tin Alley Players (a graduate group) and the National Theatre Movement. The latter, with a £20,000 sponsorship from the Victorian Government, organized an Arts Festival in 1951, staging ballet and opera as well as drama. It was during that time that the Australian ballet *Corroboree* was first presented in Melbourne. Brisbane boasts three well-established groups in the Brisbane Repertory, the Arts and Twelfth Night Players. There are several groups in Tasmania, notably the Launceston Players and Hobart Repertory Theatre, having the use of one of the oldest theatres in Australia, the charming Theatre Royal built in 1837. The West, cut off from the rest of Australia by the Nullarbor Plain, recently boasted fifteen groups, not all of them active for most of the year, to serve Perth alone. These groups have established the West Australian Theatre Council to co-ordinate the many activities there, and that organization has done very good work in organizing Festivals both in the country and the city. The leading groups in Perth are the Perth Repertory, Patch, and the University Dramatic Society, the latter body concentrating mainly on the classics. From the University in recent years, under the accomplished direction of Jean Dorrington Tweedie, have come brilliant productions of *The Duchess of Malfi*, *The Trojan Women*, *Hedda Gabler*, *Love for Love* and *Oedipus Rex*, to name only a few. In all states, these groups continue their work contributing greatly to the cultural life of Australia.

During the lean years of the professional theatre, their standards remained high, comparable to professional standards in many productions. Most support came from actors. Radio was unable to absorb all the unemployed professionals and many of the actors worked in the amateur theatre maintaining their professional standards for the day when they would be re-employed.

Since the Second World War, amateur groups have mushroomed. Some of the old-established groups turned professional overnight, and as quickly reverted to amateur status, or disappeared. This period of flux was the result of a greatly increased need for entertainment at the end of the war, and many groups hoped to take advantage of it, but they were not equipped financially or with the right backing to make a success of their ventures. Nonetheless, this indicated clearly the need for reformation and extension of the professional theatre. The amateur groups went to the Government for support, and so numerous and urgent were the requests that the Government invited Mr. Tyrone Guthrie to review, and report on, the Australian theatre with a view to establishing a National Theatre. This move was short-lived. A change of Government, a financial crisis, and the project was shelved. But by this time the move had become a matter of public discussion. Agitation from all quarters continued. It came as no great surprise when in 1954, to mark the visit to Australia of Her Majesty the Queen, a Trust known as the "Elizabethan Theatre Trust" was founded and sub-scribed to by many wealthy backers. This trust, wisely handled at its inception, not allowing any one of the already well-established groups great sway in forming its policy, selected Mr. Hugh Hunt as its Direc-tor. He, ably assisted by Miss Elsie Beyer, has already announced plans for its first production, casting on a National basis, and planning to present drama to the whole of Australia. This is in many ways a direct tribute to the steady work of the Little Theatre Movement. Whether or not it will be the answer for the many people involved in that movement, it is impossible to even conjecture, but it will mean the re-establishment of serious professional theatre and each will be given the opportunity to continue its work, either directly or indirectly con-cerned with this venture. It will be interesting to see the effect it has on the Little Theatres.

In working towards the re-establishment of the professional theatre, the amateurs have stated their case in numerous festivals since the recent war. One of the oldest, "The Intervarsity Festival" is the only annual, interstate festival and continues to bring the practical and academic aspects of the theatre together for a three-week season each year. It is non-competitive and perhaps the most successful. Miss E. M. Tildesley, of the British Drama League, is responsible for the annual one-act festival held in New South Wales, and it is a tribute to her many years of work for the Australian Theatre. The biggest theatrical event in many years was the Jubilee Festival in 1951, already referred to in this article and again largely due to the fine work of Miss Tildesley. The adult education boards of Perth and Melbourne are both very active; the former inviting overseas producers when possible to direct for the Festival of Perth, and the latter organizing extensive country tours; and both giving courses of study in Drama at summer school. Most of the work in this field has been done since the war, growing stronger each year. This work will continue. With the professional theatre more prominent than for thirty years, will the amateur festivals continue successfully? It is hard to prognosticate and perhaps foolish to attempt such a thing.

A note of regret must close this brief review. Where are the Australian playwrights? Neither the amateur nor the commercial theatre has helped them in the past, and the few notable exceptions to the cry of "no native drama" have been written in spite of them. Will the Elizabethan Theatre Trust encourage the native playwright? Or will they continue to write for the Amateur theatre, and remain amateurs? Anyone who knows Australia can vouch for the amount of dramatic material at hand; let us hope it will be used.

CANADA

by Lois McLean and Esther Nelson

In June 1953 the first season of the Canadian Stratford Shakespearian Festival opened in a small city (named after its English counterpart) in the province of Ontario. It was attended by an audience from all over the world and publicized in many nations. To a vast number of people outside Canada this was the first word they had ever heard about Canadian theatre. And perhaps the only reason they heard about it then was that the producer, Tyrone Guthrie, and the designer, Tanya Moseiwitch, together with acting stars Alec Guinness and Irene Worth, were already international theatrical names. But behind this venture, which has now completed its fourth successful season, lay the dream and planning of a young Canadian business man, Tom Paterson. In order to carry his dream to fruition he had not only to import theatre experts from abroad, but to gather together an experienced and talented group of Canadian actors and technicians. I believe that without the untiring work of the amateur theatre movement over the past thirty years in all parts of Canada, this Stratford company may never have been formed unless the entire group had been imported. I would venture to say that nearly every one of the Stratford actors had worked previously in amateur groups. Moreover, I'm sure that nine out of ten Canadians engaged in professional theatre anywhere in the world are products of the Canadian amateur movement.

In 1949, under the chairmanship of the Rt. Hon. Vincent Massey, who is now Governor-General of Canada, the government set up a Royal Commission to make a survey of arts, letters and sciences in Canada. Two years later, and based on hundreds of briefs presented by organizations all over the country, the Commission published an official report, which included a section on theatre. Regarding the amateur theatre the report recommended special reduced rail fares for groups travelling to festivals. It also noted that people everywhere desired a National Theatre, but that it should not be merely a building, but a company of players who would tour throughout the country, even to the most remote communities, and who would also give professional advice to local amateur dramatic societies in acting and stagecraft. It went on to say that "it might be desirable for gifted amateur actors of local societies to appear in minor or even major roles with the professionals, to the great advantage and pleasure both of themselves and their community". (Personally I don't think this is a very practical idea.) Also, "The members of the permanent company would be available in the theatre off-season, as directors of summer theatres, or as instructors at summer schools of the theatre; and the company could appropriately represent Canada at international festivals of the theatre." So far no National Theatre has appeared, but perhaps it will be born out of the fine work now being done at Stratford, Ontario.

Up to the present in Canada the amateur and professional theatres have been closely interwoven. There is very little active professional theatre—only a few repertory companies in large eastern cities like Montreal, Toronto and Ottawa. Growing from an amateur group is one of Canada's most exciting professional theatres, Les Compagnons de St.-Laurent, who play in French, specialize in Molière, and are directed by a talented French-Canadian priest, Père Legault. They have a theatre in Montreal, and also tour eastern Canada and the eastern United States. There have been many less successful gallant ventures, like the Everyman Theatre, organized and directed by Sydney Risk, which promoted young amateur players into the professional ranks, and the company toured to cities, towns and remote villages throughout the four western provinces in 1946-7-8. Finally it made a home out of an old vaudeville theatre-cum-cinema in Vancouver's east end, but six years after its inception the Everyman had to close its doors because of lack of financial support.

There are a handful of summer "stock" companies throughout the country, presenting weekly plays for summer seasons at resorts. In the winter many of Canada's actors, producers and technicians must turn to broadcasting, TV, or working in cafés, offices, etc., until the next summer season rolls around. But while the winter winds blow they also work with amateur little theatres, community centres, dramatic societies and educational organizations. Amateurs and professionals work together as they hardly ever do in Britain. Many actors make a fair living from radio plays done for the Canadian Broadcasting Corporation or private commercial stations, but this does not satisfy them. They long to appear on the living stage, and in order to do so they act for no fee, but for the love of their art. Thus the term "semi-professional" has arisen. These people rank alongside the thousands of "professional" amateurs who earn their living in another field but contribute the majority of their spare time and energies to the theatre.

Canada is a new country in world history, and up until fifty years ago was too busy settling her vast spaces, clearing her land, establishing industries and learning to govern her polyglot people to think about the theatre. Science and industry have rushed ahead; theatre has been part of a "cultural lag". Drama is inherent in Canada's beginnings and growth, but as yet it exists only in textbooks and has not been translated to the stage by a great Canadian playwright. The National Museum and others across the land have excellent collections of early French-Canadian folk songs, dances and games performed by the habitants as far back as the early seventeenth century, when France began colonizing eastern Canada. But there are no written plays. The Indian tribes still do their colourful Sun Dances and rituals for annual white men's gatherings, and they pass on their ancient stories. But there are no dramatizations of these set down. The 1950 *Encyclopaedia Britannica*, while giving a fairly full list of Canadian novelists, poets, essayists and historians, stated that the branch of Canadian literature making least progress was drama, and that no important theatrical works had as yet been produced.

This does not mean that no plays are being written. Good plays have come from Robertson Davies, Gwen Ringwood, Marcel Dubé, Ted Allen, Elsie Park Gowan and Norman Newton among them, and have been produced by many amateur groups. However, many playwrights are writing only for radio and television, because in these fields they are assured of polished productions and fairly large fees. Many would rather not have their plays done by amateurs, and as there is little professional endeavour, they ignore the stage. On the other hand many of the best amateur groups will not risk productions of new plays, but as in Britain, prefer to stick to the tried-and-true classics, West End successes or Broadway farces. One cannot blame them sometimes when reading examples of the so-called New Canadian Plays, written by people who not only know nothing about play construction but are blissfully ignorant of practical staging.

Many Canadians do recognize the need for playwrights, and numerous little theatres, drama leagues, universities, etc., organize annual playwriting competitions. Special prizes are also given for best productions of Canadian plays in festivals. Nothing great has yet emerged, but the signs are promising.

The majority of Canadians are woefully lacking in knowledge about the theatre. Only a very small percentage ever see plays done professionally. Back in the 1890's and in the early twentieth century a number of brave touring companies came to Canada from Britain and the United States, playing in a series of frame opera houses across the country. They didn't seem to mind travelling three thousand miles from Nova Scotia to British Columbia under primitive conditions, or even venturing up into the Klondyke during the Gold Rush. It was an exciting time, and many senior citizens remember seeing Henry Irving, John Martin-Harvey and Ellen Terry. Then the cinema came along and the opera houses were either left derelict or converted into film houses. Two generations grew up without seeing live theatre. This was particularly true in the mountain, prairie and maritime regions. Vancouver, on the west coast, and Toronto and Montreal in the east, still had occasional touring companies from abroad or across the southern border, but these companies would not, nor could not, afford to travel the two thousand miles over Canada's interior to play to scattered small audiences. This is still the case today, and the only British company to cross and play in all of Canada in recent years was Donald Wolfit's. One must admire his spirit.

A rather amusing incident occurred a few years ago when I was touring with the Everyman Theatre. We were playing in a small town in the Rockies, inland from Vancouver, and staying in its only hotel— a very old one according to Canadian lights, having been established in the 1890's. One of the actors had heard that Henry Irving and members of his company had spent a few days' holiday at this hotel, after playing on the coast. The actor asked a very intelligent desk clerk whether he knew if this rumour was true. The clerk, eager to oblige, said, "Sorry sir, I don't remember a Mr. Irving or Miss Terry. Would it have been within the last six months? You see, I've only been here since then."

I smiled with the rest of my fellow actors, but stopped when I remembered that although I was a member of a professional company, I had grown up on the prairies and had only just seen my first professional play, done by a touring company in Vancouver, a few weeks before.

To make up for the lack of professional theatre, and for the enjoyment of their increasing leisure time, Canadians turned with a great surge to amateur drama in the twenties. At this time too, immigration was at a peak, and people from Germany, Norway, the Ukraine, England, Scotland, Ireland, Wales, Italy, Poland, Sweden, Denmark, Holland, and the Orient were pouring in to mix their cultures into a Canadian pattern. Many of these immigrants missed the established theatre they had enjoyed in the old countries, and were quick to join in with new ventures. Organized amateur theatre began and has continued to grow ever since.

One of the greatest incentives towards higher standards and exchange of ideas came with the formation, in 1933, of the Dominion Drama Festival. It was founded by a Briton, Lord Bessborough, who was then

Arena setting, with audience on four sides, constructed on the floor of a student lounge, for a production of *The Glass Menagerie* by Tennessee Williams, presented by the University of Alberta Drama Society, Canada.

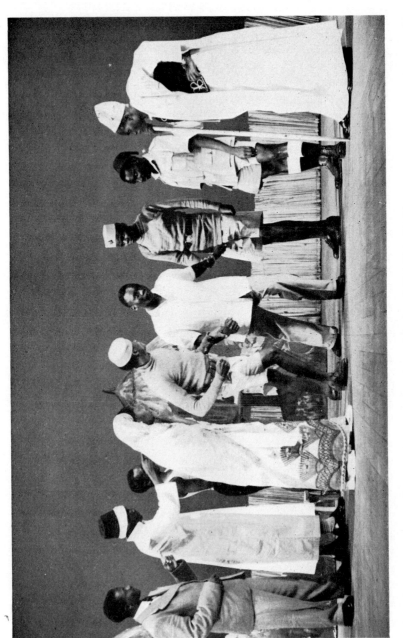

A Kenya African dramatic society in *Behold the Musician.*

Governor-General of Canada, and who presided over an inaugural meeting of representatives invited from all over the country. The first Final Festival was held in the Ottawa Little Theatre in April 1933, and except for the war years (1940–6), the D.D.F. has been an annual event growing steadily in scope and national importance. It is the greatest single unifying force in Canadian amateur theatre, bringing together French- and English-speaking groups for a week of plays, meetings and social activities. Adjudicators are brought from abroad, and among the many illustrious names who have judged Canadian productions are: J. T. Grein, Harley Granville-Barker, Michel St. Denis, Robert Speaight, Philip Hope-Wallace, John Allen, André van Gyseghem, and in 1955 the first woman to adjudicate this festival, Miss Gerda Wrede of the Finnish National Theatre. All adjudicators must speak and understand French as well as English, for Molière and other French authors are popular with French-Canadian entrants.

Originally only one-act or short plays competed, but after the war it became necessary to invite only full-length plays for the Finals, although short ones are still included in some of the regional competitions. For D.D.F. purposes Canada is divided into thirteen regions: two in Quebec, two in Ontario, and one in each of the other provinces. Festivals are held in each of the regions and around sixty full-length plays are judged by a travelling adjudicator. Based on his recommendation eight of these productions are invited to the Finals, as well as special awards being given to the winners in each region.

Major developments in the Dominion Drama Festival over the years have been: the holding of a three-day Theatre Conference during Finals week; the opening of a central office with a permanent secretariat in September 1950; the publishing of a bi-monthly Newsletter; the holding of a seminar for the directors of the competing plays during a two-day period immediately following the Finals; the inviting of the directors of the plays which win in the regional festivals but which are not invited to compete in the Finals, to attend the latter in the same manner as competitors; the formation of a Children's Theatre Section.

Such an enormous undertaking naturally requires extensive financial support, and when donations and entry fees proved insufficient two years ago, the firm of Calvert Distillers Ltd. agreed to donate 15,000 dollars (£5,000) per year. From this grant annual prizes are given of 100 dollars (£33) in each of the regions, and 1,000 dollars (£330) at the Final Festival. In addition to financial assistance the Calvert Company also presents for annual competition, thirteen regional trophies and a major trophy for the Finals, all carved in Canadian wood by three leading Canadian sculptors.

z

The D.D.F.'s permanent director, Mr. Richard MacDonald, travels across Canada several times each year organizing and attending regional festivals. Recently he came to Europe in search of adjudicators, and found it a formidable task, as not many experienced, qualified people are free to travel in Canada for some three to four months, and also have the bilingual requirements.

A great number of societies are not able to enter the D.D.F. because of the expense involved even to get to the regionals, and many smaller one-act festivals are organized by Provincial Drama Leagues, which exist in each Canadian province. These leagues also offer assistance to amateurs through short courses, lectures, bulletins and playwriting competitions. They are voluntary organizations, whose officers may be housewives, doctors, lawyers, teachers, etc. Some manage to rent an office and hire a permanent secretary. The Central Ontario Drama League has undertaken a valuable task in the compilation of a catalogue listing all one-act and three-act plays written by Canadians, whether published or not.

Nearly every city and town in Canada has an amateur Little Theatre, Community Theatre or Theatre Guild. They vary greatly in size and in standards of production. A few have professional directors, or bring different ones in for different shows. Only five or six have playhouses of their own, and the rest play in cinemas, school auditoriums, community halls, military drill halls etc., on all manner of fit-up stages. A number have managed to rent or acquire club rooms for offices, rehearsal, workshop and storage space. Very few own or have access to a great deal of modern lighting equipment. Most construct their own scenery and make their own costumes because there are only a few hire firms in the country, and they are located in the large centres. Cost of transporting hired articles is prohibitive.

The London (Ontario) Little Theatre owns a well-equipped proper theatre and employs a business staff. It has a very large active membership and reports that in a recent production of *Cinderella* one hundred members were involved—ninety on stage; the Vancouver (British Columbia) Little Theatre Association controls a fine little playhouse which is let as a cinema most of the year, and used for V.L.T.A. productions (which usually run a week) six or eight times a year; the Simcoe (Ontario) Little Theatre has a ranch-style building complete with Green Room, workshop and social centre; the Regina (Saskatchewan) Little Theatre has just begun a 50,000 dollar building campaign in order to build its own theatre; the Hamilton (Ontario) Players' Guild, probably one of Canada's oldest little theatres, being a revival of the Garrick Club formed in 1874, has bought an eighteen-room house for their activities; in B.C. the Vagabond Players of New

Westminster have converted an old fish hatchery into a small playhouse in a rustic setting among the fir trees, and construction work was done entirely by members with lumber, etc., donated by local firms.

These examples show only a small fraction of the serious activity under way towards permanent homes for amateur groups.

Luckier in this respect are societies backed by educational organizations. Canadian theatre has walked hand in hand with education, which is good in some ways and bad in others. Universities, Extension Departments, Departments of Education, Arts Boards, Civic Commissions and Physical Fitness Associations have provided a number of auditoriums in which societies may play. They have given financial assistance; provided summer schools, travelling instructors, adjudicators for school and other festivals; established drama libraries; and encouraged playwriting. However, in some cases particularly in groups connected with Universities a rather rarefied academic atmosphere has pervaded, which does not appeal to the average Canadian or persuade him to become a regular theatregoer.

Children's Theatre is receiving increasing attention in Canada, and in the last five years a number of community theatres have established branches to specialize in this. In addition, a number of groups have been formed which devote themselves entirely to children's entertainment. Educational authorities have been very co-operative in this respect and allow them to play in school auditoriums in the evenings or on Saturdays. One of the most interesting of these is Vancouver's Holiday Theatre, organized in 1953. The group has a small professional nucleus and uses amateur actors for many parts. It occupies a small theatre, seating 125, on the University of British Columbia campus, and is aided financially by that organization. Two performances are given every Saturday to which children are welcomed by the Holiday Clown, and allowed to talk to the cast after the play if they wish. Holiday Theatre has toured other communities in British Columbia and played to 40,000 children in seven months.

I think the vigour and attack of Canadian amateurs is typified in a report about a member of a society in Halifax, Nova Scotia, who in one season directed *Stalag 17*, *Journey's End* and *Harvey*, at the same time doing a full-time job on the Canadian National Railways and obtaining his B.A. degree at University. He is also the father of three boys.

Miss Esther Nelson, a young Canadian who grew up in the amateur movement, went to the United States for training, and returned to work as permanent adviser to amateur groups in the province of Alberta, has written the following article about drama in Alberta. As it is not possible to present, in a limited space, detailed reports from every province, and since development has been on similar lines across

Canada, this should give a fairly clear idea of the direction the Canadian amateur theatre is taking.

ALBERTA

Alberta, the most western of the three " Prairie Provinces" in Canada, has an area of 248,000 square miles and a population of not quite one million. In spite of the recent discovery of vast oil and gas resources, the main industry is agriculture. There are only eight cities; the largest is Edmonton which has a population of 160,000. In 1955 Alberta celebrated its fiftieth anniversary as a Province. Although amateur theatrical activity dates back to the 1890's, it is during the last twenty-five years that a distinct and fairly rapid development has taken place in Alberta's amateur theatre movement.

In 1929 a group of individuals representing the four major cities met to discuss ways and means of raising the standard of theatre work and of promoting greater activity. As a result of this meeting the Alberta Drama League was formed. The first project the league undertook was the sponsorship of a Provincial One-Act Festival which was held in 1930. The Festival proved tremendously successful and was conducted annually by the league. By 1933 the festival movement had reached such proportions all across Canada that the Dominion Drama Festival was introduced. The Alberta Festival then became a regional competition in the D.D.F. and the league became the official organization of the region.

The University of Alberta, through its Department of Extension, had always taken an interest in the amateur theatre movement and had supported the formation of the league. It was partly due to the success of the Provincial One-Act Festival that the Carnegie Foundation provided the University with a grant in 1953 for the purpose of developing the community theatre programme in the province. This grant enabled the University to appoint a full-time instructor who was to work with the Department of Extension, provide instruction and assistance for theatres throughout the province. The Extension Library, which served the entire province by mail, also stocked an extensive collection of plays and theatre books. An earlier grant had enabled the Department of Extension to establish a six-week summer school of the theatre in 1932. The site selected was the beautiful quiet little Rocky Mountain town of Banff. Now Banff has become one of the most popular summer resorts in North America and the Banff School of Fine Arts has grown to embrace all of the arts, each summer attracting between five and six hundred students from all parts of the world.

Due to the influence of one of the early instructors at the Banff School (the late Professor Koch who founded the famous "Carolina Playmakers" in the United States) emphasis was placed on the development of original Canadian plays. Through the encouragement and inspiration provided by this unusual man Alberta discovered two fine playwrights: Gwen Pharis Ringwood and Elsie Park Gowan. Gwen Ringwood's one-act play, *Still Stands the House*, is regarded by many as the best Canadian play. Time will be the judge; the play remains a most sensitive expression of the western Canadian farmer's struggle against nature and isolation.

In the early 1930's another important step was taken: courses in drama were introduced in the public and high school curriculum. This made it necessary for teachers to acquire more extensive training, and diploma courses were offered by the University and Banff summer schools.

All of these factors contributed to raising the general standard of work, even in the smaller centres. In 1939 a tiny village in Alberta with a population of barely 100 stunned the Canadian theatre world by winning the Dominion Drama Festival.

With the outbreak of war both provincial and dominion festivals came to a halt. Except for three or four amateur groups in the larger centres adult theatre work in Alberta came to a standstill. The University, the Banff School, public and high schools were able to keep their programmes going. Gradually, because of the suspension of amateur activity, certain individuals became concerned. There was a general feeling that some contact between theatre people should be maintained even though productions were out of the question for the duration. As a result, representatives from the four Western Provinces formed the Western Canada Theatre Conference for the purpose of discussing common problems and possible projects which might offset the general breakdown of activity and prepare for the future. It was decided that the Conference should sponsor a playwriting competition. By 1945 the competition was under way and was conducted annually for six years. The Conference published a booklet on planning stages and community centres in preparation for the vast amount of building that would undoubtedly take place following the war. Perhaps the most successful project had been the playwriting competition. The winning plays were published by the University of Alberta's Department of Extension. When a nationwide Canada Theatre Conference was formed in 1951 the Western Conference ceased operation as it would have been a duplication. Most people felt it had served its purpose and had, to some extent, paved the way for the larger body. In 1946 the University of Alberta student Drama Society took the lead in organizing a non-competitive Inter-Varsity Festival among the four western Universities but this was unfortunately discontinued after several years because of the high cost of transportation and lack of financial backing.

It was during the war years that the University of Alberta received a grant from the Rockefeller Foundation for the purpose of setting up the "Alberta Folklore and Local History Project". A young American writer, Robert Gard, who had previous experience with similar projects in the United States, spent two years in the Province recording the various stories and incidents of the "early" days in Alberta. The writer had an eye and an appreciation mainly for the incidents which had an American flavour. Nevertheless, the factual record will be an invaluable source of material for future Alberta playwrights. This project also sponsored a playwriting competition of plays based on regional material. The best of these plays were also published by the Department of Extension. These, together with the Western Conference plays, have been widely produced in Alberta and the other provinces as well.

Immediately following the war there was a spurt of activity. The University of Alberta set up a Department of Fine Arts with a full-time drama instructor. Courses in drama were offered for both Education and Arts students. The Alberta Government set up a Cultural Activities Branch within its Department of Economic Affairs with a full-time "co-ordinator". The Provincial and Dominion Drama Festivals were revived.

The theatre picture had changed drastically since 1939. By 1950 the Alberta Drama League had only six member groups left, and only three of those could be said to have any stability. The dozens of groups that had been active prior to the war had dissolved. The old leadership was gone. Populations had shifted, and in most places, doubled. The entire social structure had changed. The league had gladly followed suit when the change-over to three-act competition took place, but it was left with no one-act festival to encourage smaller groups to start operation, and insufficient membership to attempt two festivals.

Fortunately, the job that had to be done was not left in the hands of a struggling volunteer organization. In 1949, the drama adviser for the Department of Extension, who had been teaching part-time on the campus since the war years, was able to devote all energies once again to the provincial field. The general interest, even at that time, was at a very low level. A whole generation had grown up with no knowledge of theatre as anything more than a pleasant school activity. The public had become used to going to the movies, and could afford to do so as they couldn't during the "hungry thirties". A new sport had become the fad—curling was played on ice by young and old. The building boom that the Western Conference had foreseen had taken place, but the memorial "community centres" were mammoth arenas, devoted entirely to sports. New schools were being built all over the province with badly-planned combination gymnasium-auditoriums. The Provincial Department of Education would give building grants only to "gymnasiums", a curious contradiction of the vision shown in setting up the Cultural Activities Branch. This policy resulted in some of the strangest architectural wonders to be found anywhere in the world. Unfortunately, most of these expensive monstrosities will be the sole auditoriums for these communities for many years to come. The development of new theatres was a slow, gradual business but considerable progress was made in spite of the numerous obstacles. Without the many teachers and citizens in other fields who had received some training at either the University or the Banff School the job would have been much more difficult.

In addition to the developments within the Government and the University, another important step was taken when the Edmonton Recreation Commission appointed a full-time drama director. This was the first time in Alberta that a city department had given recognition to the field of theatre, and with the development of a similar Recreation Commission in other centres, this may set a hopeful pattern. The Edmonton Recreation Commission now sponsors a highly successful theatre for children, a field which is just beginning to open up in Canada.

The Extension drama adviser worked closely with the Alberta Drama League and in 1953 a new Provincial One-Act Festival came into being. The membership was back to where it had been before the war. In 1954 the Provincial Government recognized the work that had been accomplished and granted 1,000 dollars (£330) in scholarships in connection with the two festivals. Further recognition came in 1955 with a Provincial Government grant of 1,500 dollars (£500) to aid the league in its work. It should be pointed out that with an area of 248,000 square miles, league representatives and producing groups spend large sums of money travelling to festivals and meetings. If the grant is sustained it will provide a certain stability that the league has never enjoyed, being dependent upon the minute profits from the two festivals to cover its operating costs.

At present the University is planning to institute a degree course in drama. This, together with the expanding scholarship programme at the Banff School of Fine Arts, will make it possible for promising directors, actors, and technicians to receive their professional training at home without going to the United States and England, except for advanced work. As a result it is likely that our outstanding students will remain at home to help build the theatre in Alberta instead of going out of their country, or flocking to the larger Canadian centres in order to make their contribution. The export of Canadian talent has delayed the development of the Canadian professional theatre, as well as amateur development within the more remote provinces. In spite of this fact, the standards of work have continued to improve. The step from our best amateur theatre to a professional level is a small one artistically.

CEYLON

The two most active amateur theatre groups in Ceylon seem to be the Ceylon Amateur Dramatic Club, based in Colombo, and the University of Ceylon Dramatic Society at Peradeniya near Kandy.

The Ceylon Amateur Dramatic Club was first organized in 1912, and produced shows spasmodically until 1920, when it began a regular programme of plays presented each season. Programmes have ranged since then from small club shows to pantomimes like *Cinderella* in which 100 people were associated.

During the war the group concentrated on providing entertainment for the troops, who were stationed on the island in vast numbers, and came from all over the world. A CADS Concert Party was organized which travelled the length and breadth of Ceylon during members' spare time, using whatever transport was available, and visiting the troops wherever they were to be found; on airfields and gun sites, in camps and hospitals. Between 1942 and 1945 the CADS staged 181 performances at which they entertained well over 50,000 members of the Services. At the end of the war, when a number of ENSA parties were sent to play to troops, the CADS Concert Party disbanded to leave this work to the professionals.

At the beginning of 1946 former members of the Club began to return from the Services. Most of these were anxious to pursue their favourite interest and the Club began actively producing plays once more. Progress was slow at first, with only one play being done in 1947 and in 1948. From then on, however, the regular three or four have been presented. A variety of productions are given: Maugham, Shakespeare, Coward, Fry; Intimate Revue, Poetic Drama and Thriller.

The Club's activities include lectures and play readings as well as full-scale productions. Membership is open to everyone, regardless of nationality.

A modern new theatre, the Lionel Wendt Theatre, has recently been completed in Colombo, and it is here where the Ceylon Amateur Dramatic Club presents its plays.

The group first attempted Shakespeare (*The Merchant of Venice*) in

1954, and report that it was a very successful and satisfying experience, as well as being a complete change from the usual popular "box office" plays presented. They hope it will mean the beginning of a more experimental policy for the future.

The University of Ceylon Dramatic Society concentrates on presenting the classics and "uncommercial" modern plays. During the last twelve years their programmes have included such works as: *Marco Millions* by Eugene O'Neill, *The Star Turns Red* by Sean O'Casey, *The Twins* by Plautus, *The Good Woman of Setzuan* by Berthold Brecht, *The Little Clay Cart* by King Shudraka, and *Liliom* by Ferenc Molnar, as well as plays by Shakespeare, Shaw, Ibsen, Capek, Pinero, Pirandello, Anouilh and Bridie.

There are a large number of societies at work throughout Ceylon, because, as in many of the Commonwealth countries, there is little professional theatre, and it is up to the local inhabitants to provide their own entertainment. This they do with great enthusiasm and goodwill. They are always eager to hear about activities in other parts of the world, and when Mr. Alfred Emmet of the London Questors Theatre recently visited Ceylon, he was asked upon several occasions to speak about his own group in Britain, and about British theatre generally.

EAST AND CENTRAL AFRICA
by PETER ALLNUTT

Drama in East and Central Africa is still largely in the hands of amateurs for the reason that as yet there are, with one exception, no centres of population large enough to provide regular theatre audiences throughout the year; and, of course, without such audiences no professional company can exist. The sole exception is Nairobi, capital of Kenya and metropolis of East Africa, where in 1947 Mr. Donovan Maule established a repertory company that has been giving regular performances ever since at their Studio Theatre Club, a miniature theatre seating seventy. Although East Africa is growing rapidly, it is unlikely that any other professional company will be able to establish itself for some years and so the responsibility of keeping the British dramatic tradition alive rests with the amateur companies. For this reason the development of the amateur theatre, set about with so many more problems than in Great Britain, is of great importance until conditions are established which will enable a professional theatre to come into existence.

It is encouraging to find, therefore, that among Europeans in this area drama is a most flourishing and popular art form and in some territories the regular standard of production is remarkably high when considered in relation to the total number of civilized inhabitants. In these still largely undeveloped countries it is not surprising that the golden thread of British dramatic tradition is almost entirely in the hands of the Europeans, mainly British; but in the territories where education is most advanced African dramatic groups are emerging, though still under European direction, and their performances have shown that they have an original and exciting contribution to make to world drama. The African has a natural stage presence and with proper direction finds little difficulty in enlarging his performance so as to make it theatrically effective. The danger is, of course, that in doing so he may lose his naturalness and unique sense of fun which make his acting so memorable.

The Asian in East Africa, culturally far more advanced than the African, is faced with a different problem altogether, that of adapting an ancient Indian theatrical tradition, closely bound up with religion, to a totally different medium, that of the modern realistic theatre. Lack of suitable plays in English is the chief obstacle at the moment and the few Asian groups are chiefly restricted to costume plays with exotic settings, but they have shown that with sympathetic European guidance they too can make a valuable contribution to modern drama.

KENYA

The greatest theatrical activity is in Kenya in spite of a fair share of Africa's greatest handicaps—long distances and poor communications —and, in recent years, of the fight against Mau Mau. There have always been a dozen or more active societies both in Nairobi and in up-country centres, but during the last three years, a time when it might have been expected that the Emergency would have put a stop to all but essential activities, that number has been increased and there have been several important developments in the theatre world.

In 1952 the first National Theatre in the British Commonwealth of Nations became a reality at Nairobi when it was opened by H.E. the Governor and Sir Ralph Richardson on 6 November as the first part of the projected Kenya Cultural Centre. This fine theatre seats over 400 people and has an apron stage with an orchestra pit, being fully equipped for theatrical productions, ballet or concerts. The Kenya National Theatre is undoubtedly the best theatre between Cairo and the Union of South Africa and it enables Kenya to offer full theatrical facilities to companies passing through on their way to and from Europe. Apart from the cinemas, several of which have stages, the National Theatre is the only theatre available to amateur companies in Nairobi and the expense of hiring it does not encourage experimental productions. Therefore, in spite of Kenya's unique good fortune in possessing a National Theatre, there is an urgent need in the capital for a small experimental theatre where companies can risk bold ventures without facing heavy financial loss.

In the following year the Kenya Drama Festival began in a small way with six entries and has since developed into a flourishing National One-Act Play Festival with more than twenty entries from all over the Colony. Dramatic societies are now beginning to appreciate the value of competing against each other and so measuring the standard of their work. After the first year funds were found to bring out an Adjudicator from the United Kingdom and there is general agreement on the enormous benefit derived from his constructive criticism and advice. It is worthy of record that societies have travelled over 300 miles on bad roads to take part in this Festival and that often the most enthusiastic entries were from those areas worst affected by the Emergency where life is carried on under conditions of extreme difficulty. For instance, in 1954 the Nyeri Players had to abandon their original entry because a leading player was murdered by Mau Mau, but still continued with another play. The Festival has also provided a most useful service in Kenya's multi-racial community of enabling an African and two Asian dramatic groups to act plays in English before a mixed, but predominantly European, audience. Far from being handicapped by performing a play in another language these non-European entries in the 1954 Festival were placed high on the Adjudicator's list.

Out of the Kenya Drama Festival was born the East Africa Theatre Guild late in 1954 and it is hoped that a framework has now been established within which the amateur theatre in East Africa may develop and prosper. The initiative has come from Kenya in forming the first Branch of the Guild but it is confidently expected that a branch for Uganda will soon come into being. Later, perhaps, Tanganyika will follow suit, but there the ever-present African problems of great space and small population are far more acute than in other parts of East Africa. The aims of the East Africa Theatre Guild are to foster, promote and develop dramatic art in East Africa and to make such contacts and affiliations as may be deemed necessary; to co-ordinate and encourage liaison and mutual assistance between dramatic and kindred societies in East Africa; to act on behalf of its members in matters of common interest; and to compile records concerning dramatic art for the guidance and benefit of its constituent members and to establish a central library and wardrobe.

At the moment the Guild is in its infancy, but already it has taken over the organization of the Kenya Drama Festival. It is a Full Member of the British Dramatic League and produces a Quarterly

Newsletter. While it is true that the Guild still has a long way to go to fulfil its aims, it has started on the right road and in time should play a large part in the development of the amateur theatre in East Africa.

In the building of the National Theatre, the establishment of the Kenya Drama Festival and the formation of the East Africa Theatre Guild, the British Council has played a leading part. This organization is well placed to provide the organizing role so often lacking in the amateur theatre and in Kenya of recent years the Council has been of great service to drama.

The Little Theatre Movement is growing rapidly throughout the Colony. Mombasa boasts the first fully equipped Little Theatre, and the Nakuru Players are following suit and have already acquired a building. Societies at Molo, Eldoret and Kitale are all actively developing plans for their own intimate theatres. In addition, there are one or two charming little theatres made of local native material which enable local dramatic societies in such far-flung farming communities as Sotik to mount regular productions.

Shakespeare receives his due in Kenya and the Railway Players have been organizing regular Shakespeare Festivals in Nairobi for the past twenty-one years. Other Shakespearian productions are also mounted from time to time. Thus, at least once a year, both adults and children have the opportunity of seeing Shakespearian plays well produced. Collaboration with local musical societies produces delectable pantomimes at Christmas time, and such elaborate musicals as *Chu Chin Chow*. In all, Kenya is a rapidly developing country where the British dramatic tradition is well and truly established and promises to make a significant contribution to drama from all its races.

UGANDA

In Uganda, Kenya's most accessible neighbour, there is a limited but enthusiastic amateur dramatic activity. Uganda's European population is far smaller than that of Kenya and they are almost wholly responsible for such modern drama as can be found in the Colony.

Most dramatic activity is centred round Kampala, the capital, where there are no less than four societies, and the towns of Entebbe and Jinja, both within fifty miles of the capital. Elsewhere there is little activity but the amateur dramatic movement is spreading rapidly as the up-country centres grow and develop. For instance, at Mbale in the east of the Colony, the recently formed multi-racial "66" Club has an enthusiastic dramatic section.

In Kampala, the Amber Players have an attractive and quite well-equipped Little Theatre with a capacity of well over a hundred.

Makerere College of East Africa makes an important contribution to dramatic activity in the capital with the Makerere College Dramatic Society, a group of African students which mounts productions regularly, and the Makerere Players who draw their membership from the European staff. All productions at Makerere take place in the College Hall.

The formation of the East Africa Theatre Guild in Kenya and the establishment of the Kenya Drama Festival encouraged the Uganda amateur dramatic societies to organize their own small Drama Festival in 1955, making use of the Adjudicator whom Kenya brought out for their Festival. The British Council is again taking the initiative in bringing the societies together and it is not too much to hope that a Uganda Branch of the East Africa Theatre Guild will be formed in the near future. Later, as communications improve and East Africa becomes more developed, joint Kenya-Uganda Festivals and other theatrical activities may be held under the auspices of the Guild.

TANGANYIKA

Tanganyika is the largest and least developed of the East African territories and progress in drama, as in everything else, is severely handicapped by enormous distances and very poor communications. Amateur dramatic activity, apart from sporadic shows in the vernacular put on by Asian Clubs and African Community Centres, is confined to a few European societies.

The Northern Province, with its chief centres Arusha and Moshi close to the Kenya border, is physically part of the Kenya Highlands and communication is far easier with Nairobi than with Dar-es-Salaam. Here the only society with regular productions is the Arusha Amateur Arts Society which has converted an old hall into an excellent Little Theatre seating about 120. This Society belongs to the Kenya branch of the East Africa Theatre Guild and takes part in the Kenya Drama Festival.

In Dar-es-Salaam, the capital, the Dar-es-Salaam Players and the Railway Club Dramatic Group play in the local cinema, but plans are afoot for rebuilding part of an old Officers' Mess as a Little Theatre seating 175.

In Morogoro, the local dramatic society has converted a barn attached to an old house into a rough theatre with a capacity of about 150. Elsewhere in the territory there are a few struggling societies which spring into life whenever there are sufficient interested persons in the station for a reasonable length of time.

NORTHERN RHODESIA

Northern Rhodesia is, thanks to the mining industry, undoubtedly the wealthiest of the territories in this area and consequently amateur drama is well endowed there. Both the Government, through the Northern Rhodesia Sporting and Cultural Fund, and the mining companies have provided funds which have permitted a number of Little Theatres to be built throughout the country. One was completed last year, two are nearing completion, and three others are under way. Six theatres in two years is extremely progressive.

The Northern Rhodesia Drama Association, which was formed in 1953 with the help of the British Council, has fourteen Member Societies, all of which are actively engaged in regular play production. The Northern Rhodesia Drama Association organizes an annual Drama Festival which was started in the same year as the Kenya Drama Festival. The Northern Rhodesia Drama Festival is an ambitious Three-Act Play Festival which is held in a different theatre each year, the home society acting as host to other societies participating in the Festival. The local Municipality generally makes a substantial grant towards the Festival and every participating society also contributes a fixed amount. The extent to which Northern Rhodesian amateur dramatic societies are endowed is shown by the fact that on more than one occasion a society has flown its complete cast to take part in the Festival—something which would be quite out of the question in Kenya, for example.

An Adjudicator for the Festival is obtained from Britain or South Africa and there is room for co-operation between the territories in this area so that their respective Drama Festivals are so arranged that a single Adjudicator can adjudicate them all. In fact, the Kenya Drama Festival and the Northern Rhodesia Drama Festival did share an Adjudicator in 1954, and so reduced their expenses considerably.

The standard of production in the amateur theatre in Northern Rhodesia is high, but it is entirely confined to European groups.

SOUTHERN RHODESIA

In Southern Rhodesia the common African pattern of small centres of European population long distances apart preclude the establishment of a professional theatre for some years to come, and it is only represented by occasional visits by companies from the Union of South Africa and Great Britain. As in Kenya, amateur theatre comes into its own here and a number of European societies with activities ranging from straight drama to comic opera can be found in the larger centres such as Salisbury, Bulawayo and Umbali, each of which boasts several such societies. As yet there has been no contribution to the modern realistic drama from races other than Europeans.

The leading amateur society is the Salisbury Repertory Players who have been continuously active for well over twenty years. In 1946 the Players took over a building which they converted into the intimate Belvedere Theatre. This theatre, the first in the territory, has been progressively improved until today it can claim to be fully equipped with all the amenities that a company can expect. The terraced auditorium seats 264. The Players produce a full-length play every two months throughout the year.

Outside Salisbury, the capital, with the recent exception of Umbali, dramatic societies have to make do with the adaptation of multi-purpose halls, never a very satisfactory solution, and one society even produces plays in the lounge of the local hotel. Umbali was the first to follow Salisbury's lead and, thanks to the generosity of a local benefactor, was able to open a fully equipped theatre seating 367 in April 1955. This theatre is not only used by local amateur dramatic societies but is also available to visiting companies. However, the importance of a properly equipped theatre to the larger communities is now generally realized and in Bulawayo the City Council has taken the initiative in allocating a site for a theatre. In Salisbury, too, it is hoped that the City Council will help in providing another theatre, as the Belvedere Theatre is fully occupied throughout the year by the Repertory Players, and a site for a Children's Theatre has already been granted by a suburban authority.

Southern Rhodesian amateur dramatic societies encounter the same difficulties as societies in other parts of this area in the matter of obtaining costumes, scenery, properties, etc. All has to be borrowed, made or improvised, and because of the lack of storage facilities little can be used again. As yet, drama festivals or interchange of productions have not yet been organized but an enterprising society from the neighbouring territory of Northern Rhodesia—the Lusaka Theatre Club—did take their production of *The Cocktail Party* to Salisbury in 1954, a distance of 340 miles, which is a long way even for Africa.

INDIA
by L. K. MALHOTRA

It is most significant to note that India has never had a professional stage of the kind that is known to Western audiences. In India drama flourished at a time when this art form was not even known to the Greeks and the greatest plays within the classical framework were written before the advent of Muslim rule in India somewhere at the close of the twelfth century. But all theatrical activity in India, save on a very small scale in Bengal and Maharashtra, has been confined to amateurs. Nevertheless, the tradition of staging plays survived through various epochs and regimes and in modern times it was handed down chiefly as a folk heritage.

With the European invaders, there came a foreign three-dimensional idea of stagecraft with its picture frame of the proscenium, introducing complications which have still not been completely analysed, and of which the best elements have not yet been absorbed into the indigenous tradition. If the seeming disregard of properties, curtains and other conventions of the European stage makes the folk survivals of RAAS, NAUTANKI, KIRTANS, JATRAS and BURRAKATHA forms difficult for the comprehension of middle-class audiences in India today, fed on the naturalistic portrayals of the West End and Broadway, it is because we have overlooked the essential principles of our traditional theatre and not quite understood the despair of contemporary European producers with the box or camera play.

The most important problem, however, in this context arises with the fundamental and basic contradiction between the symbolism of the Indian heritage in drama with its poetic realism, and the naturalism of the West which permeated into India bereft of its essential sensibility, poetry and technical perfection. In the folk tradition of India, however, even in its most decadent survivals, the basis of the ancient theatre was not lost; that the actor and the audience are one:

> When the Actor beateth the drum
> Everybody cometh to see the show;
> When the Actor collecteth the stage properties
> He abideth alone in his happiness.

And the Sutradhar continued to supply the link between the various elements on the stage. He was the stage manager, producer, or prologue reciter, developed in the ancient primitive Indian theatre. In so far as he intervened as a master of ceremonies who put properties in position and asked the audience to remain quiet and won their applause with his good humour, the traditions of the village stage remained inbred, mental and imaginative. The poet and dramatist Rabindranath Tagore caught the mood of the folk theatre very correctly when he wrote: "In our country, those of the audience who are appreciative, are content to perfect the song in their own mind by the force of their own feeling." But at the same time, we cannot overlook the fact that the audience in the folk theatre was very uncritical and its attitude was compensated only by love and faith. And this attitude had an important asset in its demands on the audience because the maxim of

The Canterbury Student Players, New Zealand, in a modern dress production of *Julius Caesar*.

DHARMADATTA still applied: "Those who are devoid of imagination, in the theatre, are but as the wood work, the walls and the stones."

The gradual loss of faith in old values which had their basis in
religion and the emergence of a new urban middle class with its new
outlook and philosophy resulted in a decline of the belief in the various
arts also which depended on these values. Even before the theatre of
the West began to attract these middle class audiences the old theatre
had started losing its hold. The European theatre, mostly performed by
amateurs from the European colonies in cities like Calcutta, was
restricted to audiences of the white "sahibs" and their wives. On
20 January 1780 Hicky's *Bengal Gazette* had its first publication,
and it is significant that the first issue should have carried a notice
about the staging of the comedy *The Beaux' Stratagem* together with the
farce *Lethe*. A year later the same journal said of *The Tragedy of Venice
Preserved*: "Captain Gall played Jafar admirably well and may be
justly styled the 'Garrick of the East' . . . the actors of the inferior
parts were not totally devoid of merit."

When the richer Indians were privileged to be invited to these performances and they could peep into the lives of the European people
they naturally felt the need for projecting their own lives with advantage through the proscenium. And so gradually the secrets of the
Western theatre began to be available to the educated urban middle
class. The early history of the English theatre in India is itself wrapped
in romance just as the beginnings of the East India Company were.
But there is no doubt that the beginnings of the modern stage in Bengal
owe an immense debt to pioneers like Herasim Lebedeff, a Russian
adventurer, who came to Madras as a musician and later established a
number of theatres in Calcutta; Mrs. Amelia Bristow who lived in
Calcutta during the tenure of office of Warren Hastings and Lord
Cornwallis; Dr. Horace Hayman Wilson, a Sanskrit scholar; and
Captain D. L. Richardson, a Shakespearian scholar. The earliest
English theatre in Calcutta seems to have been the Play House which
was founded some years before the battle of Plassey and before the
reins of government passed from the Nawab into the hands of the East
India Company. This theatre along with the Calcutta Theatre and
Mrs. Bristow's Private Theatre were all intended for the staging of
plays in English and it was Lebedeff who, with the assistance of a
Bengali linguist, Babu Golaknath Das, founded the first Bengali theatre.

Under the influence of these theatres the upper middle class patrons
of drama gave private shows of which the first was Bharat Chandra's
Vidyasundar, performed in the house of one Nobin Krishna Basu at
Shyambazar in 1832. This was really the beginning of amateur theatre
in India, when a synthesis was attempted by applying the conventions

2A

of the Western stage to the prevailing indigenous traditions. Gradually opera houses built after the fashion of Covent Garden and its counterpart in Paris, with plush seats, gilded panellings and chandeliers, began to be built in the major cities. But apart from the occasional plays performed by European amateurs these theatres were filled by adaptations of Shakespeare in Indian languages, religious plays based on the RAMAYANA and the MAHABHARATA and social plays, tentatively treating of the main emotions, love, hatred, jealousy, greed, in the style of the Western ham actors. And so these theatres continued to flourish and later even original plays came to be written along the lines of English plays. In Bengal dramatists like Michael Madhusudan Dutt consciously attempted a departure from the classical form of Sanskrit drama with plays like *Eke ki bale Sabhyata* (Is this Civilization?) and *Sarmistha*. But the themes still continued to be taken from the old Pauranic legends with an occasional touch of tragedy and farce which portrayed contemporary customs and manners.

Besides Bengal, Maharashtra in Western India was another centre where the Indian theatre showed signs of development. Marathi drama also made its beginning under the influence of the British, but it attained its independence earlier, and, in fact, till the second decade of the nineteenth century, because of the very nature of its political set-up and awareness of national aspirations, it led Bengal. Towards the end of the nineteenth century and the beginning of the present, however, Bengal once again came into the forefront and the social and political revolt began to be reflected in plays like *Nildarpana*, written by Dinabandhu Mitra. This play in particular achieved unprecedented popularity and it gave rise to a wave of indignation throughout the country for it exposed the brutality of the Indigo planters of Eastern India.

During this period some of the well-known writers in different parts of India succeeded to an extent with the sincerity of serious drama but merely because these intellectuals, particularly in Bengal, realized the need for a synthesis. Rabindranath Tagore, for instance, evolved an individual style in production by emancipating Bengali drama from the influences of English forms. His plays owe a great deal to the folk culture of Bengal and he succeeded in evolving a type of poetic drama which reached great heights of simplicity and intensity. In Maharashtra similarly, when historical plays were banned by the British, dramatists evolved the humorous social play, fantasies and farcical comedies. Annasaheb Kirloskar, a dramatist who lived towards the end of the nineteenth century, introduced the "sangeet-natak" or musical play and his contribution marks an important advance in the development of the Maharashtrian stage.

But the efforts of Tagore in Bengal, or Maharashtrian dramatists like Kirloskar and Trilokekar who preferred the heroic and farcical styles, were not strong enough to influence this temporary phase of the commercial but still amateur theatre. In Northern India for instance, the theatre in the newly developing language, Hindustani, was at best a pickle of European techniques mixed with cheap conventions. Drop-curtains in glaring colours split into two at the sound of a pistol, the stage was covered with corpses, and heroes and heroines sang and spoke in a hybrid opera, comedy or tragedy, to an audience which sat through the long hours of the night enduring the rigours of happy endings or broken hearts. The Parsees revived the theatre in Bombay, drawing unhesitatingly from the folk survivals of the RAAS and NAUTANKI of the North and blending them with cheap adaptations of classical English plays, purely to promote their own commercial interests. Indeed, it would not be incorrect to conclude that what the Alfred Theatrical Company and the Parsee Ripon Theatrical Company and like produced during the earlier part of our century is more or less what most Indian films seek to achieve today; they are catering to the tastes of the masses in large cities and towns and to audiences who have hardly any tastes left!

From the welter of confusion that seemed to become worse confounded during the years, there arose, in the amateur societies of the various parts of the country, the desire to introduce the producer who would disentangle the mess. During the last twenty-five years or so any improvement that has resulted in the technique of production of plays in India has been through the growing awareness of the essential role of the producer.

Soon after the First World War and particularly in the early thirties, the younger writers in India developed a consciousness, more than ever before, of the miserable plight of their countrymen. No doubt the political struggle that was afoot for the freedom of the country unleashed intellectual forces which were reflected in nearly all the arts. The intelligentsia, more than any other class in India, became increasingly aware of the necessity to put an end not only to foreign rule but also the feudal and meaningless religious and social practices which had contributed to this enslavement. The result was the birth of a new literature in all languages, new poetry, new prose and also new dramas. And the development of the concept of democracy in the West and the progressive rebellions against nationalistic dictatorships in Europe, encouraged them to cement their own belief in the possibilities of a free India with a plentiful life for its people.

Whereas poetry and prose had easy and continuous access to the general mass of the literate middle class, India's illiterate millions, the sons of the soil, could only understand the spoken word or song and in their few hours of forgetful leisure perhaps enjoy the rhythmic movement of the body to the beat of the village drum. But there is yet another advantage which the Indian people probably have over people in other countries: they have continued to express an unceasing love for drama and even proved that they have the inborn aptitude to act. Our dramatists and theatre enthusiasts, therefore, armed with the knowledge that in drama and dance we not only possess a rich heritage but that these two forms of art could be combined to awaken the forces which have slumbered for centuries, set themselves seriously to the task of reviving folk forms. In the South, for instance, the ancient forms of the BURRAKATHA or recitals by bards and the HARIKATHA or narrative were taken up by the people's theatre groups. In Bengal similarly the scandalous Bengal famine of 1943 provided the newly formed Indian People's Theatre Association (or I.P.T.A. as it came to be known) with one of the most powerful themes through which the suffering and misery of the peasantry of Bengal could be translated into drama. For sheer art, standard of acting and stage-craft perhaps no other play has in recent years equalled the merit of *Navanna* or *New Harvest*. In Maharashtra too, Tamashas and Powadas were the simple forms which progressive writers exploited to create a new interest in the stage.

It is equally significant to record here that while plays like *Waiting for Lefty* and *They Came to a City* were being written and staged in the West parallel forces were at work in India and plays like *Zubeida* written by Khwaja Ahmed Abbas and *Aag-gari* by C. C. Mehta were becoming extremely popular with the middle-class audiences. But these plays and their like were inspired by a technique which, though realistic and modern, had no roots in the indigenous theatre of the village and, therefore, could not be taken to peasant audiences. At the same time these were only sporadic efforts which reached their culmination when the political struggle for emancipation was at its height. In Northern India the only consistent but lone effort, till a few years ago, seems to have been that of the film actor and producer Prithvi Raj Kapoor who, with his genuine love for the theatre, has spent his entire fortune in attempting to weave the simple technique of folk drama or RAAS into a pattern of modern themes like DEEWAR, PATHAN, GHADDAR and AHUTI and very recently PAISA. But the tragedy of the theatre in India, even till today, is that a city as large as Bombay cannot provide a permanent stage for producers like Prithvi Raj Kapoor. I have seen his plays performed under most trying conditions in a cinema hall called the Opera House which is available to his company only on Sunday mornings.

With the emergence of a new India a new phase has come into the life of the theatre. The younger generation of dramatists was once again inspired by the remnants of the broken tradition of our theatre. In the Punjab, Chetan Anand Rapi Peer and Rajinder Singh Bedi who had mainly attempted adaptations of Ibsen, Shaw and Gogol, found new themes in the recent partition of the country and the heart-rending stories of millions of refugees who came from the North-West into the centre. In Bengal and Bombay, the Little Theatre Group, though chiefly staging plays in English, made a distinct contribution with its high standard of acting, decor and production. Amateur actors and producers like Alkazi and Utpal Dutt, under the influence of English producers and with the experience of training in R.A.D.A. or the British Drama League, have begun producing plays which could easily be compared with some West End productions. But their audiences are mainly drawn from mercantile houses, colleges and universities and the floating Anglicized populations of big cities like Calcutta and Bombay. In Calcutta, however, which seems to have always provided the lead to the theatrical tradition of India, a group called the BAHURUPEE, with well-known stage and screen personalities like Shambhu Mitra and Tripti Mitra, is producing highly perfected modern plays in Bengali and because of the language it has succeeded in reaching much larger and varied audiences. Similarly in Delhi, which has now become the centre of all cultural activity in India, the Government sponsored an Academy of Music, Drama, and Dancing. Around it sprang up a number of amateur groups who, after a year or two of unprecedented activity, formed themselves into a larger union of the Bharatiya Natya Sangh. More recently, the Prime Minister of India has himself been encouraging the development of the various arts and the building of an ultra-modern and well-equipped theatre in Delhi where groups from all over the country could stage plays in their own language during the Republic Day celebrations in the capital. In 1954 still another organization known as the Theatre Centre of India, affiliated to the International Theatre Institute of the UNESCO, came into being. Branches of the T.C.I. have started to function in various provincial capitals and Calcutta has already had a very successful festival of plays in Bengali and Hindu.

It may appear that this could easily be another temporary phase of activity in the chequered history of the Indian theatre. Contemporary theatre in India is still groping and at best remains as amateur as it has always been. But while it is obvious that we are not going to resurrect the formalism of the ancient theatre it is also true that the modern Indian theatre cannot import the drawing-room comedy from the West. Our conditions are fundamentally different. What is certain, however, is that a new synthesis has to be evolved by combining these sporadic efforts in the theatrical life of the middle class with the simpler form of drama taken from the peasantry. We may not revive the ancient Indian theatre in its entirety, nor is it necessary that we should make any attempt but perhaps we can still profitably inquire into its old technique and content and, by adapting the remnants of the age-old folk theatre, create a new and indigenous tradition which may have something to offer even to the West. What is most important is that the necessity of theatre even in the chaotic but transitory societies of India has been realized. The realities of our life will now have to be churned up in the new theatre before they can be transformed into the higher exaltation of an art which can be the basis of a sustained and rich cultural heritage. Progress may be slow and gradual but it is certain that the theatre in India has, once again, heralded a great future.

NEW ZEALAND
by J. G. A. POCOCK

The present phase in the history of the amateur theatre in New Zealand began when the cinema made it no longer worth while for touring professional companies to undertake what is still a longish voyage to a smallish audience—our population has only recently touched the two million mark, and the centres in which we live are strung out along two sizeable and attenuated islands. For twenty (or was it thirty?) years, then, New Zealand saw next to no professional theatre, and it rested with the amateur groups to fill the gap by presenting the public with serious and ambitious dramatic work, or to leave it unfilled. This challenge produced its response, and from time to time there arose amateur theatres which took their work as devotedly and passionately as any professionals, because they had realized that they must do what there were no professionals to do. Today we are less isolated from the professional theatre than we used to be. In spite of the malignant taxation policy pursued by certain Ministers, we receive a tolerably regular trickle of overseas professional visitors, and (what is more important) we have in the New Zealand Players an ambitious and (it is hoped) established professional organization whose tours cover the whole country twice or thrice a year. Yet it does not seem that the position is essentially altered. We are glad of the Players, but one professional company cannot alter the whole theatrical situation; nor does it seem likely that our present social structure would support more than another one or two such companies. As far as can be foreseen, then, the main lines of the New Zealand theatre will continue to be

those which the amateurs lay down, and the amateurs will continue to
face the challenge which this implies.

A predominantly amateur theatre has to satisfy the needs of a provincial society of an essentially English pattern; and the classification
into which its societies fall is broadly similar to that of the English
professional theatre. The first to catch the eye are the misnamed
"repertory societies" (they do not present repertory) which flourish in
most of our larger towns. They are founded on a large subscribing
membership, often a thousand and upwards; they are opulent in funds
and assured of their audiences. The plays they present are for the most
part West End commercial successes of two or three seasons ago, and
they employ professional producers—usually imported from England
—who are happiest doing this sort of play. Now and then, and generally as a result of minority pressure, they perform a classical or an
experimental play: probably either Shakespeare or Shaw, and almost
certainly a comedy; Ibsen's *Ghosts* was thought a most daring experiment in Dunedin two or three years ago. It should be added that
willingness to attempt such plays varies greatly from centre to centre,
and from time to time; there have been several experiments in building
up a local tradition of minority work within the general framework of a
large society, and if such experiments have seldom succeeded the fault
has probably lain less with the societies concerned than with the special
difficulties that attend keeping a minority theatre alive in New Zealand. On the whole, however, it would be fair to say that the repertory
societies are the amateur equivalent of the straight commercial theatre.
Satisfying a middle-class demand for entertainment, their function is
not primarily intellectual or artistic.

Next come the minority, the *avant-garde*, the experimentalists. Struggling, impoverished, learning as they go, and usually young, they
appear and disappear wherever there is a university or any other reason
for a local intelligentsia to come into being. If they receive the lion's
share of attention in this essay, it is because they have done *most* of what
has been done to present the great plays and keep the theatre alive as a
great art. It is they who have have played Shakespeare and Sartre,
Euripides and Ibsen, and a work or two by our own poets. But just at
present they appear to be in the doldrums, and throughout their
history their curse has been that they are ephemeral. With scarcely an
exception, none has lasted long enough to establish a tradition, or for
new leaders to be acquired and trained and to step into the breach
when the founders become tired or fall away. When the original
leadership is exhausted, the group dies; that has been the rule. The
reasons for this lie in the nature of a remote provincial society with a
small population, and they may be defined as: lack of good small play-

houses, and lack of continuously active personnel. These causes can best be shown by telling the story of the rise and decline of one such group, remarkable both in itself and for its association with a notable personality: the Canterbury Student Players and the work they did with Miss Ngaio Marsh. To all the societies whose stories I do not tell, may I apologize? This history is meant to display the conditions under which we all work.

Canterbury University College—which stands in Christchurch, the second or third city of the Dominion—had possessed a Little Theatre since 1923, the work of Sir James Shelley for whom it was afterwards renamed. It seated about 200; it possessed the rudiments of a lighting system and a pair of incredibly exiguous wings; but it was made a workable theatre by the existence of a permanent cyclorama and of a grid and loft. With these assets it had stood for some twenty years, intermittently mouldering, intermittently revived, as generations of students— and their allies on the staff—with or without the power to make it run, came and went. The force that brought it suddenly and spectacularly to life in 1943 is hard to define, but arose essentially from the conjunction of personalities. Ngaio Marsh was available to produce; there was a young Englishman, Jack Henderson, whose ambition was to play Hamlet; there was a committee of students with the imagination and the organizing ability to make things happen. *Hamlet* was mounted in modern dress; and the curtain went up on a winter evening in 1943 to reveal a tin-hatted and bayonetted Francisco and Bernardo, outlined against the cyclorama.

The effect which this produced is even now hard to describe, but it could justly be compared to what we are told was going on about the same time in Welsh and Northumbrian mining villages, as the war-time Old Vic brought them Shakespeare. Many of that evening's audience were seeing "live" Shakespeare for the first time; few had seen it done professionally for many years; none had seen it done by student actors with quite the same simplicity of tragic effect, or quite the same intimacy as that small, primitive, but soon tradition-filled theatre was capable of providing. *Hamlet* was packed out, was revived, and attained rapidly the dimensions of a myth. *Othello* followed, about a year later, and an Auckland business man of theatrical and artistic interest, Mr. D. D. O'Connor, was persuaded to finance a tour. Whose the initiative was, at this distance of time, is not easy to say, but at least part of it originated with the students. In the summer of 1944–5 *Hamlet* and *Othello* were toured through the main cities of New Zealand—having been adapted to a larger stage—and wherever they went produced the same unpredictable effect as on the Christchurch first night of *Hamlet*. *A Midsummer Night's Dream* followed; then *Henry V*; then

Macbeth—either in the Little Theatre or in a larger Christchurch theatre which prestige at that time could fill—and *Macbeth* went on a second tour in 1946–7. A small group of producers and actors, not all of them undergraduates, had now formed itself, and Sartre's *The Flies* and Allen Curnow's *The Axe*—a verse play written for the theatre by a New Zealand poet—were performed in the Little Theatre as the culmination of a series of efforts by prentice hands; all of whom carried on a small but growing tradition dominated by the ideas of simplicity of décor, boldness of rhetoric, a bare but well-lighted stage and a willingness to carry the play into the tiny auditorium. In 1948 Miss Marsh returned and produced *Six Characters in Search of an Author*, which, with a revived *Othello*, was taken on a culminating tour of Australia in 1948–9.

But the rocket was at the top of its flight. Not Miss Marsh only, but the theatre's nucleus of young men and women dispersed to England and other destinations during 1948 and 1949, and for whatever reasons, the generation which followed them found it impossible to maintain the same level of activity. It began to be seen how hard it is to keep a theatre alive where the intelligentsia and artists number only a handful. The Little Theatre entered upon a physical and spiritual decline and early in 1953, about the time when some of its old guard were drifting back from overseas with ideas of resuming where they had left off, was destroyed by fire. What followed is instructive. The governing body of the College refused to replace the theatre. Miss Marsh, who was back in Christchurch after a tour with a professional company, and a devoted band of old and new helpers now presented *Julius Caesar* in the Great Hall of the College, converted for the occasion into a theatre of arena pattern. The result provided one of the most spectacular and success- ful occasions in Christchurch theatrical history, but it could not revive a lost tradition. There are two main reasons. Christchurch has now no little theatre equal to the not very exacting technical demands which university productions make, and (except when they have Miss Marsh's name to draw crowds) the students cannot fill any of the larger theatres to the point where the considerable rentals these demand can be met and a heavy loss avoided. In the second place, lacking as they now do a tradition of continuous association, the older and the younger actors no longer find it very satisfactory to work together. Christchurch's univer- sity theatre is now nothing more than a student society, which must naturally go its own way and pursue its own destiny—lacking the theatre which once gave it permanence. Some day it will revive; but a permanent and self-perpetuating tradition has not been founded.

This story has been told because it is representative. Lack of theatre buildings and lack of tradition beset the ambitious and experimental amateur in every New Zealand city. There have been instances where these obstacles have been more successfully assaulted. When the theatre attached to Auckland's Elam School of Art was destroyed by fire it was replaced by a few resolute individuals; in Wellington, Unity Theatre— an avowedly *avant-garde* group—has a record of thirteen years' continuous existence, and its own studio theatre built by its own labour is on the way. But this success rests on the basis of population. Wellington, the capital, attracts to its bureaux a high proportion of the country's intellectuals, and a theatre such as Unity may hope for a semi-permanent nucleus of resident members, who may even discover and train the replacements for those who leave. Elsewhere this does not happen, and most small theatres survive only so long as a group of five or ten dynamic individuals continue to live and work together. When these disperse, nothing is left.

Does this matter? it may be asked; the theatre is ephemeral, a phoenix not perhaps as frequent as could be wished, but still a phoenix. One group dies; there will be another. There is a great deal of comfort in this and one may put a sizeable measure of faith in its prophecy. But it implies that there will be no growth, no building by the young on foundations laid down before them, and for a raw society, still lacking traditions and artistic capital, this is a hard thing to contemplate. An extensive increase in population may contain the answer; meanwhile we do grow, though in the amateur theatre there is little sign of it at present. It would seem that, for the moment, our accumulated talent and experience is just equal to the production, sustenance, and criticism of one professional company—the New Zealand Players—which does not really meet the demands which the *avant-garde* makes on it. There must be an *avant-garde*, and for that reason alone there will continue to be amateurs; though where the next experimental impulse will come from is hard to see. The native energies bred here by depression and war seem for the present to have died out, and our amateurs imitate, at an enormous remove, the fashionable sophistications of London and Paris. Anouilh and Fry are frequently performed, but our systems really hunger for stronger meat.

Auckland conducts an annual festival of the arts to which amateur companies travel from all parts of the country, and Wellington is about to hold a Theatre Week on similar lines. What fertilizing and permanent effect these will have remains to be seen. In them, as elsewhere, the very interesting influence of the New Zealand branch of the British Drama League is bound to be strong. This devoted and practical body holds regional and national competitions in the producing, staging, acting and even writing of one-act plays, and stimulates a surprising amount of local activity in both town and country. It is permissible, however, to enter one or two mild reservations. Competitive drama (the performance of short plays in an evening before some heroic and ill-paid adjudicator) needs to be offset by the activities of other groups who prefer to perform on their own stages to their own audiences, seeking to satisfy their own powers of self-criticism, which are often considerable. If there is not enough of this sort of activity at present, it is partly because there are not enough small theatres available, but also partly because too many groups which should be engaged in free production have been led to concentrate all of their energies upon the annual festival. To immerse oneself in one-act festivals contains, besides, the danger that one will stumble into that theatrical underworld, where there exist hundreds of one-act plays written for no other purpose than to be performed at just such festivals; and there can be no doubt that too many of these desiccate the soul. The British Drama League, like the surprisingly extensive dramatic departments of the government and university adult education organizations, exists primarily to carry the drama to small towns and country districts, which in ninety-nine cases out of a hundred means the fostering of one-act play production by local groups. For this selfless, kindly and valuable activity no praise can possibly be too high, so long as one does not mistake it for what it is not: the creation and dissemination of an art. It is the characteristic fault of a colonial society to confuse creation with education, because we are driven by circumstances to start spreading our culture before it has properly taken root; and we tend therefore to confuse a laudable educational service with the spontaneous growth of a native theatrical art. This sometimes produces strange and revealing utterances. A president of the British Drama League in New Zealand not long ago declared that there was no future for the professional theatre in these islands until the country had undergone at least fifty years of prior education, after which (presumably) our grandchildren would be sufficiently broken in to the idea to be allowed to see a play occasionally. These words are only an example of the colonial and educational fallacy at its ripest, but they serve to recall us to realities. The theatre will not really be ours until we are writing, as well as producing, our own plays with some approach to regularity. This must come about through the amateur movement fully as much as—perhaps more than —through the professional theatre; since the *avant-garde* will always, here, be amateur. Therefore the amateur movement must flourish and strike roots; but I have already shown that I cannot see how, in present circumstances, it is to do so. No matter—it will probably prove me wrong. The English-language theatre is proverbially always on the verge of extinction. At all events, we can see more clearly what our present difficulties and future responsibilities may be, if we are, as seems to be the case at the moment, in the trough between two waves.

PAKISTAN
by RASHID CARRAPIETT

Pakistan is the youngest of the Islamic countries of the world but despite this lack of years, there is a basic interest in theatre which is the more heartening when we consider that there is no Islamic tradition of theatre as there is a European tradition. This could constitute a serious handicap to the natural expression of the interest in theatre that exists, but it does not; at least not directly. What in the West are today considered Victorian prejudices, still govern the attitude of most people to professional artistes of any kind, but these are social rather than religious prejudices—except the position of women who do anything in public, which is governed by a curious mixture of both kinds of prejudice, the one appearing to sanction the other. In any case, people continue to flock to the performances of those theatre companies, amateur and professional, which do exist, in spite of the fact that standards of acting and production in the professional companies practically do not exist at all. To the greater part of these audiences, however, this *is* theatre: they do not see how vulgar is the over-ripe style of acting, how artistically revolting the brightly-coloured distorted back-cloths and wings, how aesthetically unsatisfying the pseudo-historical plays with their lame construction, flamboyantly over-drawn characters and pathetically contrived spaces for pointless songs and cheap dancing-girls. (If there aren't any such spaces, the producer has to create them.) And what is more, this has been theatre ever since they or their grand-parents or great-grandparents can remember, and, for all the greater part of them care, this could go on being theatre indefinitely. There are other people, however, who have seen what theatre has grown to be in the centuries it has lived, and they are spreading the word of discontent around. They are mainly not professionals, and it is upon these intelligent amateurs that the future of theatre in Pakistan depends.

The oldest amateur company in Pakistan is the Government College Amateur Dramatic Club in Lahore. It has been in existence for over seventy years. Firmly and enthusiastically supported by the College authorities and with independent funds, the G.C.A.D.C. performs three or four plays a year. These are mainly in English, including translations from other European languages, but some plays are done in local languages such as Urdu and Punjabi. It is difficult to assess, in a general way, the standards of production and acting because it is a college group with a fluid membership; but there is tremendous enthusiasm and natural talent and a sincere striving to achieve. As long as there is no one with sufficient background and experience and knowledge to direct this enthusiasm and talent and striving, it seems destined to remain somewhat localized and frustrated of absolute achievement. Perhaps the College authorities will one day be persuaded to see the potential importance and influence of the work of the G.C.A.D.C. and extend their support to include importing a foreign expert for full-time theatre coaching.

Another regularly active amateur company is the group of Europeans in Karachi called the Clifton Players. They were organized in about 1949 by Robert and Barbara Trench-Thompson and Sir Edward Snelson, at present Secretary to the Pakistan Ministry of Law. They have been producing four plays a year, and for several years provided Karachi with its only Western-technique theatre. Their objective is, purely and simply, local entertainment. If it were not, their choice of plays might be somewhat more ambitious and universal than the standard of *Quiet Wedding*, *Arsenic and Old Lace*, and *Ladies in Retirement*, and casting would be on a sounder basis than what appears to be social eminence. Also, they would not, as they do now, exclude Pakistanis from membership. Nevertheless, their methods and technique are in the Western tradition and so they serve a useful purpose beyond the limited local one, possibly in spite of themselves. It is a pity, for this reason, that this company does not try to achieve a higher standard of production and acting particularly as they have facilities which are not open to other amateur groups. For example, their greatest advantage is that they have their own stage; it does not belong to them but they have an agreement for the regular use of it and so have been able to install, on a permanent basis, lighting and other technical equipment. Again, since most of the members of the company are in business, they have freer access to certain necessary goods and services; all of which makes their work much easier than it is for other similar companies.

When future generations of Pakistani playgoers stop to talk of how theatre developed in their country, two names will definitely be mentioned: Sigrid Nyberg Kahle and the Karachi Theatre. Sigrid is a Swedish girl married to a young German diplomat; they have been in Karachi for about three years. It is difficult for me to be completely objective about the Kahles because they are among my dearest friends and about the Karachi Theatre because I was one of the small group who, led by Sigrid, brought it to life, saw it flourish briefly and mourned its spiritual death—spiritual because there is a remnant of the original company which continues to use the name.

Sigrid believes passionately that, in addition to all else, theatre is the best sociology, and her plans for the Karachi Theatre were based on this belief. This was not to be merely a number of people with certain talents banding together for the purpose of demonstrating these talents in public for their own and other people's entertainment. This was to be a group of intelligent people with a common interest in theatre, working to achieve through this medium a better, fuller life for themselves and for their fellow-countrymen. It was to develop gradually into the first good professional company in Pakistan, producing original plays in Urdu and other Pakistani languages, using Western techniques, with sets and costumes designed by Pakistani artists, music composed and performed by Pakistani musicians—in a word, officially or unofficially, Pakistan's first national theatre. This was the ultimate objective.

In order to foster and educate the existing interest and, of course, to make money, a series of plays was to be produced to demonstrate as many aspects of theatre as was within the range of the company. An initial, rather serious handicap was the extreme difficulty of finding suitable girls and young women whose parents had sufficient faith in them and their talents to permit them to join such a group as the Karachi Theatre. It was overcome by Sigrid's personal influence with several families and her willingness to become chaperon-in-chief in addition to her other duties!

The first play was Molière's *The School for Wives*. It had magnificent costumes based on designs used for a production at the Royal Swedish Theatre in Stockholm, wigs from a Swedish firm, and a delightful period set designed by Alex Elmore, an Englishman living in Karachi, a man of considerable theatrical experience and knowledge whose principal talent, it seems to me, is an incredible ability to see at once the essence of a play and to design, in its *simplest* form, a set to bring out this essence.

The School for Wives was a tremendous success; Karachi had never seen anything like it before, and it gave the Karachi Theatre immediately a standard and a reputation. It was followed by Thornton Wilder's *Our Town*, produced by Alex Elmore. No one who saw this production will ever forget the last act in the little American cemetery; some inexpressible spiritual union of play, producer and actress took place, making it possible to bring out in all its moving beauty the terrible sadness of the impossibility of the dead coming back. The girl who played Emily Webb achieved with this performance a reputation which, in all likelihood, she will find extremely difficult to live, or act, up to.

The next production was a set of three one-act plays by Strindberg, *Playing with Fire*, *The Stronger*, and *Pariah*. An arena-theatre production, with the audience on three sides of a large room, it demonstrated to cast and spectators the almost terrifying intensity that can be built up in this form of theatre. This was followed by three short plays in

Urdu, including a translation of Chekhov's *The Proposal*. The set for one of these plays, *Outside the Serai*, was designed by a young Pakistani painter, Ahmed Parvez. The other two were detail sets against black curtains. Incidentally, *Outside the Serai* and the third play, *Talkhian*, were adapted from radio-plays, which demonstrates another problem facing amateur companies in Pakistan: the lack of good original stage plays by Pakistani writers.

These four productions took place between November 1953 and June 1954. After the Urdu plays, the Kahles went home to Europe on holiday. While they were away, the Executive Committee of the Karachi Theatre decided to use its constitutional powers rather differently than it had had opportunity to do while Sigrid was there. In two months the Committee and their Constitution had killed the spirit of the Karachi Theatre. Some of those who left in sadness and anger decided to raise their heads again with the first Pakistani production of Christopher Fry's *A Phoenix Too Frequent*.

If it appears too much space has been devoted to the activities of a single amateur company, I must make it clear that this has been done quite deliberately for two reasons. Firstly, in order to give an idea of some of the difficulties that face any amateur company, and secondly, to record that integrity and intelligence and good sense have achieved something of value in the establishment of good theatre in Pakistan. The basic qualities that made the success of the Karachi Theatre still exist; should a personality and visionary force arise again to equal Sigrid Kahle's then there will be a revival of the spirit of the theatre company she founded and led. In the meantime, plays will continue to be produced at the usual intervals but something will always be missing for those who knew the Karachi Theatre.

Apart from those I have discussed, there are several college companies that produce one or two plays a year, principally for audiences of friends and relatives. There are, as well, many small groups that come into being on the spur of someone's enthusiastic moment, do a play or, more generally, a "variety show" (a very poor equivalent of the Western revue), and then fade into the nothing they came from.

It is not only insufficient talent and organization that is responsible for the failure of these mushroom groups: amateur public entertainment in Pakistan is an unnecessarily complicated business. There are, in Karachi for example, few suitable halls and those that exist cost a quite disproportionate amount of money to rent. Again, there is a complex and exorbitant system of entertainment and other taxes to cope with. It was only the personal influence of Sigrid Kahle and various other members of the Karachi Theatre which enabled it to surmount these official and material obstacles, obstacles which cause lesser groups to founder.

The fact that, in spite of these difficulties, people do try to organize amateur groups proves again and again the basic interest in theatre on both sides of the proscenium arch (footlights are considered luxurious by most amateur companies in Pakistan), but the general rate of failure demonstrates a lack of the coherent personal integrity and single-ness of purpose which must characterize amateur theatre in Pakistan if it is to live at all and, further, if it is to serve, as it must, the additional purpose of an introduction to professional theatre.

SOUTH AFRICA
by ARNOLD PEARCE

This is only meant to be a short and general survey of the amateur theatre position in South Africa. Friends and theatrical societies will thus forgive me if I have not mentioned them.

South Africa is a country composed of many races, but is particularly derived from three main streams: the African, the Dutchman and the Englishman. The social and political structure of the country rarely allows either mixed audiences or a cast composed of both Europeans and non-Europeans. This restricts theatrical activity. The standard of education of the public varies from town to country; from race to race. Another obstacle in the way of the South African theatre is the entertainment tax which is comparatively heavy and hits particularly at professional organizations. Yet with all these attendant difficulties there is theatre in South Africa performed by both amateur and pro-fessional. It is, however, a theatre which has developed along three separate channels (channels demarcated by race and language) . . . the African, the Afrikaans and the English theatre. The latter two theatres are the most prominent and what follows deals in the main with their activities.

With the advent of the cinema, professional theatre as a living part of the community practically disappeared. Only the Afrikaans pro-fessionals kept a slight spark alive in the country districts which they traversed, and occasionally South Africa was given an English play with the whole company imported from overseas. Any large theatres that there were in the town disappeared or became cinemas. The imported companies played in cinemas converted back to theatre stages for a short period, and the Afrikaans companies kept to the village town halls. The amateur theatre thus grew in a time when there was little professional theatre to speak of. The art of acting, of produc-

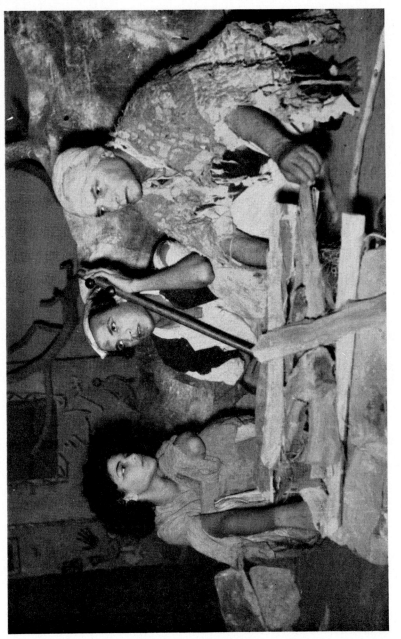

The Karachi Theatre, Pakistan, in *Outside the Serai*, by Krishen Chander.

The University of Cape Town Dramatic Society, South Africa, in *The Ascent of F6*, by Auden and Isherwood.

tion, scene designing and lighting flourished in the hands of the amateur. This had two main effects. Many people who otherwise would have joined the ranks of the professional remained in the amateur movement, and only the odd few who dared went overseas to further their work. Secondly, as the amateur theatre grew, the demand for the experienced and successful producer and actor became greater. He commercialized his talents and the amateur theatre became a new entity, a semi-professional theatre, where a few professional artists combined their talents with the larger nucleus of unpaid theatre lovers.

Most amateur organizations started off in converted halls hired for the occasion and with meagre equipment, but in the towns many small theatres began to be built . . . the Universities being the forerunners of this type of theatre. Modern equipment was bought and these theatres today are technically as efficient as most ordinary repertory theatres in England. Three of the Universities, Cape Town, Durban and Stellenbosch, have departments of speech training and dramatic art attached to their theatres. The University of Cape Town's Little Theatre is probably the oldest of the University theatres and celebrated its twenty-first anniversary in 1952 with guest productions of *Lady Windermere's Fan* and the *Oresteia* of Aeschylus. This theatre seats only two hundred and eighty-three people, but it has a good stage—twenty-two feet, proscenium opening; seventeen feet, six inches depth to the cyc. pit; and a permanent cyclorama. Donald Inskip, Controller of this theatre, is one of the most prominent theatre men in the country. The other two Universities also have small theatres and the Durban one has another leading theatrical figure at its head, Elizabeth Sneddon. The Witwatersrand University's theatre seats one thousand two hundred people, and has the largest apron stage in the Union. Emlyn Williams gave his distinguished readings from Dickens at this theatre.

There are, of course, many well-known amateur groups with their own theatres in no way connected with a University. In Johannesburg, the Johannesburg Reps. Theatre has sufficient seating for professional work and one of the finest stages I have ever played on. This theatre has often been hired by professionals for seasons. The Library Theatre is a small compact theatre in the Johannesburg Library buildings, and is hired by amateur and professional alike. The Johannesburg Reps. employed a permanent professional producer, Anthony Farmer, for last year's series of plays, and this year the Reps. have gone further and formed a permanent professional repertory company with Mr. Farmer at its head. In Durban, the Jewish Guild have their own home and in Cape Town the Reps. there bought a building and converted it into the Labia Theatre. One of the smaller groups to achieve its own theatre lately is out at Paarl, a small town in the Western Province.

The building was given them by a wealthy landowner, and Paarl has today one of the smallest and evidently nicest little theatres in South Africa.

The University theatres specialize in the classics and also present a wide selection of modern plays from all countries, especially the imaginative and unusual play. Both *Intermezzo* (*The Enchanted*) and *Leocadia* (*Time Remembered*), in translations by Donald Inskip, received productions in Cape Town long before their London seasons. The other amateur groups have tended to choose the more commercial play. In times when the professional theatre did not really exist this was a good thing and enabled audiences to see all types of work. But today with the resurgence of the professional movement, it has proved a disastrous policy. The amateur cannot compete for presentation with the professional in this type of play. He is beginning to alienate his audience's affection, and many amateur groups have tried to reorganize their planning schemes to present the more unusual plays and the classic which the professional dare not in general touch.

In time, the amateurs found the need for more co-ordination in their work, and the Federation of Amateur Theatrical Societies of Southern Africa was formed. Each year delegates from the various provinces meet to discuss their problems and a festival of plays from all the centres is put on. Competitions used to be held and floating trophies were awarded for the best productions and acting of that year, both English and Afrikaans. Today the provincial festivals are competitive, but the finalists in the national festival merely receive a criticism of their work by the judges and no actual placings are given. In this festival the producers of the various plays can be professionals, but the actors belong to an amateur group affiliated to the national body, and are not allowed to be paid for their work. The national festivals are held in a different place each year. The town that organizes the festival provides accommodation for the visiting players usually in private homes, and there is thus a social and artistic mixing of the groups. In Bloemfontein there is a library of plays with sufficient copies of each for performance, and most members of F.A.T.S.S.A. pay a nominal fee to this library and in return are able to borrow copies of plays without the expense of having to buy them outright.

After the Second World War, a metamorphosis took place in the South African theatrical scene. Professionalism in the English theatre was reborn. Permanent Rep. companies were established in Cape Town and Durban, and in Johannesburg the short seasons of all professional casts were extended. But the most important post-war development was the formation of a National Theatre of South Africa, subsidized to a certain extent by the Union Government. Mr. P.

Breytenbach, a chairman of F.A.T.S.S.A., and head of Drugersdorp Technical College, was appointed the first full-time director of National Theatre. He has built up the National Theatre to a solid company of English and Afrikaans actors covering the whole Union in their extensive tours. National Theatre, besides bringing the best in theatre to both small and large towns, has played an indirect role in the development of amateur theatre in the small towns. The people there, stimulated by the professional work, are a new and eager audience for the amateur organizations. National Theatre is also encouraging the building of theatres which can be used by both sections of the theatrical community. This year, 1955, two more permanent repertory companies are being established in Johannesburg. All this has meant a greater cleavage between the amateur and the professional, and the best talent from the amateur theatre has now directed its attention to the professional world.

Some leading professional producers who sprang into the limelight from the amateur movement are Leonard Schach, Leon Gluckman and Cecil Williams. Mr. Schach started working at the Little Theatre in Cape Town when he was studying Law at the University. Since those early days he has become South Africa's most discussed producer, having had more productions from National Theatre than anyone else, with the result that his work has been seen everywhere in the whole country. Leon Gluckman's love for the theatre was also kindled at a University—this time the one at Grahamstown. He combines the activities of producer, actor and manager, and is held in high repute. Cecil Williams was given his first production but a few years ago. His presentation of *Deep are the Roots* was so exciting and taut, that he was immediately in great demand as a producer in Johannesburg, his home town. Many professional producers have devoted much time to producing for amateur organizations. Such names as Leontine Sagan, Taubie Kushlick, Anna Romaine Hoffman, Rene Ahrenson, Costa Couvara and Hermien Dommisse come most easily to mind. Gwen Ffrangcon Davies, on one of her frequent visits to the Union, honoured the Johannesburg Reps. by directing their first major production in their new theatre. André Van Gyseghem is another overseas producer who has come out to South Africa to produce for the amateur organizations.

Professional actors stemming from the amateur movement are many. The most prominent was Wensley Pithey, who started work as head of the dramatic society at Cape Town University, and in time became controller of the Little Theatre. He was one of the leading actors of the Gwen Ffrangcon Davies-Marda Vanne company which toured South Africa during the war. After the war he went to England, where he has become a successful character actor.* Vivienne Drummond, Edna Jacobson, Hazel Casson and Joyce Bradley are some of the National Theatre stars who started work in amateur organizations. David Lytton, Lawrence Ayris, Hilda Kriseman and Diana Bester became leads with the Brian Brooke Company in Cape Town. Today's leading Afrikaans actors all stem from the old touring companies and do not have roots in the amateur theatre.

In the bigger towns professional scene designers work for both amateur and professional. This gives them a wide range of plays to work on. Some well-known names are Frank Graves, Len Grossett, Cecil Pym and Joseph Cappon. Harry Ligoff is the major lighting expert in the country and holds a position with National Theatre, but he still finds time to light the odd show in Johannesburg.

Neither the professional nor the amateur theatre has produced writers who concentrate their energies on the theatre. The English companies have a wide selection of plays from overseas to choose from, and the Afrikaans rely on translations for their diet. There are a number of South African playwrights like Uys Krige, W. A. De Klark, Professor Erlank and Professor Guy Butler, but there is not enough of their work or the various companies do not put on sufficient of their plays.

What is the future of the amateur theatre in South Africa? The amateur theatre, as I have indicated, is passing through a very important stage of its life. It has had to revert to true amateurism. If the organizers recognize that a true love for the theatre is the basis of their work; that there is scope for both the amateur and the professional theatre; that they are the training ground of new talent; that they will have to be the home of the classic, the unusual, the neglected play; then they will not fail in their task.

I have left a discussion of the African peoples to the end. They have little theatre in the straight field, but in the more musical line they have a background of old tribal songs and dances which have formed many an exciting emotional experience for the overseas tourist. The African is essentially a relaxed person, not shy of his fellow, nor over-conscious of the restraints imposed by convention. This makes him potentially a good actor, and it is a great pity that their talents are not better catered for. A start has been made, and occasionally in Johannesburg or Cape Town their shows are put on, but only occasionally.

In Cape Town there is a Cape Coloured community, a community formed years back by the admixture of European and native bloods. For their size they have a fairly large amount of theatrical clubs. The most prominent is the Eoan group which presents opera, ballet and

* He was engaged to play his first leading roles in England, by Peter Cotes, in 1948.

straight plays to crowded audiences of both Europeans and non-Europeans. The head of this organization is Mrs. Helen Southern Holt, and she has persevered through many difficulties and established this group as a living part of the cultural life of Cape Town.

Finally, I would like to mention Children's Theatre which exists in Johannesburg and Cape Town. This organization presents children's plays with adult casts and does much good work in stimulating an interest in the theatre in the young. The company usually plays in a theatre in the town both matinee and evening performances, but it also travels out to many schools and gives performances in the school hall.

As in many parts of the world, the curtain drops, the audience clap and another first night is over. Many weeks of hard work have produced an amateur show in South Africa.

XXIII. GLOSSARY OF THEATRICAL
TERMS AND EXPRESSIONS*

ACOUSTICS. The science of sound. The correct manipulation of sound is of prime importance in the theatre. In order to make a play audible to its audience great care must be taken, (*a*) that the actors enunciate clearly, and (*b*) that the auditorium is so constructed that sound is transmitted without distortion, echoes and reverberations. Solid surfaces project sound, while curtains and drapes deaden it. Low ceilings increase sound, high ones disperse it. A theatre is said to have good or bad acoustics according to the quality of the audibility in the auditorium. Shape and design of the building will alter acoustics, and this is taken into account by architects designing new theatres.

ACT. The division of a play that has one or more scenes. In Greek times most plays had five acts, and this continued until the Restoration period. Later they were reduced to three acts and this remains the standard form in the present day. The first act usually reveals the situation and poses the problem, the second act shows mounting conflict and excitement, and the third act gives a solution, a resolution and a final result.

To act is to perform a part upon the stage; to represent another person in dramatic form.

ACT CALL. The call made by a call-boy and/or over a loudspeaker to all dressing-rooms to warn actors just before the curtain is about to go up on an act, just after it has gone up, and just before it is to come down near the end of an act.

ACTING AREA. That part of the stage, in front of the scenery, on which the action of a play takes place.

ACTION. The movement of actors on stage; the movement ahead of the plot of a play. *An* action is a single movement performed by an actor.

ACTOR. A person who performs upon the stage. The first individual actor, as opposed to a group of people performing as a Chorus, was introduced by the Greeks. Until recent times his profession was not accepted as really reputable, but today he is an object of adulation by most of the general public.

ACTRESS. Women did not enter the acting profession until the sixteenth and seventeenth centuries, and were until very recent years looked upon as even less reputable than their male counterparts. Today

*Technical stage terms not found in the Glossary are explained in the appropriate chapters.

there are many more actresses than parts available for them, and competition, whether in the amateur or professional theatre, is extremely keen.

ADAPTATION. The changing of a story, novel, poem, history, etc., into dramatic form. The main ideas contained therein may remain the same but the shape and language are usually considerably altered.

AD LIB. To speak words in a performance apart from those set down in the script, in an impromptu fashion. Ad libbing is often resorted to if an actor forgets lines, another misses an entrance cue, or in informal music hall performances if an artist wishes to build laughs.

ADMINISTRATION. The general management of a theatre. (See chapter on Business Management.)

AMATEUR. A person who works in the theatre without financial reward. One who loves, and not one who is unpaid and therefore can be forgiven.

ANGEL. The financial backer of a theatrical production. This term is more widely used in America than in Britain.

ANTAGONIST. The person or force in a play against the hero or protagonist.

APRON. That part of the stage projecting between the proscenium or front curtain and the audience. It is a development from the Elizabethan forestage, and has been discarded in many modern theatres.

ARENA STAGING. A method of producing a play in a centre area, with the audience surrounding the players on four sides. This is a modern innovation, in a revolt away from the picture frame stage, and has been widely developed in America. There are very few companies, amateur or professional, using this style in Britain.

ASBESTOS. The front curtain in a theatre; made of asbestos material which is fireproof. The law states that the asbestos curtain must be lowered and raised in view of the audience before a play begins and before each act. If a fire occurs either backstage or in the auditorium the asbestos is immediately lowered.

ASIDE. A speech which an actor makes directly to the audience, on the assumption that none of the other characters in the play can hear. This device was used a great deal in earlier times, but is not often written into modern plays.

A.S.M. Abbreviation for Assistant Stage Manager. The A.S.M. is usually a novice in the theatre, who is learning his profession, and his duties vary widely. They may include prompting, keeping the prompt book, gathering and looking after properties, understudying parts, keeping time records of performances, making calls, helping to set up scenery, even making or procuring cups of tea for the producer and cast during rehearsals. He assists in all phases of stage management.

ATMOSPHERE. The mood conveyed by a play to its audience, and created by the writing, staging and acting.

AUDIENCE. Those people who come to see a play performed.

AUDIENCE PARTICIPATION. Calling upon the audience to take an active part in a production. This is usually confined to revues and music halls, but is a valuable phase of children's theatre.

AUDITION. The trying out of his ability by an actor, singer, dancer, etc., before a prospective employer. In the amateur theatre, auditions are often arranged for prospective members.

AUTOMATISM. The idea that artists should perform without relying upon conscious thought; should perform as automatons under the producer's direction. Gordon Craig developed this idea when he stated that actors should be as puppets, controlled by the ideas in the play and the staging of them.

BACKSTAGE. Any area of the stage behind the scenery and not used as an acting area. As a general term it also includes dressing-rooms, props and storage rooms, scene docks, etc.

BALLADE OPERA. This form of musical comedy became popular in the eighteenth century, beginning with works like *The Beggar's Opera*. They included spoken dialogue as well as songs, and were usually satirical.

BALLYHOO. A slang term for exaggerated publicity and stunts to promote a play or increase business.

BARD OF AVON. A nickname for William Shakespeare.

BARE STAGE. The empty stage, without scenery or properties.

BARKER. One who, by colourful, loud talk and exaggerated gestures, encourages people to attend a show. He is usually employed in circuses and sideshows, although he is sometimes incorporated as a character in a play.

BAROQUE THEATRE. A rococo theatrical style, especially in décor, which developed from the Renaissance theatre; was typical of court theatres, such as that of Louis XIV.

BEGINNERS, PLEASE! An expression used by the call-boy when going round the dressing-rooms to ask actors to take their places onstage for the opening of a play.

BENEFIT PERFORMANCE. A special performance of a play, the proceeds of which are given to a person or organization apart from the regular management. They began in the seventeenth century, and proceeds went to a star actor, usually one who was retired or about to retire; or in dire financial circumstances. Today benefits are often given for charitable organizations, and sometimes the artists freely donate their services.

BILLING. The announcement on posters, etc., of the details of a play, including title of play, author, producer, cast, place and time of performance, etc. The leading actors usually have top billing in letters larger than the rest, and in the commercial theatre position of billing is a subject of serious discussion between actors or their agents, and the management presenting the play.

THE BIRD. Derisive booing from an audience that disapproves of a play, or an actor, etc. In modern times the bird is usually given only by people in the gallery.

BIT PART. A small part in a play, usually consisting of only a few lines.

BIT PLAYER. An actor playing a bit part.

BLACKOUT. Sudden extinguishing of all the stage lights. It is used a great deal in the modern theatre for a quick scene change or to show passage of time.

BLANK VERSE. Poetic unrhymed lines, usually in iambic pentameter. First used in drama in Elizabethan times. Found extensively in Shakespeare's plays.

BLOCKING. The first working out of moves in a play by producer and actors in rehearsal.

BLURB. A publicity article or paragraph to advertise a play in newspapers, periodicals, etc.

B.O. A theatrical abbreviation for Box-Office.

BOOK. A term used to describe the working manuscript of a play. In musicals it means the words without the music.

BOOKING. Contracting a theatre for a production; or hiring an artist to appear in it, is spoken of as arranging a booking. A play is booked into a theatre; an actor is booked for a performance; and a member of the audience books his tickets at the box-office.

BORN IN A TRUNK. Being born into a theatrical family. In some cases it is literally true that the birth has taken place in a dressing-room, for many theatrical mothers work until the last possible moment.

BOX-OFFICE STATEMENT. A weekly statement of receipts compiled by a theatre management. Copies are given to the production's business manager; and to the playwright and stars if their contracts stipulate a percentage interest in the play.

BREAK A LEG. A theatrical expression used by actors to wish one another good luck on opening night.

BREECHES PART. An expression made popular in the early eighteenth century when there was a fashion for women, who were just beginning to come into their own as actresses, to play male parts in male dress.

BROADSHEET. A publicity sheet, printed on one side with particulars of a forthcoming production. Use of broadsheets was begun in the late seventeenth century, and has continued up to the present day, although today they are usually called "throwaways" or "handouts".

BUILD. The gradual mounting of tension, tempo and excitement as a play approaches its climax, worked out by the dramatist, producer and actors.

BUSINESS. The movement and actions of actors on stage, planned in advance in rehearsal by producer and actors.

BUSKIN. The thick-soled high sandle worn by actors of tragedy in the ancient Greek and Roman theatres.

CALL. Notice given to a cast, either by word or letter, of the time of rehearsals; or during a performance vocal notice that the play is about to begin, has begun, that acts have begun or ended, etc. Calls in performance are given by the call-boy, who must knock at each dressing-room door and hear an answer before he moves on to the next door.

CALL BOARD. A board placed usually near the stage door, on which special notices for the cast, dressing-room allocations, notices of rehearsals, etc., are placed.

CALL-BOY (see CALL). In the British theatre call-boys are often elderly people, who do this job as a part-time occupation.

CAST. Term for the groups of actor in a play.

CASTING. The process of choosing actors for a production. Casting is usually done by the producer, sometimes by a management in the commercial theatre, or in the amateur theatre by a casting committee. (See AUDITION.)

CASTING OFFICE. A term used in the commercial theatre in connection with large theatrical managements who have special offices and staff employed only for casting productions.

CATHARSIS. A purging of the emotions through watching a play. Term originated by Aristotle.

CHARACTER. A personality in a play. Often refers to the type of part when this is out of the ordinary, i.e. very old, eccentric or odd in any way, as opposed to a "straight" part. (See STRAIGHT.) The actor who specializes in such parts is called a Character Actor.

CHORAL ODE. Poems recited or sung by a Chorus in the ancient Greek theatre.

CHORUS. A group of people speaking or singing in unison. Originated by the Greek dramatists. In musicals there are dancing choruses and singing choruses, who provide a movement and musical background for the main action.

CIRCLE. That section of seats in a playhouse situated in the first balcony above the ground-floor level. Usually semi-circular in shape, or in the shape of a horseshoe. The first circle may be called the Dress Circle, while the next balcony above this may be called the Upper Circle. Or there may be only one Circle.

CLAQUE. A group of people specially organized in an audience to applaud a play. They may be friends of certain artists, author, etc., or paid by these to approve the play. Their lead may cause the audience as a whole to join in the applause.

CLASSIC. A work which through its repeated production has been generally acknowledged to have a high standard of excellence; also pertains to the best of Greek and Roman authors and the style in which they wrote.

CLIMAX. The point of greatest excitement in a play, towards which everything in the writing, acting and production rises.

CLOSING NOTICE. A notice, usually placed on the Call Board, to formally inform the cast and technical staff of the date a play's run will end.

COMEDIAN. An actor who specializes in playing in comedies. (See COMEDY.)

COMEDY. Drama which deals with the lighter side of life, ending happily, or treating its subject humorously. In the broadest sense it is drama in which the protagonist triumphs over the antagonist. (See PROTAGONIST and ANTAGONIST.)

COMMEDIA DELL' ARTE. Improvised farce comedy performed by groups of wandering players at the time of the Renaissance in Italy. It was the popular people's theatre of the time.

COMMERCIAL THEATRE. Theatre companies and managements whose main purpose is to make money out of the production and presentation of plays. The plays done may be worth while or they may not, but above all they must be financially successful.

COMPANY. A group of people brought together to present a play or a season of plays.

COMPS. Abbreviation of Complimentaries. An expression used to describe tickets given by a management to spectators, free of charge. If business is not good and full houses are not anticipated, "comps" are often distributed to members of the cast for their friends. They are given as a friendly exchange by managements to their fellow organizations; or to suppliers of furniture, props, etc., in the amateur theatre. (See PAPER and PAPER THE HOUSE.)

CONSTRUCTIVISM. A style of stage décor in which the settings are based upon structural units, e.g. skeleton outlines of buildings, machines, stairs, etc. Non-realistic in style, and begun by Meyerhold in Russia in the early twentieth century. (See chapter on Design.)

COPYRIGHT. Legal exclusive right to print and publish a play, etc. (See chapter on Business Management.)

CORPSE. Slang expression used in the theatre when an actor comes out of character and laughs during a performance or a rehearsal, e.g.: He corpsed in the middle of his long speech and soon the entire cast was corpsing too.

COUNTER PLOT. A minor plot to the main one in a play, which may enhance the interest by drawing the attention away from the main solution, thereby creating a surprise ending.

CRITIC. An authoritative person, with a background of theatrical knowledge and/or experience, who expresses an opinion about a play and production, usually in written form in newspapers or periodicals. Critics often influence popular opinion.

CUBISM. A type of non-realistic stage décor in which geometric forms are used to express ideas, localities, etc. Originated in painting with Picasso.

CUE. The last words or movements of an actor before another speaks or moves. When an actor is "slow on cue" the wait seems interminable to those on stage, although in most cases the pause is not noticed by the audience.

CURTAIN. This is usually the drapery which divides the stage from the auditorium, but when used in the plural, as Curtains, may mean the draperies surrounding the acting area. The front Curtain was developed around the time of the Restoration. (See chapter on Design, Part I.)

CURTAIN RAISER. A one-act play given before a full-length one. Usually performed because the longer play is of a shorter duration than is usual.

CUT. A deletion of lines in a script during rehearsal.

CYC. Abbreviation of Cyclorama, which is the backing, either of curtains or plaster, at the rear of the stage to represent the sky; usually pale blue in colour, but may be coloured by lights in other hues for non-realistic plays. (See chapters on Set Building, Design, and Lighting.)

DÉNOUEMENT. After the climax in a play comes a fairly quick resolution of the conflict, during which all the "ends" of the plot are tied together. This is the Dénouement. It usually occurs during the third or last act of the play.

DESIGNER. An artist who creates the designs for settings and/or costumes for a play. (See chapter on Design.)

DIALECT PART. An acting part which requires the actor to speak in a vocal accent other than his own.

DIRECTOR. A person who co-ordinates the work of actors, technicians, designers, etc., in a production, and who often presents a certain interpretation of the dramatist's work for the aforementioned artists to follow. Director is the term applied to this co-ordinator in America, while his British counterpart is usually referred to as the producer. (see PRODUCER and the chapter on The Producer.)

DOME. A plaster Cyclorama. (See CYC.)

DOUBLING. Playing two parts in the same play.

DOWNSTAGE. The stage area between the footlights and an imaginary line running parallel to them halfway to the back of the setting.

DRAMA. A quality in communication of ideas or action which arouses excitement, fear, sympathy and like emotions in the spectator; also a play written for the stage.

DRAMA, FOLK. Plays based on peasant legends, or myths and lore handed down from father to son.

DRAMATURGY. The art of playwriting.

DRESS. Refers to the costumes in a production; or the styles of clothing in a certain period. (See chapter on Design, Part 2—Costume.)

DRESS CIRCLE. (See CIRCLE.)

DRESSER. One who assists actors to put on their costumes for a play, and assists in quick changes between scenes. A Dresser also usually looks after the costumes of the actor for whom he is working. Stars and leading players hire their own Dressers, who perform many tasks for them apart from dealing with costumes.

DRESS PARADE. The checking of costumes by designer and producer with actors, (a) just as rehearsals begin in order to ascertain what is needed, especially in a modern play when actors often provide their own clothes, (b) at dress rehearsal to make sure that each costume is complete in every detail. (See chapter on Design, Part 2—Costume.)

DRESS THE SET. To add ornaments, draperies, decorations, furniture, etc., to the bare setting.

DROP. (a) Any material used as backing for a scene, and (b) to let a scene drag, through slow playing.

DRY. When an actor forgets his lines he is said to "dry".

DUMB SHOW. Action without words, usually written as a sketch with a plot, or as part of a play; often has a musical accompaniment.

ELECTRICIAN. The person who is in charge of the lighting equipment for a play, or the one who actually manipulates the equipment, with the aid of a cue sheet and lighting plot. (See chapters on Lighting and Stage Management.)

ELOCUTION. The art of dramatic recitation on a public platform. Unless very wisely taught and practised it can be an artificial style of delivery which is unpopular today, and especially unnatural in young children. One producer has called this false style "bellow-cution".

ENTER ABOVE. A term derived from the Elizabethan theatre, when actors came on to the Upper Stage. It now means to enter upstage, or behind (above) a certain piece of furniture, etc.

ENTR'ACTE. Literally means "between acts"; an interval, for audience relaxation; music is often played during this interval.

ENTRANCE. An actor coming on stage is said to make his "entrance".

EPIC DRAMA. A dramatic style introduced by Erwin Piscator in Germany in the twenties, and adopted by various American experimental producers and theatres; not employed to any great extent in Britain. Essentially the "epic" style involves presenting plays in a series of episodic scenes, with central characters in various situations, usually involving some larger social theme. (See LIVING NEWSPAPER.) The plays of Berthold Brecht are mainly in the epic style.

EPILOGUE. A speech given directly to the audience at the end of a play, either by one actor or several actors. Shakespeare used this technique extensively.

EQUITY. Shortened term for British Actors' Equity Association; which is the actors' trade union.

ESCAPIST. Plays which provide an escape from reality without involving any serious issues; pure entertainment.

EXIT. An actor leaving the stage is said to "exit" or "make his exit".

EXPRESSIONISM. A theatrical style developed in Germany in the early twentieth century, which expressed inner emotion and ideas in an unrealistic manner on stage. Settings, costumes, movements, effects, in expressionistic productions are far removed from the natural, and are usually violent or vivid. (See chapter on Design.)

EXTEMPORE. Impromptu acting or speaking, without prior preparation (see AD LIB).

EXTERIOR. A setting made to represent an outdoor scene, e.g. woodland, street, outside of building, etc. (See chapters on Design, Part 1, and Set Building.)

EXTRA. An actor who performs as part of a crowd onstage, without speaking individual lines. (See WALK ON.)

EXTRAVAGANZA. A very spectacular production with lavish costumes, settings, effects, etc. Large-scale musicals and ice shows fall into this category.

FADE OUT. A gradual fading of the lighting on a scene to complete darkness. Often spoken of as a "fade".

FANTASY. An imaginative unrealistic play, e.g. J. M. Barrie's *Peter Pan*, Maeterlinck's *The Bluebird*, etc.

FARCE. A highly amusing play with exaggerated comic situations and characters. (See ESCAPIST.) Some of the most famous seasons of farce were presented at the Aldwych Theatre, London, by Robertson Hare and Ralph Lynn, and were known as the "Aldwych Farces".

FAT PART. Either a large part in a play, or a smaller one with dialogue and character which will make a special impact on an audience.

FEATURE. A feature player is one second in importance to a lead or star. Feature billing means that the actor's name will appear in a prominent position on all advertising material.

FEED. In variety performances a "feed" is the person who asks questions, or gives lines to comedians to lead up to their comic lines which get the audience's reaction. In play rehearsal, and sometimes in performance, the prompter "feeds" lines to actors who cannot remember them.

FINAL CURTAIN. The last curtain which comes down at the end of a play.

FINALE. The last number in a musical show, in which usually all members of the cast are seen.

FIRE PROOFING. (See chapter on Set Building, and Appendix of Useful Information.)

FIRST NIGHT. The opening night of a play.

FIRST NIGHT NERVES. A nervous tension actors feel when about to face the audience on the opening night of a play. No matter how experienced actors may be, very few do not suffer from "nerves" on the first night. Such "nerves" may carry the performance to brilliant heights in some cases, or reduce it to a sorry state of forgetfulness in others. Each actor suffers nerves in a different way. Most try various forms of relaxing to try to overcome them.

FIT-UP STAGE. Either a stage specially constructed for a single production, or a special portable stage unit carried by a touring company, and erected in any hall in which they play. A development from the few boards, etc., which players carried about with them in medieval times.

FLASH BACK. A technique in playwriting where a central character tells the story to the audience, illustrating it with staged scenes which go back in time, e.g. Van Druten's *I Remember Mama*, and Tennessee Williams' *The Glass Menagerie*.

FLIES. All the space above the stage, higher than the proscenium. Scenery is "flown" by ropes into the "flies".

FLOP. A production which fails, either for financial or artistic reasons.

FLUFF. An actor who forgets his lines is said to "fluff"; or he may merely stumble on words, transpose them by mistake.

FLY MAN. A man who stays up in the flies, usually on a fly gallery, during a performance to manipulate the ropes which fly the scenery.

F.O.H. Abbreviation for Front of House; which means all parts of a theatre lying in front of the stage proper, including auditorium, foyer, box-office, etc. Stage lights placed in the auditorium are said to be in an F.O.H. position.

FORESTAGE. (See APRON, also chapter on Design, Part 1.)

FORMALISM. A style of production involving the use of a formal, architectural type of setting before which all scenes and acts are played.

FOURTH WALL. An imaginary wall through which the audience looks at a play, the other three walls being the background for the actors. The front curtain is in reality the "fourth wall", when it is down.

FULL HOUSE. An expression used when all seats are sold for a performance.

FUTURISM. A school of painting developed in Italy in the early twentieth century which affected stage design by stressing the importance of industry and mechanization; a revolt away from realism.

GAG. An amusing line or stunt performed in a play for the audience's amusement.

GAGGING. Impromptu ad libbing of lines for comic effect; or in such forms as Variety, joking with the audience or fellow actors.

GALLERY. The topmost balcony in the auditorium of a theatre.

GALLERY FIRST NIGHTERS. A group of people who try to attend the opening nights of all West End plays, and who approve or disapprove as a group. One management decided to close its gallery after the first nighters soundly booed a production, but the move was thoroughly unpopular, and roused so much public opinion that the gallery was reinstated.

GALLERY STOOLS. Stools placed outside the gallery entrance to a theatre (mainly in London's West End), for which numbered tickets are sold usually for sixpence on the morning of each performance. Ticketholders are entitled to sit on the stools in a queue until half an hour before performance time, when the gallery door is opened and unreserved tickets purchased for the play—the queue moving in in order of stool ticket numbers. This inexpensive system is a great boon to young people, students, and those who attend the theatre regularly but cannot afford expensive reserved seats.

GO ON. To make an entrance onstage.

GOING UP. The rising of the front curtain at the beginning of a performance; or an actor moving upstage.

GRAND GUIGNOL. Horror melodrama; highly exaggerated terror material, production, and acting, introduced at the Paris Grand Guignol Theatre at the end of the nineteenth century, and still playing there.

GREEN ROOM. A waiting-room or lounge for actors and their guests, situated near or under the stage. The first one, in Covent Garden, was painted green . . . hence the name. There are not many left in the professional theatre in Britain today, but many in the amateur theatre.

GRID. Abbreviation of Gridiron; a strong framework, usually steel, over the stage and just below the theatre's roof, over which are strung the ropes and counterweights, etc., to which scenery is attached.

GROUNDLINGS. People who stood on the ground before the stage to watch a performance in the Elizabethan theatre.

GROUPING. The placing of actors in certain positions about the stage, usually for a pleasing effect.

GUEST ARTIST. A leading player employed to work for one play or a short series of plays, with a permanent repertory or amateur company.

HALF HOUR. The call given to a cast by the call-boy half an hour (usually thirty-five minutes) before the curtain is due to rise on a play. In the professional theatre it is a ruling that all members of the cast must be in the theatre by the half hour.

HAM. A term used for over-exaggerated, pretentious acting.

HARLEQUINADE. A pantomimic performance in which the cunning beggar Harlequin is the central character. He originated in the improvised plays of the Commedia dell' Arte in Italy.

HEAVY. Either a middle-aged character actor in a play, or the villain of the piece.

HIT. A play which is a big success.

HOARDINGS. The billboards in front of a theatre, or distributed about a town or city, which give information about a production, including name of play, author, cast, time, place, etc.

HOOFER. American theatrical term for a dancer.

HOUSE. Term used to describe either the auditorium or the audience. (See FULL HOUSE.)

HOUSE BOARDS. Frames outside a theatre which contain pictures, posters, etc., with information about the play. (See HOARDINGS.)

HOUSE FULL OF PAPER. An audience which has mostly been given complimentary tickets. (See COMPS and PAPER.)

HOUSE LIGHTS. Lights which illuminate the auditorium, and which in a proper theatre are usually dimmed in and out from backstage.

IMPRESSIONISM. Begun as a movement in art, impressionism has moved to include stage décor, acting, playwriting, production, etc. It is a style which does not reproduce anything with complete realism, but is concerned mainly in giving the audience an "impression" of an

2C

idea, a colour, a mood, a time, etc. In art the works of Degas, Renoir and van Gogh are impressionistic. Such plays as O'Neill's *The Emperor Jones* and Elmer Rice's *The Adding Machine* are examples of impressionism. It is closely interwoven with expressionism, the latter being concerned not only with visual effect but with conveying an inner meaning as well.

IMPROVISATION. Improvising a role without the aid of written lines. This is a valuable technique in training an actor to develop his imagination and powers of concentration. The method was begun by Stanislavsky at the Moscow Arts Theatre in the early twentieth century for getting into the "skin" of a part.

INCIDENTAL MUSIC. Music interpolated into the action of a play for dramatic or comic effect; used extensively in the Shakespearian theatre.

INGENUE. A young girl written into a play, or the actress who plays this part. She often provides the young love interest in the plot.

INNER MEANING. A phrase introduced in the early twentieth century by Stanislavsky and his contemporaries, and further developed by the Impressionists and Expressionists. It means that there is often a deeper, hidden significance in a part, a play, a production, other than the meaning which appears on the surface. It is up to actors, producers, etc., to make this "inner meaning" as clear as possible to the audience. T. S. Eliot's play *The Confidential Clerk*, it is said, is full of inner meanings and there are many interpretations of these. Quite often the meaning of "inner meanings" is purely a matter of individual conjecture. A playwright when asked what his play meant, said, "It means whatever you think it means!"

INNER STAGE. In the Elizabethan theatre this was the alcove directly behind the forestage, and was curtained off from the audience. It has now expanded to form our stage proper behind the proscenium arch. (See chapter on Design, Part i.)

INSET. A small unit of scenery set in front of a larger set for a particular scene, and usually pin-pointed with light while the surrounding area is blacked out.

INTERIOR. A setting made to represent the inside of a room, a house or other building; any indoor setting.

INTERLUDE. A short play presented between the acts of a longer one; a technique rarely used today, but used extensively in the sixteenth and seventeenth centuries, when they were usually rude farces.

INTERMISSION. A period of relaxation between the acts of a play, during which scenery, costumes and make-up may be changed. (See ENTR'ACTE and INTERVAL.) The expression "Intermission" is generally used in America.

INTERPOLATION. Speech or movement added to a production after the script is completed; or lines ad libbed by an actor.

INTERVAL (see INTERMISSION). The expression used in Britain for the waiting period between acts.

IN THE RED. Term used when a show is not financially successful and is losing money.

JUSTIFICATION. A term used in acting when finding a reason for a certain movement, action or line; first introduced as part of the Stanislavsky method of realistic sincere acting. There should be a justification for all moves made on stage in a realistic play; they should not be made merely to create pleasant patterns or to prevent action from being static.

JUV CHAR. Abbreviation for Juvenile Character; a professional theatre term employed for the actor or actress who plays a young character part.

JUVENILE. The young male and female roles in a play; and the actor and actress who play them; often the love interest. (See INGENUE.)

LEAD. The largest or most important role in the play; also refers to the actor or actress playing it.

LEFT STAGE. All of the stage area left of an imaginary line running through the centre of the stage vertically from the footlights to the back wall, and on the actor's left as he faces the footlights.

LEG SHOW. A Variety or musical show employing lightly clad chorus girls.

LEGITIMATE THEATRE. All that phase of theatre which presents straight plays, musicals, etc., on a stage, with living artists, as opposed to radio, television, and ice shows.

LIBRETTO. The written words of a musical production, opera, etc., apart from the music. (See BOOK.)

LIGHT PLOT. A chart showing lighting equipment, light cues and light changes used during a play. It is prepared during the lighting rehearsal, and used during performance by the Electrician and his assistants. (See ELECTRICIAN.)

LIGHTING. The illumination of the stage area by light in various degrees of intensity and shades of colour. (See chapters on Lighting and Stage Management.)

LINES. The written speeches in a play spoken by the actors.

LIVING NEWSPAPER. A documentary type of dramatic presentation, which draws attention to general situations like housing, unemployment, etc., in a series of staged episodes, which are linked together by a narrator. It is a part of Epic Drama (see EPIC DRAMA), and was used extensively by the W.P.A. theatres in the thirties in America.

LORD CHAMBERLAIN. The official British Censor, who reads and either gives his approval to, or bans, all plays to be presented publicly in Great Britain. His reasons for vetoing a play may be religious, political or moral, and he was first appointed in the early eighteenth century. There have been repeated attempts to question his position, and to have banned plays released, but to no avail. In order to escape his domination many small theatres work under the club membership system, where only members who pay a subscription to the club may purchase tickets. The Lord Chamberlain's rulings do not apply to performances given in these "private" theatres. (See chapter on Business Management.)

LOVE INTEREST. The romantic element in a play; or used as a general term referring to the artist or artists involved in the love story.

MAKE-UP. Greasepaint, etc., applied by an actor so that his features will be outlined clearly under strong lights. "Straight" make-up merely heightens the actor's natural appearance, while "Character" make-up changes his face according to the age and type of character he is portraying. (See chapter on Make-up.)

MANAGEMENT. In the Commercial theatre the management is the business organization which undertakes to finance, plan, engage artists and staff, arrange bookings, etc., for a theatrical production.

MANAGEMENT, BUSINESS. Financial and business organization for a production. (See chapter on Business Management.) It is controlled by a Business Manager.

MANAGER. There are various types of Managers in the theatre. (a) Business manager (see MANAGEMENT, BUSINESS); (b) Company Manager, who acts as Business Manager for an individual production, either on tour or established in a run; (c) Theatre Manager, who deals with all phases of running a theatre building, apart from the production; (d) Stage Manager, who is responsible (often under the Stage Director) for the smooth running of all backstage departments; (e) Personal Manager, who handles all business, publicity, etc., arrangements for a leading player, either exclusively in the actor's hire, or through an Agency. (See chapters on Business Management, Publicity, and Stage Management.)

MANUSCRIPT. The typed or written pages of a play before it is published; usually used in rehearsal.

MASKING. (a) The covering from audience view of an actor by another during the action of a play; or (b) Scenery used behind doors, windows, at the edges of settings, or above them, to hide backstage areas from the audience.

MASQUE. A dramatic form popular in court society in the seventeenth century, in which people represented allegorical or mythical characters, or nymphs and shepherds and shepherdesses. Little dialogue and much music, dancing, and pageantry were employed.

MATINEE IDOLS. Actors idolized by an audience because of their good looks or personal charm; the term originated from afternoon audiences, predominantly female, who developed hero worship for favourite stars.

MECHANICS. The bare moves of actors in first rehearsals, before feeling and characterization are worked out. The mechanics are usually blocked out by the producer. (See BLOCKING.)

MELODRAMAS. Plays in which the virtues of Good against Evil were greatly exaggerated; a popular form of drama in the late nineteenth century. They always had the stock characters of Hero, Heroine and Villain, and Good always triumphed over Evil. The audience took an active part throughout by hissing the villain and cheering the hero and heroine.

MILK IT DRY. To get as many laughs as possible from an audience on a line or action, by prolonging or exaggerating them.

MILK THE CURTAIN. To get as many rounds of applause as possible from an audience on curtain calls by raising and lowering the front curtain very quickly a number of times, usually too many times.

MISE EN SCÈNE. The completed production with reference particularly to groupings of actors in relation to the setting.

MORALITY PLAY. A type of play popular in the Middle Ages, in which the characters represented abstract ideas, like Death, Friendship, Sin, etc., and the theme of the play dealt with a vice or a virtue or both. *Everyman* is a well-known morality play, still performed today.

MOTIVATION. This term may be applied to playwriting, acting or producing, and means that the cause of certain actions must be disclosed. As in real life every person in a play has, or should have, a motive for what he does. (See JUSTIFICATION.)

MOVES. The actions a producer gives an actor to carry out on stage, or which the actor suggests.

MULTIPLE SETTING. A setting which shows several locations at one time. Such a setting was used with good effect in such plays as *Death of a Salesman* by Arthur Miller, *Come Back Little Sheba* by William Inge, etc. Several different rooms in a house may be shown, even on different levels.

MUMMER. An actor who took part in a mummer play, introduced in England in the fifteenth century. They were crude rural plays, often with farmers as the principal actors, wearing masks and with their faces blackened if playing clowns.

MUSICALS. This term is much used today to describe musical comedies, in which some of the dialogue is spoken and songs are interpolated.

Operetta, light opera and opera comique are forms of musical comedy.

MUSIC HALL. A theatre in which song, dance and comedy acts are presented as a bill of entertainment. In Britain this medium of entertainment is called Variety; in America, Vaudeville.

MYSTERY PLAYS. Biblical plays presented in the Middle Ages, first by the clergy and later by trade guilds.

NATURALISM. An extreme form of realism in theatrical production and writing, which attempts to picture life exactly as it is in great detail. The novels of Zola were among the first naturalistic novels, and in the theatre Stanislavsky in Russia and David Belasco in America were exponents of naturalistic production. (See chapter on Design, Part I.)

NOISES OFF. Any sound effects performed offstage during the action of a play.

NOTICES. The reviews or dramatic criticisms appearing in newspapers after the first performance of a play.

OFFSTAGE. All the area behind the setting of a play, either at the back or sides.

ONE NIGHT STAND. A single performance of a play in a small centre not large enough to support further performances. Touring companies often do a series of one night stands, moving on each day to a new town.

ONSTAGE. All the stage area surrounded by, and in front of, the setting of a play.

O.P. Abbreviation for Opposite Prompt; literally the side of the stage which is opposite to the Prompt Corner and the Prompter. O.P. is used in rehearsal directions, e.g. a producer might ask an actor to "Move right across to the O.P. side".

OPEN COLD. To give a première of a production in the West End or on Broadway without a try-out tour in the provinces.

OPEN STAGE. A stage free of the usual setting for a play, on which scenes are played in pools of light, surrounded by darkness; or a stage surrounded by spectators on three sides.

ORCHESTRA STALLS. Seats on the ground floor of a theatre auditorium and near the front; derived from the Greek Orkestra, which was the circular flat area of ground in the centre of the amphitheatre, on which the chorus performed.

OUTER STAGE. The Elizabethan forestage, jutting out into the audience. (See FORESTAGE.)

OUT FRONT. To be in the auditorium of a theatre rather than backstage.

PACE. The tempo of a production, which may be altered by the speeding up or slowing down of actions and lines. In comedy, particularly farce, a good pace is specially important.

PACKING THEM IN. A term used to describe a production that is extremely successful at the box-office and attracting full houses.

PAGEANT. An elaborate production, usually in mime, with colourful costumes, lighting, etc., usually produced for a special historical or national occasion. Begun in the Middle Ages, when plays were travelled from place to place on Pageant Cars, which were temporary stages on wheels. (See the chapter on Design, Part 1.) The term is also applied to a type of stage light. (See LIGHTING.)

PANATROPE. Term used in Britain for the gramophone turntables employed backstage for sound effects, offstage music, etc.

PANORAMA. Scenery painted on a piece of canvas which is gradually rolled from a roller on one side of the stage to another roller on the other side of the stage, to denote a moving scene, for example behind a train, ship, etc.

PANTOMIME. Originally a performance in action without words, often accompanied by music. Today it is used loosely to describe the monster musicals presented in Britain at Christmas time, based on fairy tales and lore, with modern songs, dances and comedy routines interpolated. Certain characters in these productions are traditional: the Dame, a character comedy woman played by a man; the Principal Girl, the young heroine, played by a girl; the Principal Boy, the young hero, played by a girl; and a Villain or Opposing Force of some description.

PAPER. To paper a house means to give away complimentary tickets when business is not good. Tickets thus issued free of charge are called paper.

PAPER, TRADE. A trade paper is one which gives information for and about the theatre, including reviews, articles, employment advertisements, etc. The largest trade paper for the professional theatre in Britain is *The Stage*.

PAPIER MÂCHÉ. A paper pulp mixed with glue and used to make artificial food, vases, masks, furniture, decoration, etc. (See chapter on Properties.)

PART. The character in the play which an actor portrays. Sometimes refers to the script itself if the actor only receives sheets with his character's lines, and his cues, on it.

PEEP HOLE. A small hole made in the front curtain so that those backstage might look out at the audience without being seen. Not used to any great extent today.

PICTURE FRAME STAGE. The stage as it is today behind the frame of a proscenium arch. (See chapter on Design, Part 1.)

PIECE OF THE SHOW. The amount of money on which he will get a percentage return (usually) from box-office receipts, which a backer gives to finance a production. This is spoken of as "buying a piece of the show".

PIT. In Elizabethan times the pit was the ground area in front of the stage where the groundlings stood. It is now known as (*a*) Orchestra Pit, the space immediately in front of the stage, and running partly under it, where musicians playing in an orchestra sit for a production; and (*b*) Pit Stalls. A few rows of seats at the back of the stalls on the ground floor of a theatre auditorium.

PLACES PLEASE! The call given to actors just before the curtain goes up on a play to make sure they are in their correct places for the beginning.

PLAGIARISM. To use another's ideas, dialogue, etc., for a play and claim it as original work. This can lead to court cases.

PLANT. An actor placed in the auditorium who speaks lines from that position, and may or may not come up onstage from the audience. This technique was used, for example, in Odets' *Waiting for Lefty*.

PLAY. A story written in dramatic form for presentation on a stage; to play is to act in a dramatic performance.

PLAYING AREA. (See ACTING AREA.)

PLAY READER. One who reads plays critically for a management or a society to help select good ones for production.

PLAYWRIGHT. A person who writes plays. (See chapter on The Playwright.)

PLOT. The central action around which a play is written. There may be sub plots and counter plots which are subsidiary but add to the interest of the main story line.

POSTERS. Printed sheets in varying sizes containing information about a forthcoming production. (See chapter on Publicity.)

PRACTICAL. Any piece of scenery, property, or light which must be used or manipulated by actors onstage is said to be practical, e.g. practical balconies (which must be walked on), practical lamps (which must be switched on or off by the cast), etc.

PRESENTATIONAL. Staging which is not realistic but is aimed at conveying ideas through symbolistic effects, scenery, lighting, etc.

PRESS AGENT. The person who handles publicity for a production in connection with newspapers, periodicals, etc. He gathers news material about the cast, producer, play, and any other newsworthy ideas, which he writes into articles for release to the press; usually with photographs to accompany them. (See chapter on Publicity.)

PREVIEW. A performance or dress rehearsal of a play given to an invited audience before the play actually opens to a paying audience. It is often given to test audience reaction; and sometimes admission is charged which is given to a charity.

PROBLEM PLAY. A play whose theme deals with a social problem which may or may not be solved. The plays of Shaw and Ibsen fall into this category.

PRODUCER. British term for the Director of a play (see DIRECTOR); also used in America to describe the person who presents the play, who provides backing (not necessarily his own money), and the managing organization necessary. (See the chapter on The Producer.)

PROFESSIONAL. Anyone who is paid for his services in the theatre; in a wider sense anyone who accepts the theatre as his chosen profession and works as sincerely and devotedly in it as, say, a doctor does in the profession of medicine. A professional attitude is strong in the best amateurs, and lacking in the worst professionals.

PROGRAMME. A printed sheet either given, or sold, to an audience at a performance, which contains pertinent information about the play to be seen, such as list of characters, with the actors playing them; scene of the play; time; list of technical staff; and most important, title of play and author and producer. Most programmes contain advertisements, which often pay for their printing and guarantee a small profit. (See chapter on Publicity.)

PROLOGUE. A speech or scene given by an actor or actors before the action of a play begins, either to clarify or explain what is to follow, or for some special dramatic purpose.

PROMPT BOOK. The manuscript of a play held by the Prompter, into which he or she enters moves, deletions, additions, at rehearsal; and from which he or she assists actors who forget lines either in rehearsal or performance. (See chapter on Stage Management.)

PROMPT CORNER. The space at the side of the stage where the Prompter stands or sits.

PROMPTER. The person who takes care of, and follows the Prompt Book at rehearsals and during performances, and cues actors when they forget lines. The A.S.M. often has the job of prompting. (See A.S.M.)

PROPAGANDA PLAYS. Plays which dramatize a playwright's ideas on social or political issues, with the intention of influencing the audience's thought on the subjects.

PROPERTIES. All articles onstage apart from the actual setting, are said to be properties, or "props" (the abbreviation in common usage). (See chapter on Properties and Sound Effects.)

PROPERTY MASTER. The person who looks after the props, sets them onstage, and stores them between performances. Sometimes he is called upon to make or collect them as well. (See chapter on Stage Management.)

PROPERTY ROOM. The room backstage where props are stored when not in use onstage.

PROP PLOT. A list of properties used in a play, with an indication of where they are set onstage, and whether they must be moved during the evening.

PROSCENIUM. The opening which divides the stage from the auditorium, more correctly called the Proscenium Arch. It is closed in by a curtain. The word is derived from the Greek Proskenion: the façade of the scene building in ancient Greek theatres.

PROTAGONIST. The hero, heroine or central character in a play.

PROVINCES. Any centre outside of London where touring companies play. They are said to "play the provinces".

P.S. Abbreviation for Prompt Side; literally the side of the stage used for the Prompt Corner, and occupied by the Prompter. P.S. is often stage left, but there is no hard and fast rule about this, each theatre being slightly different.

QUEUE. A line of people waiting outside a theatre either to purchase tickets at the box-office, or to wait for unreserved seats in the Gallery or Pit. (See GALLERY STOOLS.)

QUICK STUDY. An actor who memorizes lines very quickly.

RAKED STAGE. A stage which slants from the back wall down to the footlights. This was originally introduced so that the audience seated on a flat ground floor could better see the stage, but new stages are usually now built without a rake.

RANT. To speak lines in a play in a loud, over-exaggerated manner.

RAVE. A press notice which highly praises a performance, production, etc.; also used as a slang term to denote unqualified uncritical praise.

READING. May refer to an audition given by an actor for a part, which he reads for the producer; or to the first time a cast gathers to read through a play before the first rehearsal begins.

REALISM. The portraying of characters, situations, localities, and ideas as they are in real life; "holding up the mirror to nature". Realism was first introduced in the theatre during the latter part of the nineteenth century, and Stanislavsky was its first great exponent. (See chapters on Design, Part 1, The Playwright, and The Producer.)

RÉGISSEUR. The French term for the Director or Producer of a play.

REHEARSAL. The practising of a play in private before it is presented to an audience. (For further details of rehearsals, and the way they should be conducted, see chapters on The Producer and Stage Management.)

REPERTORY THEATRE. In its true meaning this type of theatre prepares a number of plays with a permanent company, which are presented on alternate dates throughout a season, and may be revived again in future seasons. The Old Vic is an example of this, and has a repertoire of Shakespearian plays. However, in Britain there are a vast number of so-called "Repertory" companies which present a new play every week, fortnight or three weeks, as suits the community, and no plays are alternated or revived. Playing in "reps" is basic training in theatre for many young actors, and is very valuable. However, an actor who plays too long in rep, particularly the weekly type, is apt to develop tricks and mannerisms (because of having to learn so many parts so rapidly) which detract from the sincerity and freshness of a performance.

REPRESENTATIONAL. Staging which is realistic, and copies as exactly as possible the conditions of real life.

RETURNS. The amount of money collected at the box-office in ticket sales for a play. A statement of nightly returns is given by the theatre's management to the company manager of the particular play being presented. A weekly statement, which is a summary of nightly returns, is also prepared by the management. (See Box-Office Statement.)

REVOLVING STAGE. A part of the stage floor which is on a pivot and able to turn around during a production, so that one scene may be set up at the back of the revolving stage and swung quickly round to face the audience for continuous action. Scenes may thus be changed during the action of the play.

REVUE. A musical programme which is made up of sketches, songs, dances, etc., which are not related by a central plot, but which use a fixed company who play many parts.

RING DOWN. To bring down the curtain at the end of a play; derived from the old custom of ringing a bell to close a show.

RIGHT STAGE. All of the stage area right of an imaginary line running through the centre of the stage vertically from the footlights to the back wall, and on the actor's right as he faces the footlights.

ROCOCO. A florid style of décor, using detailed scroll work and ornate decoration, popular in the seventeenth century, and still used in certain period productions today.

ROMANTIC DRAMA. Plays which idealize such things as love, friendship, gallantry, etc. They may be romantic comedies, such as Shakespeare's *As You Like It*, or romantic tragedies, such as his *Romeo and Juliet*.

ROMANTIC LEAD. The leading male character in a play, who provides the love interest; a handsome physical appearance is usually the requisite for a romantic lead.

RUN THROUGH. The first time a play is rehearsed in its entirety is called the first run through. Subsequent rehearsals of the whole play are also run throughs.

RUNWAY. A ramp or platform extending from the stage into the auditorium.

S.A.E. An abbreviation used in theatrical advertisements in British stage publications meaning Self Addressed Envelope. This is expected to be enclosed with actors' applications for interviews and enagagements.

SATIRE. A play which attacks ideas, systems, individuals, etc., by ridiculing them. One of the earliest satires was Aristophanes' *The Frogs*, which lampooned Greek writers. Molière wrote many satires, e.g. *The Miser*, *The Imaginary Invalid*, etc.

SATYR PLAYS. Ancient Greek plays, usually extremely licentious, which involved a chorus of satyrs: gods which were part men, part animal.

SAVOYARD. An actor who plays in Gilbert and Sullivan operettas; derived from the Savoy Theatre, London, where many of these operettas were first presented.

SCENARIO. The outline of the plot of a play, written in some detail. Today it usually applies to films.

SCENE. May be defined as a division of an act in a play; or a section within a scene itself, one of a sequence of events. The scene also refers to the location shown in the setting.

SCENE DESIGNER. The artist who plans, makes sketches and models of, and completes construction diagrams for the scenery for a play. Sometimes he actually paints the setting as well. (See chapter on Design, Part 1.)

SCENERY. The flats, platforms, curtains, etc., which go to make up the pictorial settings for a play. (See chapters on Design, Part 1, and Set Building.)

SCRIPT. Abbreviation of Manuscript. The written or typed copies of a play used in rehearsal, before the play is published.

SECOND LEAD. The second most important character in a play, next to the leading part; also refers to the actor playing this part.

SEQUENCE. A series of scenes or events in a play, within an act or a long scene.

SET. Abbreviation for Setting (see SETTING). This shortened term is usually used rather than the longer word.

SETTING. Same as Scenery. (See SCENERY.)

SET UP. The actual placing of scenery in position onstage. (See chapter on Stage Management.)

SHARE SYSTEM. A system used in a few professional theatres, whereby the company members are not paid regular salaries, but share in the profits of a production or a season.

SHOE STRING. As in general usage, this term denotes lack of finance. A shoe-string production is done with a minimum of financial backing and a maximum of economy. A recent highly successful musical revue entitled *Airs on a Shoe String* aptly illustrated this expression.

SHOW. A general term for any type of theatrical production.

SHOW BUSINESS. A general term to describe the working of the professional theatre.

SHOW GIRL. A girl who is part of a musical production or revue, but has no lines to speak, songs to sing, nor dances to dance. She stands onstage for purely decorative purposes, and therefore is usually very attractive, and costumed in glamorous clothes.

SIDES. Parts of plays given to actors, containing only their lines, and a few words of the preceding speech as cues.

SIGHT LINES. The angles of vision from which an audience is able to see the stage from any part of the auditorium. All scenery and movement must be planned to conform with sight lines. (See chapters on Design, Part 1, and Set Building.)

SITTING ON THEIR HANDS. When an audience does not greatly applaud a production by clapping, its members are said in stage vernacular to be "sitting on their hands".

SITUATION. The plot of a play; or the play may be built on a series of "situations" which relate to the basic one.

SKETCHES. Drawings made by the designers for settings and costumes. The first sketches are usually only a rough impression by the artist of his ideas, and the finished articles may vary from the original sketches to a considerable extent. (See chapter on Design, Parts 1 and 2.)

SKIT. A short scene, usually of only a few minutes' duration, and usually comic in nature. A number of skits are included in a revue, each one being complete in itself.

SLAPSTICK. Very broad comedy actions, such as throwing pies, lighting trick cigars, exaggerated fights for comic effect, etc. The term originated from the use of two thin pieces of wood, hinged at one end, being slapped sharply together offstage when one comedian slapped another, for a sound effect. Slapsticks are still used by some comedians today.

SOCIAL DRAMA. Plays dealing with situations and problems confronting society as a whole or the particular locality in which the playwright lives. Sometimes the writer gives his particular solution for the social problem. Shaw, Ibsen, Odets, Hellman, etc., are authors of social drama.

SOCK. The light shoes worn by comic actors in the ancient Greek theatre.

SOCK AND BUSKIN. An actor is often said to "wear the sock and buskin", meaning that he performs on the stage, whether it be in comedy or tragedy. (See BUSKIN and SOCK.)

SOLILOQUY. A speech within a play spoken directly to or for the audience, and representing the character's thoughts.

SONG AND DANCE SHOW. A revue or variety show, without a central plot or dialogue; a series of singing and dancing numbers.

SOUBRETTE. A young comedy character female part; not the leading part, but often one which receives a large number of laughs.

SPACE STAGE (see OPEN STAGE).

SPECTACLE (see EXTRAVAGANZA).

"SPOTLIGHT." A British professional theatre casting service, which keeps a record of most of the actors, producers, technicians, etc., working in the theatre, and publishes the *Spotlight Casting Directory* twice yearly in which these people advertise, with photographs, information, etc. This directory is greatly used when casting by professional managements, repertory companies, etc.

S.R.O. Abbreviation for Sold Right Out; meaning that all tickets are sold for a performance. Sometimes means Standing Room Only.

STAGE. The entire area behind the proscenium arch, stretching to the back and side walls. Also used as a general term for the theatre. A person making a career of acting is said to "go on the stage".

STAGE CARPENTER. The craftsman who actually constructs the settings for a play. In the professional theatre most productions have a carpenter attached to the staff, who makes minor repairs and alterations as required on tour or in a permanent theatre.

STAGECRAFT. A general term used to describe the technical side of stage production, with particular reference to the actual building of settings.

STAGE DIRECTIONS. Instructions printed in published copies of plays, concerning the movements of actors or arrangements of scenery. Some playwrights, like Shaw, write detailed stage directions; others write none. Often the printed stage directions are those copied from the prompt script for a production.

STAGE DIRECTOR. In the British theatre the person responsible for the operation of all backstage departments concerning a production. He is the co-ordinator of these, and acts as a liaison between technicians and producer. In America the Stage Manager fulfils this function. (See chapter on Stage Management.)

STAGE DOOR. The entrance from the street to the backstage area of a theatre; always used by actors and technicians, who never enter the theatre from the front of house.

STAGE DOOR JOHNNY. A term used to describe male fans who wait to see female stars come out of the theatre, in the hope of meeting them and perhaps arranging social appointments. The practice is not as common today as it was in the early twentieth and late nineteenth centuries. Today it is more often young women who wait to see the male stars.

STAGE HAND. A backstage workman who helps to move scenery about during a scene change, manipulates ropes for drops, and any other similar tasks assigned to him by the Stage Director or Stage Manager.

STAGE FRIGHT. The nervous tension felt by artists before the curtain goes up, and often during a performance. It diminishes with experience, and often as the performance proceeds. (See FIRST NIGHT NERVES.)

STAGE MANAGER. In America the Stage Manager performs the same function as the Stage Director does in Britain (see STAGE DIRECTOR). In Britain he is second in command to the Stage Director, and performs certain tasks rather than merely supervising operations. (See chapter on Stage Management.)

STAGE PICTURE. The visual aspect of a stage-setting complete with actors, seen from out front. Clever arrangement of groups of actors greatly contributes to a pleasing stage picture.

STAGE STAFF. All the backstage technical workers on a production.

STAGE STRUCK. A young (or old) person who is not in the theatre, but who greatly admires it and wishes to be part of it, is said to be "stage struck".

STAGE WAIT. A pause in the action of a play during the performance, usually caused by an actor forgetting his lines, or missing his entrance cue or some technical fault.

STAGE WHISPER. Lines spoken by one actor to another in a feigned whisper so that the audience hears but the other actors on stage supposedly do not.

STALLS. The seats on the ground floor of a theatre or auditorium. (See ORCHESTRA STALLS and PIT.)

STAND-IN. An actor who takes the place of another, usually a leading player, at rehearsals for any reason. The term is probably used to a greater extent in films, where stand-ins are used in technical rehearsals, and in long shots, in the place of the star.

STANISLAVSKY METHOD. A method of acting and producing introduced by the Russian actor-producer Constantin Stanislavsky in the late nineteenth century, in which all characterization, movement and thought is based upon real life, and theatrical artificiality is cut to a minimum. The method requires study and thought on the part of all artists, and not merely acting and producing for effect. It might be called using a psychological approach to the theatre. Unfortunately some devotees of this method have overdone the "inner" approach, and are so completely psychologically tied up in their performance that the feeling is not projected to the audience. A happy medium must be struck between the subjective Stanislavsky approach and projection across the footlights.

STAR. The leading actor or actress in a professional commercial play is called the "star", and receives top billing, high salary and a special "star dressing-room". There is a certain brilliance of acting power in some performers that is known as "star quality", and these are the true stars, although they may not be recognized as such in the commercial theatre. The star, in the widest known sense, is a person who attracts people to see him because of great personal charm, magnetism, and usually physical beauty.

STAR ENTRANCE. The first entrance in a play's performance by the star or stars of the piece. It is often greeted by a round of applause.

STAR SYSTEM. A system of selling a play to the public on the names of its stars, not particularly on the quality of the play. The professional theatre is almost entirely under this system today, and many examples of bad playwriting, bad production, and bad casting of minor roles are covered up by the attraction of a star name in the leading role.

STICKS. A slang expression for remote towns where touring companies may play; outside the large cities.

STOCK COMPANIES. The American equivalent of British repertory theatres (see REPERTORY THEATRE). Many of these are formed for special summer seasons and are then often called Straw Hat Theatres.

STOP THE SHOW. When a performance is so outstanding that it receives special applause in the middle of a scene, the performer is said to "stop the show".

STRAIGHT. A part which in physical appearance is in the same general age group as the actor playing it, and of average outlook, without the eccentricities of a "character" part. (See CHARACTER.)

STRAW HAT THEATRE. (See STOCK COMPANIES.)

STRIKE THE SET. To take the setting down after a performance or series of performances.

STROLLING PLAYERS. Groups of actors who travel from place to place giving plays. The term is not often used today, but replaced by "touring companies". These mobile acting groups began in the Middle Ages.

STYLIZATION. Production and acting performed in a mannered way, not realistic. The "style" of presentation is the important thing, not particularly the meaning. The plays of Oscar Wilde adapt themselves well to stylized performance.

SUPER. Abbreviation for Supernumerary. Same as Extra. (See EXTRA.)

SUPPORTING ACTOR. An actor who plays a part subsidiary to the leading parts. The importance of supporting actors and roles has become increasingly recognized in many theatres, and special awards given by certain organizations each year for this work. A star "supported" by a fine actor has a greater chance of success than one who depends upon mediocre supporting talent.

SYMBOLISM. A presentation of ideas through symbols rather than realistic methods. Suggestion is used in scenic effects, rather than replicas of life; and acting and production follow the same style. Symbolism is akin to Expressionism, and was introduced in the early twentieth century as a revolt away from naturalism.

TABLEAU. A silent pictorial grouping of actors against a setting, usually held for a few moments without movement, and sometimes accompanied by appropriate music; usually used for a special effect or mood, and sometimes for a curtain call.

TAG LINE. The last line in a play before the final curtain comes down.

TAKE A CALL. To acknowledge applause at the end of a play by the cast appearing onstage with the curtain up, and bowing slightly to the audience.

TEA CUP TRADE. Audiences who come to the theatre purely for a social outing, without wanting to think deeply, and who enjoy their cup of tea at the interval as much as the presentation onstage.

TEAR JERKER. A play which moves its audience to tears; often a melodramatic type of piece, which today might jerk laughs rather than tears.

THEATRE. A general term which includes all the work done artistically, technically and in a business or organizational way in connection with a dramatic performance; also refers to the building in which a dramatic performance is given.

THEME. The general idea motivating the plot and characters in a play, e.g. war, love, hate, football pools, alcoholism, etc.

THESIS PLAYS. Plays in which the playwright develops a theme in which he is particularly interested, and on which he has strong ideas, about which he tries to convince his audience. Shaw and Ibsen wrote many thesis plays.

THESPIAN. Term for an actor, derived from the ancient Greek actor-dramatist. Thespis.

THROWAWAYS. Printed leaflets advertising a play, which are given to the public in various ways. (See chapter on Publicity.)

2D

THROWING IT AWAY. To speak a line in an offhand manner, with no attempt at dramatic emphasis is known as "throwing it away". This technique is often employed in sophisticated comedy, and requires polished and experienced actors to be completely successful.

THROW ME THE LINE. An expression used by actors in rehearsal when asking the prompter for a cue.

TIRING HOUSE. The Green Room and backstage area of an Elizabethan playhouse. (See GREEN ROOM.)

TITLE ROLE. The character in a play for whom the piece is named, e.g. "Candida", "Miss Julie", etc.

TOPPING. Speaking just a little louder than the actor who has just delivered a line, is "topping" his line.

TRAGEDY. Drama which deals with a serious subject and ends unhappily for the protagonist (hero). In tragedy the antagonist triumphs over the protagonist. (See ANTAGONIST and PROTAGONIST.) True tragedy should result in a purification of the spectators' emotions. (See CATHARSIS.)

TRAGI-COMEDY. Drama which contains some of both tragedy and comedy. (See COMEDY and TRAGEDY.)

TRAP. An opening in the stage floor leading to a lower level below the stage. Entrances and exits are often effected through traps, either by means of steps, or lifts controlled by machinery.

TREADMILL. A mechanism traversing the stage, which moves like an endless belt and conveys actors, scenery, properties, etc., for special effects.

TRIANGLE PLAY. A play whose plot revolves around three people, usually two women and a man, or two men and a woman, who are mutually involved in an affair of the heart.

TROUPER. An actor who is experienced in the theatre, and has developed a contented and practical philosophy in connection with his place in it. Real troupers are the backbone of any theatrical company.

TRY-OUT. A performance of a play either in a smaller centre before opening on Broadway or in the West End; or given for an invited private audience before its première.

TWICE NIGHTLY. Name given to the system practised in some repertory companies and most music halls, of presenting two complete performances in one evening.

TYPE. Actors who because of their looks and personalities always play the same kind of part. To type an actor is to always give him the same kind of part to play. A system of type casting is widely used in the commercial theatre, but not so much in repertory companies where actors are called upon to portray a variety of types.

UNDERSTUDY. An actor who learns another's lines and movements in a part, in preparation for performing in his place should he be unavoidably unable to play.

UNDERSTUDY REHEARSAL. Practice given to understudies in the parts they have learned; these rehearsals are usually conducted by the Stage Director who sees that the understudies' movements are exact replicas of those in the prompt book. (See chapter on Stage Management.)

UNITIES. The three unities of a play, as defined by Aristotle, in the *Poetics*. These include the unities of Time (24 hours), Place, and Action. In modern playwriting the Unities are often not observed.

UPPER CIRCLE. (See CIRCLE.)

UPPER STAGE. A balcony in the Elizabethan theatre, situated above the Inner Stage, and slightly protruding over the Outer Stage; curtained off, and with a low railing. Used for balcony scenes, scenes on battlements, etc.

UPSTAGE. The stage area between the back of the setting and an imaginary line running parallel to it halfway to the footlights. To "upstage" another actor one actor may move towards the back of the set, thus forcing the former to turn his back to the audience when speaking. Upstaging is a trick used by some experienced actors to focus the attention on themselves to the detriment of the rest of the company, and should be severely discouraged.

VARIETY. The medium of entertainment in which programmes of unrelated songs, dances, skits, acrobatics, etc., are performed. "Variety" is the term used in Britain; while in America "Vaudeville" is used. (See MUSIC HALL.)

VAUDEVILLE. (See VARIETY.)

VEHICLE. A term sometimes used to describe a play, often when it is a "vehicle" predominantly important for displaying the talents of a particular star.

VIZARDS. Masks worn by ladies who visited Restoration playhouses; for the purpose of disguising them because it was not considered quite "proper" for ladies to attend a public theatre.

WALK-ON. A very tiny part in a play, usually having no spoken lines, but sometimes just two or three. (See BIT PART.)

WALK THROUGH. In early rehearsals, when moves are being blocked in and remembered, actors often "walk through" scenes, reading their lines without due regard to expression, emphasis and meaning. This mechanical moving about enables them to concentrate their whole attention on basic movement. (See chapter on The Producer.)

WARDROBE. The department in a theatre which deals with costumes. Many companies have a permanent wardrobe from which costumes for various plays may be chosen, while others hire a wardrobe from costumiers for single productions. (See chapter on Design, Part 2.)

WARDROBE MISTRESS. The person (usually a woman) who takes care of costumes for a play. Sometimes she is responsible for making them; sometimes only for looking after them during the run. (See chapter on Stage Management.)

WORK LIGHT. A single light, usually hanging above the middle of the stage, used during rehearsals; sometimes left on when the stage is not being used.

WORKING TITLE. The tentative title of a new play, which may be changed before the first performance.

BIBLIOGRAPHY

ACTING

Boleslavsky, Richard, *Acting: The First Six Lessons* (Theatre Arts).
Bourne, John, *Amateur Acting from A to Z* (English University Press).
—— *Teach Yourself Amateur Acting* (Hodder and Stoughton).
Carroll, Sydney W., *Acting for the Stage* (Pitman).
Cole, Toby (edited by), *Acting: A Handbook of the Stanislavsky Method* (Lear).
MacKenzie, Frances J., *The Amateur Actor* (Nelson).
Selden, Samuel, *A Player's Handbook: The Theory and Practice of Acting* (Crofts).
Stanislavsky, Constantin, *An Actor Prepares* (Geoffrey Bles).
—— *Building a Character* (Geoffrey Bles).
—— *My Life in Art* (Geoffrey Bles).

BUSINESS MANAGEMENT AND PUBLICITY

Chisholm, Cecil, *Repertory* (Peter Davies).
Dean, Alexander, *Little Theatre Organization and Management* (Appleton).
Hinsdell, Oliver, *Making the Little Theatre Pay* (Samuel French).
Mason and Gibson, *Organising an Amateur Theatre Society* (Lovat Dickson).
Nelson-Smith, Alan, *The Business Side of the Amateur Theatre* (MacDonald and Evans).
Stanton, Sanford E., *Theatre Management* (Appleton).

CHILDREN'S THEATRE

Chorpenning, Charlotte B., *Twenty-One Years With Children's Theatre* (Children's Theatre Press).
Slade, Peter, *Child Drama* (University of London Press).

COSTUME

Barton, Lucy, *Historic Costume for the Stage* (Baker).
Boehn, Max von, *Modes and Manners*, 4 vols. (Harrap).
Koehler, C. and von Sichart, E., *A History of Costume* (Harrap).
Komisarjevsky, Theodore, *The Costume of the Theatre* (Holt).
Laver, James, *Fashions and Fashion Plates, 1800–1900* (Penguin Books).
—— *Taste and Fashion from the French Revolution until Today* (Harrap).
Winter, Carl, *Elizabethan Miniatures* (Penguin Books).

CRITICISM

Baxter, Beverley, *First Nights and Noises Off* (Hutchinson).
Bentley, Eric, *The Dramatic Event* (Dobson).
Hobson, Harold, *Theatre One* (Burke).
—— *Theatre Two* (Burke).
Lewes, G. H., *Actors and Acting*.
Montague, C. E., *Dramatic Essays*.
Nathan, George Jean, *The Morning After the First Night* (Knopf).
O'Casey, Sean, *The Flying Wasp* (Macmillan).
Ward, A. C., *Specimens of English Dramatic Criticism*, Worlds Classics Series (Oxford University Press).

GENERAL

Clurman, Harold, *The Fervent Years* (Dennis Dobson).
Cotes, Peter, *No Star Nonsense* (Rockliff).
Findlater, Richard, *The Unholy Trade* (Victor Gollancz).
Godfrey, Philip, *Back-Stage* (Harrap).
Grein, J. T., *The New World of the Theatre* (Martin Hopkinson).
Gyseghem, André Van, *Theatre in Soviet Russia* (Faber and Faber).
MacGowan, Kenneth, *The Theatre of Tomorrow* (Boni and Liveright).
Martin, Boyd, *Modern American Drama and Stage* (The Pilot Press).
Marshall, Norman, *The Other Theatre* (John Lehmann).
Purdom, C. B., *Drama Festivals and their Adjudication* (J. M. Dent).
Williamson, Audrey, *Theatre of Two Decades*, *Contemporary Theatre* (Rockliff).
Wilson, A. E., *Post-War Theatre* (Home and van Thal).

HANDBOOKS

Andrews, John and Trilling, Ossia (edited by), *Dobson's Theatre Yearbook* (Dennis Dobson).
Association of Junior Leagues of America, *Handbook for Children's Theatre*.
British Drama League, *The Player's Library* (3 vols., including First and Second Supplements) (Faber and Faber).
Hobson, Harold, *The International Theatre Annual* (Calder).
Markham, Harold, *Amateur Theatrical Handbook*.
Shay, Frank, *The Practical Theatre* (Appleton).
Sobel, Bernard, *The Theatre Handbook and Digest of Plays* (Crown).
Stevens, Frances (edited by), *The Theatre World Yearbook* (Rockliff).
The Stage (newspaper), *The Stage Guide*.
—— *The Stage Yearbook*.

HISTORY

Cheney, Sheldon, *The Theatre* (Longmans, Green).
Cleaver, James, *The Theatre Through the Ages* (Harrap).

Dean, Basil, *The Theatre at War* (Harrap).
Eaton, Walter Prichard, *The Actor's Heritage* (Atlantic Monthly Press).
Evans, B. Ifor, *A Short History of English Drama* (Pelican Books).
Freedley and Reeves, *A History of the Theatre* (Crown).
Gassner, John, *Masters of the Drama* (Random House).
Greene, Graham, *British Dramatists* (Wm. Collins).
Irving, H. B., *Occasional Papers—Dramatic and Historical* (Bickers and Son).
Macleod, Joseph, *Actors Across the Volga* (Geo. Allen and Unwin).
Morley, Christopher, *Seacoast of Bohemia* (Doubleday, Doran).
Nicoll, Allardyce, *The Development of the Theatre* (Harcourt, Brace).
Pogson, Rex, *Miss Horniman and the Gaiety Theatre, Manchester* (Rockliff).

LIGHTING

Bentham, *Stage Lighting.*
Corry, *Lighting the Stage.*
—— *Stage Planning and Equipment.*
Fuchs, Theodore, *Stage Lighting* (Allen and Unwin).
Goffin, Peter, *Stage Lighting for Amateurs* (Muller).
Halstead, *Stage Management for the Amateur Theatre.*
Hartmann, Louis, *Theatre Lighting, A Manual of the Stage Switchboard* (Appleton).
Knapp, *Lighting the Stage with Homemade Equipment.*
McCandless, Stanley R., *A Method of Lighting the Stage* (Theatre Arts).
—— *Glossary of Stage Lighting* (Theatre Arts).
Ridge, C. H. and Aldred, F. S., *Stage Lighting: Principle and Practice* (Pitman).
Williams, R. Gillespie, *The Technique of Stage Lighting* (Pitman).
Wilson, *The Small Stage and its Equipment.*

MAKE-UP

Baird, John, *Make-up* (A Manual) (Samuel French).
Bamford, T. W., *Practical Make-up for the Stage* (Pitman).
Strenkovsky, Serge, *The Art of Make-up* (Dutton).
Ward, Eric, *A Book of Make-up* (Samuel French).

PLAYWRITING AND DRAMATISTS

Archer, William, *Playmaking* (Dodd Mead).
Baker, George Pierce, *Dramatic Technique* (Houghton Mifflin).
Gassner, John, *Masters of the Drama* (Random House).
Henderson, Archibald, *European Dramatists* (Grant Richards).

Lawson, John Howard, *Theory and Technique of Playwriting* (Putnam).
Platt, Agnes, *Practical Hints on Playwriting* (Stanley Paul).

PRODUCING

Browne, E. Martin, *Putting on a Play* (Lovat Dickson).
Clark, Barrett H., *How to Produce Amateur Plays* (Little, Brown).
Desmond, D. J., *Amateur Acting and Producing for Beginners* (C. Arthur Pearson).
Fernald, John, *The Play Produced* (H. F. W. Dean).
Gassner, John, *Producing the Play* (Dryden Press).
Heffner, Hubert C., Seldon, Samuel and Sellman, Hunton D., *Modern Theatre Practice: A Handbook for Non-Professionals* (Crofts).
Mitchell, Roy E., *Shakespeare for Community Players* (Dutton).
Purdom, C. B., *Producing Plays* (Dent).
Seldon, Samuel, *The Stage in Action* (Crofts).
Sladen-Smith, F., *The Amateur Producer's Handbook* (University of London Press).

SCENE DESIGN AND CONSTRUCTION

Bell, Stanley; Marshall, Norman; and Southern, Richard, *Essentials of Stage Planning* (Muller).
Brandon Thomas, Jevan, *Practical Stagecraft for Amateurs* (Harrap).
Cheney, Sheldon, *The Open Air Theatre* (Mitchell Kennerley).
—— *Stage Decoration* (Chapman and Hall).
Coles, E. C. and Burris-Meyer, H., *Scenery for the Theatre* (Little, Brown).
Craig, Gordon, *Scene* (Oxford University Press).
—— *On the Art of the Theatre* (Heinemann).
Gorelik, Mordecai, *New Theatres for Old* (Dennis Dobson).
Jones, Robert Edmond, *Drawings for the Theatre* (Theatre Arts).
Melvill, Harald, *Designing and Painting Scenery for the Theatre* (The Art Trade Press).
Myerscough-Walker, R., *Stage and Film Décor* (Pitman).
Simonson, Lee, *The Stage is Set* (Harcourt Brace).
Somerscales, Marjorie, *The Improvised Stage* (Pitman).
Southern, Richard, *Proscenium and Sight-Lines* (Faber and Faber).
—— *Stage Setting* (Faber and Faber).
Theatre Arts Prints (4 vols):
  Vol. 1. *A Collection of Photographs from the Days of the Greeks to our Own.*
  Vol. 2. *Modern Stage Design.*
  Vol. 3. *Shakespeare and his Times.*
  Vol. 4. *Stages of the World.*
Whitworth, Geoffrey, *Theatre in Action* (The Studio).

SPEECH

Fogerty, Elsie, *Speech Craft* (Dent).
Rippmann, Walter, *The Sounds of Spoken English* (Dent).
Woolbert and Nelson, *The Art of Interpretive Speech* (Crofts).

STAGE MANAGEMENT

Bax, Peter, *Stage Management* (Lovat Dickson).
British Drama League, *Basic Equipment for the Small Stage.*
Napier, Frank, *Noises Off: A Handbook of Sound Effects* (Muller).
Parsons, Charles S., *Amateur Stage Management and Production.*
Strand Electric and Engineering Company, *Stage Planning and Equipment for Multi-Purpose Halls, in Schools, Colleges, Little Theatres, etc.*

APPENDIX I

USEFUL INFORMATION FROM THE N.O.D.A. YEARBOOK

AMATEUR PERFORMANCES

In some cases Societies will discover in their contracts with the Holders of Performing Rights a clause which makes it incumbent on the Society to announce clearly in all publicity that the performance is by amateur players. This clause should not be misconstrued as making it obligatory for the word "Amateur" to be incorporated in the Society's title.

CHILDREN IN ENTERTAINMENT

According to the Children and Young Persons Act, 1933, children of any age may take part in Amateur productions without a special licence providing they do not appear on more than six occasions in any one period of six months. Children over twelve may take part on more than six occasions but only under licence. There is no power to grant a licence to children under twelve, so that they must be restricted to six occasions in six months. These six occasions mean six actual performances. A child is defined as a person who is not over the compulsory school age of fifteen years, or in the case of special schools, sixteen years. Children are deemed to be of compulsory school age until the end of the term in which they attain the age of fifteen or sixteen as the case may be. If required, licences may be applied for to the Local Education Authority. Copies of the Children and Young Persons Act, 1933, may be obtained through any bookseller for two shillings.

CONTROL OF ADVERTISEMENTS REGULATIONS, 1948

On 1 August 1948, under the Town and Country Planning Act, 1947, regulations came into force with regard to advertisements. Existing advertisements at that date may stand for a period determined by the length of time they have been in existence. New advertisements may not be displayed without consent granted by the local planning authority. Societies are advised to investigate conditions locally as there are many penalties for contravention.

FIRE-ARMS

The Fire-arms Act, 1937, places restrictions upon the purchase, acquisition and possession of fire-arms and ammunition. If a Society wishes to buy, hire or borrow fire-arms a certificate, costing five shillings, continues in force for three years, when application for renewal may be made, for which a fee of 2s. 6d. is payable. An individual taking part in a theatrical performance or rehearsal may have a fire-arm in his possession without holding a certificate *only during* the performance or rehearsal. The owner of the fire-arm, or person who has hired it, must hold a certificate. A dummy pistol which can be converted into a lethal fire-arm capable of discharging a missile is, in its converted state, liable to the provisions of the Fire-arms Act.

The following fire-arms are exempt from restrictions and need for certificate:

(*a*) Smooth-bore guns having barrels not less than twenty inches in length.

(*b*) Air guns, air rifles or air pistols not being of a type declared by rules made by the Secretary of State to be especially dangerous (no rules have hitherto been made);

as are the following types of ammunition:

(*a*) Cartridges containing five or more shot, none of which exceeds nine twenty-fifths of an inch in diamater;

(*b*) Ammunition for an air gun or air rifle or air pistol;

(*c*) Blank cartridges not exceeding one inch in diameter. Special application for authority to possess and acquire machine-guns or sub-machine guns for theatrical use must be made to the War Office. If this authority is granted, application for a fire-arms certificate must then be made to the Chief Officer of Police.

FIRE PROOFING

Societies that make their own scenery must make sure that it is fire-proofed, to conform with the laws regarding licensing of theatres. Reputable scenic contractors supply their goods already fire-proofed. Specially prepared crystals may be obtained from certain chemists and theatrical suppliers, but the following preparation may be made by the Society: for coarse fabrics: 1 lb. Phosphate of Ammonia, 2 lb. Sal. Ammoniac, 1½ gal. Water; for delicate fabrics and cotton: 10 oz. Borax, 8 oz. Boracic Acid, 1 gal. Water.

LOTTERIES

A misunderstanding of the provisions of the Betting and Lotteries Act, 1934, may possibly involve Societies and their officials in serious trouble.

Only "private lotteries" are lawful. This means that lotteries may be promoted by a society under the written authority of its governing body, but the sale of tickets must be strictly confined to members of the promoting society. It is unlawful for the society to sell tickets to members of another society, or to the general public. No tickets may be sent by post. A fine not exceeding £100 may be imposed on a society convicted of promoting an unlawful lottery.

POSTERS, CARDS AND BILLS

Posters are produced in the following standard sizes:

18-sheet Double Crown	...	120 in. wide × 90 in. deep
12-sheet Double Crown	...	80 in. wide × 90 in. deep
6-sheet Double Crown	...	40 in. wide × 90 in. deep
4-sheet Double Crown	...	40 in. wide × 60 in. deep
Quad Crown ...	...	30 in. wide × 40 in. deep
Double Crown ...		20 in. wide × 30 in. deep

The sizes having the greatest vogue are 12-sheets, 6-sheets and double crowns. The two former sizes for the hoardings and theatre boards, and the double crowns for shop windows and small hoardings.
Billposting charges are reckoned per double crown sheet.

Window Bills

Half Double Crown	...	10 in. wide × 30 in. deep (usual Theatre Daybill)
Crown	...	15 in. wide × 20 in. deep
Crown Folio ...	...	10 in. wide × 15 in. deep
Double Crown Thirds	...	10 in. wide × 20 in. deep

Hanger Cards (for Box Office, Trams, etc.)—holed and corded.

Royal Folio ...	...	$12\frac{1}{2}$ in. wide × 20 in. deep
Royal 4to ...	...	10 in. wide × $12\frac{1}{2}$ in. deep
Royal 6mo ...	...	$6\frac{1}{4}$ in. wide × 10 in. deep

Souvenirs, Circulars, Handbills, etc.

Crown 4to ...	...	$7\frac{1}{4}$ in. wide × $9\frac{3}{4}$ in. deep
Demy 8vo ...	...	$5\frac{1}{2}$ in. wide × $8\frac{5}{8}$ in. deep
Crown 8vo ...	...	$4\frac{7}{8}$ in. wide × $7\frac{1}{4}$ in. deep
Demy 16's ...	...	$5\frac{5}{8}$ in. wide × $4\frac{3}{8}$ in. deep

In the case of souvenirs and circulars the number of pages should be divisible by 4, i.e. 8 pp., 12 pp., 16 pp., 20 pp., etc.. and circulars are usually 4 pp.

Date Slips. For use with pictorial posters, giving details of theatre, times and prices:

Half Double Crown, 30 in. × 10 in., for 6-sheets and larger posters.
Demy 16's, 5⅝ in. × 4¾ in., for Double Crown.

SUNDAY PERFORMANCE

Permission of the Local Authority (or in the case of London, the L.C.C.) is required for a public Sunday performance in aid of charity. A rigid condition is that stage make-up shall not be used by the performers and no stage costume be worn. Stage patter, cross-talk and duologues must not be introduced into the performances. Private clubs are permitted to give stage presentation of plays on Sunday.

UNIFORM OF H.M. FORCES

The wearing of exact replicas of current uniforms of H.M. Forces on the stage or elsewhere is not permitted. On the stage, however, more latitude is permitted than in the street. A slight deviation of badges, buttons, formation signs and flashes, etc., overcomes the difficulty. With the exception of such distinguishing marks, accuracy of cut and colour is considered desirable.

APPENDIX 2

THEATRICAL PUBLICATIONS

PUBLICATIONS

Amateur Stage, 57 Church Hill, London, N.21 (PALmers Green 4281). (Published on 1st of each month. Ads. to be received by 14th of the month preceding issue. Cost 1s. 3d. per copy.)

Drama, British Drama League, 6 Fitzroy Square, London, W.1 (EUSton 2666). (Published quarterly. Ads. to be received a month before publication. Cost 1s. 6d. per copy.)

Plays and Players, 21 Lower Belgrave St., London, S.W.1 (SLOane 0394). (Published monthly, 30th preceding month. Ads. to be received ten days before 30th. Cost 2s. per copy.)

The Stage, Carson and Comerford Ltd., 19/21 Tavistock St., London, W.C.2 (TEMple Bar 5213/4). (Published weekly (Thurs.). Ads. to be received four days before publication. Cost 6d. per copy.)

Theatre World, Practical Press Ltd., 1 Dorset Buildings, Fleet St., London, E.C.4 (CENtral 1555). (Published 1st of each month. Ads to be received on 12th of preceding month. Cost 2s. per copy.)

APPENDIX 3

THEATRICAL SUPPLIERS

COSTUMES

Angel, Morris & Son, Ltd., 117–119 Shaftesbury Ave., London, W.C.2. Telegrams: Teatridio London; TEMple Bar 5678 (5 lines).

Bamber, R. Sheldon, Ltd., 12 & 13 Charing Cross Mansions, Glasgow, C.3. Douglas 1471; Telegrams: Bamberre, Glasgow.

Benjamin, D. & J., 22–23 Dean Street, London, W.1. GERrard 1019.

Citizen House Ltd., 21 Green Park, Bath. Bath 5157; Telegrams: Period, Bath.

Drury, B. & H. Ltd., 23 New Road, Brighton. Brighton 26588; Telegrams: Drury, Brighton.

Errol, Doreen, 8–9 Carlisle Street, Soho Square, London, W.1. GERrard 4136.

Faith House Wardrobe Ltd., 7 Tufton Street, London, S.W.1. ABBey 6218.

Fashion Hire Ltd., 7 Shorts Gardens, Upper St. Martin's Lane, London, W.C.2. TEMple Bar 9541.

Fox, Chas. H. Ltd., 184 High Holborn, London, W.C.1. HOLborn 9557–9. Telegrams: Theatricals, Westcent, London.

Homburg, W. A. Ltd., 31 Call Lane, Leeds, 1. Leeds 28425.

Hume, W. A. and Sons, 88–94 Oxford St., Manchester, 1. CENtral 2244.

Mutrie, Wm. and Son Ltd., Proscenium House, Bell's Brae, Dean Bridge, Edinburgh, 4. Edinburgh 27107; Telegrams: Proscenium, Edinburgh.

Nathan, L. H., 12 Panton Street, Haymarket, London, S.W.1. WHItehall 5245.

Sally Spruce, 49 Greek Street, London, W.1. GERrard 3162.

Simmons, B. J. & Co., Ltd., 7 & 8 King St., Covent Garden, London, W.C.2. TEMple Bar 5568; Telegrams: History Rand, London.

Smith, F. A. Ltd., All Saints, Manchester, 1. Ardwick 2642; Telegrams: Masque, Manchester.

Theatrical Supplies, 268 Rockingham St., Sheffield, 1. Sheffield 21698.

Watts and Co., 18–20 New Brown St., Manchester, 4. Blackfriars 5826/27.

MAKE-UP

"Bert" (see under Wigs).

Leichner, L. (London) Ltd., 44A Cranbourn St., London, W.C.2. GERrard 1086.

Max Factor Ltd., 16 Old Bond Street, London, W.1. HYDe Park 6720.

Mutrie, Wm. & Son (see under Costumes).

Nathan Wigs (see under Costumes).

Smith, F. A. Ltd. (see under Costumes).

Theatrical Supplies (see under Costumes).

PRINTING

Inprint Ltd., 66 Shaftesbury Ave., London, W.1. GERrard 8738.

Potten, Baber and Murray Ltd., 78 Milk St. & Clark St., Bristol. Bristol 24784; Telegrams: Potten, Bristol.

Stafford and Co. Ltd., Netherfield, Nottingham. Carlton 58214.

PROPERTIES AND/OR SOUND EFFECTS

Bishop Sound and Electrical Co. Ltd., 48 Monmouth St., London, W.C.2. TEMple Bar 7484-5.

Floral Decor, 15 Gerrard Street, London, W.1. GERrard 1957.

Robinson Bros. Ltd., 5/7 Hampstead Road, London, N.W.1. EUSton 4894.

Stage Properties Ltd., 13 Panton Street, London, S.W.1. WHItehall 8528.

SCENERY

Bamber, R. Sheldon, Ltd. (see under Costumes).

Bert Loman Ltd., Head Office: Mericourt Mere, Cheshire. Bucklow Hill 2203. Studio: Bloomsbury Hall, Rusholme Rd., All Saints, Manchester. Ardwick 2796.

Brodie and Middleton Ltd., 79 Long Acre, London, W.C.2. TEMple Bar 3289, 3280.

Cape of Chiswick (T. Ireby Cape Ltd.), Sutton Lane, Chiswick, London, W.4. Chiswick 2828.

Cape (Northern Ltd.), Councillor Lane, Cheadle, Cheshire. GATley 4205.

Crossland, James Ltd., 50 Temple St., Wolverhampton. Wolverhampton 25054.

Dodsworth and Spencer, Wellington Road Studios, Bradford. Bradford 37137; Telegrams: Dodsworth.

Drury, B. and H. Ltd. (see under Costumes).

Fredricks (James) Studios Ltd., Langford Rd., Weston-super-Mare. Weston-super-Mare 4791.

Garrick Curtains Ltd., 44 Amhurst Road, Hackney, London, E.8. AMHerst 3171.

Hall and Dixon Ltd., 19 Garrick Street, London, W.C.2. TEMple Bar 1930–8331.

Howard, Rex (for curtains), 12 Connaught Street, London, W.2.

Mutrie, Wm. and Son Ltd. (see under Costumes).

Scenic Display Services Ltd., Norcroft Studios, Listerhills Rd., Bradford. Bradford 24377.

Skelton, Penny, 8 Cleland Lane, Glasgow, C.5. South 3558.

Stage Furnishings Ltd., 346 Sauchiehall St., Glasgow, C.2. Douglas 6431–2; Telegrams Stagelite, Glasgow.

Stage Scenery Ltd., 13 Short's Gardens, Monmouth St., London, W.C.2. TEMple Bar 9541–4; Telegrams: Scenery, Westcent, London.

Star Scenic Studios, 78 Elms Road, Clapham Common, London, S.W.4. MACauley 6401–2.

Sudden Scenic Contractors, 40 Oxberry Ave., Fulham, London, S.W.6. RENown 4779.

Watts and Corry Ltd., 305/317 Oldham Road, Manchester, 10. Collyhurst 2736.

Whyatt, A. and Son., Hartley St., Wolverhampton.

Williams, John, Scenery Makers, 1 Meadow Studios, Bushey, Herts. BUShey Heath 2914.

STAGE JEWELLERY

Robinson Bros. Ltd. (see under Properties).

White, Robert, and Sons, 57–59 Neal St., London, W.C.2.

STAGE LIGHTING

Furse, W. J. and Co. Ltd., 65 Traffic St., Nottingham, also at London, Manchester, Derby, Bristol. Telephone: Nottingham 88213.

Major Equipment Co. Ltd., 22 Gorst Road, London, N.W.10. ELGar 8041 (5 lines).

Northern Stage Electrics, 8 Barrowby Lane, Austhorpe, Halton, Leeds. 10 Bryn Arden Road, South Yardley, Birmingham, 26.

Strand Electric and Engineering Co. Ltd., 29 King St., London, W.C.2. 313 Oldham Road, Manchester. 62 Coawson St., Dublin. 481 Malvern Road, Melbourne, Australia.

WIGS

Bamber, R. Sheldon, Ltd. (see under Costumes).

"Bert", 46 Portnall Road, London, W.9. LADbroke 1717.

Fox, Chas. H. (see under Costumes).

2E

Homburg, W. A. Ltd. (see under Costumes).

Hume, W. A. and Sons (see under Costumes).

Mutrie, Wm. and Son (see under Costumes).

Nathan Wigs (see under Costumes).

Smith, F. A. Ltd. (see under Costumes).

Theatrical Supplies (see under Costumes).

Walker, Vivienne, Flat 4, 36 Nottingham Place, London, W.1. WELbeck 0140–0149.

Wig Creations Ltd., 69 George St., Baker St., London, W.1. HUNter 0771.

APPENDIX 4

SAMPLE PRODUCTION BUDGET

EXPENDITURE	INCOME
Scenery	
Set Construction	
Hires	
Painting	Ticket Sales
Properties and Wardrobe	Sale of Programmes
Costume Making	Programme Advertising
Hires	Refreshments
Properties Bought	
Hires	
Lighting	
Equipment Bought	
Hires	
Publicity	
Press	
Posters and Handbills	
Special Publicity	
Printing	
Tickets	
Programmes	
Miscellaneous	
Hire of Theatre	
Hire of Rehearsal Space	
Salaries (if any)	
Orchestra (if any)	
Royalties	
Lord Chamberlain's Licence	
Theatre Licence (if any)	
Performing Rights Fees	
Phonographic Performance Fees	
Entertainment Duty	
Insurance	
Photographs	
Cartage	
Scripts	
£ _____	£ _____

INDEX

Paul Twyning, 259
Pavlova, 283
Payne, B. Iden, 298
Peace in our Time, 263
Peach, L. du Garde, 267, 268, 269, 270
Peake, Bladon, 261
Pearce, Arnold, 352
Pearse, Patrick, 292
Peer Gynt, 287, 293, 296
Penny for a Song, A, 275
People's Theatre (Newcastle-upon-Tyne) 35, 236, 286-88
Pepper's Ghost Effect, 142
perches, see lighting
Percy, Edward, 255
Perfect Woman, The, 300
Performing Right Society, 59, 60
permanent formal sets, 107
personal contact, re publicity, 69, 78
Peter Pan, 198
Petticoats Preferred, 296
petty cash float, 68
Phelps, Samuel, 3
Philp, Peter, 276
Phoenix Too Frequent, A, 304, 351
Phonographic Performance Ltd., 60
photographs, re publicity, 70, 72, 75, 77; use in set designing, 103
Picasso, Pablo, 364
Pickles, Wilfred, 251
Picnic, 23
picture frame stage, 99; drawing of, 101, 375
Picture Post (magazine), 103
Pilgrim Players, The, 246
Pilgrim Trust, 222, 264
Pillars of Society, 297
Pinero, Arthur Wing, xix, 5, 250, 329
pin hinging, 124, 131
Pink Champagne, 188
Pinocchio, 284
Pin to See the Peep Show, A, 57
Pippa Passes, 285
Pirandello, 270, 285, 290, 329
Pithey, Wensley, 355
Planchette, 187
Plant in the Sun, 307
Plautus, 329
Playboy of the Western World, 274
Playfair, Nigel, 222
play of ideas, 5
play readings, 42; re publicity, 77

play-reading committee, 39, 40, 42
playwriting, 241, 243, 248; 19th century, 3, 4, 5; 20th century, 6-7; courses by B.D.L., 224-25; Victorian, 4
Playwright, The, 1-7, 376; 19th century, 3; and publicity, 70; royalties to, 55-56
Player's Library, The, 222
Playing with Fire, 350
Plays and Players, 72
plot, 376
Pochin, R. Eric, 278
Pocock, J. G. A., 342
Poet's Corner, 279
Pollitzer, S., xxi
Pontypool Educational Settlement, xviii, xxii
Popplewell, Olive, 279
Portia, 2
Posford, George, 189
Postage book, 68
posters, 71, 73-75
poster holders, see bill holders
Pot Luck, 286
Potter, Peter, 225
Powell, Douglas, xx
president, of an amateur group, 36
press publicity, 71-73, 76
press relations officer, 70
Priestley, J. B., 7, 253, 256, 257, 258, 265, 272, 288, 296, 298, 300
Pringle, Harry, 79
Prior Bolton, 303
Prisoner Before You, The, 279
Prison Without Bars, 301
Producer, The, 8-16, 365, 377; of an amateur group, 38, 39; as an actor, 13; and author, 9; blocking movement by, 47, 48, 49; casting by, 11; and costume designer, 10; and dances in plays, 178, 194; decision of, 14, 15; definition of, 8; and designer, 96, 102-03, 106; as demonstrator, 14; development of, 8; in drama festivals, 210; and dress rehearsal, 15, 16; and first reading, 46; functions of, 9; and lighting, 10, 11; and lighting rehearsal, 92-95; and loyalties, 11; and make-up, 10; and music between acts, 32; of musicals, 191; and publicity, 70; and rehearsals, 12-16, 46-53; and scenic artist, 10, 45; and set up, 50; and stage director, 45; and stage management, 80, 81;